ALSO BY ANDREW NAGORSKI

Reluctant Farewell

THE
BIRTH OF
FREEDOM

SHAPING LIVES AND
SOCIETIES IN THE NEW
EASTERN EUROPE

Andrew Nagorski

SIMON & SCHUSTER
New York • London • Toronto • Sydney • Tokyo • Singapore

SIMON & SCHUSTER
Simon & Schuster Building
Rockefeller Center
1230 Avenue of the Americas
New York, New York 10020

Designed by Levavi & Levavi
Manufactured in the United States of America

1 3 5 7 9 10 8 6 4 2

Library of Congress Cataloging in Publication Data
Nagorski, Andrew.
The birth of freedom / Andrew Nagorski.
p.   cm.
Includes index.
1. Europe, Eastern—History—1989–   I. Title.
DJK51.N34   1993
947—dc20   93-1750
                                                                CIP

ISBN 13: 978-1-43915-426-7
ISBN 10: 1-439-15426-0

ACKNOWLEDGMENTS

FAR MORE PEOPLE than can be mentioned here have extended their generous cooperation, and in many cases their friendship, during the years that I have been reporting from Eastern Europe. Many of these new Europeans figure prominently in the pages that follow; others, who do not, also provided invaluable insights and guidance as I attempted to chronicle the collapse of the old system and the emergence of new societies based on new principles. To all of them, I wish to express my deepest gratitude.

I am also indebted to my editors at *Newsweek* for readily agreeing to my request to base myself in Warsaw so that I could experience the transformation of the region on a daily basis, not simply flying in and out to cover specific stories. Throughout my assignment and during my previous postings, they provided me with the kind of leeway to pursue my interests, to explore any angle, or to travel anywhere that struck my fancy, that correspondents can often only dream about.

My thanks, too, to my agent, Robert Gottlieb, who urged me to propose this project at a time when most people were preoccupied with the collapse of communism rather than with what would replace it; to Marie Arana-Ward, my editor at Simon and Schuster, who was an unfailing source of good cheer and encouragement even as she gently prodded me to stick to my deadlines; and to Andrzej Wiecko, my office assistant in Warsaw, who performed any number of tasks that helped make juggling my normal reporting routine and writing a book possible.

All of my children contributed to this project as well. The oldest ones did so in very specific ways: while she was an exchange student at the University of Wroclaw, Eva arranged student contacts for me that proved very helpful; while she worked during the summer as an intern at the environment ministry in Warsaw, Sonia moonlighted as my researcher on environmental and health issues, providing me with much of the data that I used in chapter five. As for the younger members of the family: Adam was the in-house monitor of my progress; the knowledge that I would have to report to him on how many pages I had written each week was another incentive to keep going. Alexander provided me with the release I needed, the moments when I could escape into his always colorful, joyful, and spontaneous world.

The key link in all this was Christina—or Krysia, as most people here in Poland know my wife. I find it extremely difficult to try to summarize her role. She has educated me about the country of her birth for more than two decades; she immediately established our house in Warsaw as a meeting place for many of the people who are playing such important roles in the political, intellectual, and cultural life of Polish society; she instinctively knew when I was overlooking something important or losing my sense of perspective. We sometimes argued over what I had written, and more often than not I later reluctantly had to admit that her criticisms were right on target. I can say *dziekuje* or "thank you," but that is hardly enough.

For my parents, Marie and Zygmunt,

and for Alexander

CONTENTS

INTRODUCTION

ON AUGUST 20, 1990, exactly eight years after my family and I left the Soviet Union following my expulsion from that country for "impermissible methods of journalistic activities" in the twilight of the Brezhnev era, we flew to Warsaw to take up residence in a new postcommunist Eastern Europe. It was a journey I had always longed to make, but one I had vaguely assumed would only take place much later in my life, if at all. That I would be arriving in a transformed Eastern Europe at the beginning of the 1990s, where the people I had long known as dissidents would be in power and the people I had known as communists would be largely powerless, was something that I cannot claim to have envisaged. Nor had I envisaged that the story I would be coming to cover would be the re-entry of the Poles, Czechs, and Hungarians into the political, economic, and cultural entity known as Europe, the making of the new Europeans.

Shuttling back and forth across the European divide throughout the 1980s, I had attempted to chronicle the emergence of novel forms of opposition in Eastern Europe, and I was increasingly convinced that I was witnessing a serious and sustained assault on the postwar order. But this was an assault from below, led by dissidents outside the existing power structure, and, like the dissidents themselves, I was cautious in making predictions. In May 1988, when Polish workers were engaged in what looked like another hopeless confrontation with the government, I spent an evening in Warsaw discussing the mounting signs of crisis, across Eastern Europe and within the Soviet Union, with Adam Michnik, the leading intellectual theoretician of the still-banned Solidarity movement. His conclusion was that all this signaled "the beginning of the end of the Soviet empire," but he added as we parted: "This is a very long beginning." I agreed—and we both were proved wrong on his second point.

But what a delight to be proved wrong.

The liberation and continuing transformation of Eastern Europe was and is not just another story for me; it is the culmination of a personal journey that began long before I became a journalist, a journey preordained by family history. My job as a *Newsweek* correspondent would later give me the opportunities to expand this journey far beyond my original expectations, but I had instinctively pushed to discover the land of my family's origins even as a teenager and, like a magnet, the region would keep pulling me back in subsequent periods when my professional assignments took me elsewhere.

As I was growing up, I sometimes played a "what if" game. What if the Second World War had not intervened and I had been born in Poland instead of Scotland in 1947—what kind of person would I have turned out to be, and in what kind of a country? What if my parents had decided to return to the newly communist Poland instead of emigrating to the United States shortly after my birth? What if I had confronted the choices that my Polish contemporaries faced between at least tacitly cooperating with the system or risking my education, future job possibilities, and personal freedom by openly opposing it? What if, instead of taking part in civil-rights projects in Mississippi in the 1960s designed to implement goals supported by the federal government, I had had to oppose or accept an officially inspired anti-Semitic campaign of a communist government?

I knew enough about my family background to recognize the extent to which individual fates are subject to the broader sweep of history, the extent to which chance plays a role in determining the setting for each person's life. My mother's family, the Bogdaszewskis, had lived on an estate in Byelorussia since the eighteenth century. There were tales of how the men of the family had participated in the 1863 Polish uprising against Russian rule, and how my grandparents, with their newborn daughter, had had to flee the family estate near Minsk during the Bolshevik Revolution. Like the other Polish families from the region, they had abandoned most of their belongings and settled in areas that would become part of the newly independent Poland that emerged in the wake of the First World War.

That part of the family history had always seemed dreamily distant to me; the most direct reminder I had of it was my mother's indignant protests whenever someone suggested that she had been born in the Soviet Union. But she knew little about her birthplace near Minsk, except that it was called Wiazyn and situated seventeen versts—a Russian measurement slightly longer than a kilometer—outside of Minsk. A surviving photograph showed beautifully sculpted gardens, a chapel, and part of a formidable tower. My mother always assumed that no traces of that past remained, and I never made it to Minsk when I lived in the Soviet Union in the early 1980s to see if that was indeed the case; the chances of discovering something seemed too remote to make this a high priority.

Then, in the spring of 1991, I visited Minsk to do a story about Byelorussian political discontent. With a sense that I was merely going through the motions, I started making inquiries whether a village called Wiazyn still existed, only to learn that there was a place called Viazan that looked to be about the right distance from Minsk. It seemed worth a try, although I doubted I would learn anything. I dutifully drove there, to find a cluster of tumbledown peasant cottages, garages, and a two-story wooden house belonging to the local collective farm, whose dismal state was perfectly obvious from the first glance. I asked two women sitting on a bench, their boots planted in the mud, whether they knew if Poles had lived there before the revolution. One of them indicated that she had heard that Polish families had lived there, but she knew nothing specific.

Another woman came up and joined in without any preliminaries. She wore a cheap print dress, a brown coat, and a white scarf tied babushka-style around her head. Yes, she remembered the Polish church, she said in a singsong voice, which had stood just beyond where the garages now stand. She was born in 1928 and, as a little girl in the 1930s, she remembered when the graves in the church were pulled out by people looking for valuables. Someone had pulled out the grave of Mrs. Bogdaszewska, she continued. . . .

Incredulous, I interrupted her. "Mrs. Bogdaszewska?"

"Yes, yes, the Bogdaszewskis lived right over there," she said, gesturing to a space between the garages where a lone tree now grows.

I went on to find an old woman whose parents had worked as servants for my grandparents, and learned a good deal more about the family in the final years before they fled, and how my great-grandmother had been disturbed by the savagery of the 1930s even in her grave. That chapter of the past no longer seemed dreamily distant, but an indication of why someone like Tadeusz Konwicki, a gifted contemporary Polish novelist, writes about "history which flows behind us, beside us, ahead of us." Little wonder that history is not seen in this part of the world as a classroom abstraction but as a living, breathing force.

The legacy from my father's side of the family was the conviction that it is a force that each individual can and should try to influence, whatever the odds. When Poland was still partitioned among Russia, Prussia, and Austria, at the beginning of the century, my grandfather was expelled from universities in St. Petersburg and Berlin for his involvement in Polish nationalist movements. After Poland gained its independence, he became a prominent lawyer in Warsaw who participated in the codification of the country's legal system and was active in the Peasant Party. This was undoubtedly the most satisfying period in his life: he enjoyed tremendous professional success, which not only provided material rewards but, more important, made him a highly respected public figure. His wife, a woman who loved the arts and entertaining, ensured that their home was a vibrant meeting place for Warsaw's intellectual and cultural elite. In later life, they would both look back at this period as their golden age.

But my grandfather never allowed personal success to blind him to the more troubling political and social trends within Poland, which gathered momentum during the interwar years. Following Marshal Jozef Pilsudski's coup against the chaotic new parliament, he harbored considerable misgivings and turned down offers to join the government. He went on to serve as a defense counsel at the major political trial of opposition leaders in Brest in 1930, whose arrest he denounced as "an evident abuse of power." He was particularly saddened by the increasing anti-Semitism of the far right, which, like many moderate Catholics, he vigorously deplored. Elected to the executive board of the Polish Bar Association with the strong support of the Jewish lawyers who played a dominant role in that profession, he was attacked as a "Jew lover." He later wrote movingly of the disillusionment of colleagues he admired with "the victory of might over right, force over justice." But his commitment to a free Poland, however strongly he criticized its failings in the interwar years, was unwavering.

My grandparents and my father's new bride escaped the country at the outbreak of the Second World War; my father fought as a tank-battalion officer in the doomed September 1939 defense against the Germans. After the surrender, he, too, escaped, mostly on foot to Hungary, then making his way to France to rejoin the Polish forces and his family there. After France fell, they went to Britain, where my grandfather was a member of the Polish government-in-exile and my father served in the Polish forces under British command. Stalin's imposition of a communist government in Warsaw decided the family's fate: there was no going back. With my older sister and me in tow, the family headed across the Atlantic.

So history determined that I grow up an American instead of a Pole, although speaking Polish at home and conscious of my Polish origins. At age seventeen, I visited Poland for the first time, only to discover as soon as I boarded the Polish-airline flight in Vienna how limited that consciousness really was. I suddenly found myself laughing to myself because of the irrational thought that all of the strangers on that flight were speaking my family's private language; it was then that I realized how little I knew about the country I was about to see.

My first visit there did not satisfy my curiosity, and in the fall of 1968 I returned for a semester as an exchange student at the Jagiellonian University in Krakow, my father's alma mater. That was a particularly grim year. In March, the Polish authorities had brutally suppressed student demonstrations and blamed the unrest on "Zionists." In August, Warsaw Pact troops had invaded Czechoslovakia, putting an abrupt end to the Prague Spring. During the first cold, rainy days of September, after my arrival, the grayness of the town, with its lovely but often dilapidated buildings, felt overwhelming, matching the dispirited mood of many of the students.

But in the gray planet of state socialism, I quickly discovered patches of private greenery. Suffice it to say that I met and married Christina there, unexpectedly adding a new Polish connection to our family. The greenery could also be found in my intense personal relationships on other levels, revealing political and moral convictions that were for the moment camouflaged in public. I left Poland convinced of the superficiality of the image of conformity that a period of repression conveys.

It was a conviction reinforced by a small incident in Prague, where I made a stopover on my way back to college in February 1969. A month before, a twenty-one-year-old philosophy student named Jan Palach had set himself alight on Wenceslas Square to protest the Soviet occupation. As someone visiting Prague for the first time, I could find no hint of the passion that had inspired his suicide—only the sullen, drawn faces of people who seemed intent on avoiding eye contact as they scurried home to their private worlds. All hope seemed to have vanished. But then a middle-aged man quickly confirmed his impression that I was a foreigner and delivered a curt message: "Don't think we all accept this."

That message stayed with me throughout the 1970s, when I traveled only occasionally to Eastern Europe but continued to monitor developments there, and also when I arrived in the heart of the Soviet empire to take up my posting in Moscow in 1981. I was always on the lookout for the hints of defiance and individual aspirations that surfaced even in the similarly grim late Brezhnev period, which was marked by the invasion of Afghanistan, martial law in Poland, and a crackdown on dissent at home. I found them often—among Lithuanian nationalists, young Muslims in Tajikistan who were terrified by the prospect of serving in Afghanistan, Russians in provincial cities disoriented and outraged by worsening food shortages and other economic hardships. After fourteen months of such reporting, the Soviet authorities sent me packing.

From 1985 to 1988, I worked out of Bonn, at the time *Newsweek*'s base for coverage of East-Central Europe. I roamed throughout the region, watching as, amid the familiar grayness and despair, the dissidents steadily broadened the range of their activities, undercutting the control of the communist regimes over ever-widening circles of life. Those experiences led me to conclude that the Eastern European opposition forces would no longer be content with anything that smacked of reform communism; their goal was the creation of a democratic political system and a capitalist economy.

That was a conclusion not everyone wanted to hear: it was not only the Kremlin but also some Western neighbors who were uneasy about the course of developments in the region. In 1988, when I started a fellowship at the Carnegie Endowment for International Peace in Washington, D.C., I spelled out those views in an introductory presentation. A foreign-policy strategist for West Germany's Social Democratic Party was visibly upset with my account of Eastern European aspirations; his party had cultivated contacts with communist "reformers" and largely skirted the dissidents, assuming that most Eastern Europeans should be grateful for any incremental reforms and that full democratization was out of the question. "What do they want—a revolution?" he demanded.

The answer was yes and no. Yes, in the sense of the scope of the changes they were demanding. No, in the sense of a repetition of the bloody, revolutionary experiences of this and previous centuries, where all too often the revolutionary path led straight to a new tyranny. At least that was true for Poland, Czechoslovakia, and Hungary, the three countries best prepared to defy the present and historical odds to launch a transformation as startling for its lack of violence at birth as for its breadth and daring. When I arrived in Warsaw in 1990, I intentionally focused on those three countries, recognizing that they were best equipped to succeed in their goal of "entering Europe." They would be the pacesetters, demonstrating the opportunities and the dangers. Others, like Bulgaria and Romania, had greater historical and current obstacles to overcome; the Baltic states, the Ukraine, Byelorussia, and Russia could aspire to similar goals, but they would be slowed by the difficult process of disentangling themselves from the badly torn but still-sticky remains of the Soviet web. As a region that was absorbed into an existing state, East Germany was a case apart. So was Yugoslavia, that disaster which did not wait long to happen.

But would Poland, Czechoslovakia, and Hungary demonstrate the same ingenuity in building the new as they did in overthrowing the old? Their first instinct was to rename streets, metro stations, and other public facilities, either restoring their precommunist names (President Wilson Square instead of Paris Commune Square in Warsaw) or honoring new heroes (John Paul II Street instead of Lenin Street in Czestochowa; Jan Palach Square instead of Red Army Square in Prague). The elimination of the most galling reminders of the subservience of the communist period prompted understandable satisfaction—after all, who could fail to wince whenever the recording on Line B of the Prague metro announcing stations along the way blared out "Next Stop: Moscow"? But often there was confusion as familiar if despised names disappeared, to be replaced by names that a new generation did not remember. "Let's ask Grandmother—she might remember the new street name," young people joked in Budapest.

And I had to wonder if the confusion might go deeper, if the peoples of the region would be able not only to draw upon the positive elements of their precommunist history but also to avoid repeating old mistakes and arousing old demons. I was reasonably confident that many of the former dissidents were acutely aware of those dangers, since they had so imaginatively broken the cycle of rebellion and repression in 1989. They knew the difference between national pride and xenophobia, between the use of national symbols to rally a people's best instincts and the use of such symbols to mobilize the hatred of the mob. Or so I wished to believe.

But I also was aware of the equally firm conviction of many of the region's best writers, thinkers, and artists about the mixed traits of their own people. Poland's turn-of-the-century novelist Henryk Sienkiewicz described his people as "the last Indians of Europe" and "a dying race," defeated by all its neighbors. Since Poland was still swallowed up at the time by Russia, Prussia, and Austria, his verdict sounded less melodramatic at the time than it does today; but it reflects a martyr complex that can inspire either feats of national heroism or a fetish of "Polishness" in the face of a host of enemies, real or imagined. Like many Poles who were as appalled by their countrymen's internal feuding as by their ability to unite against an external threat, playwright Witold Gombrowicz reached a sweepingly damning verdict. "The air of freedom has been granted us so that we could deal with an enemy more tormenting than our former oppressors—with ourselves," he wrote of the period of Poland's independence between the wars. "After the struggles with Russia, with Germany, a battle with Poland awaited us. No wonder, therefore, that independence turned out to be more burdensome and more humiliating than subjugation."

Poland's southern neighbors are capable of equally scathing self-criticism. Historians like to point out that Czechoslovakia had the healthiest political system in the region between the wars, anchored in a middle-class nationalism of a liberal-democratic orientation. But older national traits reasserted themselves under both brands of totalitarianism that followed. "Dad was thoroughly Czech," says the protagonist of Czech émigré writer Josef Skvorecky's piercing novel *The Engineer of Human Souls.* "He always did his duty conscientiously while thinking the opposite of what he was expected to think. But he did his duty." Duty—or, more accurately, collaboration—enabled successive rulers to do their own renaming, relabeling, rewriting with minimal opposition. As Czech writer Ivan Klima put it in his novel *Love and Garbage:* "In our country everything is being forever remade: beliefs, buildings and street names. Sometimes the progress of time is concealed and at others feigned, so long as nothing remains as real and truthful testimony."

Both between the wars and during the communist era, the frictions between the Czechs and the Slovaks were suppressed rather than addressed, with far-reaching consequences. My assumption that both peoples would be among the pacesetters of change proved to be wrong. Those frictions played themselves out only in the postcommunist era, splitting the country into two and consigning the Slovaks to a slower track.

In *The Loser,* one of Hungarian novelist George Konrad's characters makes quick work of all of his countrymen. "We are not a nation that makes history," he declares. "Our revolutions have failed, in wars we always end up on the losing side. Whenever we have to make a stand, we get beaten, but when we lie low we come out ahead. When foreign hordes plundered this land, my ancestors, who were serfs, hid in the marshes. They sat under the water and breathed through reeds. . . . We served the Turks, then the Germans, and now the Russians. Two empires have come and gone; the third will also pass from the scene." But,

Konrad's character is saying, no thanks to the Hungarians themselves.

It can be argued that all of those judgments are too harsh, since the Soviet empire in Eastern Europe passed away precisely because of the efforts of the Poles, Czechs, and Hungarians; because of their tenacity, their commitment to truth, their imaginative forms of resistance, they did make history. True enough, but those negative judgments cannot be lightly dismissed, since they raise troubling questions about the psychological scars that a complex and often tragic history left on all the nationalities of the region.

Perhaps somewhat paradoxically, I also found something very encouraging in those somber assessments: nothing nurtures the democratic spirit more than the ability of a people to criticize themselves. I returned to Eastern Europe convinced that history would play its role but so would the individual choices of the inhabitants as they sought to define their new identities: there is nothing predetermined about the outcome of the transformation currently taking place.

A decade ago, Luigi Barzini wrote *The Europeans,* a wonderful book describing the British, the Germans, the French, the Italians, the Dutch, even the Americans. At the time, he did not feel obliged to explain why he did not write anything about the Eastern Europeans; his tacit assumption was that their political subjugation meant that they were not really part of a contemporary Europe. In that sense, the Poles, Czechs, and Hungarians are seeking to become the first of the new Europeans, leading the march back to a continent, defined by its political, economic, and social system and values, that they and the other nations of the region were long excluded from.

This is a very different book from *The Europeans,* in terms of both subject and style, which I certainly did not attempt to match. Barzini was describing well-established and, for the most part, comfortable nations. I am describing the often painful rebirth of countries attempting to find their way through uncharted territory, since they had no precedents to look at as they began to dismantle communist structures and replace them with representative governments and market economics. This is also a psychological process, requiring major adjustments of thinking about almost every other aspect of life—personal habits and beliefs, arts and culture, the environment, to name only a few areas. Above all, it is a process still very much under way, which means that I can only offer an impressionistic and far from comprehensive eyewitness account of the birth of freedom and new societies in the making.

But the very rawness of that process endows it with tremendous intensity and excitement. I felt extremely fortunate to be there, at their creation. On a visit to Budapest in 1989, when communist governments were rapidly losing control, Miklos Haraszti, a leading Hungarian dissident writer and activist, advised me to take up residence in the region rather than continue to commute in and out. "This is the time to be here," he said. "It'll still take a while before we become normal, boring countries." He was absolutely right.

RESISTANCE,
REBELLION,
AND LIFE

Early one muggy summer evening in 1985, I arrived at a pre-arranged meeting point in the Mokotow residential district in Warsaw. Surveying the prosperous one-family houses with neatly groomed garden plots, I wondered what I was getting myself into. Probably nothing, I told myself, deliberately dampening my expectations. The signal that I had received about the possibility of an interview with Zbigniew Bujak had provided no assurances. As the underground leader of Solidarity, Bujak had been Poland's most-wanted fugitive for three and a half years, since General Wojciech Jaruzelski's government outlawed the independent trade union and declared martial law in December 1981. Constantly on the move to elude the police, he had not risked a meeting with a Western reporter for nearly as long. My instructions were to wait at the prearranged time and place, but not to be surprised if no one showed up; that would simply mean that the underground had not managed to make safe arrangements for such a meeting.

I knew I would be disappointed if nothing came of this tantalizing prospect, but I was equally worried about the alternative. When I was asked by a friend with connections to the underground whether I would be interested in an interview with Bujak, I had not masked my eagerness—but I had also insisted that I only wanted to go through with it if the underground was certain that the meeting could be arranged in a way that did not jeopardize his safety. The last thing I wanted was to be responsible for his arrest. As an American journalist of Polish background, whose recent experiences in the Soviet Union had only made me more suspect, I had to presume that I was under surveillance. So did the underground, which knew that this was my first working visit to Poland since my expulsion from Moscow; the authorities had refused ny earlier requests for a journalist's visa. And I had no illusions that I could lose or even detect whatever surveillance they had established.

But, right on schedule, a short, bearded man walked up, nodded, and indicated that I should follow him. There were no introductions, only a couple of words, and we were on our way. My anonymous escort was calm but all business, while I somewhat nervously realized that he was truly intent on leading me to Bujak, and that this was a major operation involving several people who were all taking significant risks to pull it off.

We switched cars three or four times, getting out at various points in the city, walking through crumbling courtyards and back lots to the next street, where another car cruised by for a quick pickup. Only once, when we reached a street corner and were not immediately picked up, did my escort look agitated, glancing at his watch and up and down the street. No more than a couple of minutes later, a young woman drove up in a *maluch*, a tiny Polish Fiat, apologizing profusely that her car had stalled in traffic. As we weaved back and forth through Warsaw and its outskirts in our different vehicles to throw off anyone who might have been tailing me, I lost all sense of direction. I was impressed by the professionalism of the operation, but still far from sure that it had been fully effective.

Finally, my escort led me through a standardized cluster of drab concrete buildings to an upper-floor apartment, whose owner offered me tea and quietly disappeared. A couple of minutes later, a beefy man with a goatee and mustache appeared; the face underneath looked vaguely familiar, but I was not certain it was Bujak until he started talking. Before he had gone underground, he had looked very much like what he was: a young worker at the Ursus tractor factory outside of Warsaw, whose boyish features and wavy, somewhat unkempt hair looked typically Polish working-class. That had proved essential to his ability to elude the police. "I noticed a very long time ago that I have such a typical face," he told me, describing his close calls with the police. "I just take anybody's ID." He was clearly exaggerating, but as I looked at the transformation he had accomplished—by growing out his hair and the goatee and adding some extra pounds, which made him look considerably older than his thirty years of age—I could almost believe him.

As we began a talk that would last three hours, I felt reassured by his evident confidence that no one had observed my arrival. In some ways, the elaborate arrangements to get me there were as impressive as the meeting itself. During our talk, Bujak branded as "wishful thinking" General Jaruzelski's assertions that the underground was dying; he noted that about fifty to seventy thousand people participated in its work directly, and perhaps another 200,000 to 250,000 were involved with it in some form from time to time. "We can say that every hundredth Pole is engaged in our cause," he said. "Poland never had more people engaged in conspiracy."

There was no way of checking those numbers, but the sense of people's double lives was brought home to me the very next day, as I drove through a Warsaw intersection; out of my window, I suddenly glimpsed the young woman who had driven us in the Polish Fiat walking down the street, to all appearances a normal citizen going to work or to shop. I found myself smiling in silent admiration.

But Bujak's message was not all upbeat. He spoke candidly about the problems as well as the accomplishments of the underground. If the numbers he cited were a source of pride, he also admitted that the "great enthusiasm" of the resistance had diminished as people were worn down by the burdens of their everyday lives. Some supporters had stopped helping the underground, and others were taking advantage of the government's willingness to allow them to emigrate. He saw no prospect of a short-term victory, speaking instead of a struggle that could last ten to fifteen years. "Something will certainly move. I am convinced I am going to see it," he insisted.

Could he remain underground for so long? He wasn't sure, conceding both that he might be apprehended and that the notion of an open-ended conspiracy, however justifiable, somehow defied normal logic. He shrugged. "We are living in a country where there is no normal life, so insane gestures must be performed in order to win something."

Bujak did not mean to be dismissive of any of the underground's activities, but his reference to insane gestures seemed perfectly reasonable: there was an element of blind faith, rather than careful calculation, in the whole underground movement, however well it performed its functions. Given the forces arrayed against Solidarity at the time, would a sane person bet on its success? Later, when such defiance produced results that far exceeded anyone's expectations all across Eastern Europe, it also seemed natural to speak of insane transformations.

Take Jiri Dienstbier, who likes to talk about the job he held after the

Soviet invasion of Czechoslovakia in 1968, when, as a journalist who had supported the Prague Spring, he found himself barred from his career. Like many talented professionals, he ended up as a manual laborer; reporters like me who sought him out in Prague in those days often had to make a couple of visits to his apartment, which had no phone, to catch him before or after one of his rotating shifts as a stoker. With evident relish, Dienstbier points out that he remained on that job right up until the day in December 1989 when he was sworn in as Czechoslovakia's foreign minister, exchanging the subterranean world of furnaces for a Baroque seventeenth-century palace on Prague's majestic Castle Hill. "There was something absurd in it," he told me on my first visit to his new office. "But in a country where the heritage of Franz Kafka, *The Good Soldier Schweik*, and Joseph Stalin have all been combined, nothing can be absurd anymore."

President Vaclav Havel, the former dissident playwright who appointed Dienstbier, carried with him that sense of the absurdity of it all long after his inauguration. "I am the kind of person who would not be in the least surprised if, in the very middle of being president, I were to be summoned and led off to stand trial before some shadowy tribunal, or taken straight to the quarry to break rocks," he told the Hebrew University in Jerusalem a few months after taking office. "Nor would I be any more surprised if I were suddenly to hear the reveille and wake up in my prison cell, and then, with great bemusement, proceed to tell my fellow prisoners everything that had happened to me in the past six months."

Both the resistance to communist regimes in Eastern Europe and its outcome contained elements of insanity and absurdity, but they also were rooted in an eminently sane if highly risky reaction to the absurdities and insanities of a system based on false premises or just plain lies. In talking to a Bujak, a Dienstbier, or a Havel in the days when they were fighting against what appeared to be overwhelming odds, I marveled at their courage but I also attempted to understand what inspired them, why they and others like them were willing to expose themselves to inevitable retribution. Were they romantic crusaders, or were they privy to insights that eluded most of their countrymen and outsiders? Were they as idealistic as they often sounded, or pragmatists who were as motivated by personal ambition as by the chance to serve a greater cause?

After the dissidents emerged triumphant, such questions did not lose their immediate relevancy. The answers to them are important, not just to future historians but also to those seeking to evaluate the new leaders of the region, since their beliefs and behavior as dissidents have a direct bearing on their performance as establishment politicians. And their behavior as establishment politicians has a direct bearing on the kind of societies that are replacing communism. Beginnings can offer revealing clues about possible endings.

For Bujak, the beginning of the most crucial episode in his personal odyssey was marked by a fortuitous circumstance. It was pure chance that he and Zbigniew Janas, a fellow Solidarity activist from the Ursus tractor factory, did not find themselves arrested on December 13, 1981, when the Polish authorities imposed their "state of war." They had been attending a meeting of the Solidarity leadership in Gdansk, which broke up unexpectedly before midnight on December 12. While Lech Walesa returned to his apartment and the other activists went to the Monopol Hotel, Janas told Bujak that he was going to catch the overnight train to Warsaw. Bujak did not want to go, and he urged Janas not to, either, since their wives were in close touch. "Listen, if my Wacia finds out that you've gone home and I've stayed here, there'll be the most almighty row," he pleaded. But Janas refused to change his mind, and convinced Bujak to come along.

As they waited for the train, they saw riot-police units in front of the station and around the Monopol. They were not unduly alarmed right away, since Bujak's first instinct was to dismiss this as a training exercise. But the train did not arrive, and the police activity began to make them jittery. As soon as the police cars pulled off, they decided to go to the hotel to see what was going on. There the frightened assistant of one of their colleagues told them that several activists had been rounded up and that the police were still going from room to room looking for others.

Bujak and Janas remained calm, still not recognizing the dimensions of what was happening. "We could not imagine that the leaders of a legal labor union could become the objects of the hunt," Bujak recalls. Today he ascribes his disbelief to his inexperience and the illusion that the authorities would prove incapable of mounting an action that would stop the "avalanche" known as Solidarity. "I was young, only twenty-six," he notes almost apologetically. It was only when they sought to leave the hotel and the concierge began nervously to search for the key to unlock the door that Bujak discovered his heart was beating faster and he made his decision that he would not be caught like the others. "I decided I would not follow them," he says. He positioned himself by the window, so that he could break it and jump through if the police showed up. But the concierge found the key and let them out.

Running into a local Solidarity activist, they learned that Walesa's apartment was surrounded and that arrests were taking place all over the city. They decided to split up to increase their chances. Janas spent the night at the apartment of some friends and managed to board a train to Warsaw the next day. Bujak spent two nights at a monastery, which immediately gave him refuge, and then another few days in a private apartment. By that time, the escape routes were being carefully monitored, but Bujak put on the first of his many disguises. With the help of Solidarity supporters among the railwaymen, he dressed in a conductor's uniform, donned glasses, and eluded detection on his trip back to Warsaw.

Thus, in the midst of the crackdown aimed at crushing Solidarity, the underground resistance was born. Bujak quickly emerged as the leader of that resistance, eluding police dragnets for four and a half years, until he was finally captured in May 1986. It was a resistance that defied all the odds of past Soviet bloc crackdowns, when force always had prevailed. "There was no rational reason for hope, just an emotional basis," Bujak recalls. "The political strength of Solidarity was such that I was sure that we would never build something that strong again. If we were going to continue the struggle with that system, it could only be with Solidarity. I knew there was no room for doubt. If I said we would win sooner or later, this involved some mental discipline. If you concluded your strongest weapon is Solidarity in this political struggle, you couldn't allow any doubt to enter your mind."

Both in its underground incarnation under Bujak's leadership and in its more open incarnation under Walesa after his release in November 1982, Solidarity's story was a saga of stubborn determination, of the refusal of activists to be cowed even when defeat seemed inevitable. In that sense, it is a classic tale of human courage and daring, of the commitment to the elementary ideals of human rights in the face of an ideological system that felt mortally threatened by the assertion of those rights. But the drama that played itself out in Poland was far more complex than that, and a variety of factors contributed to the final stunning outcome, which heralded the collapse of communism throughout Eastern Europe and, ultimately, within the Soviet Union.

On one level, the struggle was a magnificent battle of ideas, an intellectual liberation without precedent in terms of its practical consequences. On another, it was an all-too-familiar contest of competing political and personal ambitions—sometimes noble, sometimes petty—both between and within the opposing Solidarity and communist camps. On still another, it was the instinctive rejection of an alien system whose failure in every aspect of life was progressively more evident.

• • •

That rejection came naturally to many Poles, especially those who had been brought up in the tradition of the formidable Polish resistance during the Second World War. Teresa Wisniewska was thirteen when the war erupted in 1939. Seventeen days after German troops invaded from the west, Stalin ordered his armies to invade from the east, implementing his secret agreement with Hitler to divide up the Polish nation. Teresa, who lived in the eastern Polish city of Bialystok, remembers that her school suddenly switched to Russian language instruction. In protest, she and some of her friends threw several busts of Stalin out the window. Although a sympathetic headmistress managed to convince the Soviet occupiers that this was merely an irresponsible childish prank, Teresa's mother was horrified. She pointed out to her daughter that her action could endanger her father, who, by virtue of his position as a minor Polish treasury official, was already a prime candidate for arrest.

It was then that Teresa's father intervened, offering her advice she has never forgotten. "Don't say that," he told his wife. Turning to Teresa, he added: "Always act according to your conscience and sense of obligation, because there are more important things than even your own family."

Teresa's father was arrested two months later, and he perished somewhere inside the Soviet Union without ever seeing his family again. But Teresa took his lesson to heart. After the Germans occupied Bialystok on their drive eastward, she attended a clandestine Polish school and began running errands for the Home Army, the main Polish resistance group, which was dedicated to achieving independence for Poland from both Germany and the Soviet Union. By the time the Soviet Army recaptured the city from the Germans in the summer of 1944, she was taking on increasingly dangerous assignments. She survived, but just barely.

After helping to hide several Home Army partisans in her own and other apartments in the city, she was captured by the NKVD, the Soviet secret police. During one interrogation, two officers grabbed her by her ears, rocked her back and forth on a chair, and banged her head repeatedly against the floor. During a two-week train ride to a Soviet labor camp, she nearly starved; the prisoners were jammed into railroad cars and received almost no water, never mind food. Some had managed to bring along a few pieces of dried bread, which they shared, but most resorted to eating bits of wood that they stripped off the insides of the cars. Many died. Life in the camp was only marginally better. Teresa's ears, which were severely inflamed and infected, caused her constant pain.

Released and sent back to Poland at the end of 1945, she found that the persecution was far from over. The new Polish communist regime was engaged in its own terror campaign, and ideologically suspect families like the Wisniewskis were automatic targets. Teresa's mother was imprisoned, and Teresa had to bounce around between different jobs since many employers were afraid to hire her for anything more than short stints. But she did manage to support a younger sister, study education, and eventually start teaching Polish at a Warsaw high school.

Throughout thirty years of teaching in a communist Poland, she never accepted defeat. In the classroom, she slipped in as much as she could about the long history of Polish resistance to Russian domination. She repeated her father's admonition about higher goals. "I always told my students that," she recalls. "How many fathers would act that way now?"

Outside the classroom, Teresa immediately became involved in the efforts to build a free trade union in the 1970s, culminating in the emergence and legalization of Solidarity in 1980. When the crackdown came a year later, she was imprisoned with other Solidarity activists; after seven months, she was released but not allowed to go back to teaching. Aside from remaining involved with Solidarity, she became active in the Siberian Union. Its purpose was to gain recognition for the estimated two million Poles who were deported to the Soviet Union during 1939 and 1940; over half, like Teresa's father, never returned. Following the collapse of the communist regime, she was readmitted to the classroom, although she could have simply collected her pension. Teaching was her personal vindication.

For veteran Polish resistance fighters like Wisniewska, there was never any question of accepting the political, economic, and social system imposed by the Kremlin and Polish communists. Poland was remarkable for the number of people it had of that mold, who kept chipping away at the system. But far more numerous were the people, both young and old, who for a long time attempted to find a place for themselves in the new order without confronting the authorities, whatever their misgivings and disappointments. And that was even more true of Czechoslovakia and Hungary, where there was nothing like the long Polish tradition of resistance. Hungary erupted in 1956, and Czechoslovakia attempted a peaceful transformation in 1968, but Soviet tanks swiftly suppressed both revolts. In the aftermath of those actions, all three countries at times looked largely pacified, with outright opposition limited to relatively small groups of activists.

But appearances were deceptive. Something new was emerging in the midst of the curious limbo that followed the invasions of Hungary and Czechoslovakia, and the successive internal crackdowns by the Polish authorities against periodic worker unrest. Even as the governments of the region were asserting their authority by repression, liberalization, or sometimes a combination of both, the potential base for resistance was gradually expanding far beyond the veteran resistance fighters. The reason was simple: the system was failing to provide even the meager rewards that it had once seemed capable of assuring to those of its citizens who were willing to go along with it.

It may be hard to recall now, but communist rulers were once able to claim that they were providing steady if modest improvements in the living standards of their peoples. Although the gap between living standards in the East and the West remained enormous, Eastern European leaders promised that the basic human needs of their people would be fulfilled and that, over time, more of the amenities of modern life—such as decent housing, a wider array of consumer goods, and cars—would be provided. After 1956 and 1968, Eastern European governments sought to strike a bargain with their citizenry. If the people agreed to remain politically passive, the tacit understanding went, they could anticipate better economic conditions.

In Hungary, that promise was based on steps toward economic reform and, later on, foreign-financed economic expansion. In Czechoslovakia, it was based on the diversion of funds from investments to the consumer sector, which eventually led to the steady deterioration of the country's once-formidable industrial base. In Poland, in the 1970s, party leader Edward Gierek created the illusion of an economic takeoff by borrowing heavily from the West, most of whose loans either were used to boost consumption or were squandered on nearly bankrupt state industries; some ended up lining the pockets of corrupt officials.

In retrospect, the results were hardly surprising. Czechoslovakia, which ranked among the top ten industrialized nations when it was founded in 1918, found it increasingly difficult in the 1970s and 1980s to compete in Western markets with its low-quality manufactured goods. The share of its total trade with the less demanding socialist countries rose steadily, from 65 percent in 1980 to 79 percent in 1987. Prime Minister Lubomir Strougal privately joked to Western delegations that a sign stood on Czechoslovakia's border: "Welcome to the Museum of the Industrial Revolution." Despite its pioneering efforts at economic reform, Hungary found itself saddled with the highest per capita foreign debt in the Soviet bloc and declining living standards; none of its reforms had gone far enough to produce a turnaround. Throughout the 1980s, Poland was a basket case, struggling with $40 billion in foreign debt, an inflation rate of Latin American proportions, and rationing combined with constant shortages of basic foodstuffs, medicines, and other necessities.

No one needed convincing that the system was a failure when a young Polish couple could expect a waiting period for a new apartment of anywhere from twenty to forty years, or when hospitals began to run out of anesthesia for some routine operations. Every gap between East and West was widening instead of narrowing: the technology gap, the productivity gap, the life-expectancy gap. In the 1950s, some of those gaps had narrowed—but no more. The question was what could the peoples of the region do that had not been tried, and suppressed, before. Violent revolt, in particular, had never had a chance against the overwhelming force that the authorities could mobilize, either at home or from inside the Soviet Union.

Something new and imaginative was required.

"In 1970, as I was leaving the Gdansk shipyard defeated, between two rows of tanks, I may have sighed, asking God how this system could be overthrown and this army defeated without bloodshed," Lech Walesa told the first freely elected Polish parliament in November 1991. "Here today, as Poland's president, I can say before a democratically elected parliament: we have a free Poland now."

How did this come to pass? No single answer can fully encompass the forces at work in Poland and throughout the region that made this transformation possible, but one response comes closest: the power of ideas. No, such an assertion is not an exercise of poetic license; it is the recognition of a complex process based on an intellectual commitment to principles that spawned a creative but immensely practical strategy of undermining the political system. The something new and imaginative turned out to be an aggressive commitment to truth.

The relationship between ideas and activism is never easy to sort out, since activism breeds ideas and ideas breed activism. The activism that began to well up in the latter half of the 1970s and blossomed in the 1980s did not spring from an overall intellectual blueprint, but such a blueprint was in the making, and the activism of that period spurred its further development. In 1976, Polish intellectuals organized the Committee for the Defense of Workers (KOR), which constituted the first effective independent group to bridge the gap between workers and intellectuals, and thus paved the way for Solidarity; up till then, workers and intellectuals had usually protested separately—making it easier to suppress each group separately. In 1977, Czechoslovakia's dissidents launched Charter 77, a loose association of human-rights activists, and in the early 1980s Hungary's "democratic opposition" grew increasingly active. They all contributed to the blueprint that emerged, founded on a common belief in the liberating impact of truth in the face of a system based on lies.

The notion of the importance of truth, of keeping truth alive in the midst of the daily profusion of official lies, was hardly new. That is why Teresa Wisniewska and countless other Poles defied the authorities by contradicting their rewrites of history, passing on to the younger generation the truth about their national legacy, about the long tradition of resistance to Russian and then Soviet domination. That is why Hungarian parents told their children the true story of 1956, and why Czech parents told their children about 1968.

The worst nightmare for someone like Czech émigré writer Milan Kundera was that the truth would be forgotten, not just because it was deliberately contradicted by communist propaganda but also because of the fleeting attention span of the modern world. In *The Book of Laughter and Forgetting,* he wrote: "The bloody massacre in Bangladesh quickly covered over the memory of the Russian invasion of Czechoslovakia, the assassination of Allende drowned out the groans of Bangladesh, the war in the Sinai Desert made people forget Allende, the Cambodian massacre made people forget Sinai, and so on and so forth until ultimately everyone lets everything be forgotten."

But that bleak vision is contradicted by another strain in the literature of exiles from the region, an almost mystical belief that nothing is forgotten, that no despot or despotic system can ever prove successful in instilling collective amnesia. Polish émigré poet and Nobel Prize winner Czeslaw Milosz wrote bitterly about the outlawing of truth and the transformation of those who clung to it into criminals: "The laughter born of the love of truth / Is now the laughter of the enemies of the people." He also offered a stark warning, which in 1980 Solidarity activists chose to engrave on the monument outside the Lenin Shipyard in Gdansk, dedicated to workers killed a decade earlier:

> *You who wronged a simple man*
> *Bursting into laughter at the crime,*
> *Do not feel safe. The poet remembers.*
> *You can kill one, but another is born.*
> *The words are written down, the deed, the date.*

If in the early years of communist governments in Eastern Europe the truth was stored in people's consciousness as a means of quietly preserving their identity and dignity, it was transformed into a more overtly offensive political weapon in the late 1970s and the 1980s. If the state structures still looked impregnable, individuals could at least liberate themselves by driving totalitarianism "out of our own souls," as Havel would later write. That meant banishing the fear of speaking the truth, of acting according to the dictates of conscience, not just within tight circles of family and friends but in public. This was nothing less than a new strategy of liberating Eastern Europe by undermining totalitarianism "from below."

The task that the dissidents had set for themselves was to chart a course between the extremes of resignation and violent revolt that had marked the postwar history of the region up to that point. The latter was always a danger, since a spreading feeling of hopelessness among the broader population could well breed desperate acts. But the dissidents argued against violence on both practical and moral grounds. In practical terms, they knew that, unarmed as they were, they could not prevail in a show of force. In moral terms, they felt that they could hardly combat a totalitarian system, based as it was on the violence of repression, by resorting to more violence. They did not want their chapter to be titled "Resistance, Rebellion, and Death" but "Resistance, Rebellion, and Life."

The most extensive application of the new strategy could be found in Warsaw, but the first comprehensive explanation of its theory emerged from Prague. In his 1979 essay "The Power of the Powerless," Havel made his debut as a political writer and offered what still ranks as the single most compelling explanation of the ideas that shaped the decade that followed. His focal point was the impact of individual actions on totalitarian regimes.

Taking the example of a greengrocer, Havel explained how his participation in the rituals of communist societies—voting in nonelections, putting up party posters, and endorsing positions he did not believe in at public meetings—was essential to maintaining the pretenses of the system. This contradicted the commonly held assumptions about the emptiness of those rituals. The rituals may have seemed meaningless, Havel pointed out, but they served a vital purpose of involving the greengrocer in the game of transforming rituals into a reality with its own rules. The greengrocer, Havel concluded, "has himself become a player in the game, thus making it possible for the game to go on, for it to exist in the first place."

Up till that point, Havel had concentrated on explaining how the communist rulers maintained power, but the essential part of his essay demonstrated the impact of the opposite kind of behavior:

> Let us now imagine that one day something in our greengrocer snaps and he stops putting up the slogans merely to ingratiate himself. He stops voting in elections he knows are a farce. He begins to say what he really thinks at political meetings. And he finds the strength in himself to express solidarity with those whom his conscience commands him to support. In this revolt the greengrocer steps out of living within the lie. He rejects the ritual and breaks the rules of the game. . . . By breaking the rules of the game, he has disrupted the game as such. He has shattered the world of appearances, the fundamental pillar of the system. He has demonstrated that living a lie is living a lie. . . . He has said that the emperor is naked.

The greengrocer's example was meant to be contagious, sending the signal to others that they are not alone in perceiving that the emperor is naked and that they, too, should abandon the pretenses of their lives. In his famous letters from prison in the early 1980s, Polish activist Adam Michnik urged his countrymen to live according to the credo "freedom is self-creation." "You score a victory not when you win power but when you remain faithful to yourself," he wrote. Implicit in such statements was the realization that the political odds against victory were very long, and that it would be a mistake even to begin calculating them. Shortly after he became president, Havel responded to a question at a press conference about his earlier beliefs by saying: "When a person believes in keeping with his conscience, when he tries to speak the truth, and when he tries to behave as a citizen, even under conditions where citizenship is degraded, it may not lead to anything, yet it might. But what surely will not lead to anything is when a person calculates whether it will lead to anything or not."

Yet both Havel and Michnik sensed the broader possibilities of their actions, however carefully they avoided making specific forecasts or raising hopes that could easily be dashed. In his subsequent essays and in conversations, Havel developed a favorite theme—the "radioactivity" of words in a totalitarian state. "When free speech is suppressed, speech paradoxically has a special weight and power," he explained to me when I first visited him in 1986. "A proper word in the proper time is able to influence the situation more than five million voters of some political party in the West." And it was more than a fanciful, near-mystical impulse that prompted Michnik to predict, in a prison letter a year earlier, that the dissidents' seemingly quixotic dedication to following the dictates of conscience could produce an unexpected turnaround. "Here, on a spring morning, one may wake up in a changed country," he wrote.

Individual actions mattered, Michnik repeatedly insisted. In the somber aftermath of martial law, he paraphrased a Milosz poem to the effect "that the course of the avalanche depends on the stones over which it rolls." He then added prophetically: "And you want to be the stone that will reverse the course of events."

As a dissident, political writer, and historian who had confronted successive Polish regimes since his student days in the 1960s, Michnik had been striving for some time to become one of those stones. It was no accident that in the real world it was the dissidents rather than the greengrocers who spoke out first, regardless of the price they had to pay. Russian physicist Yuri Orlov, the founder of the Moscow Helsinki Watch Group, who spent nine years in Soviet prisons and labor camps, once noted that dissidents "can be compared with people who openly throw themselves on barbed wire, hoping that there will be others who will step on their bodies to cross the wire." The barbed wire included loss of jobs, continual harassment by the secret police, repeated imprisonment, occasionally even death. But the dissidents were not easily deterred.

Most activists did not have an overarching vision when they first became involved in the dissident movement. "When I started I had no conscious plan," recalls Grzegorz Boguta of his initial involvement with KOR, the Committee for the Defense of Workers, in the late 1970s. "My goals had the character of a Christian mission: people are being beaten and we need to help them." Boguta had just graduated from the university and started work as a biochemist when he joined the struggle for human rights, and he quickly became a leading organizer of underground publishing operations. His first efforts met a specific need: he published manuals for workers on how to organize.

Such activities, which foreshadowed the far more extensive Polish underground culture that would emerge in the 1980s, began as highly primitive operations. Today Witold Luczywo is a specialist in the computerization of Polish government operations, and he looks back with bemusement at the much more basic challenges he faced when, as a young electronics engineer, he served as an editor and chief printer of *Robotnik* (*Worker*), the underground publication of KOR. As he helped prepare the first issue in 1977, he realized that there was a serious technical problem. The editors had access to mimeograph machines, but mimeographed copies were too bulky for distribution on factory floors, since they could be too easily detected.

Luczywo came up with the idea of employing a simple silkscreen printing process. All he needed was a wood frame stretched with material, which had the added advantage that it could be easily replaced if confiscated. The print was photographically reduced in size but remained quite readable; one page of this process could contain six pages of mimeographed material. He produced ink from a substance he discovered in a common detergent, and he was particularly elated to discover that he could speed up the repetitious lifting motion of the wood frame by using the elastic band found in men's underwear.

At first hundreds and then thousands of copies were printed and distributed by workers. Some workers were caught and arrested, and their copies confiscated. Luczywo was detained twenty-four times for forty-eight hours each, the maximum someone could be held before formal charges were brought. Although the authorities considered him a prime suspect, they failed to catch him with incriminating evidence. When Solidarity won legal recognition from the government in August 1980, he took charge of its printing operations in the Warsaw region. He also ran training courses for activists from all across Poland, teaching them the techniques of silkscreen, stencil, and offset printing. Boguta, who focused primarily on book publishing, says this period of open operations also generated considerable profits, instilling the lessons of the market. "It was good preparation for martial law," he says. "We became more professional in our activities. A large group of people lived from this—printers, distributors, editors."

Once martial law was imposed, activists like Boguta and Luczywo simply resumed their underground operations, but in a far more professional manner than before. As riot police broke down the doors to Solidarity's offices in Warsaw, Luczywo escaped, to go into hiding for two years. "It's very easy to hide in Warsaw. It's a big city," he now says, dismissing that accomplishment as nothing special. He organized the printing of the first issue of the Warsaw-region Solidarity weekly, *Tygodnik Mazowsze,* in February 1982, developing an increasingly sophisticated network of printing operations in the basements or attics of Solidarity supporters' homes on the outskirts of Warsaw. At its peak, sixty to eighty thousand copies of the weekly were published each week. Most of the printing was done on offset presses smuggled in from the West, and some of the layouts were composed on personal computers.

Boguta operated Nowa, the largest of about a hundred leading underground publishing operations, which churned out books and also produced audio- and videotapes. Though many books had a direct political message, the idea was to build up a truly independent culture. "First of all, we published good literature," he says. The authors were an eclectic lot: Milosz, Vonnegut, Grass, Solzhenitsyn, Sakharov, to name a few. Such operations took place under the noses of the secret police, who were constantly looking for printing shops and people distributing the illegal literature. To purchase paper, whose distribution was controlled by the state, the underground publishers used rubber stamps of bogus printing plants and publishers, and they even had their own censorship stamps. When people were arrested and their publications confiscated, this meant big financial losses. Whereas most of the people involved felt they had a political mission, others saw their involvement as a valuable addition to their livelihood—for example, printers in state publishing houses who quietly printed up dissident literature after hours.

Western support played a vital role by providing funds and equipment. Among the most prominent supporters were the AFL-CIO and the National Endowment for Democracy, which understood that, as one Solidarity activist put it, "printing presses were our submachine guns and bazookas." George Orwell had predicted that modern technology would allow totalitarian regimes to extend their control, and the secret police did use new technology, like small video cameras, to monitor dissident activity. But the revolution in communications technology proved to be a boon to opposition movements. Underground video studios produced documentaries and news reports, which were shown on the growing number of VCRs in private homes and church basements. (Parish houses were also used as lecture halls and stages, thus avoiding any state sponsorship or censorship of scholars and performers.) Kenwood Scanners, provided by the AFL-CIO, allowed the underground leaders to listen in on police frequencies and get early warning of impending raids. Western radio stations like Radio Free Europe, the Voice of America, and the BBC provided their invaluable steady input, extending the reach of underground publications by broadcasting their contents.

After a major amnesty for political prisoners in 1986, most of the arrests stopped, but anyone caught printing or distributing underground literature still had to pay a price. The police would confiscate not only whatever literature they found but also property on the premises—radios, televisions, and other items. They levied steep fines. If they caught someone with a significant amount of underground literature in his car, they would confiscate the car. But here, too, the organizers came up with an ingenious free-market response. Boguta set up an insurance fund, to which all of the underground publishers contributed—and which repaid people for their material losses. "But if someone was caught, his insurance premium also shot up," notes Boguta. "It was Western-style insurance. We were learning about the market."

For all their imaginative initiatives and responses, many activists did suffer from serious moments of self-doubt. "In the mid-1980s, I had a crisis, a feeling that we were deceiving ourselves," says Boguta. "I thought that we underground publishers and authors were trapped in a black box, that our activities were only medicine for our frustration, that we were simply writing, publishing, and reading for ourselves." None of the top Solidarity leaders accepted the regime's cynical offer to free them from prison if they would go abroad. In a letter to Interior Minister Czeslaw Kiszczak, Michnik poured scorn on the proposal. "To offer to a man, who has been held in prison for two years, the Côte d'Azur in exchange for his moral suicide, one would have to be a swine." But many lower-ranking Solidarity activists did quietly leave the country in those years, convinced that any change, if it came at all, would be too late for them to benefit from it. "You had to have a certain blind optimism," Boguta told me in discussing his own commitment to activism despite his doubts. "I believed in what I was doing."

My experience in 1985, when I interviewed underground leader Bujak, had led me to underestimate somewhat how many activists found it similarly difficult to convince themselves. At a diplomatic party in Warsaw in 1991, I suddenly found myself looking at a familiar bearded face. Its owner introduced himself as Zbigniew Lewicki, the director of the North and South American department of the Foreign Ministry—and reminded me that we had met in 1985, when he had served as my escort to Bujak. I was delighted: at long last, I was able to learn who he was and about his double life back then. Officially, he had taught American literature at Warsaw University; unofficially, he had arranged Bujak's hideouts and logistics. But Lewicki, the anonymous foot soldier who had looked to me like the quintessential picture of commitment, conceded that he had acted more out of a sense of duty than of any conviction that such actions could produce results; communism, it seemed to him, would last another fifty years.

"In those days, it all seemed a lost cause. You had to do this, but you didn't have the feeling that this would end in triumph. It became quickly apparent that the police were stronger. It was a period when, honestly, a lot of people had had enough of all this. Only Bujak was still saying, 'When we win . . .' "

Perhaps it was in the nature of intellectuals like Lewicki to entertain more doubts than workers like Bujak. Zbigniew Janas, Bujak's colleague from the Ursus tractor factory, says flatly: "I never had doubts whether to act, only how." But they were also the ones to take the highly theoretical message of Havel's essay "The Power of the Powerless" to heart, recognizing that it not only represented a moral argument but also provided a broader political rationale for their activism. When the essay was published in the underground Polish press in 1979, they treated it as "a great discovery." Everything made sense, even to Bujak, who was not quite as zealous an optimist as Janas. "When we were working at Ursus, there came a moment of doubt: I could not see how this could lead to a bigger success, how it could lead to a weakening of the system. Then Havel's essay came and lifted our spirits," he says. He adds wryly: "The Czechs had excellent theoreticians of opposition, and we had the opposition."

In fact, the Charter 77 movement in Czechoslovakia had demonstrated surprising resilience, and it had helped spawn a "parallel culture" like Poland's, even if it was considerably smaller. In 1979, Kundera, by then in exile, bemoaned "the massacre of Czech culture." That was accurate as far as officially sanctioned culture was concerned. The post-1968 "normalization," that favorite euphemism of terrified despots, did enforce a deadening conformity in public life and, at first, private resignation. The initial attempts to act according to Havel's credo of carving out space for independent activity had resulted in arrests and long jail terms; many of the dissidents felt not only persecuted but psychologically isolated. By the mid-1980s, however, there was an almost palpable, if still-labored, reawakening of the citizenry.

The samizdat press focused on human-rights abuses, the disastrous state of the environment, and religious affairs. In early 1988, five hundred thousand Catholics signed a petition demanding religious freedoms and an end to the government's suffocating control of church appointments, which had left most of the country's dioceses without bishops. In private homes, Czechs studied everything from ancient Greek and Hebrew to the Bible and astrology. On a visit to the home of dissident philosopher Ladislav Hejdanek in Prague, I stumbled into a gathering of Czech scholars listening to a lecture by a Belgian visitor on an obscure academic debate about logic, whose tortured reasoning left me and, I suspect, some of the courteous audience less enlightened than confused. But the important point was that each such unlicensed gathering defied government controls, weakening what had once been a to-

talitarian state, and forming the basis for what activists began to identify as an emerging "civil society."

As in Poland, the government's monopoly on information was also
undermined by new technologies. The spread of VCRs produced a flourishing black market in uncensored movies from abroad, including politically charged offerings like Andrzej Wajda's Solidarity-era films about
Polish workers. When Karel Srp finished serving a sixteen-month prison
sentence in early 1988 for his leadership of the Jazz Section, a popular
independent music club and publishing operation, he was astounded to
be immediately interviewed for the first independent video journal,
which, as in Poland, circulated clandestinely on video cassettes. All of
this helped contribute to a feeling that the dissidents were no longer
alone, that their message was spreading and seeping into the popular
consciousness of a population whose passivity masked rather than
demonstrated its true feelings.

Speaking after the collapse of the communist regime, Foreign Minister Dienstbier recalled thinking that the dissident label had been mis-
applied. "I always resisted that word," he said, adding about the
communists: "I felt they were the dissidents." Or, as a bit of Prague graf-
fiti put it, referring to the "normalization" campaign: "They tried to
normalize us, but we were normal all the time."

Whatever the differences in scale, the similarities with Poland were
no accident. Charter 77 and other activists were encouraged by the Polish example and also offered some encouragement of their own. In 1986,
Petr Pospichal, a young Charter 77 member, managed to establish contact with Zbigniew Janas. Pospichal wanted to know if the Poles would
be willing to set up some form of cooperation with them; Janas quickly
agreed. Soon the two sides worked out a pattern of meetings in the
mountains on the Polish-Czechoslovak border, using codes to set the
time and place. In areas scouted out beforehand, activists from each side
held several meetings. Aside from Pospichal and Janas, they included the
likes of Havel, Michnik, and other leading dissidents of both countries.
The meetings actually took place on the Czechoslovak side of the border, so that the Poles would be guilty of crossing the border illegally instead of the Czechs, who faced tougher penalties under their hard-line
regime.

Pospichal spent four months in prison in early 1987 for arranging
those contacts, but strong protests from Solidarity, which were subsequently echoed in the West, helped get him released and the border activism expanded further. The Poles arranged to send across samizdat

journals and books; some were in Polish, but others were prepared by the Czechs in their own language and then published on the far more sophisticated Polish equipment. Two groups of "hikers"—one Polish, one Czech—would meet at the mountain paths along the border, carrying identical knapsacks. They would sit down not far from each other without exchanging a word, and when they got up to leave they would take each other's knapsacks.

Such exploits bolstered the spirits of both sides. For the Czechs, it gave them access to the far broader resources of the Poles. "The barrier between dissidents and ordinary people was very great here," Pospichal points out. "We could not count on the help of ordinary people. It was only later, in 1988, that the situation here began to resemble the situation in Poland in the early 1980s and people began to come up and offer help." As a result, the feeling that they had the support of their Polish counterparts provided an important psychological boost. For the Polish activists, the effect was similar. "This was a period when a lot of people here had doubts whether our activism served any purpose," recalls Janas. "This gave us a feeling we were needed and recharged our batteries." The push for liberation was now a movement not only from below, breaking through barriers of the mind and internal political structures, but also through the barriers of international borders.

Those international barriers were both physical and psychological. However stridently Western politicians berated the Kremlin for dividing the European continent, they all too often tacitly acquiesced in the assumption that the division was all but officially permanent. When policy-makers in Washington, Bonn, or Paris spoke of "Europe," they meant Western Europe—those countries either allied with the United States or formally neutral. Eastern Europe, an area similarly defined by politics rather than by geography, was excluded, its nations and peoples branded separate and unequal because of the political system imposed on them by the Soviet Union at the end of World War II.

For Eastern European intellectuals and activists, one of the greatest challenges was to debunk such thinking. Past frontal attacks on the "naïveté" of Westerners in dealing with the Soviet Union rarely produced positive results, only bitterness on both sides. Whatever the historical merits of their case, Eastern Europeans who simply recycled old arguments about the West's responsibility for caving in to Stalin at Yalta, thus sealing the region's fate, made little political headway. But the Helsinki agreement of 1975, Jimmy Carter's emphasis on universal human rights, and Ronald Reagan's rhetorical assault on "the evil empire" provided them with new openings. There was a chance to present Eastern Europe in a new light, challenging the tacit assumptions produced by decades of subjugation by presenting a new frame of reference for examining the processes at work in the region.

It was hardly surprising that the impulse for such an initiative came from Hungary, where Janos Kadar had accomplished a remarkable transformation. Once known as "the butcher of Budapest" for his role in suppressing the 1956 revolt and the execution of the popular Prime Minister Imre Nagy, Kadar had doggedly worked at recasting his—and his country's—image. He launched economic reforms that, by the standards of the time, were far-reaching. His government abolished farmers' compulsory deliveries to the state, ensuring well-stocked food markets. It also loosened industrial central planning, and allowed for the emergence of a small private sector in the 1980s. Kadar coupled such measures with a gradual easing of political repression. "Whoever is not against us is for us," he proclaimed in 1961, reversing the old Stalinist dictum that "Whoever is not with us is against us." Slowly, he won a measure of recognition, both at home and abroad, as the leader of the most liberal regime in Eastern Europe.

The "democratic opposition" that emerged in the 1980s acknowledged that they faced far less brutal treatment than their counterparts in Czechoslovakia and Poland, but they, too, were harassed, denied jobs and travel abroad when they refused to accept the expanded but still-definite limits that the system imposed. Dissident Miklos Haraszti argued, in his 1981 book *The Velvet Prison: Artists Under State Socialism,* that intellectuals were experiencing not freedom but entrapment in an alluring web, a "velvet prison." The new regime made it easier for artists to engage in politically "neutral art," sometimes daring in form, that made it possible to retain the illusion of self-respect. But Haraszti maintained that real change could take place only if intellectuals rejected the compromises that, however seductive, brooked no questioning of the state's power to demand loyalty.

Nonetheless, Kadar's determination to project an enlightened image provided a valuable tool to his critics. The Hungarian leader wanted to be seen as someone in charge of a country that occupied a special place in Europe, commanding the respect of both East and West. The activists considered this a sham, but they could exploit his reluctance to resort to new repression by triggering an open political debate about how genuinely to overcome the East-West divide.

In October 1986, on the thirtieth anniversary of the Hungarian uprising, 122 prominent dissidents from Hungary, Poland, Czechoslovakia, and East Germany issued what at the time was a remarkably bold joint declaration. Asserting that Hungary's revolutionaries had sought "independence, democracy, and neutrality," they announced: "We declare our joint determination to struggle for political democracy in our countries, pluralism based on the principles of self-government, peaceful reunification of divided Europe and its democratic integration, as well as the rights of minorities."

The philosophical underpinnings for that declaration had been spelled out by Hungary's George Konrad in his book *Antipolitics* two years earlier. His prose was aimed primarily at Westerners, who were caught up in an impassioned arms-control debate, forgetting that arms-control issues were merely a symptom of a much larger problem. And he was determined to spell out the nature of that problem:

> It is pleasant to commiserate with the unfortunate Eastern European cousins, but let no one think the West is going to make any trouble on their account. They got détente, they got credits, what more do they want? What more? They want a creative initiative, a concrete, tangible peace proposal, a plan to take down the Iron Curtain. They want Western Europeans to understand that while Eastern Europe remains under occupation, Western Europeans cannot live in security. . . . Western Europe rests its back against a wall of dynamite, while blithely gazing out over the Atlantic. I consider Western Europe's good fortune as uncertain as our misfortune.

Then, in a prescient observation, he summed up the significance of the disparate strands of dissent that still appeared so fragile at that time. "A European movement for emancipation has begun, and it will inevitably become a movement against Yalta," he wrote. Konrad's specific recommendation for a "post-Yalta" formula: a radical Western proposal for German reunification, the dissolution of NATO and the Warsaw Pact, and the creation of a European federation. Among the dissident community, especially in Poland and Czechoslovakia, there were very mixed feelings about the usefulness and merits of such a proposal, but there was agreement on the underlying premise motivating it. "What threatens peace in Europe is not the prospect of change but the existing situation," Havel explained.

The contribution of *Antipolitics* was to make that case dramatically, however questionable Konrad's proposals proved to be. To change the frame of reference of the East-West debate further, Konrad and others revived an old concept: "Mitteleuropa" or Central Europe. On both sides of Europe's political divide, Mitteleuropa became the subject of a mushrooming debate on a topic that was once thought to have been buried in the rubble of the Third Reich and by the decisions made at Yalta. The lack of any clear definition of precisely what Mitteleuropa meant made it an ideal subject for intellectual dissection and controversy. Suddenly, it was the topic of seminars, kitchen debates, and proclamations. On a visit to Budapest in early 1987, I found Konrad a bit stunned by what had happened. "I was one of those who started this discussion, but I never expected it would become so fashionable," he told me.

Those who promoted the concept were a diverse group: not just dissident intellectuals in Hungary and Czechoslovakia, but also former leftist activists of the 1960s along with some members of the radical Greens and conservative Christian Democrats in West Germany, and a smattering of Austrians, Poles, Slovenes, and Italians of varying political hues. The single conviction they all shared was that, as Konrad had spelled out in *Antipolitics,* the division of Europe was unnatural and that, at least in psychological terms, it had to be overcome. The term Mitteleuropa, West Berlin writer Karl Schlögel argued in his book *Die Mitte liegt ostwärts: Die Deutschen, der verlorene Osten und Mitteleuropa* (*The Middle Lies Eastward: The Germans, the Lost East and Mitteleuropa*), was a challenge "to the wall in our heads." Those proponents did not have to be reminded that Prague is farther West than Vienna and that the political divisions did not respect the cultural roots of the region.

In his famous essay "The Tragedy of Central Europe," Milan Kundera put the history of the successive revolts in the region in perspective. "The deep meaning of their resistance is the struggle to preserve their identity—or, to put it in another way, to preserve their Westernness," he wrote. Though Kundera asserted that Central Europe's borders cannot be drawn exactly since "it is a culture or a fate," he argued that the Central European culture is fundamentally Western, set apart from Russia, which is "a singular civilization, an *other* civilization."

The Mitteleuropa concept strengthened the sense of common cause, especially among those who were painfully aware that separately their countries had never been able to throw off Soviet domination. Some of the sentiment was reminiscent of the "Austroslavism" of the Austrian empire. Even in 1848, when nationalist feelings were on the rise, a Pan-Slavic Congress meeting in Prague was dominated by the "Austroslavs." They advocated national development within the framework of the Austrian empire; otherwise, they feared they would not be able to survive, wedged in as they were between the Germans and the Russians.

Such historical analogies were more than coincidental, since the Hapsburg period was enjoying an emotional comeback. In Czechoslovakia, official histories still offered a standard Marxist interpretation of that era, but many young Czechs took an uncritically nostalgic view when comparing it with their bleak contemporary conditions. In Hungary, even official history books had begun to describe the creation of the Dual Monarchy of Austria-Hungary in 1867, which granted Hungary local autonomy, in generally positive terms. A statue of Elisabeth, the wife of Hapsburg Emperor Franz Josef, was put up again in Budapest in 1986; it had been taken down in 1962.

Although dismissing Konrad's notion of a neutral Mitteleuropa as "political fiction," Hungarian officials were eager to boast about the dramatic improvement in the ties between their country and neutral Austria. Economic and cultural ties were flourishing, and since 1979 visas had no longer been required for travel between the two countries. They did not want to make Moscow nervous with any talk of creeping neutralization, but they were happy to convey the impression to Westerners that their Warsaw Pact membership did not establish their full identity, that they were in fact a part of that hazy cultural region known as Mitteleuropa.

In that sense, the strategy of Konrad and other Mitteleuropa proponents of using the notion to change the frame of reference of the East-West discussions was working. By defining themselves as Central Europeans, with common roots transcending the East-West division, they were making a political as well as a cultural statement. If Westerners began to think of them as Central Europeans, they could hardly be indifferent to their fate. If Hungarian communist leaders began to reorient their thinking in the same direction, the country could start to redefine its role. And if the Kremlin even tacitly accepted such an evolutionary course, the Iron Curtain would begin to disappear.

Such sweeping scenarios were far from the minds of many of the Western politicians attracted to the Mitteleuropa concept. They had more modest aims, centered on the regional cooperation and contacts that proved to be the first practical manifestations of Mitteleuropa thinking. If Soviet domination could not be exorcised, they figured, these arrangements would at least offer a bit more breathing room for those who considered themselves Central Europeans. "It's a little piece of freedom for them," explained Vienna's Deputy Mayor Erhard Busek, co-author of the book *Project Mitteleuropa*. The conservative politician urged further cultural and academic exchanges, the creation of an East-West scientific academy, and Austrian television and radio broadcasts in the languages of neighboring communist states.

Those proposals were far from purely altruistic; the Austrians, in particular, were also motivated by their own concerns. Austrian intellectuals recognized that their country had lost touch with its heritage by accepting the notion that it was part of Western instead of Central Europe. Busek's special concern was Vienna's demotion to the status of a provincial capital, since it was cut off from its Central European roots. "If Vienna wants to be a city a little bit bigger than Austria is in a cultural sense, it has to look to Mitteleuropa," he told me.

As the Mitteleuropa debate took on momentum, many of the participants warned that it also contained hidden dangers. Austrian historians cautioned that it should not lead to a romanticizing of the country's past, especially the creation of a myth that all nationalities had lived happily under the Hapsburgs. Any reluctance to confront Central Europe's dark legacy of this century—two world wars, the Nazi era, and, particularly, the anti-Semitism that brought on the Holocaust—could lead to actions that exacerbated tensions rather than eased them. In West Germany, many adherents of the Mitteleuropa idea were acutely aware of those dangers. In discussing his book about Germany's Central European identity, Schlögel emphasized the need for acknowledgment of German ties to the East as well as to the West, but he was uncomfortable with calls by either the left (for neutralization of the two Germanys) or by the right (for reunification).

"I of course wish for the reunification of Europe and of Germany and Berlin, but we don't as yet have the conditions to free ourselves from the suspicion that we want to manipulate the Mitteleuropa discussion for our own aims of reunification," Schlögel said. "That suspicion is justified by the whole history of this century."

If West Germans remained badly divided on how to handle the touchy reunification issue only a couple of years before the Berlin Wall came down, the Mitteleuropa discussion helped forge somewhat unexpected *de facto* alliances on some of the practical aspects of how to deal with those on the other side of the European divide. The Greens and Christian Democrats agreed on at least one point: their mutual contempt for the traditional Social Democratic view that they must deal primarily with the governments of the Eastern bloc. The party that had won applause for its innovative *Ostpolitik* of the 1970s had compromised itself by shying away from the new democratic movements that emerged in Eastern Europe, preferring instead to meet with communist officials. In December 1985, the party's chairman, Willy Brandt, met with government officials in Warsaw and refused to see Lech Walesa.

The Mitteleuropa debate had produced growing criticism of such actions. "I would assert that the inner aversion of many West German intellectuals to the people of Eastern Europe is the result of successful blackmail," wrote Peter Schneider, author of *The Wall Jumper* and like Schlögel a former New Left writer in West Berlin. The blackmail in question: that those who wish to keep peace with Moscow should largely ignore human-rights abuses and popular aspirations within the Soviet bloc. In this situation, according to Mitteleuropa proponents, the traditional West German left had become the most faithful defender of the *status quo,* barely concealing its satisfaction, for example, when Solidarity was crushed and "order" was restored in Poland.

Through its emphasis on popular aspirations, the Mitteleuropa debate also forced the Eastern Europeans to examine their own feelings about eventual German unification. In Czechoslovakia and Hungary, many intellectuals were open to the idea of reunification, but they insisted that it should not be achieved by submitting to Soviet terms. "If we insist on the self-determination of all people, that has to include the German people," said Jiri Hayek, who served as Czechoslovakia's foreign minister during the Prague Spring of 1968. Polish intellectuals were more wary of German aspirations—as they were of the entire Mitteleuropa discussion. "The concept does not exist as far as Polish writers are concerned, because Poles think of themselves as belonging to the West," argued Michnik. He also disagreed with Kundera's notion that Mitteleuropa should exclude Russian culture. "What kind of European culture would it be without Dostoevsky, Tchaikovsky, Prokofiev, Chekhov?" he asked. "Mitteleuropa ought to be an antixenophobic idea."

But, for all the reservations and disagreements, the debate started by Konrad had a tremendously positive impact, spreading the message that the region's broader cultural identity would eventually prevail over a political system that had been imposed on its inhabitants. In retrospect, the fact that such seemingly utopian logic was translated into reality endows the Mitteleuropa proponents with a visionary mission. At the time, Konrad conceded that his proposal for the neutralization of Central Europe was construed as "more of a stimulus for thought" than a practical means to that end. "I believe that political ideas come from intellectual discussions," he told me. He was right on both counts: neutralization was not a proposal that caught on, because Eastern Europeans had no desire to come up with a solution akin to what the West sometimes called "Finlandization," a neutrality favoring the Soviet Union; nonetheless, the intellectual discussion produced tangible political results.

The degree to which Mitteleuropa thinking seeped into the consciousness of Hungary's communist rulers became apparent at a critical moment in 1989, which marked the beginning of the end of the Iron Curtain. Admittedly, the Hungarian leaders acted only after Poland had already achieved its breakthrough agreement between the Jaruzelski government and Solidarity that led to the creation of the first noncommunist government in Eastern Europe. But this did not diminish the momentous nature of Hungary's actions in September of that year. Faced with a crisis, the Hungarian authorities could either respond as Central Europeans, people motivated by the cultural traditions of the West, or as captives of the communist political system; they could not reconcile the two by fudging their stance, as they had attempted to do in the past.

That summer, Hungary had opened its borders with Austria, ostentatiously beginning to take down the barbed-wire fences that separated the two countries. Since Hungarians had been able to travel freely to Austria for a decade, this was primarily intended as a symbolic gesture, aimed at demonstrating that Hungary should no longer be considered as merely a member of the Soviet bloc. The Hungarian leaders were trying to shelter their country from the economic disintegration of the rest of the bloc, and they were eagerly seeking Western approval and financial support. But the decision had far-reaching implications. East Germans were allowed to visit Hungary and other "fraternal socialist countries," and they quickly discovered that they could freely cross the Hungarian-Austrian border, prompting a mass exodus.

Erich Honecker's regime was enraged, and demanded a prompt reversal in Hungary's policy. Budapest faced a clear choice: either it could honor its international human-rights commitments, which it had embraced to prove it could meet those "Western" standards, or it could honor a twenty-year-old treaty between Hungary and East Germany in which the countries pledged to prevent each other's citizens from moving west without permission.

There was no ambiguity about the Hungarian decision. Referring to the Hungarian–East German treaty, Foreign Minister Gyula Horn declared: "Such agreements should be annulled or modified." In the midst of the ensuing uproar, I asked Istvan Foldesi, a special assistant to Communist Party General Secretary Karoly Grosz, what the reasons for this action were. "We thought that, if we wanted to meet the requirements of joining Europe, this was the test," he explained.

Suddenly, the Iron Curtain had a gaping hole—and this spelled the beginning of the end of the East German state, which could only survive if the exits were blocked. For activists in Czechoslovakia, this was also a signal that all hard-line governments in the regime were vulnerable, including their own; up till then, they were still not sure if the earlier breakthrough in Poland heralded a broader transformation or merely reflected that country's stubborn long history of struggle, which might have to be repeated elsewhere to achieve similar results. Mitteleuropa was no longer an abstract notion but a reality in the making.

What kind of reality did the inhabitants envisage for themselves if they could finally shape it?

As an exchange student in Krakow in 1968, I found Polish students depressed, beaten down. The two blows they had just suffered had proved devastating: the brutal suppression of their protests in March, which had called for the kind of broad liberalization that they were witnessing in neighboring Czechoslovakia, and then the crushing of the Prague Spring itself. Nonetheless, they still held out hope for what Dubcek had popularized as "socialism with a human face"—a middle way between the totalitarianism of Soviet-style systems and Western "bourgeois democracy."

Back in Poland in May 1988, the mood among a group of Warsaw University students I met at a café was equally depressed. Strikes had once again erupted in Gdansk, and the government appeared unyielding in its refusal to recognize Solidarity or relinquish any of its dictatorial powers. But when I reminded them of the faith of the 1960s generation in democratic socialism, they scoffed at the naïveté of anyone who could have held such beliefs. Among their generation, a sociology student volunteered, "Nobody is for socialism."

In the new Eastern Europe or Mitteleuropa taking shape in the 1980s, the most striking philosophical change was the complete abandonment of middle-way thinking. The belief in a middle way required a modicum of faith that communist leaders could be found who would institute genuine reforms, honestly seeking humane solutions under that fuzzy rubric of democratic socialism. But harsh experience had proved that any leader who seriously pursued reforms would be stopped, as Dubcek was, by Soviet tanks. Other self-proclaimed reformers, like Poland's Gierek or Hungary's Kadar, balked at any changes that would have touched the core of the communist system. As for middle-way economic solutions, Yugoslavia had amply demonstrated how any effort to break new ground guarantees only decades of confusion and crisis.

The earlier search for a middle way was also based on a justification tacitly employed by almost every Eastern European communist leader since the war: that they had to operate within the constraints of a system imposed by the Kremlin, which may have offered some limited room for maneuver but only within strict boundaries. However, the activists of the late 1970s and the 1980s were no longer willing to accept those rules or the rationale for them. If most dissident movements steered clear of openly endorsing multiparty systems and free-market economics until the mid-1980s, this had less to do with the evolution of their views than with survival tactics. "Antisocialist" behavior still sent dissidents to jail or cost them their jobs; in the eyes of the authorities, anyone who advocated pluralism and capitalism was effectively signing his own confession. As repression eased, those goals were openly acknowledged with increasing frequency.

The revulsion against anything labeled as socialist was readily apparent. "What is the relationship between democracy and democratic socialism?" asked a joke making the rounds in Poland in the mid-1980s. "The same as between a chair and an electric chair." The dissidents might debate whether a Swedish model of capitalism, with its broad safety net, or the American model, with its relatively narrow one, was more appealing, but they recognized that neither represented a middle way in the old sense of that term. Their goal was the establishment of Western institutions within their countries, displacing the system they loathed. "The vision behind the notion of Mitteleuropa is that communist rule is temporary," Hungary's Haraszti explained in 1987, when such a statement required a leap of faith.

This did not mean an uncritical endorsement of everything Western. In his early dissident writings, Havel wrote not only of the dangers of totalitarianism of the East but also of "the omnipresent dictatorship of consumption, production, advertising, commerce, consumer culture" in the West. The other prominent figure who issued similar warnings was, by no accident, the Polish pope, John Paul II. But those reservations had more to do with the philosophical or spiritual realm than with specific political or economic mechanisms.

After the upheavals of 1989, both Havel and the pope made clear that they were not seeking to avoid capitalism, only to infuse it with a greater sense of moral responsibility and less greed than is evident in the West. An unintentional by-product of communist repression, Havel told a joint session of the United States Congress in February 1990, was that it allowed people to take a longer view. "A person who cannot move and live a somewhat normal life because he is pinned under a boulder has more time to think about his hopes than someone who is not trapped that way." What the newly liberated Europeans have to offer, he concluded, is "our experience and the knowledge that comes from it." This was a lofty sentiment of what could be labeled middle-way morality, which would prove difficult to maintain in the transition to democracy and capitalism. And for many activists in the 1980s, these were increasingly abstract and largely irrelevant considerations.

In the struggle against the old system, the shedding of any illusions about the viability of middle-way solutions strengthened the dissident movement. Oddly enough, Mikhail Gorbachev's obstinate clinging to his illusions on the same score speeded up their victories. Gorbachev was a self-described product of the 1960s, who rejected Stalinism in favor of the vague concept of reform socialism. When he first came to power, his ideas about reform reflected less of Dubcek than of his late mentor, KGB chief and party leader Yuri Andropov. Like Andropov, Gorbachev initially believed that cosmetic reforms and the instilling of greater "discipline" at the workplace could make the command economy function efficiently; based on that assumption, he launched his disastrous antialcohol campaign, which failed to curtail the consumption of alcohol but succeeded in alienating much of the population. He began to understand the broader dimensions of the crisis after such tinkering produced dismal results, aggravating an already alarming pattern of decay, but he refused to give up on the notion of reform socialism throughout his six years in power.

But, significantly for Eastern Europe, Gorbachev began to view the relationship between economics and politics in a fundamentally different light from his predecessors. For the previous Kremlin leaders, the taboos for Eastern Europe were easily identifiable: no challenges to the Communist Party's monopoly on power, and no talk of leaving the Warsaw Pact. If a choice existed between enforcing political control and achieving economic gains, there was no doubt which decision would be taken. Gorbachev understood that the exercise of strict political control, at the price of deepening economic disarray, was self-defeating at home and in Eastern Europe. In a high-tech age, the Soviet Union could not count on maintaining its military might unless the country's economic base underwent major repairs; the old insulation between a well-oiled military machine and a Third World civilian economy could come apart. That, in turn, would undermine the Soviet Union's political status as a superpower, even if—and this was far from certain—popular discontent with deteriorating economic conditions did not produce significant social unrest.

Once he had made the decision to focus primarily on seeking to repair the Soviet economy, Gorbachev almost inevitably had to take a radically different tack on Eastern Europe. From his vantage point, the ideal solution would have been for reform communists within that region to come up with strategies for economic progress that would satisfy popular aspirations, eliminating the threat of new unrest. His obstinate belief in a middle way led him to conclude that such a solution was genuinely possible. He envisaged not the abolition of the communist system but its salvation through reform. And after being tested in those smaller laboratories, the successful strategies could possibly be applied in the Soviet Union itself, helping him with his domestic agenda.

All this turned out to be self-deception, as subsequent events proved. "He didn't realize the consequences of his actions. He couldn't imagine them," Professor Svetlana Falkovich of the Institute of Slavic and Balkan Studies in Moscow later pointed out. As late as October 1989, when East Germany was celebrating its fortieth anniversary, his message to Honecker was, in essence, to preserve a more humane East Germany. He did not understand that any weakening of the long-standing Soviet commitment to use force if necessary in Eastern Europe, which his actions signaled, would trigger a process that would sweep away not only the hard-liners but also communist reformers. If he had, he might never have sent those signals. As perhaps the last believer in a middle way, Gorbachev blundered into a *de facto* alliance with the opposition movements in Eastern Europe, whose goals were radically different from his own.

Those opposition movements triumphed because of what has to rank as this century's major creative intellectual achievements: the development of a nonviolent strategy, an entire philosophy of resistance, that undermined the seemingly invincible military and political might of the Soviet empire. But the result was not only the product of the happy coincidence of the internal struggle, the grand crusade for democracy "from below," and more favorable external conditions; it was also determined by the sometimes brilliant, sometimes idiosyncratic behavior of the people who were in the forefront of the opposition movements— and particularly of the person who played the leading role, Lech Walesa.

As the leader of Solidarity, Walesa was a one-man generator, a shipyard electrician generating his own electricity. His fame and stature prompted the authorities to pamper him during his eleven-month detention after martial law was imposed. Instead of serving in an internment camp, he lived in comfort in government villas and was fed a rich diet that caused him to put on jowls. He had attained such a privileged position because of his instinctive political genius, his ability to galvanize the constantly feuding Solidarity activists and to lead negotiations with the government; the Jaruzelski team felt that they could not afford to treat him like just another political prisoner—he was a special case, no matter how eagerly they tried to dismiss him in public as an ordinary citizen with no more official function.

Walesa was surrounded by intellectual advisers, but at key moments he was the one who made the decisions that proved essential to the next breakthrough. "I saw the personality of a leader," notes Andrzej Celinski, a young sociologist who served as one of his closest advisers throughout the 1980s. "I was not put off by his lack of education, by his primitive language, by his inability to express a coherent game plan. That didn't matter."

What did matter was Walesa's enormous personal ambition and his ability to think several steps ahead of the others. Celinski recalls driving with Walesa from Warsaw to Gdansk in April 1981, during Solidarity's legal existence but in a period when the danger signals were everywhere. Walesa turned to Celinski and said jokingly: "I'll make you foreign minister." When Celinski wondered how, Walesa replied without hesitation: "I'll be the leader."

Walesa understood that he had an informal power that could propel him to the top, even if it was hard to imagine what that top might be. And he was determined to position himself politically against future potential rivals who might stand in his way. When he was freed by the authorities in 1982, he was especially concerned about not being eclipsed by Bujak and other underground leaders who were still in hiding. "He was fighting not only for victory, he was fighting for his position after the victory over the communists," Celinski says. "And that was during the worst period, when no one dreamed of victory." When the underground leadership of Bujak called for a strike, Walesa often countermanded the order at the last moment. Since Walesa knew that many of the strike calls would go unheeded anyway, because workers were tired of high-risk, low-gain protests, he could accomplish two goals: he won the quiet gratitude of those workers who wanted an excuse not to strike, and he reinforced his image as the reasonable leader who made the decisions that counted.

Celinski describes Walesa's use of such tactics in uncompromising terms. "Walesa is a cold, calculating SOB. He is incredibly self-centered. He wants everything for himself. And he exploits his position with cold calculation." But Celinski also openly admires the political skills Walesa displayed in his shadowboxing with the underground leadership, whose activism was essential to maintaining his own authority since it demonstrated the strong pro-Solidarity sentiment in the country. "He was pushing Bujak into the position of a crazy underground activist, an extremist who was ineffective at the same time," Celinski points out. As for Bujak, he only shakes his head now at what happened during that period, admitting that he did not realize Walesa saw him primarily as a political rival. "I underestimated to what extent Lech was worried about my standing and how far he was willing to go to lower it."

If Walesa's overwhelming personal ambition drove him to play hardball with his allies, it also fueled his struggle against the communist system. He knew that his future depended on his ability to best his real opponents. In that, he had no equal. When the Jaruzelski team decided at long last it had to negotiate, it turned to Walesa. Despite warnings from more militant activists that he might be trapped into long deliberations designed to undercut Solidarity's authority, he agreed, putting his personal reputation on the line by calling for an end to strikes even before the negotiations finally were formally launched.

At the round-table talks in early 1989, he led the Solidarity team in hammering out an agreement that once again represented a major political gamble. The accords lifted the seven-year ban on Solidarity and called for partially free elections, but they still apeared to guarantee communist domination of the next government. When Solidarity won a stunning 260 of 261 contested seats in parliament, the fact that the communists had reserved a majority of the seats for themselves and their allies no longer loomed so large; two smaller parties ended their alliance with the communists, tipping the balance in favor of Solidarity. Walesa took the offensive once again, overriding his intellectual advisers and demanding that Solidarity form the first noncommunist government in Eastern Europe, assuming responsibility for a country that was near economic collapse and for a political system suffering the equivalent of a nervous breakdown. With his critics shouting that he was walking straight into a trap, Walesa achieved the breakthrough that triggered all of the subsequent events of that momentous year.

It was a year filled with risks and delicious ironies. Wiktor Kulerski, a leading underground activist who managed to elude the authorities until they stopped the arrests altogether, readily admits that he was among the most hardened of the skeptics about Solidarity's chances from the very beginning. He recalls that he told his father in 1980: "On this communist dung heap, a flower like Solidarity cannot blossom. It must die poisoned by the soil from which it grew." In 1989, after he won a seat in parliament on the Solidarity ticket, he suddenly found himself in a parliamentary corridor opposite the man whose job had been to hunt him down, Interior Minister Czeslaw Kiszczak. Kulerski was not sure how to behave, and he thought of trying to slip by unnoticed. But Kiszczak spotted him and rushed up to shake his hand.

"Ah, Wiktor," the general said, "how we searched for you—our best people searched for five years."

"Ah, General," Kulerski replied, "if I'd only known—I really didn't want to cause you so much trouble."

With such scenes playing themselves out in Poland, other regimes were finding it increasingly difficult to command the modicum of obedience that had been so essential to keeping dissent within bounds. A giddy feeling of new possibilities was sweeping away previous inhibitions. The process of driving totalitarianism "out of our own souls," as Havel put it, was in its final stages.

Shortly after he was elected to parliament in June, Janas and three of his colleagues who had been active in the Solidarity–Charter 77 contacts decided to pay their first open visit to Czechoslovakia. The Czechoslovak authorities did not prevent them from entering the country, but kept them under close surveillance as they made the rounds of local activists. When the group visited Havel in his country house, they found their host troubled about where events might lead in Czechoslovakia, since he had received signals that the government was ready to use force if the opposition decided to stage new demonstrations. Havel wanted to step up the pressure against the authorities, but he was worried about the possibility of bloodshed.

Despite Havel's concerns, spirits were high among the veteran activists; the transformation in Poland, and the Poles' personal transformations from dissidents into politicians, prompted a lot of joking and jubilation. Olga Havel cooked a hearty meal, which was accompanied by large amounts of beer and champagne. Afterward, Havel had a flash of inspiration: instead of using the bathroom, he led his guests outside to urinate in full view of the secret-police surveillance cameras he knew were routinely deployed in a cottage opposite his house. Czechoslovakia's final confrontation was still a few months away, but a police state that prompted such open mockery was already deprived of its most potent weapon, the ability to inspire fear, and its fate was all but sealed.

THE
COMMUNIST
AFTERLIFE

THE BORY PRISON, on the outskirts of Pilsen in western Bohemia, is a ponderous yellowish structure built in 1876, when the Hapsburgs still reigned, surrounded by a twelve-foot-high concrete wall. Cell blocks radiate like spokes from a wheel along corridors shooting out from a central hub, whose heavy doors of iron bars clang continually throughout the day. During the communist era, about twelve hundred inmates were housed there at any one time, a mixture of common criminals and political prisoners, including its most famous former resident, Vaclav Havel. After 1989, the prison population declined to a more comfortable number of about seven hundred, offering the prisoners more living space and better overall conditions, more time to watch television, and a more relaxed atmosphere. But the prisoner I came to visit in October 1991 insisted that, at least in one respect, there was continuity rather than discontinuity in the new era: as the only former senior Communist Party official to be tried and convicted in the region, Miroslav Stepan maintained that he was the country's last political prisoner.

Stepan's prison cell offered few clues to the past of its occupant. A map of Washington, D.C., hung on the wall, a souvenir of a visit he had made to the United States as part of an official Czechoslovak parliamentary delegation in 1988, when he was chairman of the foreign-affairs committee. His pencil holders were converted Coca-Cola cans, and his cigarettes were Camels. His reading materials included books on Czechoslovakia's Velvet Revolution, a French novel, the essays of Francis Bacon, an exercise manual, and a few Western and Czech magazines and newspapers. But, sitting in his blue prison garb, the former Prague Communist Party boss, once considered the prototype of a new, young breed of hard-liners, still exuded his old contentious personality, even if his graying hair and confinement provided stark evidence that, at forty-six, he was no longer a rising young star. Speaking quietly but insistently, he portrayed himself as a victim of both his old communist comrades and the former dissident movement, with no reason to utter a single *mea culpa* for anything.

Arrested in December 1989, Stepan was initially accused of responsibility for the violent attack by Prague's security forces on the last big demonstration before the communist regime collapsed. When the new authorities had problems making that accusation stick, they switched their focus to his role in suppressing earlier demonstrations, in October 1988, charging him with abuse of power. Sentenced to a two-and-a-half-year term, he served a total of seventeen months before and after his trial, obtaining his release shortly after my visit. Stepan maintained his innocence all along, but his early release was the result of his good behavior rather than any reconsideration of the verdict by the courts. In prison, he worked his way up to the position of "brigadier," the head of a seven-man team of prisoners responsible for distributing food and cleaning chores. "You can't change his views, but his behavior is perfect," Prison Director Karel Slajs told me before I paid my visit to his cell. But his lack of repentance, Slajs added, meant that he could not be considered a model prisoner.

Whatever the legal merits of the specific case against him, Stepan was representative of a breed in a larger sense: his attitudes mirrored those of much of the old ruling class, particularly concerning the question of moral responsibility for the past. Somehow, almost every former communist, whatever generation he belongs to, absolves himself of any such responsibility and presents himself as, at a minimum, a closet reformer who had been seeking to liberalize the system all along. Like Stepan, they argue that they are well qualified for "normal, honest citizenship" in the postcommunist political and social order, and that any actions against them smack of new repression. "I'm against having political prisoners at all now," Stepan somberly intoned. "We should not have political prisoners in the last decade of the twentieth century."

Stepan was happy to spell out his personal innocence on all counts. In 1948, when the communists took over in Czechoslovakia, he pointed out, he was "too small" to be blamed for anything. During the Soviet invasion of Czechoslovakia in 1968, he was "an ordinary soldier in the armed forces." "During the subsequent twenty years, I was not involved in internal changes," he continued, since most of that time he was an official, and then president of the International Students' Union, a job that involved shuttling constantly to Moscow, which called the shots in that organization. "So my hands are quite clean," he insisted with a shrug, as if to ask why anyone could have suspected otherwise.

This may have been news to the former dissidents who once feared him as a total opportunist, ready to justify any policy in his bid to rise to the top, but Stepan offered ready explanations for his actions even as Prague party chief in 1988 and 1989. If he exhorted security forces to deal harshly with "antisocialist elements," he was merely echoing the party line, he said, and he had nothing to do with the actual security arrangements. In reality, he continued, he was working as a quiet in-house reformer: "My concept was to make changes within the party to make change possible within Czechoslovakia." Then, settling into his victim role, he added: "Maybe that was a mistake. In political life, it is very difficult to work for both sides. I had the possibility of declaring different views but, if I had, I might have been in jail earlier. My idea was to bring more clever, educated colleagues and friends from party life into more responsible positions." And, although he did not assert this directly, to rise to the post of general secretary of the Communist Party, something that once looked almost within his reach.

Stepan asserted that his people began investigating abuses, such as party officials purchasing villas at token prices, and that he made "revolutionary" personnel changes, displacing the old guard. Such tactics, he charged, incurred the wrath of his older comrades, who began plotting "a coup," a murky theory that he claimed he would spell out at length in his forthcoming memoirs. To hear Stepan tell it, the Velvet Revolution may have been no more than a marriage of convenience between party hard-liners and the dissidents, whose chief target was none other than Miroslav Stepan. "Those we investigated [within the party] finally found a common language with the opposition," he said. The dissidents had been effectively hindering his work for reform by their public demonstrations, which strengthened the party hard-liners; once the communist regime began to collapse, they were happy to accept him, from those same hard-liners, as a sacrificial lamb. "The communists offered me up, saying I was responsible for everything," he concluded. "They offered me to the streets."

Something in Stepan's hardened, pasty look, even when his chunky

frame was in prison garb, still smacked of the former apparatchik lurking within. And that aspect of his personality pushed its way to the forefront when I began questioning him about the old regime. "I reject the
generalization that everything was bad in the past," he said, although I
had not made any declaration of the sort. He conceded that prison conditions had improved now, but argued that life in general was more "humane" then, with its "social guarantees," such as full employment.

I asked him about past political prisoners like Havel who had served
time in the same cells. "I was not responsible for the fact that Havel and
others were in jail," he replied defensively, missing the more general
point I was trying to make. When I pressed him further, he summoned
the standard response of an earlier era: "The border between normal
crimes and political crimes is not clear."

He was willing to concede that changes were necessary in the old system, but they should have been carried out gradually—in other words,
according to his timetable. As he escorted me from his unlocked cell to
the door at the end of his corridor, he made a significant addition to the
litany of villains who prevented him from doing so: Mikhail Gorbachev.
The Soviet leader had undercut communist regimes in Eastern Europe,
and after the failed coup inside the Soviet Union in August 1991, he had
left millions of the party faithful in the lurch by disbanding their organization. "I don't like that," Stepan added, throwing in a jibe at his policy vis-à-vis the Third World as well. "It's not right to support
national-liberation movements and then to say we'll have nothing more
to do with you." When he had served as president of the International
Students' Union, he had been a propagandist for those movements, an
instinct that clearly had not died.

By the time we were saying our final goodbyes, Stepan had warmed
considerably to his assault on the Soviet leader, whose erratic behavior
had at first mystified and then infuriated him. "Gorbachev should apol-
ogize for what he did," he concluded, returning to the question of his
role in Eastern Europe. He did not specify to whom, but he was much
too modest to suggest that Gorbachev should have apologized to him
personally.

The upheavals of 1989 were nothing like the French Revolution and the
Bolshevik Revolution: they were revolutionary in impact but radically
different in their methods, suggesting that their aftermaths should be
equally different. And they were. In Poland, Czechoslovakia, and Hungary, the old system collapsed and another was born without bloodshed,
at least in that final stage of a long struggle, and without violent retali-

ation against the former oppressors. Retribution of any sort was rare: Stepan's prison term served as the exception that proved the rule.

Nonetheless, communism and its legacy continued to cast a long shadow over the newly free countries, sometimes constituting a noxious fume that threatened to poison the political atmosphere and do almost random damage to individual careers and reputations. Everything that the former dissidents stood for suggested that they would not indulge in the kind of mindless retribution that had turned the aftermath of previous revolutions into a nightmare. But the balance between forgiveness and justice is difficult to establish, especially when those who are to be forgiven behave as if they deserve to be thanked rather than chastised, when they suddenly speak of tolerance and virtue, when they abruptly wrap themselves in the cloak of democratic values and an honest work ethic that they claim always to have upheld.

"Politics is choosing the lesser evil, holding your tongue and sometimes playing with marked cards," the early postwar Polish communist leader Edward Ochab once remarked. Some of his colleagues from the Stalinist era maintained until the bitter end that they had been involved in a utopian experiment, denying the existence of the Gulag and claiming that only "traitors and enemies" were ever convicted of crimes. But most, like Ochab, defended their actions on the grounds that they did the best they could for their country operating within the rules imposed by the Kremlin. Unlike Stepan and others in Prague who ensured that Czechoslovakia remained a bastion of hard-line thinking until the old order collapsed, the Polish communists who ruled in the 1980s could more credibly argue that they had truly tried to represent "the lesser evil." The degree to which they were successful in convincing their countrymen on that score, or at least raising serious questions in their minds, had a significant impact on the postcommunist political climate.

No one had worked harder at portraying himself as a Polish patriot, who had the country's interests at heart, than General Wojciech Jaruzelski. He had served the communist cause all his life: as defense minister, he oversaw the Polish Army's participation in the Warsaw Pact invasion of Czechoslovakia in 1968; as the leader of the Communist Party and prime minister, he imposed martial law in his own country in 1981, outlawing Solidarity, arresting its leaders, and ushering in a new period of repression. But Jaruzelski's government later agreed to sit down with Solidarity at the round table, an unprecedented action at that time. That mixed record left Jaruzelski's behavior open to a broad range of interpretation.

Thanks to the round-table accords, Jaruzelski had managed to cling to the presidency during a prolonged transition period, even after the first Solidarity government took power. It was not until Lech Walesa's push for the presidency in 1990 forced new elections that he had to step down, at the end of that year. In November, shortly before he did so, Jaruzelski held a farewell gathering for the press in the Belvedere Palace, the official Polish presidential mansion. Dressed in a dark blue suit and wearing his famous dark glasses, he kissed the hands of the women journalists and was every bit the Polish gentleman.

"What was the best moment for you?" asked one woman.

"Meeting you," he replied with a slight bow.

But Jaruzelski was also intent on some serious spin control. He knew that this was his chance to influence the stories about his political legacy that would be churned out in the coming days, and he took full advantage of it, parrying the inevitable questions about martial law and stressing that his role in history should be seen from the proper perspective, his perspective. "What is important is the historical truth," he said when he reached me in his rounds. Even after he declared martial law, he argued, Poland was "an island of heretics, because some of our actions were far ahead of what was taken up later by perestroika." He insisted that the long period of stalemate between his government and Solidarity "was not wasted, because it created the basis for our initiative, the round table—it was my initiative—and it allowed us to make the subsequent transformations step by step."

Though acknowledging that he had not anticipated the speed of Poland's evolution into a democratic state, Jaruzelski was eager to cast himself as the prime mover in that process, arguing that his actions in 1981 in no way contradicted such a portrayal of his role. General Czeslaw Kiszczak, his interior minister, would later make the same point even more explicitly in his memoirs. "There exists, even though this sounds paradoxical, a general unity of intentions and goals in martial law and the round table," he declared in *General Kiszczak Mowi . . . Prawie Wszystko (General Kiszczak Tells . . . Almost Everything.)*

Is this historical truth? Jaruzelski repeatedly argued that the "purgatory" of martial law was necessary "to prevent us from ending in hell." The "hell" he had in mind was the prospect of a Soviet invasion or some other punitive action almost as devastating. Jaruzelski's backers compare his actions to those of Marshal Jozef Pilsudski, whose 1926 coup and mild brand of authoritarianism held Poland together in the turbulent interwar period. His critics consider an analogy with another marshal more apt: France's Philippe Pétain, who collaborated with the Germans to spare France total occupation in World War II. He, too, was convinced that he was saving his nation from the brutal arm of an over-powering neighbor.

Neither contention is possible to prove, and this debate will never be fully resolved to anyone's satisfaction. In October 1992, Gorbachev appeared to undermine Jaruzelski's case by telling a correspondent for the Polish Press Agency: "Soviet forces were not to intervene in Poland under any circumstances." In its December 12–13, 1992, issue, the Polish newspaper *Gazeta Wyborcza* published extensive excerpts from meetings of the Soviet Politburo about the Polish crisis that appeared to buttress Gorbachev's assertion. In a transcript of a Politburo meeting that took place on October 29, 1981, KGB chief Yuri Andropov is quoted as saying: "The Polish leaders sometimes talk of military aid from fraternal states. However, we should decisively carry out our own policy—not sending in our troops to Poland." To which Defense Minister Dmitri Ustinov added: "In general it should be said that our troops should not be sent into Poland. They, the Poles, are not ready to accept our troops."

But the transcripts left no doubt that the Kremlin bosses were outraged by what Solidarity was doing, and they wanted it stopped. They fully expected the Polish leadership to launch its own crackdown, which it did. What the alternative would have been remains a subject for often angry discussions. Jaruzelski could take heart from opinion polls taken on the tenth aniversary of martial law, in December 1991, which showed that a slight majority of Poles felt that the imposition of martial law had been justified. Such sentiment helped doom efforts by one political party, the Confederation for an Independent Poland, to push for a trial and conviction of the officials responsible for imposing martial law. In early 1992, the Polish parliament branded the imposition of martial law an illegal act, but it kept putting off the initiatives to mete out punishment to its authors. Although both Jaruzelski and Kiszczak found themselves testifying later that year and in early 1993 before parliamentary committees and prosecutors about their role in declaring martial law and the circumstances surrounding the deaths of nine striking coal miners in the crackdown that followed, there was no groundswell of public sentiment to try and convict them.

The willingness of many Poles eventually to give Jaruzelski and his colleagues the benefit of the doubt on martial law does not necessarily translate into an acceptance of their revisionist version of subsequent events. The evidence suggests that Jaruzelski's later rule was not so benign or forward-looking as he would have everyone believe. Nonetheless, once he was out of power, the former communists almost uniformly accepted his interpretation as gospel, thus absolving themselves of all guilt.

Jaruzelski argues that he was for dialogue and reconciliation all along, but that Moscow's hostility and Solidarity's unwillingness to compromise produced a deadlock after martial law was imposed. This conveniently overlooks the fact that it was Jaruzelski who refused to accept Solidarity as an opposition force, insisting that history had passed it by. He rebuffed repeated appeals from his country and the West to negotiate with Solidarity. As late as May 1988, when the Kremlin looked much less threatening than before, he sent out the riot police to break up peaceful strikes and demonstrations.

On a visit to Warsaw during that confrontation, I watched one particularly chilling minidrama unfold. The *Newsweek* office, where I was staying, overlooks Castle Square, the broad entrance to the city's reconstructed old town. At dawn one morning when demonstrations were expected, I looked out my window and saw bus after bus disgorging secret-police plainclothesmen, who were immediately recognizable by their premeditatedly casual dress and movements as they dispersed throughout the old town. All day they waited, mingling in the evening with the crowds attending a mass at St. John's Cathedral. Standing amid the worshippers, I could spot members of their contingent.

As we left the church, there were shouts of "Solidarity" and antigovernment slogans; several people warned their colleagues not to get caught up in the action, knowing that the riot police were lined up at the entrance to Castle Square. "Provocation," they shouted. I skirted the crowd and crossed the police lines to avoid getting caught up in the action.

The secret policemen in the ranks shouted louder and swept some of the crowd along onto the square, then turned to chase, beat, and capture them. They caught mostly older people, especially women, who were slower to flee. In front of a crowd of dismayed onlookers standing behind the police lines, they dragged their captives ostentatiously across the square to the waiting riot police and their vans, to be driven away for booking.

Those were not actions of a government seeking reconciliation but of one that still believed force could prevail. During that unrest, I discussed the situation with Mieczyslaw Rakowski, a Politburo member who would later take over as prime minister of the last communist government and eventually serve as the last leader of the party. Rakowski, a former journalist, has always attempted to portray himself as a leading

[margin note: Plac Zamkowy]

reformer, but he bristled when I asked why the government would not finally sit down to negotiate with Solidarity. "Because we are here on the Vistula, and we are responsible for this country, not you or Reagan," he replied. "Today what is decisive is the economy, not whether I smile at Walesa."

When I reminded Rakowski of our talk years later, long after he had lost power, he admitted the obvious. "I still thought that the country could be calmed [then], that reforms could be instituted with a dominant role for the party." He claimed that he was undergoing "an intellectual process" that would lead him eventually to see the recognition of Solidarity as inevitable, but he conceded that the authorities had long been reluctant to consider that possibility. "It can be said that the party and the government of which I was a part were not mentally prepared to recognize a second equal or even stronger force," he said, although he claimed to be in the forefront of those pushing for a change in that stance in the late 1980s.

The timing and motivation of the change in the government's stance are keys to understanding what role the communists really did play in the dramatic breakthrough that followed in 1989—particularly whether Jaruzelski's revisionist claims that he had been seeking a compromise all along can be taken seriously. Interior Minister Kiszczak dealt metaphorically with the question of the timing of his loss of faith in preserving communism and his recognition of the need, in light of the country's economic and political crisis, to enter into a power-sharing agreement: "This is impossible to pinpoint exactly; it's a bit like going bald. Every day I shave and don't notice anything. Until I suddenly look closely, and then I'm bald."

That was certainly closer to the truth than Jaruzelski's own assertion that he had been seeking genuine reconciliation all along, something that was incompatible with the standard communist view that the party's monopoly on power had to be preserved at all costs. "He was genuinely convinced until January 1989 that socialism in this form could be cleansed of Stalinism and reformed," his former aide Colonel Wieslaw Gornicki told me. "He was never a turncoat." In a revealing passage in his memoirs, Kiszczak says flatly that even after the partially free elections in June 1989, when he tried unsuccessfully to form a government for the communists and their allies in parliament, on the basis of the rigged majority, the party "did not want to give up power."

Faced with a collapsing economy, mounting social discontent that threatened to explode, and no possibility of Soviet support for a new crackdown, the communists had negotiated the round-table accords, hoping to cling to power by giving a portion of it away. As Stanislaw Ciosek, another member of the Jaruzelski team, explained in Moscow, where he served as Polish ambassador for the new governments that followed, this was a period "when it was obvious that our plane had lost its undercarriage, the engines were not working—but you had to make some sort of landing." The round table constituted the party's last hope of controlling their landing.

Such tactics might have worked earlier, when Solidarity was weaker, as some of the former party leaders now point out a bit wistfully. In the wake of martial law, Solidarity's chances of maintaining its hold on the imagination of the nation were endangered as the stalemate dragged on; its leaders would have welcomed an accommodation that legalized the movement's existence and allowed for a measure of participation in the political system. But, as both Solidarity activists and the former communist leaders now point out, the 1984 murder by secret-police agents of Father Jerzy Popieluszko, the popular activist priest, served as a rallying point for the opposition, reversing its fortunes.

Jaruzelski and Kiszczak insist that the "concrete" faction within the party, their hard-line critics, had conspired to discredit their "moderate" policies. The murderers were tried and convicted, but doubts remained about how high the conspiracy went. In any case, the Jaruzelski team felt increasingly embattled, seeing themselves as threatened both within the party and, on the outside, by Solidarity. Any hopes for compromise all but vanished in this dark period.

Though acknowledging their efforts to cling to power, Kiszczak and his colleagues offer what they call their moderation as evidence of their goodwill. The former interior minister even suggests that the group intentionally tolerated much of the underground activity led by Zbigniew Bujak. Praising Bujak as "a great conspirator," he nonetheless conveys the impression that his security forces could have caught Bujak earlier if they had wanted to. "The existence of Bujak was rather convenient for us, because he was a rival of Walesa's," he argues. "[That's] an old method."

I asked Bujak for his reaction. "I don't believe it," he said. "The political price they paid for us was huge. The price was that this whole system of power was disintegrating, because it was shown to be ineffective." In fact, the security forces had come close to catching Bujak on a couple of earlier occasions and failed, and their frustration at these near misses was evident.

So was the anger of the authorities when I interviewed Bujak while he was still in hiding. Jaruzelski's aide Colonel Gornicki sent livid protests to *Newsweek* after the interview ran, threatening that I would never again be able to interview anyone representing the "real Poland." In a letter to the chief of correspondents, he wrote:

> Seeking various or opposing viewpoints is a perfectly legitimate journalistic practice. . . . Nobody ever objected in this country to foreign correspondents interviewing church representatives or persons quite unfriendly to the present government. The Polish lunatic fringe, however, of which Mr. Bujak is a typical product, certainly has nothing newsworthy to say on current realities of our country. What Mr. Nagorski did was not political reporting but an attempt to resuscitate a small, isolated, and meaningless group, politically bankrupt and morally dubious. Thus not press freedoms were at stake but a political manipulation of the sort that shall not be tolerated in Poland.

Referring to my earlier request for an interview with Jaruzelski, Gornicki accused me of "cheating" him, presumably by not informing him that I also had plans to interview Bujak, as if I should have tipped the authorities off to allow for his capture. "This kind of cheap trick may be perhaps passable down the Limpopo River but not in the center of Europe," he wrote. For the next two and a half years, I was repeatedly refused visas to Poland. That hardly constituted the reaction of a government that had been happy to play along with Bujak's "game" of hiding in the underground.

Whatever the merits of the argument about the necessity for martial law, Jaruzelski wasted nearly a decade afterward trying to avoid the outcome that eventually proved unavoidable. Poland paid a high price for that decade. In economic terms, those were wasted years. As Jaruzelski tinkered with a failed system, the country fell further behind the West, experiencing the twin agonies of socialist-style shortages and capitalist-style inflation. Measured by any normal standard—housing, health care, the environment—Poles were living in appalling conditions with no hopes of improvement. Hundreds of thousands left for the West, while demoralization of the people reached alarming proportions. The last years of communist misrule were not a foundation for change, as Jaruzelski claims, but a heavy part of the burden inherited by the governments that followed.

And yet the old ruling class acted offended that its "contributions" have been so vastly underestimated by an ungrateful populace. Instead of remaining silently appreciative when subsequent governments resisted political pressures to punish them, they waxed indignant about the slights they had endured, real or imagined. Shortly after Prime Minister Jan Krzysztof Bielecki traveled to Bonn to sign a long-negotiated Polish-German friendship treaty on June 17, 1991, I talked with Rakowski, the head of the last communist government. I had heard that he was offended that he was not invited by Bielecki for the ceremony—something I found hard to believe, since Bielecki could hardly afford to be seen as embracing a man who symbolized the old system. After all, the transition in Poland in 1989 could not be compared to a normal change of government in the West, where both the outgoing and incoming teams can claim equal legitimacy.

I asked Rakowski whether he really felt he should have been invited. "Of course; that was required by political civility," he replied. "I did do a lot for Polish-German reconciliation. It was I who started the talks with [Chancellor Helmut] Kohl. I don't want to comment on the lack of political manners."

Rakowski went on to recount a conversation he had had with a Western European who had organized a conference he had attended in Basel.

"Don't you have a diplomatic passport?" the organizer asked.

"No, it was taken away from me."

"What do you mean? Here any politician who was ever head of state or government has a diplomatic passport for life."

"You see," Rakowski explained, "we're just moving toward Europe."

Among the members of the former ruling class, the notion that they had never really served an alien ideology, that they were merely the vanguard not of a totalitarian system but of the forces pushing for democratization, was taken as accepted fact. This was equally true for communists like Hungary's Imre Poszgay, who could legitimately claim to have pushed the party to accept and negotiate with opposition forces, and for those who had resisted the changes all along.

In the case of older party functionaries, such behavior can be explained as normal self-justification, an unwillingness to admit that they had spent most of their lives serving the wrong cause. But I was more intrigued by the younger breed of leaders who emerged at the forefront of the old, often renamed and revamped communist parties in a postcommunist world. What prompted them to continue their association with parties tied to a discredited and mocked past? Lubomir Ledl, a young Czech communist, recalls that, when he told his wife in 1990 that he had agreed to run the party's campaign for the country's first free parliamentary elections, she had only one comment: "I knew you were an idiot, but I didn't know how big an idiot."

Remembering her reaction, Ledl laughed. He could do so because the Czech communists had won 13.7 percent of the vote in those first free elections and 14.4 percent in the second elections, in June 1992. In Hungary's first free elections, the former communists, who had renamed themselves the Hungarian Socialist Party, won 8.5 percent. In Poland, where fully free parliamentary elections did not take place until late 1991, the Social Democratic Party, which is how the communists renamed themselves, won 12 percent in a badly fragmented field, emerging as the second strongest party. However despised they were by a good portion of the population, the former communists proved to have a strong base of support among people who in some way identified with the old regimes. The younger party activists who assumed increasingly high-profile leadership positions were no idiots; they were using their communist tickets to advance their careers just as they had in the past, even if their political opportunities were no longer as extensive as in an earlier era.

Label them opportunists or, as they prefer, pragmatists. By whatever name, this was the generation of communists who entered the party without the blind faith in the system that at least some of their predecessors had had. Their justification was that they were serving to reform the party from within, although they make no secret that they also saw the party as a vehicle for their personal ambitions. And they have continued to do so.

A new young leader emerged even in the Hungarian Socialist Workers' Party (HSWP), a hard-line splinter group of the old Communist Party which refused to go along with the majority that formed the Hungarian Socialist Party (HSP). First elected to head the new party at the age of thirty-six in late 1989, Gyula Thurmer explains that his group kept "Workers" in their name to symbolize their commitment to Marxist ideas that the HSP has abandoned. "We decided to build up a party with a more concrete social basis," he says. "We want to represent the interests of workers and peasants along with intellectuals. We don't want to become a social-democratic party. We don't accept the capitalist way as the single possible way of development. We also don't want to become an old Bolshevik party. We would like to become a modern labor party."

Thurmer acts and talks like the young functionary with ambitions to go places, even if he is now only the proverbial big fish in a small pond. His party won 3.8 percent of the votes in the 1990 elections, falling just short of the 4 percent barrier required for parliamentary representation. But he has a desk, a steady salary, and what he believes is the prospect of a future parliamentary role, assuming that disillusionment with the hardships of economic reforms wins his party a few more supporters. He also throws around the old party jargon without betraying any self-consciousness about how anachronistic he sounds.

Why did he join the party at age eighteen in 1971? "First of all, I believed that there were really important, sound principles, like the equality of people, and that something can be built on those principles. Certainly later everyone from my generation could see the mistakes made by Kadar. Our generation felt strong enough that we could take an active role in correcting those mistakes."

I asked if a simpler explanation wasn't that party membership was the ticket for a career. He smiled and shrugged. "I don't think it was the most important thing for us. In the last ten years, party membership was not so important."

But Thurmer had joined the party much earlier. He had started working his way up the foreign-affairs ladder in the mid-1970s, serving first in the Foreign Ministry and then in the Hungarian Embassy in Moscow. In the early 1980s, he worked in the Central Committee's international department and, in 1988, when Karoly Grosz replaced Kadar as party leader, he served as the new general secretary's foreign-policy adviser.

None of that inhibited him from portraying himself and his party as committed democrats. "Our party is a new party—we have a lot of members who criticized the Kadar system in the last decades. No one in our leadership held any top position in the Kadar period. Why can't we support democracy?"

What he failed to mention was that much of their criticism was directed at the reformers within the party, whom they considered too "soft," just as they would criticize Yeltsin and sympathize with the hardliners who tried to stop the Soviet Union's disintegration. I was supposed to be impressed by how far his group had come, not how firmly they were anchored in the past.

When I pointed out that his office bookshelves contained only the old tired volumes of Marx and a Soviet *Who's Who,* looking very much outdated as we met in 1992, after the formal dissolution of the Soviet Union, he grew defensive. "Why throw them out? They're good books. I don't have much space. If I did, I would bring in some other books." Then he added, perfectly seriously: "But you don't see any pictures of Lenin here, or of Marx."

Other new young leaders are smoother, and certainly make a point of restocking their bookshelves and their rhetoric. Aleksander Kwasniewski, the leader of Poland's Social Democratic Party (the renamed Communist Party), does not preface his remarks with talk of Marxist ideals. "I represent a special generation—of people born after Stalin, people who attended university in the 1970s. My generation joined the party for purely pragmatic reasons. We were convinced that reforms would be more likely from within. Here we differed with those who decided to join the opposition. During the 1980s, I worked for more civilized conduct by the authorities. I am more of a pragmatist than a revolutionary, so I believed you have to move step by step to change things."

He made one admission: "I probably underestimated, as Gorbachev did more recently, the power of inertia in such great structures as the party. So sometimes you do have to demolish in order to change something."

Unlike Thurmer, Kwasniewski openly applies the same "pragmatism" to the new economic situation. In the face of widespread allegations that the communists were the first to enrich themselves under the cover of economic reforms, and anger at the speed with which some of them transformed themselves into capitalists, Kwasniewski sounds more like an exponent of survival-of-the-fittest capitalism than a committed communist. "If there's any legal proof of fraud or other crimes, the court should step in, but I'm against accusations of dishonesty against anyone who's made money," he told me. Then he broke into a broad grin. "Rockefeller, when asked if it's possible to earn a million dollars honestly, supposedly replied: 'The third or fourth million, yes, but not the first.'"

Wealth was not something normally associated with communism, but certainly it was associated with the old communist ruling class. And never more so than in the era of transition from communism to capitalism. Communism at death and capitalism at birth provided the *nomenklatura,* the communist ruling class, with an abundance of opportunities to ransack what they could from amid the chaos of disintegration and initially largely unregulated rebuilding. The extent to which members of that caste took advantage of those opportunities proved to be a source of continuing dispute, providing an emotional backdrop to the more general debate about what should be done in the name of "decommunization."

The communist parties controlled vast holdings of property and funds, which the new governments passed legislation to reclaim for the state. Buildings such as the massive party headquarters, the infamous "white houses" of Budapest and Warsaw, could hardly be hidden, and they were quickly put to new uses. The Budapest party headquarters was transformed into an office building for members of the revived parliament; the Warsaw headquarters became a banking and business center, housing the country's first postwar stock exchange, the Polish-American Enterprise Fund, and other symbols of the new capitalist era. But money was another matter. There are no records of what may have disappeared earlier, but on January 29, 1990, when the Polish Communist Party officially dissolved itself, banks reported that they were holding $11.5 million in its name, mostly in Swiss francs. On February 27, 1991, when a law on the confiscation of the party's property came into force, the accounts showed only $4,000 left. Money appeared, money disappeared.

The Polish communists were further embarrassed in late 1991 by revelations in the Russian press that they had taken an interest-free loan of $1.2 million from the Soviet Communist Party in January 1990 to help fund the new party they were forming. Gennady Yanayev, the man who later led the aborted Kremlin coup in August 1991, recommended to Gorbachev: "We deem it advisable to come to the assistance of our Polish friends." Rakowski, who had negotiated the loan, claimed that it was repaid, but a report in the Russian press that the first installment was repaid in cash through KGB couriers in November 1991 hardly helped the Polish party's image.

The mysteries of party accounting were only a portion of a tale of financial shenanigans that, at least in the popular imagination, represented outright highway robbery. Throughout the region, stories abounded about how members of the *nomenklatura* had set themselves up in new private companies, appropriating state property and funds for themselves on a massive scale. By engaging in elaborate shell games, so the stories went, they quickly covered up the money trails leading from their initial raids on state property and funds. By the time governments got around to trying to deal with the problem, much of the damage had already been done, and pinning the blame on anyone proved extraordinarily difficult.

Bribery and embezzlement were commonplace throughout the communist era, but the introduction of putative economic reforms opened up a whole new range of get-rich-quick possibilities in the late communist period. In the 1980s, Polish governments had permitted the creation of new joint-stock companies. Although the major shareholders were usually state organizations, and the private component only began to expand later, the idea was supposed to allow for the creation of companies that would be under fewer constraints than the traditional state enterprises, permitting them to become more autonomous and efficient.

In 1985, 1,220 such companies were registered, whereas in the political transition year of 1989 the number shot up to forty-one thousand. But, in practice, it turned out that at least a portion of them served as little more than cash cows for the *nomenklatura*. In one popular ruse, factory directors and local officials would rent out space and equipment for a nominal fee to a new company, which they controlled themselves. This often meant that the same workers would be working on the same machines in the state enterprise, but nominally for a company commissioned by the factory to do the work. The factory continued to cover most of the costs while paying the new company for the full price of their products. Workers rarely complained, since they were usually paid better under this arrangement, while the directors raked off the profits.

Such schemes provided endless possibilities for siphoning money from the state enterprise, whose financial plight would go from bad to worse, to the new companies, where the directors awarded themselves handsome bonuses. As Jan Bieda, the spokesman for the Supreme Chamber of Control, pointed out later: "If a director makes three times as much for the company as he does in his role as the director of the state enterprise, whose interests will he care about?" In some cases, the state enterprise bought raw materials at the going rate and sold them to the company for 10 percent of cost, and the company would then sell the finished product to outside firms at full price. In others, "trading companies" were established, which charged as much as 25 percent commissions for their alleged services. Since the trading companies might be represented by a single employee who would take the orders, this amounted to pure profit. The losers were not just the state enterprises but the buyers, who often were forced to pay artificially inflated prices.

After the communists lost power, a study conducted by the Ministry of Justice of about fifteen hundred companies formed in the first half of 1989 found at least seven hundred directors and deputy directors of state enterprises, nine provincial governors, and fifty-seven mayors among their corporate officers. In 1990, the government passed a law prohibiting such conflicts of interest among directors of state enterprises, and there were fewer reports of flagrant abuses. At the very least, state-enterprise bosses recognized that they had to watch their step.

But the rules were still loose, and a lot of situations wide open to interpretation. When I visited a large state railroad repair facility in southeastern Poland in early 1992, director Jan Szpunar, a holdover from the communist era, explained that he was doing everything possible to keep his yard in business. That included allowing three former employees to set up a private "marketing" firm to arrange the state-enterprise contracts, which receives a 1 percent commission. "They get this to take care of everything," Szpunar said. That meant either covering their costs to get the order or, as he indicated by demonstrably shoving his hand into his jacket pocket, taking it for themselves. But he immediately sought to dispel any impression that he could have a financial interest of his own. "I'm only interested in getting the work and not having to fire my people," he assured me.

For all the stories of questionable dealings, many members of the *nomenklatura* bounced back in the postcommunist era because they had management experience and specific talents to offer. What bothered many Poles was that they often moved into positions it would seem logical for new people to take over. Grzegorz Boguta, the former underground publisher who is now the managing director of PWN, the state scientific publishing company, pointed out a specific example from his domain. In 1990, an open competition was held for the position of director of the state enterprise that serves as the largest wholesaler of books. The winner was Kazimierz Molek, a former deputy minister of culture under the communists, who had hounded underground publishers and opposition writers. "We hated this person," noted Boguta, who had served as one of the judges of the competition, "but he turned out to be the best candidate." Despite the controversies surrounding such decisions, the willingness of people like Boguta to admit as much underscored the degree to which Poland remained open to those representing the old system. If someone from the *nomenklatura* had apparent skills, he could still use them.

When I met Ireneusz Sekula in May 1989, his spacious office in the Council of Ministers mirrored his own stiff formality. A neatly arranged desk stood at the end of the room, and he received visitors at a rectangular conference table that stretched practically to the door. At forty-five, he was young to be the deputy prime minister in charge of economic affairs, and he took his mission very seriously. A heavyset man with a broad pale face and a gray crew cut, he offered a lengthy exposition of the government's economic reforms and how they were allegedly creating all the preconditions for "revolutionary" changes and market mechanisms. Alluding to the elections scheduled for the following month under the round-table accords, in which the communists and their allies had a guaranteed majority of uncontested seats, he maintained that the government's initiatives had already attained "a critical mass" and would be continued "even if a new team entered this build-ing after the elections."

"I don't think it will come to that," interrupted one of the two aides who flanked him during our discussion.

"Everything is possible in a democracy," Sekula replied with a grin.

His aides laughed appreciatively, one of them knocking the wood of the conference table in a mock appeal for the good luck that he was con-vinced would prove unnecessary. After all, the upcoming elections could hardly be described as democratic, and their outcome, as far as the com-munists were concerned, was not in doubt. He was delighted by his boss's rare display of humor in front of an American journalist.

After the subsequent Solidarity landslide that humiliated the com-munists, and the rush of events that swept them from office, I would have expected to find Sekula somewhat chastised, disoriented. Nothing could have been further from the truth.

In late 1990, when I revisited him for the first time, he was smoking a Cuban cigar in his new office as president of Polnippon, a Polish-Japanese joint venture. Sekula had comfortably settled into his new role as capitalist entrepreneur. During that and subsequent visits, he con-veyed the impression of a man who had found his calling, which, in the new world of business opportunities, he could far more effectively pur-sue than his old political career in a dead-end regime.

Sekula wanted to make sure I understood that Polnippon should not be considered a *"nomenklatura* company," a term that connoted not just participation by members of the *nomenklatura* but the hijacking of state assets. "We have clean hands," he told me. "I have always been very careful that there should not be a single zloty of state property in this company. We do not have any state shareholders. We've never re-ceived, bought, acquired, or leased anything from the state, so that there can't be any discussion whether we got something too cheaply. We don't even do business with state enterprises so there would be no talk that we sold something too expensively."

The initial investment in Polnippon in 1990 was small: $50,000 by the Polish participants, and the same amount by their Japanese part-ners. Two years later, Sekula estimated that the market value of his firm was between $3 million and $3.5 million. In those wild years of early capitalism, this was impressive but nothing spectacular; others had built bigger empires. Sekula, however, insisted that, contrary to many of the meteors which had streaked across the Polish business horizon and dis-appeared, his emphasis was on laying a firm foundation for long-term growth. "Poles are generally impatient: this is the beginning of capitalism, and they want results in a week or two," he said between puffs on his cigar. "But we're not oriented toward making a quick buck—to buy something and then quickly resell. We're thinking long-term."

During its first two years of operation, Polnippon prepared studies for Japanese government agencies like the Ministry of International Trade and Industry and organized the program for visits by about twenty Japanese business groups. Its data bank listed about five hundred Polish firms seeking foreign partners, and about one hundred foreign firms, not only Japanese, seeking investment opportunities. Sekula reeled off potential deals: an ambitious project to employ Japanese biotechnology to revive flax production in Poland, with the output destined for the large Japanese market; the sale of a new generation of environmentally clean furnaces for waste disposal and heat generation, with financing provided by Western aid earmarked for environmental protection; the list went on and on.

Sekula's most sweeping vision concerned the energy sector in Poland and Russia. From the time he launched Polnippon, he began drawing up plans for brokering a major deal for the expansion of off-loading, storage, refining, and distribution facilities for oil and liquefied natural-gas imports through Gdansk. The financing would be provided by a London-based international consortium with Saudi Arabian, Nigerian, and British money, which had proposed an investment of $700 million to build those facilities. With Russia dramatically cutting back energy exports, Poland's need to expand its capacity to import supplies from the Middle East and elsewhere was indisputable.

On an even larger scale, Sekula envisaged putting together the Western financing and expertise for a deal to modernize the energy sector in Russia, which had been allowed to degenerate because of lack of investments. "In the Tyumen basin alone, six thousand kilometers of piping has to be replaced," he explained. "The pipes cannot withstand normal pressure, and this results in leaks. A train passes a pipeline that leaks gas and the whole thing blows up. . . ."

Sekula was convincing in his arguments about both Polish and Russian requirements, although it was hard to tell how much, if any, of this would translate into concrete business deals. The stakes were enormous and, at least in Poland, there was political resistance for him to contend with. Local officials in Gdansk and other Baltic ports were worried about the effect of allowing a top former communist to put together and profit from a major port-expansion deal. In 1992, Sekula claimed that the resistance had diminished, but his open scorn for the officials he had to deal with hardly indicated that he had established a good relationship with them. "The local authorities are extremely incompetent," he complained. "It's hard for them to tackle long-term projects. Secondly, if a deputy mayor of a large Polish city stubbornly insists that one hectare equals a thousand square meters and not ten thousand, then it's not easy to communicate with him."

Whatever the fate of his more sweeping plans, Sekula had already proved that he was capable of making money in the aftermath of the collapse of communism. Seven hours before Germany was officially reunified on October 3, 1990, he put together a bargain-price deal with the East German airline Interflug: for under $1.5 million, he bought two Ilyushin 18-D airliners along with twelve spare engines, extra propellers, and other spare parts, enough equipment to keep the planes flying for a long time. By the following summer, Polnippon Cargo was operational, with Polish pilots hopping between Europe, Africa, and Asia, mostly carrying non-Polish cargo. By early 1992, Sekula was looking into the possibility of leasing extra planes, perhaps Boeing 727s or 737s, if he could get the financing. "Right now our planes are not enough for all our orders," he pointed out with satisfaction.

My meetings with Sekula convinced me that he had developed into a serious businessman, and no one had provided any evidence to question his claim that he had made the transition from communist to capitalist legitimately. But I was far less impressed with his political vision, his view of the broader changes that made his own metamorphosis possible. In that respect, he was still very much a product of the old thinking.

"It is perfectly normal all over the world for former politicians to go into business," Sekula told me in one of our talks. But I reminded him that Poland had not been a normal country run by a normal leadership, and I wanted him to deal with the question of the link between his past in the communist system and his current incarnation.

"How do you reconcile what I do as a minicapitalist with my left-wing roots?" Sekula asked rhetorically. His answer was long on the alleged achievements of the last communist government, and not just short but devoid of any self-criticism.

"First, a short theoretical digression," he said, leaning back in his chair. "There has never been communism in Poland. There was a small group of communists in the 1920s and 1930s, but the system that emerged in Poland after 1945 was not a communist system. It has been described as communism, but that's an abuse of the term, for a simple reason: communism assumes total nationalization of property."

Pointing to the fact that over 80 percent of farmland remained in private hands and that a small private-business sector also existed, he argued: "So what kind of communism was it? If anything, we could speak of socialism, and socialism more of the social-democratic variety. Now, if you refer to Marx, the socialist system is defined in a very simple and beautiful way: it's a system that ensures development and happiness. That's all."

The implication was clear: he and his cronies had chosen the most practical way of achieving those aims under the conditions that existed at that time; later, after the political upheaval, they could turn to purely capitalist ventures—but also thanks to their own earlier initiatives. "I belonged to a group of reformers in the party, which was absurdly described as a 'Communist Party,' which it was not," he insisted. This group, he continued, had introduced the fundamental shift toward a market system, allowing for more private enterprise and a host of measures which he claimed triggered the economic transformation that followed its departure. "In effect, the subsequent governments only added symbols to this. They changed the name of the country, crowned the eagle, changed street names, and started pulling down monuments. We dealt with the substance, we plowed the field."

While he was no longer in the government, he won re-election to parliament in the first fully free elections in 1991 as a member of the Social Democratic Party, proclaiming that the former communists stood for tolerance, equal chances for state and private enterprise, efficient management, and the providing of a social safety net for all citizens. As a communist or a capitalist, Sekula never had any cause for self-doubt: he could only congratulate himself for making the changes in Poland possible. He may have learned the ways of capitalism, but he had not shaken the habit of cynically rewriting history to suit his current needs. The notion of absolute truth does not exist for self-proclaimed Marxist reformers like Sekula, any more than it does for their more doctrinaire former comrades. To them, the discourses of Havel, Michnik, and others on the subject were either the abstract babbling of innocent fools or simply a clever political weapon that proved more potent at a critical moment than they ever expected.

The arrogance of those who had fallen from power produced understandable resentment among the citizenry of the nations of the region, who, unlike most of the former communist leaders, were paying a heavy price for the disastrous policies of the previous four decades. In a period of new economic hardships caused by the painful adjustments of the transition from communism to capitalism, the ease with which someone like Sekula slipped into another privileged life-style was, at the very least, a cause of bewilderment among many ordinary Poles. They could hardly be blamed for thinking that somebody had to be responsible for the sins of the past, that somebody should pay for them.

"Detective writers have apparently overlooked the only truly perfect crime: the one in which an entire society is complicit," German author Peter Schneider wrote in his book *The German Comedy*. He was referring to East Germany, but expressing a frustration that could be felt in any country that had emerged from communist rule. Was no one guilty? Had the crimes committed in the name of an alien ideology been the work of some extraterrestrial force?

There were attempts at punishment, or at least at rectification of what were perceived as earlier failures of the justice system. In October 1991, the Polish parliament recommended the investigation of eighty-eight suspected political killings in the 1980s. In December, the courts began to act: six former secret policemen were sentenced for up to five years for kidnapping, torturing, and threatening Solidarity activists in 1984; a secret policeman was sentenced to eight years' imprisonment for killing a protester in 1982; and the Supreme Court overturned on a technicality the 1987 amnesties of three secret policemen convicted for their roles in the murder of Father Jerzy Popieluszko. In the summer of 1992, two generals who held top positions in the Ministry of the Interior were put on trial for allegedly ordering the murder of the dissident priest.

In Hungary, the parliament passed a law in November 1991 that waived the twenty-year statute of limitations on crimes such as murder, treason, and aggravated assault, allowing for the prosecution of crimes committed by communists as far back as 1944. The real objective of the law was to punish the perpetrators of specific crimes during the suppression of the 1956 uprising. But in March 1992, the Constitutional Court threw out the bill, arguing that it ignored a constitutional requirement that the laws of the time when the alleged crimes were committed had to be taken into consideration.

In both Poland and Hungary, the issue of what to do about people who collaborated with the former secret police was initially put off by the authorities, who harbored serious doubts about the accuracy of the secret-police records and worried that delving into them might prompt new injustices rather than rectify old ones. Though "decommunization" was a popular slogan in election campaigns, the impulse to punish was kept largely under control. Bursts of impassioned rhetoric about the crimes of the old regime did not translate into sweeping measures designed to ban those who had served it from political life; most former dissidents turned politicians did not lose sight of the need to ensure that the means justified the ends of any such action, and most citizens were willing to accept the constraints that the new democratic system imposed. Considering what might have happened given their accumulated grievances against their previous rulers, Poles and Hungarians largely behaved on this issue like the new Europeans they aspired to be, playing by the rules of the new instead of the old Europe.

But Czechoslovakia was a case apart. In this country, which had prided itself on its prewar democratic record but which endured a much harsher brand of communism than Poland or Hungary, the pressures to take more drastic action proved far more intense; the past cast a longer shadow. The means employed to rectify old wrongs collided with the fundamental principles of a democratic society, with President Havel placed in the uncomfortable position of trying to reconcile two contradictory impulses. A drama unfolded that raised the most basic questions about justice, individual rights, and due process—and about the nature of the people themselves, especially what they had learned from their experiences under communism. Czechoslovakia proved to be the primary laboratory for an experiment that can be labeled "settling accounts with the past."

A dual national by virtue of having been born in England of a Czech father and a British mother, Jan Kavan had gone to study in England in the late 1960s and then remained there when the "normalization" campaign following the Soviet invasion of Czechoslovakia left no doubt that a long, dark chapter was beginning. During the two decades that followed, he developed into a one-man support group for dissidents in the country he considered his homeland. From London, he organized dozens of shipments of "subversive" literature into Czechoslovakia, publicized human-rights abuses in the Palach Press news agency he headed, and even slipped into the country several times under an assumed name to meet with Havel, Dienstbier, and other prominent activists. Above all, he was always there for the dissidents when they needed him, providing a lifeline to the outside world.

"Kavan was the only person in the émigré community whom you could call at any time, at two in the morning, and he'd never complain," Petr Pospichal, the former dissident who later became a foreign-policy adviser to Havel, told me over a dinner in Prague. "But he's also an unlucky person."

How unlucky? Kavan recalls an incident in 1976 when he had flown from London to Brussels to pick up a van that had broken down there after making a clandestine delivery of opposition literature to Prague. At the airport in Brussels, he lent a hand to a young woman who was pushing a baby in a carriage and lugging a heavy suitcase. At that point, "just as in a bad James Bond film," the police surrounded them, tipped off by the British authorities that the young woman was smuggling marijuana in the carriage. They were both arrested. Although the woman testified that Kavan knew nothing about the drugs, he was not released until six weeks later, after Scotland Yard had vouched for him.

When he returned to Prague on November 25, 1989, for the final days of the communist regime, it looked as if he had shaken his bad luck. Although he was detained at the airport and questioned by the StB, the dreaded Czechoslovak secret police, he went on to participate in the Velvet Revolution and later won a seat in the new federal parliament on the ticket of the Civic Forum, the loose grouping organized by former dissidents to encompass all those eager to attach themselves to their movement. But that happy ending was not to be. On March 22, 1991, a parliamentary commission read out ten names of deputies whom it labeled as StB collaborators; the most famous name on the list was Jan Kavan.

Kavan promptly began a fight to clear his name against a charge he flatly denied and a process he claimed threatened his country's newfound democracy. "There is the presumption of guilt here," he told me, when I first talked with him during a break in a parliamentary session. "You can't build a democratic state when you adopt Stalinist principles." He freely conceded that the situation was dramatically different from that in the Stalinist period: he was not threatened with arrest or execution, only with the loss of his reputation and probably his parliamentary seat.

But if there was no comparison in the price to be paid, Kavan argued that this did not alter the fundamental nature of the injustice he felt was taking place, with him cast in the role of innocent victim. In his first reply to the charges in parliament, he warned of the consequences of not learning from the mistakes of past revolutions. "Throughout history, the activities of various Committees for Public Welfare led mostly to situations about which it was said later that the revolution began to devour its own children," he said. "I hope that those images of the past will remain forever in the past."

For Kavan, the past kept crowding in. The StB had assembled a hefty file on him over the years, which had fallen into the hands of the parliamentary commission that had declared him a collaborator. "My file is thick in terms of number of pages, but the pages do not amount to any evidence," he insisted. He was labeled a collaborator on the basis of his contacts with a Czechoslovak diplomat named Frantisek Zajicek in 1969 and 1970, which were reported in the "Kato" file, the code name the StB assigned to him. At the time, Kavan was head of the Czechoslovak Union of Students in Great Britain, and Zajicek described himself as the London Embassy's education counselor, so their meeting was not unusual. But in light of the 1968 Soviet invasion of Czechoslovakia, any official contacts could be suspect.

Kavan freely admitted to the meetings with Zajicek. At the time, he argued, most Czech and Slovak students studying in Britain planned to return home, which meant there was no desire to cut off all official contacts. In 1969, since he did not have any money, Kavan said, he asked Zajicek for £10 to hire a hall for the founding meeting of the Czechoslovak Union of Students in Great Britain, and he signed a receipt for that amount, which, it later turned out, became part of his file. Kavan also claimed that Zajicek talked and behaved like a "Dubcekite," a supporter of reform leader Alexander Dubcek. When Zajicek was recalled in 1970 and there were subsequent reports that he was expelled from government service, Kavan took that as evidence that he really had sympathized with the Prague Spring.

In his parliamentary speech replying to the charges, Kavan did make one concession. "I do admit that it is of course possible to sharply criticize me or to condemn as naïve the twenty-two-year-old student who failed to see through Mr. Zajicek's 'cover' and allowed him even, as the file says, to pay for the food and drink he consumed during the meetings." But he insisted that naïveté was his only sin.

Fellow parliamentarian Petr Uhl, one of the prominent former dissidents whom Kavan had regularly helped in the old days, examined the StB file carefully and concluded that one key piece of evidence backs up Kavan's version of events. In his report on his final meeting with Kavan, Zajicek indicated that he was afraid to ask certain questions since they might arouse Kavan's suspicions about his role. "That exculpates Kavan," Uhl maintained. But, by a narrow margin, the commission voted against Kavan, ignoring his requests that several of his supporters be allowed to testify in his behalf. There was nothing like a court procedure, a trial, or a chance for both sides to make their case and present their evidence. The committee ruled, and those named, like Kavan, had to decide how to respond. Only then could they begin a lengthy court procedure to try to clear themselves.

When I talked to Kavan about his case in the fall of 1991, he alternated between dealing with the specific details of his life two decades earlier and his broader judgments about the implications of the process that had ensnared him. "It's very painful, because I had great expectations for this country, and I worked for twenty years to bring this democratic change about. I believed that, once this country made the change, we would be more democratic than our neighbors, simply because we had a long democratic tradition. I believed this would prevent us from embarking on a McCarthy-type witch-hunt. But it worked out the other way around: we seem to be at the top of the league of witch-hunts."

As we sat in the largely empty parliamentary chamber, he harked back to Havel's notion, expressed in "The Power of the Powerless," that each person shared a measure of guilt for allowing the old totalitarian system to function, for participating in its rituals. "When I read 'The Power of the Powerless'—and, ironically, Palach Press was given the copyright for it, and I distributed it in the West—I felt that this was very true," he recalled. "But I didn't feel very guilty myself. Not because of any great achievement on my part, but because I didn't spend the last twenty years here, so I didn't have to go through those motions. And I felt that I had spent the twenty years the best way I could to help. Today, ironically, I'm accused. . . ."

In part, he saw the fervor of his accusers as an expression of the broader sense of collaboration that existed in Czechoslovakia than in a country like Poland, where dissent was far more commonplace. "Havel said it and I repeat it: those who are today the loudest, the most vociferous, the most radical are those who are drowning their own feelings of guilt for not helping the opposition in those years, for being conformist." Although he advocated establishing a legal framework for preventing people who were "genuinely guilty of hurting other people, causing arrests, persecution, harassment" from holding top government positions, he was alarmed by the lack of such procedures in his case and others, which presumed that righting perceived old wrongs was more important than adhering to democratic procedures.

"You cannot build a democratic state with undemocratic methods. You cannot create a democratic state without full respect for civil rights," he told me. "There is a Czech proverb which was used in the 1950s, when my father was arrested: 'When you cut wood, splinters fly.' It's pitiful, this principle—people may have to be sacrificed for the greater good of cutting the wood."

The woodcutting process is called *lustrace,* the Czech word for "lustration" or "purification." To its proponents, this is a form of preventive surgery: it is necessary to screen government officials, they argued, to make sure that StB agents and collaborators do not infect the country's new democratic institutions. Those who are identified as "StB positive" are asked to quietly resign, and if they do their past is not publicized. The parliamentary *lustrace* commission, as it was commonly called, based its findings on the StB registry of files, which contains about 140,000 names. The listings include "enemies" of the system, but the majority are people who provided information or assistance. The names are classified according to a range of categories, from "residents," who ran networks of agents, to "trustees," who may have served unwittingly as sources of information.

The chief woodcutters of the *lustrace* commission were Jiri Ruml and Petr Toman, who could not have looked more different. Ruml, the chairman of the commission, was in his late sixties, with a weathered, heavily lined face. Commission spokesman Toman, his youthful face framed by a neatly trimmed beard, was not yet thirty when he announced the findings of the commission about Kavan and the other alleged StB collaborators within their ranks. But they shared an implacable faith in the StB register, which they treated as nothing less than a Bible. "Everything that is in the register is very reliable. It was impossible to falsify the register," Ruml told me in the offices of the commission, just off Wenceslas Square. In the basement coffee shop of parliament, Toman echoed those sentiments: "We don't have a single case of falsification of the register."

Their identical zeal in trying to convince everyone that the StB had been flawless in its reporting was no accident; any doubts about the accuracy of its information would undercut the entire foundation of their work. Thus, they spoke of the StB documents with unrestrained awe, convinced that they had a priceless treasure in their hands. Registers gathered from offices around the country were then placed in a large closet in the commission's office; wax seals indicated an attempt to maintain security, but the precautions looked rather perfunctory. Some StB files had been destroyed or disappeared in the immediate wake of the Velvet Revolution, yet the registers, which served as indexes with summary information, had survived. Ruml shook his head in apparent wonderment. "To this day I am surprised they were not destroyed," he said.

Ruml asserted that, by combing through the 140,000 names in the register, he and his colleagues had identified sixteen thousand people in categories that left no doubt that they had knowingly worked as agents or collaborators of the StB. Among the three hundred members of parliament, the commission identified sixteen as collaborators. Each was given a chance to avoid formal public exposure by resigning. Six did so, but ten—including Kavan—refused. When their names were read out in parliament, they protested their innocence, and several filed lawsuits demanding a public retraction of the charges. Several officials in top government offices were also identified; those who refused to resign were fired.

The surest sign that someone had collaborated was a signed agreement to that effect, Ruml explained, something that might occur after an informer had been entrusted with several assignments and performed well. The informer was prepared for the signing of this binding act by his StB handlers, who then had to get the approval of two immediate superiors before proceeding to make the relationship official. But Ruml conceded that this was not always the case. "In the last twenty years, it was not a strict rule for collaborators to sign an agreement if this would complicate their situation. They could collaborate without signing. It's a real mess, because you have to figure out who collaborated without signing the agreement."

And how was that possible? The classification of the informer, indicating whether he was in the categories constituting conscious collaboration, would be entered into the register, even if he had not signed an agreement. The person who entered an informer's name would not be the same as the agents running him, thereby providing a vetting procedure, with agents checking on the work of other agents. Once again, Ruml assured me that the system was marvelously foolproof.

At the same time, Ruml conceded that it was not always possible to ascertain the exact nature of the collaboration, but he denied that this posed problems for the commission's mission. "This commission is not a court," he said. "Our task is not to determine what kind of collaboration there was, but only which people were collaborating knowingly." The assertion that the commission was not a court also served to justify its refusal to call the witnesses Kavan had put forward; the normal rules of a court did not apply. According to Ruml and Toman, they were not trying and punishing but merely seeking to cleanse the parliament of collaborators, which was something quite different. As Toman argued: "No one has the right to be a member of parliament."

An inherent contradiction ran through my discussions with both men. On the one hand, they argued that their methods were foolproof; on the other, that they did not have to be held to the same standards as in a court of law. The argument that they were not inflicting punishment rang hollow, since the public humiliation and the destruction of people's reputations were all too visible. And underlying the entire debate were the lingering questions about the reliability of the StB records, upon which all these cases depended, and the broader issue of who was qualified to judge whom.

Ruml had begun his career as a radio reporter in the Stalinist era, even attending the show trial of Communist Party General Secretary Rudolf Slansky, who was hanged in 1952 as "an enemy of the people." He had had "no doubts" about what he was witnessing, because he was a communist believer at the time. "Since 1945, I was a fighter for justice, and we had the feeling that not everything was going well here, so we got the impression that there must be an enemy who was fighting against our development," he said. Later, Ruml gradually grew disenchanted and shifted sides; he was expelled from the party in 1969 and, in the 1980s, became a prominent dissident, landing briefly in jail on several occasions.

Reminiscing about his own run-ins with the StB after his expulsion from the party, Ruml recalled their asking him about a trip they thought he had made to Switzerland in 1953 to cover an ice-hockey championship. The death of Czechoslovakia's leader Klement Gottwald had led to the cancellation of the trip, both for the country's team and for Ruml, but that apparently never made it into his records. "I've never been in Switzerland," he said, laughing. Didn't this prove that the StB files could be wrong? Clearly discomfited by my question, Ruml refused to concede the point, spinning an elaborate explanation that they only would have begun maintaining a proper file on him after he joined the ranks of the dissidents.

Some of those listed as collaborators did fight back by claiming that the files were inaccurate. In particular, they argued, overzealous recruiters were prone to falsify their reports. Jaromir Gebas, a former deputy director of a national park who was elected to parliament on the communist ticket, was supposedly signed up by two border guards. When Gebas took his case to court, the two border guards testified that they had "recruited" him without his knowledge and forged his signature on a collaboration agreement. Lubomir Ledl, who ran the communists' election campaign, claimed to have irrefutable evidence that he was in Algiers on the 1984 date when he was allegedly signed up in Czechoslovakia. Both Gebas and Ledl won their cases in court in late 1992; two other deputies who had filed similar suits to clear their names emerged victorious in their own court battles in late 1992 and early 1993.

In my talk with Toman, I had again raised the question about the accuracy of the records. I knew from my own experience in Moscow in the early 1980s how the KGB had concocted charges against me by putting in their files patently false reports about my reporting trips. It was a dialogue of the deaf. "Why would they falsify the files?" he asked. "They were powerful organizations then."

Giving up on that tack, I asked him whether he could say he had not collaborated with the system. "Everyone collaborated, except a few dissidents," he said with a shrug. "I can talk about collaboration in terms of being silent under the old regime. I moved to northern Bohemia knowing I would not be forced to become a member of the party there, but I was silent." As a lawyer, he had specialized in divorces and criminal cases, never involving himself directly in politics.

"When I study the files of agents and the circumstances under which they signed agreements of collaboration after they were blackmailed, I cannot say for certain I would not have signed," he conceded. "Only those who refused can say so. As a human being, I can fully understand that they signed. The man who signed an agreement does not lose anything in my eyes. But the man loses in my eyes if he doesn't step down from political life now."

I asked him to consider, at least hypothetically, a case based on misinformation, where the person identified as "StB positive" was truly innocent. Toman's tone immediately hardened. "Even the man who thinks he is innocent may have to step down to make it possible for others to step down," he declared. "If someone told me I was in the register, and even if I knew I was innocent, I would step down. If I create doubts about that [the commission's findings], I might help myself, but it would also help the real agents."

Then, without any prompting, his argument became less abstract. "If Kavan is such a proponent of democracy, he should step down and not create doubts about the whole screening process." The refrain was familiar: individual injustices may be necessary for the good of the cause. Here was Toman, a member of the new generation of politicians without either a dissident or communist past, talking in terms that would have been perfectly understandable to those who had conducted the purges in the 1950s. Then guilt had had to be admitted for the good of the party; now guilt had to be admitted for the good of *lustrace*. The circumstances and punishment were indeed vastly different, but the logic was the same.

From the very beginning, the ethical lines in *lustrace* turned out to be far more blurred than its proponents anticipated. Take the case of Bedrich Moldan, who was sacked in early 1991 as environment minister of the Czech Republic. He admitted he had talked several times with StB agents who had approached him. "I did not throw them out the door, because I was convinced that this was a normal part of life under a communist regime," he explained. "I definitely wasn't a hero." But he insisted that he had turned down their appeal to sign on as a collaborator, and the StB records listed him only as a "candidate" for recruitment. In firing him, the Czech government admitted that no evidence had been found that he acted as an informer. But it determined, rather vaguely, "certain aspects of Dr. Moldan's contacts with the StB to be of such a nature that their misuse cannot be ruled out."

Even proven cases of collaboration could raise troubling questions. On a student fellowship in Austria in 1961, Rudolf Zukal at first rebuffed requests from a Czechoslovak diplomat to report on his meetings with American students. But when the diplomat threatened to expose an affair he was having with a married Austrian woman, Zukal agreed to talk. He insists that he warned the American students they were under surveillance, and that he told the diplomat nothing incriminating. That was the only time Zukal was classified as a collaborator in the StB register, since the economist went on to become a well-known member of the dissident movement, earning him an "enemy" classification. Detained, harassed, and beaten over the years, Zukal was elected to parliament in the first free elections. Then the *lustrace* commission demanded that he resign because of his 1961 collaboration; when he refused, his name was among the ten publicly identified.

Zukal looked weary when I discussed his case with him. "If I had killed someone so many years ago, it would not have been mentioned," he said, referring to the statute of limitations on ordinary crimes. "We live in the country of Kafka, and this is Kafkaesque." The process had hurt not only him but also his family. What hurt worst of all was that most of his accusers were people like Toman, who had never taken any risks themselves to confront the old regime. "Some of those idiots can kiss me on the face, because they were silent all the time," he added, alluding to Judas' famous kiss of betrayal. Others were afraid to speak up, he continued, because they feared taking a politically unpopular stand. "There is fear in this parliament, fear governs in this parliament," he said. Whatever happened, he had decided to retire from political life at the end of his term, his dreams of a new democratic age shattered by his personal ordeal.

But those kinds of experiences did not prevent the parliament from passing a sweeping *lustrace* law in October 1991. It banned agents and collaborators, along with former senior Communist Party officials and members of the People's Militia, from holding jobs in the state administration, state media, and state enterprises for five years. For a $7 fee, it allowed anyone over the age of eighteen to file a request with a new *lustrace* commission for a verdict on whether he or she was "StB positive." Many independent journalists, teachers, and others who were not obliged to submit to *lustrace* felt they should do so in order to prove they were clean. In the meantime, the law triggered esoteric debates about who was obliged to undergo screening. Were school cooks required to undergo *lustrace*? No, the Ministry of Education eventually ruled, but anyone who managed a school cafeteria had to be screened— and, in some cases, that might be the cook.

Although the *lustrace* procedure was supposed to provide for quiet resignations of those who were found to be tainted by the StB records, it contributed to a general climate in which the presumption of guilt became widespread. Rumors abounded about who had been found "StB positive," and an "anticommunist alliance" even began to publish highly suspect lists allegedly of everyone in the files; all the claims that lustration was needed in order to prevent an explosion of unsubstantiated charges of collaboration evaporated in the ensuing avalanche of lists. Any resignation by a top official prompted the public to conclude that the reason was StB collaboration. "Unless you suffer a massive heart attack, you can't quit your job right now without finding yourself labeled as an agent," Jaroslav Veis, the editor-in-chief of the daily *Lidove Noviny*, told me. Unfortunately, he was hardly exaggerating.

What had produced this runaway phenomenon? "Any revolution throws up fantastic expectations," Kavan pointed out. "There is a general need here to have a clear-cut internal enemy to explain why those expectations have not been met." Rudolf Slansky knows something about internal enemies. The son of the Communist Party leader who was executed in 1952, he became a prominent dissident. Appointed by Havel as Czechoslovakia's ambassador to Moscow, he could maintain a certain distance on developments in his homeland. *Lustrace,* he told me, is "a means of political struggle—it is a means for removing from power one's political rivals."

But if on occasion *lustrace* served that purpose, the reality was that it was a scattershot weapon. Though the top communist officials were banned from public life, most of them had nothing to fear from the StB files. After all, the StB had had no reason to maintain files on them or to recruit them; its efforts were directed against anyone considered to be hostile to the old order. In discussing the possibility of a similar law in Hungary, I asked Gyula Thurmer, the leader of the hard-line faction of former communists, whether his group had anything to fear. "We don't have members who worked with the secret police," he replied.

"We had orders that party members could not be made collaborators of the secret police—only by special dispensation of parliament." Of course, many collaborated on a daily basis, but not in a way that would appear in secret-police records.

The other cruel irony of *lustrace* was that it gave the StB a new lease on life, since its files had acquired new importance; an organization that had specialized in determining people's fates was still doing so. Their work kept reaping rewards, poisoning the political atmosphere of the society, which was supposed to shed the legacy of the past. But the most avid proponents of *lustrace* refused to concede any of those points, seeing all criticism of the process as evidence of new conspiracies. They began muttering about a convoluted plot orchestrated by Kavan, the StB, Western intelligence services, and the Western media aimed at discrediting *lustrace;* during a parliamentary debate in early 1992, one deputy held up what he considered particularly damning evidence: a *Newsweek* story I had written on *lustrace.* The feature had opened on a two-page spread, with large photos of Kavan and Ruml facing each other, but the deputy showed only the page with Kavan's picture to make his point about Kavan's insidious influence on the press.

The mood in parliament was summed up by its adoption, in December 1991, of a measure equating communism with fascism and declaring that both ideologies were illegal. The sentiment may have been understandable, but there was little doubt that this was a misguided attempt by parliament to dictate its own ideology—a reflex more in tune with the old system than with a democratic state. Jiri Svoboda, the chairman of the Communist Party, promply pinned a red Star of David on his chest in a gesture that was, to put it mildly, tasteless. And Georges Marchais, the French communist leader who had been a faithful apologist for communist repression, indignantly denounced the measure, which he claimed was unprecedented "except in the darkest period of contemporary European history."

In fact, the parliamentary vote had no practical implications, since it was treated as a symbolic declaration rather than a law requiring enforcement. Nonetheless, leaving aside the self-serving apocalyptic talk of the communists themselves, it indicated the pent-up anger in a society where communism had proved to be far more suffocating in everyday life than in Poland and Hungary. In this respect, Czechs were similar in their reaction to the East Germans, who also decided to try to "settle accounts" by prying open secret-police files.

Alexander Vondra, an aide to Havel, once suggested another reason for the dramatic difference in the national approaches to these issues:

Poles and Hungarians are mostly products of a Catholic culture, whereas the East Germans are mostly products of a Protestant culture and the Czechs, unlike the Slovaks, cannot be truly described as the products of a Catholic culture; 39 percent of the inhabitants of the Czech Republic describe themselves as Catholic, but Bohemia in particular has never taken strongly to Catholic traditions. As Havel himself put it in an interview with Michnik, there is "the tradition of sin, toward which Catholicism is far more understanding than Protestantism." But if forgiveness is a part of Catholic tradition, he concluded wryly, so is the Inquisition. In other words, no single explanation suffices.

If Havel could discuss *lustrace* with his usual intellectual verve, he nonetheless found himself facing a frustrating dilemma. As a moral philosopher, he was keenly aware of the dangers of blaming others for the sins of the past. The totalitarian system, he told his countrymen in his first New Year's address as president, on January 1, 1990, was a product of the complicity of all members of society. "In other words, all of us are responsible, each to a different degree, for keeping the totalitarian machine running. None of us is merely a victim of it, because all of us helped to create it together." But as a politician, he hesitated to confront the *lustrace* issue openly because of the clear danger of finding himself on the losing side.

According to his moral philosophy, that risk should not have affected his judgment. But he temporized again and again. In September 1991, Deputy Prime Minister Vaclav Vales, a coordinator of the economic policy and a veteran of the communist reform movement of the 1960s, resigned amid speculation that he may have been linked to the StB. "I cannot go on like this," Vales declared in a broken voice. Havel denounced the "smear campaign" against Vales, which never produced any concrete evidence, but he did not accompany this with warnings about the dangerous direction that the entire *lustrace* offensive was taking. In November 1991, he spent three hours with Kavan in a Prague restaurant, but he never took a public stand on Kavan's ordeal in parliament, asserting that he could not comment on individual cases.

When the *lustrace* law was passed by parliament, Havel signed it. But, at the same time, he proposed amendments designed to soften its impact. Coming after the parliamentary debate and voting, this was a purely symbolic gesture with no chance of winning approval or even being seriously considered. In his 1992 New Year's address, Havel sounded a far different note from two years earlier. He talked about how "we all underestimated the extreme cunning of our former opponents," indicating some sympathy for the popular desire to settle accounts. "But it must be done and handled in a cultured, legitimate, and civilized manner," he added. As Czech editorialists commented later, this was a classic case of trying "to square the circle." He offered no practical clues on how such a goal could be accomplished.

But Havel's uneasiness with the process was apparent when, in May 1992, he revealed that he, too, had figured on StB lists as a candidate for recruitment for three months in 1965. "Apparently I behaved civilly enough that they decided to cultivate me," Havel declared in one of his regular Sunday radio broadcasts. "But after three months they changed their minds." Later, Jaroslav Basta, the chairman of an independent commission that heard appeals in lustration cases, revealed that among those listed as "candidates" no case of conscious collaboration had been discovered. In September 1992, after a year's work by his commission, he conceded that the evidence of collaboration of those listed in higher classifications was also hardly foolproof. The StB, he admitted on television, "was just as dishonest an institution as all others in a totalitarian state." Such declarations indicated that the lustration drive was finally running out of steam.

But not in Kavan's case. In October 1992, Basta's commission upheld the finding that Kavan was guilty of "conscious collaboration." Basta himself dissented from the verdict, which was eagerly endorsed by right-wing deputies. Calling the verdict "unjust," he pointed out that there was nothing extraordinary about the fact that Kavan as a student met with a government official, since at the time many officials had indeed sympathized with the reform movement that had been crushed. "I know how it was in 1968. I have my own personal experience," Basta declared. But many of the younger deputies on the commission did not know, or did not seem to care to know.

Havel came closest to revealing his true feelings about *lustrace* in an interview with the magazine *Mlady Svet* in which he talked about the rich material the new period could provide for him as a writer. Asked to be specific, he replied:

> Just imagine someone who was importuned all his life by the secret police, and has learned how to take evasive action, to prevaricate and equivocate. At last, he thinks he has just escaped their clutches, that he has successfully deceived them. After the revolution, this person feels an enormous sense of relief; now he can breathe easily because they, the secret police, can no longer bother him. . . . And now, suddenly, there is a new fear: he hears how, one

after another, people who were marked as secret police collaborators swore they had never been collaborators, that someone had
put them on a list without their knowledge, that on the basis of a
single meeting in a cafe they were entered on a list of "candidates"
for secret collaboration or something worse, just so some cop could
get to chalk up the credit. . . . It's exactly what would interest me
in a play, the situation of someone who felt he'd made it through
the system unscathed and suddenly is terrified that maybe he hasn't
after all.

The problem was that *lustrace* is real life, not a play. Injustices may be
part of any new society that is seeking to shake off the legacy of totalitarianism, and they do not prevent democracy from evolving into a system that guards against the kind of excesses that were a part of the
lustrace drive. But, in failing to confront those issues head-on, Havel
proved himself to have been transformed into more of a practical politician than a moralist. He knew that he could not stop *lustrace* or even
modify it; instead, he straddled the fence and talked about the existen-
tial problems he could address if he were still writing plays. He had
moved from antipolitics to politics, a journey that inevitably meant an
attrition of idealism. But it was a journey that he was far from alone in
making.

OUTSIDERS
AS INSIDERS

T HIS WAS NOT the Lech Walesa I had been used to seeing during his long struggle with the communist authorities or even during the intense infighting within Solidarity. Nor was it the Walesa I had observed during his drive for the presidency that had torn the old opposition movement apart. In each of those cases, Walesa had methodically undermined, pushed, and outmaneuvered his opponents, displaying a singleness of purpose that not even his often circuitous and deliberately contradictory pronouncements could mask. In deciphering his responses to my questions in earlier encounters, I had quickly found a pattern even in the most frustratingly oblique exchanges, a message that emerged from the jumble of words, mixed metaphors, and rhetorical flights of fancy that characterized a Walesa interview.

But, walking into the Belvedere, the Polish White House, in February 1992, I found Walesa to be somehow diminished, a politician who had ostensibly achieved his ultimate ambition but who looked more trapped than triumphant. More than in any earlier crisis of his political life, he seemed uncertain about what to do, where to direct his efforts to shore up his sagging authority, and how to regain the initiative as he had so successfully done repeatedly in the past.

Even as I observed Walesa before the interview we had scheduled for that day, I was struck by a sense that he was at loose ends. Standing in the ground-floor entry hall with his chief aide, Mieczyslaw Wachowski, Walesa watched the honor guard line up in the courtyard in preparation for the arrival of a new ambassador from Argentina, who was coming to present his credentials; Walesa was chatting idly with Wachowski, as they both regularly peered out the window. When the honor guard snapped to attention, signaling the ambassador's arrival, Walesa beat a hasty retreat to the room where he would receive him to avoid giving the impression that he had been killing time. But that was exactly what he had been doing. The man who occupied the highest office in the land did not seem to have much to do at that moment except wait for this purely ceremonial occasion.

Of course, too much could be read into that brief glimpse; every leader has his idle moments, and schedules are often less than packed. But Walesa was going through one of the lowest points in his presidency. His approval ratings were hovering at no more than about 40 percent, and only 20 percent of Poles believed that he was still playing the role of an "arbiter" on the chaotic Polish political stage. In another survey, which asked who had led the country most effectively, a plurality rejected all the listed leaders, with Wojciech Jaruzelski, the last communist president, actually scoring slightly better than Walesa among those who expressed any preference. The legendary leader of Solidarity, whose critics had branded his drive for the presidency as an expression of dictatorial ambition, was increasingly dismissed as a largely powerless figure. The government of Prime Minister Jan Olszewski, the third team since the downfall of communism, was openly flaunting its disdain for him. Walesa could hardly afford to waste much time in seeking to repair the damage.

But his efforts to do so lacked the drive and spark of his offensives during earlier periods when he had been down if still far from out. After receiving the ambassador, Walesa marched into the green room— outfitted with nineteenth-century green furniture, landscapes of Warsaw, and a seventeenth-century Gobelin—where I was waiting to interview him. From the start, he was on the defensive, putting in less than a sparkling performance in trying to refute criticism of his leadership. "I am not powerless," he protested. "I have a question for Poland, for anyone who knocks me: is it good or bad that I've done ten times the task assigned to me? If I only did what was allotted to me, I also should get top marks for getting the job done. But I've done much more."

Then, referring to a 120-page booklet his staff had put out simply listing his meetings and official functions during his first year in office, he talked about anyone who might want to oppose him in the future: "If you want to run against me, write a book the way I did, and we'll give the people our books and then let them judge who did what." Like a worker in the communist period, he made a claim based on his alleged overfulfillment of his quota—as if his output as president could be measured by a production chart.

I pointed out that many people were saying he was not the kind of strong president they had expected.

"Just a second: let us reflect. Can you be a dictator when democracy is being constructed?" he replied. "Of course I am capable of being strong, but in another system. In a democracy, you cannot expect that a single individual will solve everything by himself. So, for the sake of democracy, we all suffer losses—and I personally have suffered the greatest ones."

Calling himself "a great democrat," he went on in that vein, combining his insistence that he was not powerless with a barely concealed tone of frustration about his limited influence on events in a democratic system. "My commitment to democracy diminishes my effectiveness to the point where I am not steering things," he complained. He declared that he had another option, but he was refusing to take it. "Nobody knows what demands could be made of me tomorrow by the dissatisfied masses," he said. "With that in mind, I've had to say: 'If things don't come off the way you want them, I'm ready to restrict democracy and rule by decree.' I'm ready for that. But I am not resorting to this because I want to reach the same goals democratically."

What was the bottom line? Was he really powerless, or a leader preparing to justify an authoritarian solution? What did the remarkable rise and slumping fortunes of Walesa say about the prospects for the evolution of a stable, democratic system in Poland? What did this say about Walesa himself? Or about the perils of the transformation of dissidents into establishment politicians, from outsiders to insiders, something occurring throughout the entire region, not just in Poland? How much of Walesa's problems, which were visible in particularly stark relief at that moment, stemmed from his own personality, and how much from the general difficulty of making the psychological switch from the politics of resistance to normal democratic politics?

Three weeks before Poland's first free presidential election on November 25, 1990, Walesa began his campaign pitch in the southeastern city of Rzeszow on a somber note. "I ask you not to let yourselves be directed by emotions, even toward me," he told his supporters assembled in a sports arena. But then he played the crowd's emotions like a virtuoso stump politician. "I am one of you," he assured them, pointing to his rural origins and his working-class pedigree. He was seeking the presidency, he explained, to accelerate Poland's transition to democracy and higher living standards. "The richer you are, the richer Poland will be." As for Tadeusz Mazowiecki—the Catholic journalist he had tapped for the prime minister's job a year earlier, who was his challenger—Walesa dismissed him as so slow that "he won't even catch a flea." The crowd alternatively applauded and laughed, then emerged entertained and recharged—and convinced, as one woman put it, that "Lech is the only candidate."

In the northwestern city of Szczecin two days later, Mazowiecki's supporters provided an elaborate welcome: a marching band, a hot-air balloon, and an enthusiastic, largely student audience—in other words, a bit of American-style campaign hoopla, and the kind of crowd that was eager to be charged up by Mazowiecki. But, as always, the prime minister delivered a solemn message in his painfully slow cadences, which dampened rather than built on the expectant emotions. Poland had come a long way since his government came to power, he told the students, and new opportunities for young people were emerging. Nonetheless, more hardships would lie ahead, including greater unemployment. "We must get through these difficult times," he said, warning against putting faith in "storytellers and magicians who promise to fulfill all our wishes." His supporters applauded politely, but with none of the enthusiasm that they had displayed when he first appeared. He had succeeded in deflating his own balloon.

Walesa versus Mazowiecki was the first electoral contest in Poland that could not be reduced to a battle between the remnants of the evil old system and its noble opponents. Both men had fought on the same side of the barricades throughout the previous decade, and both won tremendous respect—Walesa, the charismatic shipyard electrician, and Mazowiecki, his cerebral adviser. But their personalities defined their campaigns, in terms of both style and substance, and the sharp contrast determined its outcome. Mazowiecki's strategists tried to portray their man as the turtle plodding along against Walesa the hare, but in this story the hare kept racing farther ahead.

The presidential contest marked the official dissolution of the Solidarity camp. The strains of keeping that diverse movement together in the aftermath of the collapse of the communist system had been glaringly evident long before then, and Walesa's declaration of a "war at the top" in order to launch his bid for the presidency was only the final blow. No one doubted that eventually different political parties would have to emerge from the ranks of the old opposition; after all, Solidarity had fought for a pluralistic system. It could not continue indefinitely as a broad umbrella for groups that had dramatically different ideas about what kind of society they wanted, now that the common enemy was defeated. Nonetheless, the timing of Walesa's offensive sparked intense debate.

The split between Walesa and Mazowiecki occurred at the very beginning of the implementation of a bold new economic program, producing a sudden shift in focus to the simmering resentments between the two camps. Throughout the campaign and long afterward, both sides blamed each other for not finding a way to continue working together at least until the economic situation had somewhat stabilized; each accused the other of putting political ambitions above the broader interests of the nation. The mutual recriminations proved only to be a foretaste of a series of ever more acrimonious battles, all with Walesa at the center, that would revive the old questions about whether the Poles, who throughout their history so valiantly fought for freedom, were capable of effectively governing themselves once they no longer had the unifying threat of an external enemy.

When Mazowiecki became prime minister in August 1989, the conventional wisdom was that his government might last only a few months. Its mission, orchestrated by Finance Minister Leszek Balcerowicz, was to introduce economic "shock therapy" designed to curb the country's hyperinflation, stabilize the Polish zloty, and fill the shops with goods—but at the price of a sharp drop in real wages, the slashing of subsidies, and the beginnings of unemployment. After the program was introduced in January 1990, the initial response was overwhelmingly positive. Looking perpetually exhausted, his eyes sunk deep in a doleful face, Mazowiecki came across as the hardworking leader who was willing to level with his people about why they needed to take this bitter medicine, which they never would have accepted from any communist government. Even his closest advisers were astonished when, in March 1989, Mazowiecki's approval rating stood at 89 percent—eclipsing Walesa's by ten points.

Relations between Mazowiecki and Walesa, who had chosen to remain on the sidelines as the Solidarity leader in Gdansk rather than holding any state office himself, had grown increasingly cool, and such poll results only aggravated the tension. Mazowiecki had declared from the beginning that he would be his own man, leaving no doubt that he did not see himself obligated to take orders from Walesa—even if the latter had chosen him for the job. The Solidarity leader began sniping at the government, criticizing the government's performance in one breath and, in the next, offering assurances that his support for its program was as strong as ever. Walesa's rhetorical zigzags were famous, or infamous. "I am for and even against . . ." he would often say. At the beginning of an interview, he once instructed me: "You should listen when I say something—and half an hour later it is no longer binding."

Mazowiecki's popularity began dropping. According to Walesa and his followers, the government was to blame: it had demanded too many sacrifices without moving fast enough on reforms that would produce tangible gains. According to the Mazowiecki camp, Walesa was to blame: he was deliberately undercutting its efforts. Direct communications between the Solidarity leader and the prime minister became less and less frequent. Members of the Walesa entourage again blamed Mazowiecki, arguing that at the very least he should have called their man in Gdansk more often, giving him the feeling that he continued to have an important role to play. "That phoning to Walesa is a lot of nonsense," Mazowiecki told me over a year later, displaying his continued sensitivity to the charge. "First of all, I did call from time to time. And, second, how could I call Walesa the day after he said that one couldn't catch a flea with me?"

Whoever was at fault, Walesa felt increasingly ignored and frustrated by his sense of being on the sidelines. The combative instincts of the man, which were apparent in the 1980s both in his fight against the communists and in his often one-sided competition with underground leader Zbigniew Bujak, were aroused by his inactivity. In his best-selling book *Wodz* (*The Leader*), Jaroslaw Kurski, who served as Walesa's press secretary from the fall of 1989 to the summer of 1990, when the "war at the top" was launched, pointed out: "Walesa needs an opponent. When he defeats him, in order to live he must find another one."

That impulse was strengthened by the fact that Walesa saw others gaining power and recognition. Despite his earlier denials as spokesman, Kurski confirmed in his book that Walesa refused to meet Vaclav Havel on his first trip to Warsaw as Czechoslovakia's president out of petty jealousy: "He was hurt that after a couple of demonstrations Havel had attained what [Walesa] would have to seek with prolonged, great effort."

If Walesa felt slighted, so, too, did numerous other Solidarity activists, who looked on with open envy as the Mazowiecki team enjoyed the spotlight of national and international attention. Within the government and parliament, veteran activists like Jacek Kuron, Bronislaw Geremek, and Adam Michnik played leading roles, while activists who had not been so well known nursed their grievances and rallied around

Walesa. The twin brothers Jaroslaw and Lech Kaczynski began putting together the Center Alliance, which they hoped would emerge as a major political party by engineering Walesa's presidential drive. Others openly admitted that they were motivated by a desire to sweep the Mazowiecki crowd from office. "One Solidarity elite has been at the top for ten years," Zdzislaw Najder, a Walesa adviser during the presidential campaign, told me. "It's time for a change in elites."

Walesa was careful to couch his public pronouncements in terms that emphasized his sense of public duty rather than personal ambition. "I don't want to but I have to," he would say about running for the presidency. His opening was provided by the incomplete nature of the political changes produced by the 1989 negotiations between the communists and Solidarity. Since the round-table accords had apportioned 65 percent of the seats in the lower house of parliament to the communists and their allies while the smaller Senate was freely elected, General Jaruzelski had narrowly managed—with the tacit support of some of his former opponents—to be elected president by a joint session of both houses of parliament. With Walesa's blessing, Mazowiecki had formed a Solidarity government that still included members of the old regime; at the time, this was a tremendous breakthrough, although it required leaving communists in charge of the key Defense and Interior ministries. When Walesa launched his drive for the presidency, he insisted he only wanted to accelerate the process of full democratization in order to defuse growing popular discontent with the high price Poles were paying for the economic reforms.

At the start of his offensive, Walesa developed a new interpretation of why he had tapped Mazowiecki for the job of prime minister. He claimed that he had seen Mazowiecki as only a "transitional" figure. "He was best at that moment because the party tolerated him. He was slow and would not do anything foolish," Walesa said. But once the Communist Party fell apart, Walesa charged that Mazowiecki's instinctive caution was no longer a virtue. He forced the hastening of new presidential elections, warning that all reforms had to be accelerated. "The reforms have bogged down," he told me during the campaign. "I see this, I see the danger. And I know what to do to pull Poland out of the crisis and press on with the reforms."

The Mazowiecki team knew they had a Walesa problem, but they had allowed themselves to be somewhat lulled by their early successes and high approval ratings. A mood of self-congratulation crept into their private conversations, fueled by the sense of importance of their mission as the pioneers of the postcommunist era. It was unfortunate that Lech was unhappy in Gdansk, they told themselves, but he had opted to stay there, so it was primarily his problem. The Polish people were proving so understanding of the need for belt-tightening measures that maybe they could do without Walesa's help; in the early months of the economic reforms, popular discontent hardly looked like a serious threat. Maybe the Poles were ready to accept the intellectual arguments for short-term sacrifices for long-term gains.

As Walesa began to signal his increasing restlessness, an old undercurrent reasserted itself. Solidarity's remarkable achievement was to bring Polish workers and intellectuals together, overcoming the traditional barriers between the two groups, whereas the emerging split between the Walesa and Mazowiecki camps threatened to drive them apart again. The two sides were far from clearly divided along those lines, since many intellectuals sided with Walesa, and Mazowiecki initially could claim considerable support among workers. But the tone of the two camps reflected the positions of their leaders, and the tendency for workers to identify with Walesa and intellectuals with Mazowiecki was strengthened as the rivalry heated up.

In talking about Walesa, the intellectuals who favored Mazowiecki began privately to make him the butt of the kinds of jokes that had once been reserved for particularly primitive communists. According to one story, the Walesas were attending a performance of *Swan Lake* and Lech dozed off in the middle of the performance. Waking with a start, he asked his wife, Danuta: "Did anyone notice I was asleep?" "I don't think anyone in the audience did," she replied, "but the actors began walking around on tiptoes."

Another story was about Walesa's bedtime routine. At night, he has two glasses—one with water, and the other empty. The first is for when he is thristy, the other for when he isn't.

Walesa's reading habits were a particularly easy target. His library burns down and he is in despair. "Don't make such a fuss," Danuta scolds him. "There were only three books." Lech replies: "But I hadn't colored one of them yet."

Such jokes kept people laughing at Warsaw dinner parties, but they also reflected a vast underestimation of Walesa's innate skills at a time when Mazowiecki's supporters were overestimating their own abilities. As tensions increased, Walesa proposed a deal: he would be elected interim president by the parliament, pending general elections at a later date; parliamentary leader Geremek would be elected vice-president; and Mazowiecki would remain as prime minister. Mazowiecki turned the offer down, making a counteroffer: they should both pledge not to run for president and designate a third candidate. That would have thwarted Walesa in his goal, and he dismissed the proposal out of hand.

In retrospect, Mazowiecki and his followers made a serious mistake in not accepting the deal Walesa proposed. Such a solution would have extended the life of their government and slowed down the disintegration of the Solidarity camp, allowing economics, not politics, to dominate the agenda a bit longer. It would have saved Mazowiecki from going down to a humiliating defeat. But they did not see that then. This was not a period when the dissidents-turned-politicians maintained a good grasp on their own limitations. For all their anger at Walesa's naked ambition, they, too, had acquired a taste for power. Wladyslaw Frasyniuk, a former bus driver and a talented Solidarity leader from Wroclaw, was the rare exception. When Mazowiecki asked him whether he would take a Cabinet post in his government, Frasyniuk replied: "I could be your driver but not your minister."

As Walesa pressed for elections, Mazowiecki's supporters in parliament put forward the idea of immediate popular elections for president, in the mistaken belief that their man might have the advantage in such a contest. But their political strategy was as weak as their predictions. Looking back after the elections, Mazowiecki offered an astounding admission: he had not been consulted by his own parliamentary backers before they began to float the idea of general elections. "I learned about that afterward," he told me. Since the Walesa camp could not afford to oppose a vote of the people openly, general elections were quickly agreed upon, and Mazowiecki hesitantly threw his hat into the ring.

There may have been too much bad blood by then to allow for a cooler assessment of the situation and a compromise. Mazowiecki's backers charged that Walesa was making a power grab that could lead to chaos and a virtual dictatorship, derailing Mazowiecki's steady economic and political reforms, which had put Poland "on the road to Europe." In the process, they added, Walesa was casting himself as a populist, making promises that he could not possibly fulfill, and tapping into dangerous emotions like anti-Semitism and the desire for revenge against former communists. They derided Walesa's proposal to offer every Pole a certificate worth more than $10,000 for the setting up of new businesses, which he called an interest-free, twenty-year loan, as an outrageous ploy. And they charged that Walesa's loose talk about issuing decrees and wielding an "ax" to sweep away former communists and corruption proved that he would not respect democratic rules. Adam Michnik, the editor of the daily *Gazeta Wyborcza* and a former close adviser, flatly declared: "Lech Walesa will not be the president of a democratic Poland."

Walesa's supporters responded that it was the Mazowiecki camp that sought to block a multiparty system, and that their man was the victim of a smear campaign. "The same people who created his great legend in the world are accusing him of all this," said Andrzej Micewski, who served as a Walesa adviser during the campaign. "Before, he was made into a king; and now he is made into a devil. This hurts our country."

All such exchanges were intensely personal. Michnik, who comes from a mixed Catholic-Jewish family, was particularly incensed by Walesa's statement the previous summer that people "should declare their origins." "He never asked me about my origins when he served as the godfather of my son," he told me. Privately, Walesa's advisers claimed that their man had not understood the impact of his words, and after the campaign Walesa offered a rare apology for them. Nonetheless, his supporters turned the tables on Michnik, charging that he was responsible for stirring up the anti-Semitic feelings of a small minority to justify his attacks on Walesa. Whatever the size of that minority, it was visibly aroused. Rumors about "Jews in the government"—including stories that Mazowiecki himself was Jewish—reached the point where Bishop Alojzy Orszulik felt compelled to note that the prime minister's "genealogical tree based on his baptismal certificate dates back to the fifteenth century."

The campaign was dominated not only by such raw, atavistic undercurrents but also by the more understandable mixed emotions stirred up by the choices facing voters who continued to identify with Solidarity. Some of Mazowiecki's supporters were distinctly uncomfortable with the notion of rejecting Walesa, who remained the most prominent symbol of that movement. When Mazowiecki met with a group of local officials on his campaign swing through Szczecin, one of them explained that, though he backed the prime minister, the decision was painful. Like many activists, he claimed to have slept on the shipyard floor with Walesa during one of the strikes. In the back of the room, Henryk Wozniakowski, Mazowiecki's press spokesman, muttered: "It seems everyone slept with Walesa. I never slept with him." But such jokes should not have obscured the message of those kinds of declarations: the Walesa legend still radiated a powerful mystique.

A portion of the electorate was thoroughly disillusioned with both major candidates and the now divided movement they represented. As Walesa and Mazowiecki's supporters tore each other apart, they looked for an alternative and came up with a seemingly improbable choice from among the four other candidates: Stanislaw Tyminski.

Having spent half of his forty-two years outside of Poland, Tyminski was the ultimate outsider. A citizen of Poland, Canada, and Peru, he had founded a moderately successful computer software company in Canada and a cable television company in Peru before returning to Poland to promote his book *Swiete Psy* (*Holy Dogs*), and run for the presidency. Speaking slowly in a simple Polish marked by an accent acquired abroad, he offered up a mixture of incredible promises of instant riches and wild accusations of anti-Polish conspiracies.

Tyminski's press conferences and interviews were marked by incoherent utterances and a seemingly endless series of non sequiturs, delivered with his eyes completely unfocused. But in the free daily television slots assigned to all candidates, he hammered away at a few simple messages, producing a different impression. He was the self-made man, who arrived in Canada with no money and returned to his homeland as a wealthy "American," fulfilling the fantasy of so many Poles. As president, he told them, he could show them how to achieve similar success in their own country. Defying all early predictions, he came in second behind Walesa, knocking Mazowiecki out of the race and forcing a runoff with the Solidarity leader: Walesa had won 40 percent of the vote, Tyminski 23 percent, and Mazowiecki a paltry 18 percent.

The two Solidarity camps were stunned, but their reactions once again demonstrated their differences. Geremek, the historian and former Solidarity leader in parliament, a Mazowiecki supporter, wondered whether Poles were "mature enough" for democracy. "We need many, many lessons in democracy," he declared. When the returns rolled in, a shaken Walesa refused to face the television cameras. But, characteristically, he was not long at a loss for words. As soon as he emerged, he declared that he was appalled to be running against a "nobody" like Tyminski. He told a Solidarity gathering that Tyminski represented "counterrevolution" and that Polish reforms were "threatened by populism." Nonetheless, he rejected the interpretation that Polish society was not ready for democracy, arguing instead that the entire Solidarity camp had underestimated the level of popular discontent associated with the hardships of economic reform and the running battle between his supporters and Mazowiecki's. "They gave us a fatherly spanking," he said when I saw him in Gdansk a few days after the first round. He vowed to crush his opponent in their face-off and called him a "con man," but he did not demean the electorate in the process.

Tyminski had indeed tapped into a rich vein of discontent and a parallel vein of xenophobia. The "second Poland" of young working-class voters in small cities and towns made a receptive audience for his message that, with his experience as a businessman in Canada, he could immediately start putting money into their pockets and bringing them up to Western living standards. A typical refrain from young Poles who voted for him was: "He lived in the West for twenty years, and he knows how things work." In his book and speeches, he offered up a variety of conspiracy theories about why Poles were the "white Negroes" of Europe, earning only a fraction of Western wages, and warning of a Mazowiecki-led conspiracy to sell Poland's industries to unnamed "foreigners," with the clear implication that he was talking about Jews.

Emerging into the spotlight after his strong finish in the first round, Tyminski was not able to gain ground against Walesa. The press, which had largely ignored him before, began raising questions about his past and present affiliations. He was surrounded by people associated with the old regime, and during the 1980s he was reported to have repeatedly stopped at the Polish consulate in Libya when traveling from Canada to Poland. There were reports that he had been found "mentally unfit" for the Polish Army and that he had been deep into drugs during his "mystical" period in Peru. Tyminski called the stories about psychiatric problems and Libyan stopovers "lies," but his momentum was slowed, and he was very much on the defensive.

In confronting Tyminski, Walesa rapidly switched roles. He was no longer running against the first postcommunist government but as the defender of the new establishment, although he still vowed to improve on its performance; he was appealing for social stability, while Tyminski was endorsing all protests and strikes. When I asked Walesa for his assessment of Mazowiecki, he struck a completely different note from a few weeks before. "Some things could have been done better, but the Mazowiecki government could not have leapt straight from communism into capitalism," he said. "I accuse Mazowiecki of many things, but if I were in his shoes I probably would have made other mistakes. I'm not defending the government—I'm just appealing for common sense. There was just no avoiding mistakes."

Walesa won the runoff easily, with 74 percent of the vote, and Tyminski quickly faded from politics and Poland, complaining that he had been done in by the Jews. But the wounds of the campaign were not easily healed. Some Mazowiecki supporters bitterly maintained that Walesa himself had set the stage for Tyminski's demagogic approach, blaming him for stirring up the discontent and hatred that the interloper exploited. "Tyminski is in essence a caricature of the political style you, Lech, initiated at your meetings," charged Michnik at an emotional meeting of Solidarity's parliamentary group after the first round. The hyperbole in Michnik's angry broadside was evident, but so was at least a small, discomfiting grain of truth.

The truths that Mazowiecki's supporters failed to face were their own shortcomings in dealing with spreading dissatisfaction that they had largely ignored, preferring instead to express doubts about the ability of Poles to handle democracy, and privately to express their sense of disenchantment with Polish workers. "I was brought up with the myth of the Polish worker—first the communist myth and then the Solidarity myth that Polish workers were simple but wise, incredibly articulate, concerned about social issues," one woman, a polyglot intellectual in her mid-thirties, told me after Mazowiecki was trounced. "Now that myth has been shattered."

Looking back at those events from the distance of more than a year, Mazowiecki also naturally focused on the faults of Walesa, not his own. But his assessment of the link between Walesa's insurgent candidacy and his subsequent weak start as president was right on target. "He found himself in the trap of his own method of operation, that of the people's tribune whose promises should then be implemented by a responsible president," Mazowiecki explained. "It is very difficult to reconcile these two roles." He summed up Walesa's thinking as follows: "In order not to lose, I must always move with the tide—and later, somehow, I'll try to put things right." Reverting to his own thoughts, Mazowiecki concluded: "But he does not recognize that sometimes he causes the tide, which he must cope with later."

The tide of events had swept Walesa into the presidency before the powers of that office were defined. The original expectation had been that the first fully free elections would be for a new parliament, which would then have the popular mandate to write a new constitution, spelling out the division of powers. If Walesa had been elected interim president by the old parliament, that still could have been the case. But the insistence on a direct popular vote for president changed everything. Suddenly, Poland had a president with a popular mandate, and a parliament whose mandate could easily be challenged as illegitimate, since it had not been chosen by free elections.

Such a situation should have favored Walesa, allowing him to assert his authority broadly and dictate the political agenda. And, at first, it seemed to. He was able to select a new prime minister who had no strong political base of his own. Jan Krzysztof Bielecki, the leader of the small Liberal Democratic Congress, quickly developed a good working relationship with Walesa, with relatively few internal conflicts. "There was a simple reason: I was the president's 'child,' even though I had never been a close associate of his," Bielecki recalled later. "He treated me as his prime minister, his appointment." But in the larger battles to shape the country's future, Walesa was weakened by the lack of clarity about his powers, the endless personal infighting among his aides, and his own failure to provide effective leadership. Poland soon became a poorly governed country, although the failure of leadership was far from Walesa's alone.

Polish history was littered with warnings about the need for sensible rules that minimized the chances of government paralysis. In the eighteenth century, Polish nobles enjoyed the right of *liberum veto,* which meant that one dissenting voice could torpedo any proposal. Predictably, as the country was increasingly threatened by its imperious neighbors, the nobles could not agree on what measures to take in response. This paved the way for the successive partitions of Poland by Russia, Austria, and Prussia, until Poland disappeared altogether from the map in 1795.

When the country re-emerged after the First World War, the new parliament, operating under rules of proportional representation, quickly fragmented, providing a vivid example of dysfunctional democracy. Historian Bruce F. Pauley described the Polish parliament as "a pen full of hungry dogs with fifteen parties fighting over political bones." In 1926, Marshal Jozef Pilsudski staged a coup, dissolving the ineffective body, which he dismissed as "a sterile, jabbering, howling thing that engendered such boredom that the very flies on the walls died of sheer disgust."

For a people as acutely conscious of history as the Poles, the warning provided by those experiences should have been obvious: this time, write the rules better. Yet, in 1991, the first parliament of the postcommunist era promptly drafted a new electoral law based on the same principle of extreme proportional representation that had doomed its predecessor in the 1920s. Rather than providing incentives for political groupings to unite into larger parties, the law effectively encouraged a splintering process, playing to the worst tendencies in Polish political life. Unlike most Western European countries, or even Czechoslovakia and Hungary, which had already held free parliamentary elections, Poland opted for a law that set no minimum percentage of the votes as a requirement for a party to win seats; in most other countries, the barrier was about 5 percent, which kept small parties out or encouraged them to unite into larger ones.

Everyone was eager to shift the blame for such a disastrous law. The most common explanation was that the former communists and their allies, who were sitting in seats allotted to them in parliament, were afraid that in free elections they would not muster enough votes to break through such a barrier, so they avoided setting one. That was true, but only part of the story. Everyone in the post-Solidarity camp, from the defeated Mazowiecki partisans regrouped as the Democratic Union to the newly created right-wing Christian Democratic movements, went along with the principle of unchecked proportional representation. Some of the post-Solidarity groups had the same fears as the former communists about their electability; others seemed simply to have turned a blind eye to the historical precedents and common practices elsewhere.

In theory, Walesa could claim to have been the most active opponent of the law. When it reached his desk in June 1991, he vetoed it, warning that the law was too complex and encouraged a fragmented parliament. Both arguments were accurate, but Walesa concentrated his energies on changing specific provisions that had nothing to do with its fundamental defects. He demanded the rescinding of a ban on campaigning in churches, a provision vigorously opposed by the Catholic Church, and the elimination of a provision that required prospective candidates to have been Polish residents for at least five years. A roaring debate ensued, with Walesa attending rallies designed to show that the people were eager for him to dissolve a parliament that did not reflect the popular will, although he had no legal basis for doing so. While his foes from the Mazowiecki camp again suggested that he was flirting with authoritarian solutions, he helped fuel such speculation by declaring to a gathering of the Solidarity trade union: "I wonder if evolution from communism to democracy is possible or whether other, tough methods are needed."

Eventually, parliament revised the law to satisfy most of Walesa's demands—dropping the ban on conducting campaigns in churches, for example—and the immediate crisis blew over. But not the larger crisis prompted by an abysmal piece of legislation. The first fully free parliamentary elections were held in the fall of 1991, and twenty-nine political parties won seats in the lower house of parliament. That made the task of forming a government coalition maddeningly complex, even if the key players had been willing to approach the negotiations in a spirit of compromise. But that was hardly the case. During the first year of Walesa's presidency, the rifts within the old Solidarity movement had deepened further. The same politicians who had been among Walesa's most enthusiastic boosters for the presidential race had turned into his most avid political opponents. The subsequent battles would make the Mazowiecki-Walesa exchanges look mild by comparison.

• • •

Close associates of Walesa describe him as a man who displays instinctive distrust, which may be perfectly natural for someone who maintained his position so effectively throughout the unpredictable 1980s. As president, he did not lose those instincts. He steadfastly read every letter or document he had to sign, refusing to place complete trust in his staff not to allow something possibly compromising to make it to his desk. He demonstrated the same distrust of Jaroslaw Kaczynski, who had served as his top campaign strategist and later as chief of the presidential chancellery. Walesa proved right on this score, since Kaczynski's only loyalty was to his own political ambitions. But that raised questions about why someone like Kaczynski had been elevated to such a lofty position in the first place. Instead of providing an anchor of stability for the nation, the early period of the Walesa presidency was marked by chronic internal conflicts.

According to Kaczynski, who constantly quarreled with his boss during the year he served in the Belvedere, Walesa made one fundamental mistake. "He let himself be persuaded that a president can manage without his own political group," he explained. "So, ultimately, he found himself in political isolation." After Kaczynski left the Belvedere, he charged that Walesa's entire staff deserved to be fired: "He has surrounded himself with people who have no political qualifications." Among the most frequent targets of such criticism was Mieczyslaw Wachowski, Walesa's former driver, who had ascended to be head of the president's office and served as his constant companion. If Wachowski was indeed short of political qualifications, much of the resentment stemmed from his role as the palace gatekeeper, jealously guarding access to his boss. "Since it is difficult to hit the president, you aim at his arms and legs," Walesa told me. "And since Wachowski is a kind of gate that has to be passed, it is he who is hit."

Walesa was also repeatedly hit. After the parliamentary elections in the fall of 1991, he resisted pressure by Kaczynski and a right-wing coalition to name lawyer Jan Olszewski as the country's third prime minister since the downfall of communism. But Walesa was unable to drum up enough support for an alternative candidate, which meant that he was forced to accept Olszewski in the end. He had turned to that group of frustrated Solidarity activists when he had needed them to mount his drive for the presidency, but then he was no longer able to block them from taking advantage of their new political positions. His formal and informal powers did not allow him to keep playing one group off against another without ultimately paying a heavy price himself.

The Olszewski government proved to be the most inept team to hold power since communism fell. It focused on settling personal scores rather than on solving Poland's problems. And among the most personal of those scores was their desire to make Walesa pay for his opposition to them. In April 1992, Defense Minister Jan Parys accused Wachowski and other presidential aides of offering promotions to top military officers in exchange for their political support against the government. The subsequent outcry led to two parliamentary investigations and the conclusion that such hints of a possible coup were groundless; Parys was finally forced to resign in May. But Olszewski's team remained unrepentant about their continued assaults on Walesa's authority.

In public interviews, they accused Walesa of supporting the old communist structures. Any opposition to their attempts to launch purges in the military and other institutions was portrayed in those terms. "The president is defending communists," Krzysztof Wyszkowski, a top Olszewski aide, told me. At the same time that they warned of Walesa's allegedly dangerous ploys, they mocked his powerlessness. "Walesa is too weak a personality to be a dictator," Wyszkowski declared in an interview for *Gazeta Wyborcza* published on April 22, 1992. Zdzislaw Najder, Olszewski's chief adviser, spoke disdainfully of Walesa's efforts to define his role in the early days of the skirmishing between him and the government. "The president behaves like a player who during the game says he's bored with basketball and decides to switch to volleyball, and then he decides he doesn't like volleyball and he switches to soccer," he told me. "He would better display his extraordinary talents if he were confined by an ironclad framework of regulations."

Walesa had different ideas. Battered by his former supporters, he struck back. In a speech to parliament in May, he deplored "the Bermuda triangle" of a splintered parliament, a weak government, and his own frustrating presidency. He urged the lawmakers to grant him more power, arguing that only a strong presidency based on the French system could arrest Poland's political slide. "We cannot look on passively as our country sinks into stagnation and disorder," he warned. "Once again it is said that the Poles are incapable of making use of the freedom they attained at such a high price."

That speech failed to produce any immediate initiative for expanded presidential powers, but it helped crystallize a growing sentiment that the government had been wrong in waging war against Walesa. The president was regaining at least some of the political touch he seemed to have lost. As the battle between Walesa and Olszewski reached a critical point, the prime minister responded to a question from reporters about the tension between them by saying: "You should ask him. Electricians know all about tension." A few days later, in front of the television cameras, Walesa greeted Olszewski at the Belvedere with his reply: "Anyone who knows anything about electricity knows that an electrician's job is to remove short circuits and bring light."

Along with delivering rhetorical zingers, Walesa encouraged the emergence of a new coalition in parliament that could dislodge Olszewski. Patching up his differences with Mazowiecki and other members of the liberal wing of the old Solidarity movement, he encouraged them to make common cause with Waldemar Pawlak, the young leader of the Polish Peasant Party, which was ready to bolt from the Olszewski coalition. In the face of a common foe, the adversaries of the first round of "the war at the top" rallied to topple Olszewski.

Not before the outgoing team set off some final fireworks, however. As the parliament met to take up the no-confidence motion in early June, Interior Minister Antoni Macierewicz distributed "top-secret" lists of politicians who had allegedly served as agents of the former secret police. During the televised debate, one deputy shouted, "Walesa is on the second list." As other deputies pounded their desks in disapproval, Walesa laughed and offered mock applause.

But the president was in no laughing mood. Charging that the lists were full of fabrications, he furiously denounced the government's action. "It paves the way for political blackmail," he declared. "It completely destabilizes state and political structures." The Olszewski team had made little pretense of its intentions. A few days earlier, it had tried to save itself by winning the support of Leszek Moczulski, the leader of the populist Confederation for an Independent Poland. When Moczulski turned the government down, officials accused him of being an agent, suggesting to his aides that they dump him. "Even the communists during martial law did not resort to such methods," said deputy Adam Slomka.

After that brush with Czech-style lustration, the "war at the top" cooled down somewhat. The next government that emerged, a broad-based if somewhat tenuous coalition led by Prime Minister Hanna Suchocka of Mazowiecki's Democratic Union, sought to maintain a nonadversarial relationship with Walesa, although the president had originally promoted a different team. By November 1992, Walesa was able to sign an interim constitution passed by parliament. It spelled out the respective rights and responsibilities of the government and the president, at least partly eliminating that major source of earlier friction.

The Olszewski partisans continued to hurl ever more hysterical accusations against Walesa, and the late-blooming lustration debate led to the introduction of several proposals for dealing with the issue. But as such measures languished in parliamentary committees, the new team was able finally to focus more on governing than on settling personal scores. Suchocka, an articulate lawyer with a no-nonsense approach, made continued economic reform and defusing government-labor tensions top priorities, while backing the efforts of parliamentary leaders who won approval before impending early elections for a sensible new electoral law in May 1993. Under its provisions, only political parties that garner at least 5 percent of the national vote will be awarded parliamentary seats.

For Walesa, the scorecard looked better than it had for a long time. He had managed to regain some of his lost authority by demonstrating that he could still call the shots at a critical moment, retaliating against a government that had sought to discredit him. Although he subsequently had to accept a new government not of his own choosing, he had demonstrated his ability to remove at least one of the short circuits.

But the short circuits were also of his own making. The behavior of some of his opponents may have been wildly irresponsible, seriously damaging Poland's image, which had been so high in the immediate aftermath of the downfall of communism. Nonetheless, Walesa was partly responsible: he had helped to elevate them to their positions, displaying singularly bad judgment in many cases. His sporadic efforts to be a healer and a source of stability were at odds with his more constant instinct for political combat, which all too often proved destructive for the country and for his own standing. In those early transition years, Poland's political lights flickered disturbingly often, and the country's most famous electrician was frequently both the source and the fixer of the problem.

When communism began to crumble in Eastern Europe, the conventional wisdom was that Poland enjoyed a unique advantage over its neighbors: the broad opposition movement known as Solidarity had spawned an alternative political elite that was ready to move into positions of power. But even Walesa, the most overtly political of the practitioners of the antipolitics of the old days, proved to be only a mediocre postcommunist leader. His place in history is undoubtedly assured: in the next century, his name will dominate any short history of Poland's re-emergence as a fully independent state. But that does not mitigate the disappointments of his presidency.

Poles offer various explanations for the generally poor political performance of the new ruling elites. Veteran activist Jacek Kuron, who served as labor minister in the Mazowiecki government and returned to that post under Suchocka, argued that the qualities required of dissidents proved in many cases to be the opposite of those required of political leaders in a democratic system. All dissidents had to have a stubborn, unrelenting quality, he explained over dinner one evening. They had to be able to withstand all sorts of psychological pressures, refusing any compromises designed to break them down. They also had to be able to spot the conspiracies directed against them. But a political leader who is completely uncompromising and prone to see others as conspirators against him can hardly be effective in a more normal environment.

Kuron maintained that some dissidents were able to transcend those qualities, leaving themselves open to genuine compromises and demonstrating an ability to play by new rules. But he claimed that most of those former dissidents had participated in the Mazowiecki government; once they were swept from office, he concluded, the dissidents who demonstrated only the negative qualities were present in the Olszewski government. Despite the obvious self-interest in his breakdown of who belonged to which category, his psychological portrait of the dissidents was revealing.

Many Poles were inclined to blame "communist" thinking, which they assumed had seeped into the psyches of their countrymen regardless of their political views. "I do sometimes reason the way the system reasoned," Walesa told a Solidarity meeting in Gdansk in March 1992. "They have got it into my head, they have stuffed me with it. They've done the same to you."

But others searched for deeper roots for the disorder of postcommunist Polish political life, with the conspiratorial communist era only reinforcing thought processes that could be traced back further. "This is a country that missed the benefits of the nineteenth century," Ewa Letowska, who served as the country's first ombudsman and commissioner for civil rights, told me as she concluded her term in early 1992. "It was in the nineteenth century that democratic institutions took shape in the world: the administrative court system developed in France, parliamentary democracy was consolidated in England, the period of conquests ended in the United States, and a more decent order prevailed. But Poland was partitioned in the nineteenth century, and all those institutions were foreign."

In his novel *The Polish Complex*, which was originally published in 1977, Tadeusz Konwicki offered a similar judgment. Referring to the successive heroic but doomed uprisings by Polish patriots, he wrote: "The nineteenth century was the era of our greatness and our downfall."

It may have been precisely because the tradition of rebellion and dis-

sent was so strong in Poland that the process of constructing a work-
able new political system proved so difficult. Maybe only a new generation, no longer steeped in the battles of the communist days, would be
able to draw up more effective rules and govern more wisely. But such
judgments may be overly harsh. For all his failings, Walesa was able to
put events into perspective, avoiding the extremes of euphoria or despair. "The West must understand that we are undergoing an accelerated course in democracy," he told me during the heat of his presidential
race. "If this could be spread over forty or fifty years, you wouldn't have
the same intensity. If things are brought into sharper focus, it is because
changes are more concentrated." And the changes kept coming. Despite the missteps of its dissidents-turned-politicians, Poland was stum-
bling toward a new political order.

———

Even in his dissident days, Vaclav Havel lived fairly well. His top-floor
apartment in a building that had once been owned by his father looked
out on the Vltava River; during the middle and late 1980s, when I visited Havel several times there, it underwent a complete renovation, giving it a clean, modern feel that was totally at odds with the building's
decrepit look from the outside. He also was able to escape regularly to
write and relax in his country house in a village whose name means "little castle," which was how his dacha was dubbed long before anyone
could have imagined him working in Prague's real Castle. When he was
elected president, Havel decided not to live in the Castle, the spectacular structure that overlooks the city, but to return home at night to his
apartment. He felt comfortable there, and probably welcomed the sense
the commute across the river afforded him that he had not given up all
of his normal life.

Although Havel likes to recall that he first treated the possibility of
his running for president as an "absurd joke," he fit into his new sur-
roundings with relative ease. The Castle may have been a lavish stage,
but he quickly added enough of his own touches to give it a less pretentious feel. Sitting in one of the outer offices waiting for an interview
with him in July 1991, I was struck by the degree to which the atmosphere was dictated by Havel and his staff instead of by the splendid
Baroque setting, which could have easily overwhelmed them. A body-
guard with a ponytail lounged nearby, while a secretary wearing a long
white T-shirt featuring sunglasses and green trimmings that matched
her opaque green panty hose explained why her boss was running late.

Along with ornate chandeliers, velvet armchairs, and Oriental carpets, the rooms featured numerous bright modern paintings, and, walking into Havel's office itself, visitors encountered a metal sculpture of a head with a huge screw entering the right temple. The stamp of history may have been everywhere, but so was the stamp of its current occupant.

Havel had just presided over the meeting that formally dissolved the Warsaw Pact and met with the various leaders of neighboring states who had flown in for the occasion, and he wandered in clearly exhausted. He carefully responded to my initial questions about the disarray in the Soviet Union and Yugoslavia along with the possible implications for Czechoslovakia, although there was little doubt that he longed to bring his day to an end. His answers were thoughtful as always, putting the upsurge of nationalism in its proper historical context, but he had little enthusiasm for his task. I felt that I was playing the dutiful journalist, hitting the issues of the moment, while he was playing the dutiful head of state.

But, with that required ground behind us, Havel began to warm to questions about his personal role and broader philosophical concerns. He puffed on a successive Dunhill and sank more comfortably into his chair as he ruminated about the current application of his earlier concerns about "unrestrained consumerism" or his core belief in the "radioactivity" of words, the impact of a single word of truth in totalitarian societies. "The special radioactive power of the truthful word, of the solitary word, has ceased in the present conditions, where anyone can say what he wants," he mused, adding with a wry smile: "I must say, God has punished me. I got myself into a situation where I have to talk from morning to night, and any tired, poorly thought out word can damage something or cause trouble."

He carped about the constraints and burdens of office. "There are some parallels between prison and life as president," he said. "The difference is that in the communist prison I was responsible just to myself and to God; right now my responsibility is broader."

I asked him what he missed the most from his old life. "I miss many things—for example, that I could walk the streets without anyone recognizing me. Now everybody knows me. Nonetheless, if I put on dark glasses, walk quickly, and tell my bodyguards to be as inconspicuous as possible, I manage to walk the streets. I miss solitude. I am alone only in the bathroom. This is very similar to prison, except that one was never alone there, because there was no bathroom."

He also complained about the lack of time for himself, for reading, writing, and friends. He did manage to sneak away for about half an hour every couple of days to a pub, he said, but otherwise he was constantly busy with official duties, and his reading consisted almost exclusively of the press and official papers. He claimed not to have had much time for self-reflection, but he had reached one conclusion: "It is much easier to sit at home and write about things than to rule."

But he did not sound like someone who was eager to go back to sitting at home, since he was enjoying his role as, in Arthur Miller's words, "the world's first surrealist president." When I reminded him of that characterization, he responded with perfect seriousness: "Some intellectuals sometimes consider me their ambassador or spy in the world of the political establishment. I was afraid that the politicians might not like that, that they would see me as an alien element, and that they would look at me as an amateur or a dreamer who forced himself upon their community. But I must say, my experience has been totally the opposite. I get along with the politicians very well, and they take my presence as refreshing."

As for the future, he sounded reasonably confident about his country's prospects. The violent breakup of Yugoslavia should serve as "a bad example" for Czechoslovakia. He argued, as he had frequently over the previous months, for a referendum to allow Czechs and Slovaks to decide directly what they wanted, pointing out that a majority of Slovaks indicated in opinion polls that they wanted to maintain a common state. "Even if the improbable happens and they decide for an independent state, the separation must take place in a constitutional manner," he said. "It is not the case that Czechs would prevent Slovaks from becoming independent if they want that."

When it came to his own prospects, he hedged like any good politician. With elections for another term in office not scheduled until the summer of 1992, he claimed not to have made up his mind about running again. But it was a singularly unconvincing claim. "I can only say one thing," he told me. "If, under certain conditions, I accept to run, I would not do it because I've liked the presidency so much."

I came away convinced that, for all his complaints, which were genuine enough, Havel not only wanted but expected to win another term. He may have reached office by the power of his ideas about "antipolitics," but he had also found satisfaction as a practicing politician. The problem was that he underestimated the dimensions of the crisis brewing in Slovakia, the extent to which the political dynamic there was pulling the country apart. He also overestimated his powers of persuasion, as did many of his former Czech dissident colleagues, who were rudely awakened to the realities of the new politics in the period that followed: they were already branded as the old politicians in a new game.

Within a year, Havel did run for re-election, only to find himself blocked by Slovak opponents. More important, his hopes of preserving the federation were dashed. He was elected president of the newly independent Czech Republic on January 26, 1993, but the very fact that such a new post had to be created symbolized the failure of his earlier policies aimed at keeping the Czechs and the Slovaks together. The Velvet Revolution had given way to the velvet divorce. Instead of seeking to join Europe together, the Czechs and the Slovaks began to chart separate paths.

On a visit to the headquarters of Vladimir Meciar's leftist Movement for a Democratic Slovakia in the Slovak capital of Bratislava in the late fall of 1991, I was treated to an unexpected view as I climbed the stairs that overlooked the building's inner courtyard. There an older man was skinning a hare, which he had strung up over a jumbled assortment of battered garbage pails, its blood dripping into and around the containers. As I entered the hallway leading to Meciar's office, I spotted several more dead hares through the open door to a back room. The hunting season was in full swing, I was told, and some of the staffers had gone out to do some shooting.

If Havel's entourage and the president himself radiated their intellectual and artistic origins, the most popular politician in Slovakia and his followers radiated a red-meat populism that stemmed from their completely different background. As I stepped into Meciar's office, the ruddy-complexioned former boxer grasped my hand in a knuckle-crushing handshake. "We suspect that Czech politicians want to destroy the Czechoslovak state and blame the Slovaks," he told me, getting straight to the point. He complained that the Czechs were winning the propaganda war, since the Slovaks did not have good communication channels to the West. "The Czechs are seen as the good guys. The Slovaks are seen as fascists, nationalists, anti-Semites, cryptocommunists," he added, scoffing at the absurdity of such charges as a couple of aides nodded their heads in smiling agreement.

"There is a very hostile campaign against me," Meciar continued, warming to the counterattack. "They accused me of being an agent of the StB, the KGB; there is the accusation that I manipulated the security apparatus, or that I am trying to make Slovakia into a new communist country. I've heard all possible lies about myself."

Who was behind such attacks? Meciar reeled off the Federal Ministry of Interior, the Federal Assembly, and the Castle, including Havel himself, along with the Slovak parliament and rival parties—particularly the Christian Democrats, led by Jan Carnogursky, who was the republic's prime minister at the time. If he claimed that the underlying cause of Slovakia's problems and his problems were Czech feelings of superiority, he left little doubt that he had plenty of enemies in Bratislava as well as in Prague. "Still, the Slovak people trust me," he said proudly. "I don't leave anyone indifferent."

That he didn't. After the downfall of the communist regime, Meciar had first served as Slovakia's interior minister and then as prime minister. His tenures in both posts were marked by bitter controversy as Public Against Violence, the broad political movement akin to the Civil Forum in the Czech lands, split into rival factions. Meciar's enemies accused him of abuse of power, running roughshod over democratic procedures and stirring up nationalist sentiments. In April 1991, he was ousted as prime minister and replaced by Carnogursky. To Meciar's supporters, this amounted to a palace coup which they suspected was orchestrated from Prague.

In theory, Carnogursky was an ideal leader for Slovakia in the new era. Like Havel, he had impeccable dissident credentials, although he was from a region where the tradition of dissent was much weaker than in Bohemia. After graduating from law school in 1971, he defended religious activists and political dissidents until he was disbarred by the authorities in 1981. He then continued to dispense legal advice to opponents of the regime on an informal basis and edited an underground publication called *News of Bratislava*. Like Havel, whom he knew during those dissident days, he was arrested and served time in prison right before the collapse of the communist regime in 1989. After the Velvet Revolution, he served briefly in the federal government in Prague, but then returned to Bratislava to lead the Christian Democrats and concentrate on Slovak issues. As Havel and other Czech politicians looked on with increasing irritation, he demanded that more attention be paid to Slovakia's aspirations and historical grievances.

Meciar's personal record was hardly as impressive. Born in 1942, he worked for the Czechoslovak Union of Youth, the local equivalent of the Komsomol, in the 1960s, and he joined the Communist Party in 1962. After the Soviet invasion in 1968, he was swept up in the purges: he lost his job at the Union of Youth and was expelled from the party. While working at a steel mill, he obtained a night-school law degree; from 1984, he worked as a lawyer for a glass factory. There was never any indication he was active in the dissident movement, but during our discussion he claimed that he had had some contacts with dissidents and that he had been twice listed by the StB as an enemy of the state. He made an oblique reference to what he called his "personal feud with the old regime," but he did not elaborate. "I never talk about it," he said.

In fact, Meciar had repeatedly to deny charges that he worked for the StB and that he may have destroyed his own files during the time he served as Slovakia's interior minister in 1990. No direct evidence had surfaced to make the StB collaboration charges stick; existing files only showed he was listed as a candidate for recruitment in the mid-1980s, just as Havel had been two decades earlier. But the more serious charge leveled by his political opponents was that he used his early access to the files to try to intimidate them.

Meciar portrayed all of the charges against him as a devious plot aimed at discrediting his efforts to bolster Slovakia's standing, and none of the StB-related accusations took much of a toll. Unlike in the Czech lands, the lustration drive to purge alleged StB collaborators never gained momentum in Slovakia. Even more than the Czechs, most Slovaks had accepted the old system. There were far fewer dissidents, and few Slovaks felt a strong compulsion to settle scores with collaborators, whether real or imagined.

A radio reporter in Bratislava described the kind of conversations that took place when someone was identified as "StB-positive."

"So you worked for the StB," one of his colleagues might say. "Did you ever say anything against me?"

"No, no, I never did," the agent would assure him.

"Fine. Then let's have a beer," his questioner would suggest, signaling that the subject had been exhausted.

In that atmosphere, neither Carnogursky's dissident record nor the charges against Meciar made much of an impact. Instead, while he was out of power, Meciar could consistently take the offensive by upping the ante on the nationalist issues. During his stint as prime minister, Carnogursky attempted to push the Slovak cause forward and also keep the more extreme nationalists in check, but this proved to be a losing battle. He was not helped by the contrast between his stiff, somewhat standoffish personality and Meciar's man-of-the-people routine. Long before the June 1992 elections which propelled Meciar back into the post of prime minister, the contest was effectively over. Meciar, not Carnogursky, would define Slovak nationalism.

In the first few months after the overthrow of communism in 1989, Czech politicians somewhat derisively dismissed the Slovak issue as "the hyphen problem," referring to the parliamentary debate over whether the country's name should be written with a hyphen to stress the separate identity of the Slovaks. Eventually, the two sides agreed to use the name "the Czech and Slovak Federal Republic" formally, but officials in Prague made no secret of their impatience with the entire discussion. As they saw it, the carping of the Slovaks amounted to little more than an irritating distraction to the real challenges facing the newly liberated country.

Despite their close linguistic ties and common statehood from the time Czechoslovakia was created in 1918, the Czechs and the Slovaks have vastly different cultural and historical experiences. The predominantly rural, Roman Catholic Slovaks were subjected to Hungarian rule for centuries, while the more urban and secular Czechs lived under relatively enlightened Austrian rule. On June 30, 1918, Czech leader Tomas Garrigue Masaryk concluded "the Pittsburgh Pact" with Slovak Americans to win their support for a common state, promising Slovakia autonomy once that goal was achieved. But he later failed to fulfill his pledge, offering the flimsy excuse that he had no obligation to adhere to an agreement with foreign nationals on such a matter.

This was only the beginning of what many Slovaks felt were a steady series of slights and broken promises. During the period between the two world wars, Slovakia remained the less developed part of the country, and Czech officials often took their superiority for granted. After the Second World War, Slovakia was once again promised a degree of autonomy, and once again the promise was not kept. The communist takeover meant that decentralization and autonomy would only amount to empty slogans. During the Prague Spring, new promises of autonomy were made to the Slovaks, but these vaporized along with the other reforms once the Soviet tanks rolled in.

As a result of that history, many Slovaks felt that they had never had the chance to establish their own identity. For all the insecurities of the Czechs and their own history of domination by outside powers, they knew that their lands had long been an important center of European culture and industry. Slovaks were acutely aware of their different feelings. "The Slovaks always see themselves as people who are trying to win their sovereignty," Boris Strecansky, a history student at Bratislava's Comenius University, told me in early 1991. "The Czechs do not lack this feeling of sovereignty."

The relative security of the Czechs and insecurity of the Slovaks were evident in the degree of self-criticism among each group. According to studies conducted by the Institute for Social Analysis in Bratislava in 1990, both groups had negative feelings about the other: 69 percent of

Czechs viewed Slovaks in a negative light, while 65 percent of Slovaks had similar feelings about Czechs. As a rule, the Czechs tended to view the Slovaks as nationalistic and backward, and the Slovaks saw the Czechs as smugly superior. But what was most striking was that 76 percent of the Czechs had negative feelings about themselves as a people, and only 31 percent of the Slovaks held a negative view of themselves.

The Slovaks were clearly searching for a national identity that they had never been able to establish, but sometimes that search took bizarre, troubling forms. A prime example was the controversy surrounding Monsignor Jozef Tiso, who served as president of the Slovak puppet state created by Hitler during World War II. Tiso presided over the deportation of about sixty thousand Slovak Jews to concentration camps, even paying the Nazis for the transports, and he welcomed the Nazi suppression of an uprising by the Slovak Army in 1944. In 1947, he was executed as a war criminal. But because he was a priest and the leader of the only separate Slovak state, some Slovaks justified his behavior, claiming that, even while he collaborated with the Germans, he sought to rescue his countrymen, including some Jews who were exempted from deportation. "He was a remarkable politician who saved as many lives as possible," Father Stefan Herenyi, the pastor of a Bratislava church, told me. "He saved the nation."

Other Slovaks vehemently disagreed. Historian Jan Mlynarik, who served as a member of the federal parliament, warned against "false history." "Tiso bears the main moral responsibility for the genocide of the Slovak Jews," he asserted. But many Slovaks were openly ambivalent about Tiso, not knowing whether to assign him to the ranks of villains or heroes.

An even more crucial difference that emerged in the Czech and Slovak viewpoints focused on their more recent history. During the communist era, the authorities boosted Slovak living standards by locating heavy industries like arms production in the less developed region. For Czechs, the communist era meant a steady backsliding in living conditions as compared with its western neighbors, whereas many Slovaks felt that this was a period of ascendancy. But the postcommunist era proved far more painful for the Slovaks than for the Czechs. Their heavy industries found it hardest to adjust to a competitive market environment. By mid-1992, the unemployment rate in Slovakia had reached 12 percent, more than triple the Czech rate.

A survey conducted by the Center for Social Analysis in Bratislava in early 1992 indicated just how wide the gap in perceptions about the communist period had grown. Thirty-seven percent of the population in the Slovak Republic considered themselves supporters of the old regime; the corresponding number for the Czech Republic was 15 percent. Sixty-three percent of the Czechs saw more advantages to the present system than the old one, but only 41 percent of Slovaks felt that way.

During his term as prime minister, Carnogursky took for granted that the Slovaks, like the Czechs, were particularly eager to rejoin Europe and to make the transition to a Western-style market economy. Their aspirations for a separate national identity, he believed, did not have to impede those goals. He devised a program he characterized as "the golden middle way." "Czechoslovakia should go together into an integrated Europe," he explained. "I know that the disintegration of Czechoslovakia before we enter the European Community would harm the chances of both republics for membership." But his goal was for the Czech Republic and Slovakia to receive separate memberships in the EC around the year 2000. In a future integrated Europe, he argued, national boundaries would lose much of their importance anyway, and such a solution would fulfill the need of Slovaks to establish their own identity.

What he underestimated, however, was the extent of negative Slovak feelings about the West. According to the 1992 survey, 63 percent of Slovaks felt distrust toward the European Community; the corresponding figure for the Czech Republic was 37 percent. Even the fact that Carnogursky was a conservative on social issues, strongly tied to the Catholic Church, did not help him. Although the majority of Slovaks are Catholic, 63 percent of the population feared church interference in politics. When Carnogursky's Christian Democrats attempted to introduce antiabortion legislation, they met with an overwhelmingly negative response.

In the face of growing nationalist sentiment that was not tied to the church, Carnogursky tried a new approach to relations with Prague. In April 1991, he declared that the Czechs and the Slovaks should negotiate a state treaty before they adopted a federal constitution. At first, the Czechs rejected the proposal, arguing that a state treaty could not be concluded between the two republics, since that implied that they were two sovereign states, not part of a federation. But it was precisely that bow to the concept of sovereignty that Carnogursky was looking for, hoping it would satisfy his people. For months, the two sides bickered over what should be done. By the time the Czechs came around to the idea and the terms were negotiated, Carnogursky had lost too much political support to be able to deliver on any compromise. In February 1992, the Slovak parliament rejected the draft treaty by a one-vote margin.

Meciar worked hard to derail any resolution of the crisis, knowing that a sense of thwarted nationalist aspirations offered him the best chance of winning in the upcoming elections. But Meciar was too clever to call for outright independence, like the militant Slovak National Party, recognizing that most Slovaks still rejected that course. For similar reasons, Meciar and other Slovak politicians had steadfastly rejected Havel's proposals to hold a referendum to determine support for the federation or partition. Even if they resented what they saw as their subordination to Prague, many Slovaks indicated they wanted an equal partnership, not an outright break whose consequences they feared.

Meciar delivered the deliberately vague but promising message that many Slovaks wanted to hear. On the campaign trail, he called for "sovereignty" but not "independence." "We are now half-autonomous and half-dependent on the Czech Republic," he told a rally in the town of Zlate Moravce. "All we want is to preserve the Slovak nation and its identity." Once his party won the elections, he explained, Slovakia would declare its sovereignty, adopt its own constitution, elect its own president—and then negotiate with the Czechs about the future relationship between "two equal states." Slovakia would resolve its economic troubles with a separate economic policy, involving more state intervention and spending, he argued. Somehow, this was supposed to produce a loose confederation, culminating in separate representation of Slovakia in the United Nations and other international organizations.

Meciar's major accomplishment was to make his demands for "sovereignty" so ambiguous that he won the support of voters with diametrically opposite views. "Meciar will make Slovakia independent," Michal Borze, a retired worker in Zlate Moravce, told me. At another rally of Meciar's party in Bratislava, Ladislav Orem, an airport technician, asserted with equal conviction: "He'll try to preserve a common state with the Czechs." Both proceeded to vote for Meciar.

The Slovak leader may have really believed that he could drag out the country's ambiguous status after the elections, amassing more power in Bratislava without triggering a final break with Prague. As long as Havel and many of his former dissident colleagues were in power, they had kept trying to finesse the Czech-Slovak differences, expressing impatience with escalating Slovak demands but accepting the defeats of their successive proposals and avoiding a final showdown. However, the political landscape was changing in the Czech lands as well, bringing to the fore a new brand of political leadership, far less willing to search endlessly for an accommodation where none seemed possible. The June 1992 elections produced diametrically opposite results in the two parts of the country. While Meciar's leftist party emerged as the clear-cut victor in Slovakia, Vaclav Klaus and his right-wing Civic Democratic Party won decisively in the Czech Republic. Czech politics took on a different look and a different tone.

When Klaus launched his bid to forge a right-wing political party from the ranks of Civic Forum, the coalition that toppled the communist regime in 1989, his detractors calculated that he was too arrogant to be successful as a politician. They were wrong. By tirelessly campaigning for free-market economic reforms that he vowed would allow Czechoslovakia to regain its proper place in Europe, the finance minister established himself as the embodiment of many of his countrymen's aspirations. On the campaign trail in 1992, he proved highly effective, even learning to crack an occasional joke to counter his grim technocratic image. As an adviser to Havel grudgingly admitted: "Klaus radiates certainty. That means a lot in these uncertain times."

Certainty came naturally to Klaus. "He never changed his ideas and attitudes," noted his wife, Livia, with no trace of irony in her voice. He developed his faith in the free market in the 1960s as a postgraduate student at the Institute of Economics of the Czechoslovak Academy of Sciences, where he studied in the department that was supposed to criticize non-Marxist economics. "Instead of criticizing, I spent fifteen hours a day studying basic economics," he told me. "This was an enormous advantage. Probably nobody in this country has such solid [economic] roots, because I was young and free to study, not just to read one book when I was thirty-five."

He quickly identified with Milton Friedman and the Chicago school and proudly pointed out that, after the Soviet invasion of Czechoslovakia in 1968, he was forced out of the institute as an "anti-Marxist," not a "revisionist," as reform communists were called. Subsequently, while working in a branch office of the state bank, he continued to study Western economic models, reinforcing his belief in what he viewed as purist capitalist solutions.

During the 1992 electoral campaign, Klaus belatedly claimed to have a social as well as an economic policy, which he had disdainfully dismissed as unnecessary before. "SOCIAL IS NOT SOCIALIST," his campaign billboards proclaimed. But he had displayed an instinctive reluctance to regulate, even opposing consumer-protection measures. That left him wide open to attacks from critics who charged that he was as doctrinaire about the market as his predecessors were about central planning.

Initially, Klaus looked as if he might be on a collision course with

Havel, whose pronouncements on the dangers of "unregulated consumerism" suggested that he was hardly comfortable with Klaus' brand of economics. In 1990, Havel backed his friend Martin Palous for the job of chairman of the Civic Forum, only to watch Klaus soundly trounce him. But the two men made their peace. Havel strongly endorsed the economic reforms, and Klaus had only public praise for the president, recognizing his personal popularity at home and abroad. Klaus also made support for Havel's re-election for the federal presidency a centerpiece of his 1992 campaign.

But there was no doubt that this was an alliance of convenience more than conviction. In *Summer Meditations,* the short book Havel wrote during his presidency, he strenuously denied that he was for any "softening" or slowing down of economic reforms. Nonetheless, he added: "The only thing that genuinely bothers me, because I think it is dangerous, is the way aspects of the reforms have become an ideology, and the way intolerant dogmatism, even sheer fanaticism, sometimes accompanies this process." He never mentioned Klaus, but he did not have to.

Klaus responded to all attacks by branding his critics as "leftists," lumping together former dissidents who expressed moderate reservations about his program with former communists who opposed it. That was no accident, since he was particularly sensitive to any reminder that he had not joined the dissident movement. I raised the issue with him during the 1992 campaign, only to be treated to a revisionist rendition of the collapse of communism in Czechoslovakia, with Klaus casting himself in the starring role.

"It's an easy label, this 'dissident,' " he said. "For me, 'dissident' has many dimensions, many layers." Rather than openly attacking the old system, he added, "my preference was to go to the margin of the acceptable." Pointing out that he had led controversial but officially tolerated economic seminars in the 1980s, he claimed that even then he was laying the groundwork for sweeping economic reforms. "Those seminars and the bulletin we published were more important than the dissidents' meetings of five or ten people. I'm sure I was doing much more than the so-called dissidents." Scoffingly, he added that he had not worked in a boiler room "like Mr. Dienstbier."

Such egregious claims only fueled the feud between Klaus and the former dissidents. Even Pavel Bratinka, one of the leaders of a conservative party closely allied with Klaus' party on most issues, pointed out: "His seminars could only exist because we were the lightning rods for the police. They were possible only because we made ourselves public enemy number one of the state." Unlike Havel, Foreign Minister Dienstbier did not mask his antipathy toward Klaus, especially during the 1992 election campaign. When I asked about the differences between him and Klaus, Dienstbier shot me a sardonic grin. "Maybe it's that he's a sportsman and I have a sense of humor. He's a nonsmoker; I'm a smoker. He's a banker; I'm a journalist. What next? He's a decent man; I'm a dissident."

The latter jab had a particularly bitter edge because Klaus had managed to convince many Czechs, without ever directly saying so, that a dissident past was suspect. "Being a dissident is no longer a qualification for political office," Dienstbier told me as he tried to drum up support. "But it's not a disqualification. The chances should be equal." That was no longer the case, however. Many of the former dissidents recognized that they had seriously underestimated Klaus' political skills, even if they were convinced that they were right on target about his arrogance.

Klaus' party had staunchly backed the lustration drive, the purging of alleged secret-police collaborators, ridiculing the objections of former dissidents whose names frequently appeared in secret-police files. At a Klaus rally before the June 1992 elections, one of his supporters earnestly explained to me: "It's better to have someone who wasn't involved in the politics of the former regime." He clearly lumped together the dissidents and the communists as similarly involved. The people who had stood on the sidelines, like Klaus, were considered more acceptable. The results of the 1992 elections confirmed that trend: Dienstbier's Civic Movement, which included many of the former dissidents who espoused centrist policies, failed to win the required minimum 5 percent of the vote to make it into parliament.

One explanation for such a stunning reversal of fortunes was the polarization of the electorate. Klaus had managed to convince many voters that only his brand of right-wing politics could guarantee continued reforms, and those who were opposed were more likely to vote for the former communists as the clear-cut alternative. The specter of a leftist victory in Slovakia by Meciar's party only accelerated the polarization. The intellectuals who had made up the dissident movement instinctively shied away from what they considered to be simplistic slogans of either the left or the right, offering more complicated—and less easily marketable—answers. Though the former dissidents still enjoyed widespread respect as moral authorities, they had not learned to translate that into political power, or to play the power game with the kind of single-minded determination that characterized their more calculating opponents.

Havel was the prime example. His moral authority and popularity were beyond dispute: he consistently received over 80 percent approval ratings in the Czech lands and about 50 percent in Slovakia, despite the steady deterioration of Czech-Slovak relations. He was seen as a tireless campaigner for the common good, a leader who kept up a dialogue with his people in regular Sunday radio shows, and whose immense prestige abroad was a source of local pride. But if, unlike Poland's Walesa, Havel had managed to remain extremely popular after making the transition from dissident to president, his political authority proved just as weak. Although he was unquestionably the country's leading statesman, he could mobilize little support for his political proposals. His efforts to broaden presidential powers, which would have permitted him to take such measures as calling a referendum on the Czech-Slovak issue without parliamentary approval, went nowhere in parliament.

Father Vaclav Maly, a leading dissident under the old regime, could observe the fortunes of his close friend with relative detachment, since he devoted himself to his priestly duties instead of continuing with politics after 1989. He praised Havel for exerting a consistently calming influence on the country but also identified what he called "his greatest mistake." "He underestimated the importance of political tactics and of normal power politics," he said, adding that Havel had never maintained good channels to parliament, thus depriving himself of information and influence.

But Maly was uncertain whether any of the former dissidents could have fared better, even if they had proved to be more adept politicians. He was convinced that a major psychological factor had played a significant role in their defeats. More Czechs were involved in open dissent than Slovaks, but they were still a tiny minority. "Many people had collaborated in some way," Maly said, with a fatalistic shrug. "People don't like to see people who struggled against the communists. It's a covert pleasure to push them out of politics." The presence of the dissidents in high places, he concluded, constituted a constant unspoken challenge to their past behavior.

That resentment also began to be directed against Havel, especially after he stepped down as federal president and quickly signaled his interest in running for the Czech presidency. He was attacked by right-wing publications like *Cesky Denik,* which derided his alleged leftist leanings, and his suitability for the presidency was called into question by both the former communists and some members of Klaus' Civic Democratic Party (ODS). Members of the latter group began openly discussing the possibility of backing another candidate. Even after ODS and its coalition partners declared their support for Havel's candidacy, some of Klaus' followers did not bother to mask their disdain for him. ODS parliamentary leader Jiri Honajzer suggested Havel knew little about politics and should leave his party to run things as it saw fit. "I hope he's not going to speak first and think about it later," he declared. The sniping took its toll. His approval rate, which had already slipped to 60 percent in July 1992 when he resigned as federal president, dropped to 45 percent in December.

Some of Havel's allies believed that Klaus had deliberately tried to bring him down a notch by allowing the discussion of alternative candidacies and the venting of such attacks. While Klaus recognized that Havel's election to the presidency was important to the new Czech Republic's image abroad and that his rejection would anger even some of his followers, he wanted to leave no doubt that he—and not Havel—would wield the real power. The prime minister made sure that the Czech constitution provided for a president with tightly circumscribed responsibilities, especially in daily politics. He also rebuffed Havel's bid to call for direct presidential elections, something which would have given Havel a power base of his own. He was elected instead by a parliament controlled by Klaus.

Havel may have weakened his position by seeming overeager for the job, once again demonstrating his failings as a political tactician. "He re-entered politics too soon," argued Maly. "If he had waited patiently, the politicians would have come to him themselves. This was a political mistake." Dienstbier disagreed. "What could he do?" he said. "He was asked every day if he wanted to be president. If he had said something else, he would have been seen as playing games."

When I visited Havel in January 1993 a few days before he was voted back into office, he continued to insist that he was not enamored of politics, denying that he was motivated by personal ambition as many of his friends and foes alike suspected. "I have done many things in my life because of an inner feeling of responsibility, even if these things brought me more suffering than joy. For example, I was imprisoned when I could have avoided jail quite easily." Then, harking back to the parallels between life in prison in politics from our earlier discussions, he added: "This is true also in the case of politics."

I pressed him on the issue of personal ambition, asking again if it had not played a role in his decision to run. "I don't feel that I am a person enchanted by power, someone who longs for power, who wants to hold any office," he replied. "The point is that I want to work for something, that I cherish some values, that I want to continue this struggle or work. If I were only concerned about being president at any price, I would have behaved somewhat differently than I have. I would have behaved so as not to have any adversaries, and I have plenty of them."

Havel was undoubtedly sincere in hoping to instill a loftier, more idealistic tone to Czech politics to temper the brash style of Klaus. But in talking about his motives, he refused to acknowledge other feelings. He had been more open the previous September when he had visited Poland and admitted that "politics is the kind of beast that, once it seizes someone, does not let go." He, too, had been seized by the beast, even if his real strength was his moral voice that transcended politics as it is narrowly defined.

Many other former dissidents also remained in politics. But others shrugged off their setbacks and returned to fields such as teaching and journalism, from which they had been banned before, or explored new fields such as private business. Shortly after the 1992 elections, I chatted with Jaroslav Koran. He had served as mayor of Prague after the Velvet Revolution, only to be ousted in a power struggle in September 1991. Trying to recall his thoughts during his dissident days, he explained: "We never thought we would be real politicians. We probably thought we were preparing the way for someone else. It's probably time for us to retire. The real professional politicians are probably somewhere else. There are other fields for us to plow."

Koran had already taken his own advice. After he lost his job as mayor, he launched the Czech edition of *Playboy,* which proved to be an instant commercial success. The "real politicians" like Klaus took over the job of sorting out the future of Czech-Slovak relations.

During the campaign, Klaus had run on a strong profederation platform. Disregarding warnings from some rival Czech politicians to attack Meciar directly, to make Slovak voters reconsider their choice, he insisted that he would try to negotiate with the Slovak leader if he won. But he indicated he would stand firm on two points: the continuation of the federation, which meant that Czechoslovakia had to be represented as one country abroad, and a common economic policy. Both points were at variance with Meciar's platform. Havel and the previous federal government had taken the same position, but they had not forced a confrontation over the issue. Klaus was determined to take a different course. He told his supporters at campaign rallies that he would seek to keep the federation together, but would also not prolong its limbo state should the Slovaks refuse to accept his minimum conditions. "If we have to, we'll have a civilized divorce," he said.

The Czech populace, which had supported the federation at almost

all costs before, was increasingly impatient with Slovak demands, reinforcing Klaus' determination to play tough. In subsequent negotiations,
Klaus and Meciar agreed that they could not come to terms, and the
process of dissolution formally began, with the split becoming official
on January 1, 1993. Predictably, both sides blamed each other for that
outcome. Meciar claimed that Slovakia was forced into translating its declaration of sovereignty into all-out independence, although it had
wanted to maintain a confederation with the Czechs. Klaus insisted the
Slovaks had forced the split. Significantly, neither leader was willing to
risk holding a referendum to ask the people if they approved; the split
was presented as a fait accompli.

In an era when new states were cropping up all over Eastern Europe,
Slovakia's emergence as an independent state was not all that startling.
Its population of 5.3 million is only about half that of the Czech Republic, but it is still larger than those of such Western countries as Ireland and Norway, and considerably larger than those of the Baltic states.
Nonetheless, all the indications were that the breakup would exact a
heavy price on Slovakia.

Meciar's plans to slow down economic reforms and pump new subsidies into faltering industries could produce devastating results. An increased deficit and inflationary pressures were almost certain to scare off
foreign investors. Before the split, Slovakia had only received about one-
tenth of the foreign investment in Czechoslovakia. The IMF and the
World Bank were likely to be cool to renegotiating existing agreements.
The European Community, insisting that Czechoslovakia's association
accord would have to be renegotiated by both the Czechs and the Slovaks, was certain to take a more critical look at Slovakia's plans.

Czech economists dreaded the complications of dividing up the federation's assets, such as railroads, oil and natural gas pipelines, and
telecommunications. But they argued that the Czech Republic would
bounce back quickly, since it would be freed of the burden of supporting the weaker Slovak economy. Klaus' unquestioning commitment to
economic reform also reassured foreign investors, keeping them interested even in the midst of the process of dissolution. But the Czechs,
too, would have to pay a price during the period of uncertainty and reorganization.

None of those predictable consequences had stopped the nationalist
agitation in Slovakia which precipitated the split, even if Klaus accelerated the process in the end. Many Slovaks had seemed indifferent to the
broader impact of their actions. "They are not interested in the effects
abroad of what is happening here," said Zora Butorova of the Center

for Social Analysis in Bratislava. "They do not accept arguments about geopolitical destabilization."

Although Czechoslovakia was not remotely comparable to Yugoslavia and the split was nonviolent, tensions between the Slovaks and the ethnic Hungarian minority of six hundred thousand were immediately exacerbated. Meciar insisted that only the Slovak language could be used for official business in the country, although some communities were completely Hungarian. Fearing that their rights would be infringed upon, Hungarian political groups began calling for local autonomy, which Meciar promptly branded an attempt by Budapest to create a pretext for annexing Hungarian areas. The ensuing charges and countercharges only reinforced the impression that Slovakia could be written off as part of the region's belt of chaos, stretching from the Balkans to the former Soviet republics, even if no real crisis had yet occurred.

Other nationalist phobias were also on the rise. Along with their distrust of the West, opinion polls indicated that more than half of the Slovak population feared Jewish influence, although only about three thousand Jews still lived there. While careful to point out that many Slovak groups were seeking to maintain good relations with Jews to allay such fears, Thomas Kraus, the president of Bratislava's Jewish community, spoke of the nervousness members of the community felt about the changing status of Slovakia. "After independence, the standard of living will quickly drop and people will look for someone to blame," he predicted in May 1992. "At that point, we could have a revival of anti-Semitism."

Even if some of those fears prove to be exaggerated, there is little doubt that independence will be a mixed blessing for the Slovaks. For the first time in their history, they are on their own. However, instead of finding themselves in the company of not only the Czechs but also the Poles and the Hungarians, who are making the fastest progress in rejoining Europe, they are likely to slip backward into a crowded second tier of troubled new nations with little hope of keeping pace. They will no longer be considered part of the first group of new Europeans.

Could the split-up of Czechoslovakia have been avoided—and with it the loss of the Slovaks to that second tier? Even some of Havel's advisers conceded that he should have tried to take preventive action sooner. They believed that, if Havel had prodded the Czechs to provide a quick, positive response to Carnogursky's pleas for a state treaty between the two regions, a deal could have been struck. But his initial underestimation of the dimensions of the problem kept him from doing so. "Slovakia is the part of the country that Havel did not consider to be very important," Carnogursky told me during a conversation in early 1991, pointing out what he saw as a grievous error. Later, when I talked to him in December 1992 right before Slovakia officially became independent, Carnogursky was in a more charitable mood, pointing out that Havel "went the furthest toward meeting Slovak proposals than any Czech politician." The problem, he added, was that Havel did not have the political skill or clout to force the other Czech politicians into line.

Given the rise of nationalism throughout the region, Havel may not have been able to prevent the final outcome no matter how he had played his cards. Meciar could have always escalated his attacks, even on a completed deal. Carnogursky conceded as much in looking back at his defeat. "Meciar discovered the power of nationalism and used it to pursue his goals much faster than I did," he told me. "I was not able to win the race with him." As a populist nationalist, Meciar's appeals incorporated both leftist and rightist slogans, making for a potent brew.

Havel's steady voice of calm and reason at least made it possible for the divorce to take place peacefully. His consistent message that the Slovaks were free to choose their fate and that the Czechs would accept their choice kept emotions within reasonable bonds. Otherwise, the Czech Republic would also have dropped out of the first tier of nations pushing their way back into Europe. Havel made plenty of tactical mistakes, but, on balance, he probably salvaged what he could from a chain of events that had quickly taken on a life of its own.

———

If an interview with Walesa always offered an element of exciting unpredictability, and an interview with Havel offered the promise of a personal and genuinely intellectual meditation that addressed but also transcended the politics of the moment, an interview with Hungarian Prime Minister Jozsef Antall offered neither. A historian by training, Antall came across as the plodding teacher and librarian that he had been for most of his earlier career. Dressed in a gray suit, his gray hair brushed back, he delivered long circular answers in a monotone that gradually dulled the senses and made it hard for an interviewer to summon the energy to pin him down on anything. He was the ultimate Mr. Blandness, cutting so unprepossessing a figure that, when he stood beside Havel and Walesa at summits of the "triangle," the three leading states of Eastern Europe, he was often hardly noticed.

But Hungary under Antall proved to be politically the most stable country in the region. Even with civil war raging across its southern border in what had been Yugoslavia, and with Slovakia on its northern border extricating itself from Czechoslovakia's old federative structure, Hungary remained an oasis of relative stability, making it the favorite haven for foreign investors who were initially discouraged by the problems and uncertainties they faced elsewhere. Serious problems and tensions also existed in Hungary, but they were dealt with in a less shaky, more functional framework than that of its neighbors. Though Antall's blandness could be maddening, it proved on balance to be more of an asset than a liability in the larger process of making postcommunist Hungary work.

Unlike Walesa and Havel, Antall was a truly evolutionary, not a revolutionary, figure. As a young man, he did play a modest role in the Hungarian revolution of 1956, serving as the chairman of the revolutionary committee at Eotvos High School, where he worked, taking part in the reorganization of the Independent Smallholders' Party and helping to found the Christian Youth League. His official biography states that he was subsequently arrested, although when I once pressed him on that point he conceded that he had never been sentenced. He did lose his teaching job, however, and he was professionally blacklisted until 1962. That brush with repressive policies appeared to reinforce his instinctive sense of caution. He never joined the Communist Party, but he also stayed clear of openly dissident movements.

Like Vaclav Klaus, Antall could be defensive about his lack of dissident credentials. When I asked him during an interview about the contrast between his background and the dissident past of Walesa and Havel, he replied: "It is not I in question but Hungary. There were no well-known opposition figures in those years. In Hungary the Kadar period was special. It had the characteristic that it didn't have a mass popular opposition movement like Solidarity. And in the last years, there was no severe dictatorship that could have created a solid opposition, as in Czechoslovakia. So nobody had a background similar to Havel or Walesa."

Antall admitted that Hungarian dissidents had existed. "There was a small group consisting of philosophers and sociologists in Hungary's democratic opposition," he said. "It was a very small circle within the intelligentsia." Aside from downplaying their importance, he dwelled on the radical roots of those who were students in the 1960s. "They were associated with the Western left, and several of them were Maoists," he said. "And when they were enthusiastic about the events in Prague in 1968, they still considered the 1956 events as counterrevolutionary."

The group he was referring to eventually formed the core of the Alliance of Free Democrats, which emerged as the main opposition party to his government. "The other group was constituted by historians and writers who could work in legal conditions," Antall added, referring to his grouping that eventually developed into the Hungarian Democratic Forum. "They had an ideology close to the center, and Christian Democratic, nationalist trends."

Unlike Poland and Czechoslovakia, Hungary already had two well-defined political currents outside of the Communist Party before the collapse of communism. The open dissidents, known as the "democratic opposition," were primarily Budapest intellectuals; in many but by no means all cases, they were drawn from the capital's relatively large Jewish community, which was the largest to survive in Eastern Europe. The other group of populists or nationalists had begun cautiously meeting in the mid-1980s and launched the Democratic Forum in 1987 with the tacit support of some reformers within the Communist Party, such as Imre Poszgay; some were from smaller cities and towns, and—like Antall—they usually had avoided direct involvement in either the Communist Party or dissent. Although they were not strictly divided by age, many of the prominent leaders of the democratic opposition were members of the 1960s student generation, whereas Antall and some of his best-known colleagues were older and thus more influenced by 1956.

The psychological legacy of those formative years was considerable. Foreign Minister Geza Jeszenszky, a close colleague of Antall's, was a teenager during the 1956 uprising, which left an indelible impression on his thinking. "People of my generation, who never believed in Marxism, felt that '56 taught us a lesson," he explained. "We learned that you cannot overthrow the system if you will not be supported by outside countries. The West would not stand up for the uprising, so we had to work for survival. We had to have children to prepare for the time, probably in the next generation, when communism would come to an end."

Jeszenszky viewed the openly confrontational activists as dangerous, both in their more radical 1960s phase and later, as committed human-rights crusaders in the 1970s and 1980s. "They showed a kind of radicalism which I could not associate myself with," he recalled. In the late 1980s, as the Democratic Forum began to take shape as something in between an opposition and a government movement, he still felt that way. When members of both groups met, he was alarmed by what he took to be their militant rhetoric. "We felt it was dangerous, because a peaceful transition requires the collaboration of the authorities to some degree, and an open challenge could lead to a crackdown and endanger not only our personal safety but what had been achieved," he said. "So

I continued to believe the gradual approach was the right one."

In September 1987, the nationalists gathered for a meeting in Lakitelek, a small town outside of Budapest, in what would prove to be effectively the beginning of the Democratic Forum, although it was only officially registered as an organization a year later. Even then, Jeszenszky recalled, he felt "very dubious" about how much they could push for change—and what the reaction of the authorities would be. Along with one other member of the rival democratic opposition, dissident novelist George Konrad had been asked to attend, and Jeszenszky gave him a lift. Since Konrad was late, Jeszenszky had to drive fast to make up for lost time. He vividly recalled telling Konrad that the authorities could use his speeding as a pretext to arrest them, thus stopping the meeting. "I still felt that we might end up in prison because of that meeting," he told me.

I asked Konrad about his recollection of the incident. He did not remember anything particular about the ride itself. Did he feel any anxiety? "Not at all," he said, laughing off my mention of Jeszenszky's nervousness. "People who were in the democratic opposition were not dominated by any sense of fear at that time. They didn't take it [the threat of repression] very seriously." By 1987, the dissidents had been through their worst experiences and knew that the authorities were more eager to prove their "liberalism" than to demonstrate any ability to act tough. But for Jeszenszky and others in his group, their meetings still seemed daring, since they represented their first tentative steps toward open activism. Although both groups were working to prepare the way for the transformation that would soon take place, their different histories colored not only their views but their perception of the possible personal consequences as the momentum for change began to build.

Before the fall of communism, Miklos Haraszti was one of the most persistent critics of the system, a publisher of a samizdat journal and blacklisted writer whose books and articles appeared only in dissident publications or abroad. But he had once, as he put it, been "one of them." His father was a factory foreman, his mother an office worker—and both were dedicated communists from the prewar years. Their beliefs were so strong that, like many Hungarian Jewish communists, they never told him he was Jewish, although Miklos had been born in Jerusalem in 1945 during the period when they had sought refuge there.

"As communist Jews, my parents were part of the first and only Jewish generation in this five-thousand-year-long history who would not tell their children they were Jewish," he told me during one of our first encounters, in the mid-1980s, in his Budapest apartment. "It was so with all my [Jewish] friends." They would discover their Jewish roots, usually during their early teens, from encounters with their peers which were often tinged with anti-Semitic accusations. When Miklos asked his parents if he was Jewish, they replied: "You are of Jewish origin, but first of all we are communists, and then humans, and then Hungarians, and then . . ."

Although his parents did not hold anything approaching senior positions, they had managed to place Miklos at age six in the Maxim Gorky Russian-Hungarian School to receive what he now describes as "a classic colonial education." This was an elite institution for the children of the faithful, where all subjects except Hungarian literature were taught in Russian, and teachers were addressed, Russian-style, by their Russified first names and patronymics. Miklos' gym teacher was Istvan Kovacs; since his father's first name was also Istvan, which is the equivalent of "Stefan" in Russian, he was called "Stefan Stefanovich." Predictably, the children were taught about the glories of socialism and the dangers of imperialist enemies. "Hungarian society was a rosy victory scene," Haraszti recalled. He was fired up by the idealism of "serving a good cause."

But 1956 changed all that. The Hungarian-Russian school closed its doors for good on October 23. Haraszti's parents were frightened by the uprising, and they welcomed the announcement of a new government headed by Kadar and the Soviet suppression of the revolt "with joy and relief," Haraszti said. "I was in one of the very few families where at home the uprising was spoken of as a counterrevolution." When he transferred to the normal neighborhood school, he continued, "young, violent working-class children told me very directly what they thought of 'Russian agents' such as me."

The lesson that his earlier vision of Hungarian society, based on his ideological upbringing, was "entirely false" came as an enormous shock. This sowed the seeds of dissatisfaction with his family and Kadar's brand of politics. "I needed food for my idealism, and this wishy-washy Kadarism didn't give me any," he explained. "Quite naturally, my first means of expressing this dissatisfaction was a sort of true, pure communism learned from textbooks." His early heroes were Mao and Che Guevera. Laszlo Rajk, the son of the famed former Hungarian interior minister and foreign minister who was executed after a Stalinist show trial in 1949, has been friends with Haraszti from way back. "I had crazy fights with Miklos then," he recalls. "But it was always on a friendly basis with him." Because of his family background, Rajk never went through what he terms "a romantic '68 period," when Haraszti and others, like their counterparts in the West, embraced a radical brand of Marxism.

In 1970, Haraszti was expelled from the university on charges of subversion, and four years later, in one of the last political trials in Hungary, he received an eight-month suspended prison sentence for his book *A Worker in a Workers' State,* which was based on his brief stint in a tractor factory and published in samizdat as well as in the West. As he battled the censors of the Kadar regime, Haraszti underwent a complete transformation of his views, rejecting the dogmatic Marxism of his youth and becoming a tenacious advocate of civil liberties. "I realized that in all my ideological adventures all I felt was a lack of freedom, all I needed was the possibility of an uncensored life, and that the best thing that I can offer is a widening of the possibilities of free speech," he told me in 1986.

After the Polish government and Solidarity reached their round-table agreement in April 1989, the pressure for change intensified in Hungary. The gradual reforms instituted by the communist authorities were no longer deemed adequate, even by communist reformers like Poszgay, who was appointed chief negotiator for the party in Hungary's own version of the round table. But Haraszti and other members of the dissident movement were openly suspicious that the Democratic Forum would be willing to cut a deal with Poszgay that would preserve the communists' hold over key institutions. Haraszti and his colleagues instinctively sensed that they did not have to agree to the kind of compromises that were necessary in Poland, since Hungary's Communist Party had been promoting evolutionary changes for a long time and had demonstrated a willingness to anticipate rather than react to events. The communists were also weakened by the declining threat from the Kremlin.

Haraszti's assessment of the Democratic Forum proved correct. As relative newcomers to the opposition, Antall, Jeszenszky, and other leaders of the Democratic Forum were focused on winning an agreement for free elections, but they were still uncertain of their own leverage and willing to go a long way toward reassuring the communists. In early September 1989, as the talks between the opposition groups and Poszgay were nearing conclusion, I met with Jeszenszky. He told me that, if the Democratic Forum won a plurality in the elections, it would not be averse to offering the communists the Defense Ministry to reassure Moscow, possibly along with some other portfolio. "I wouldn't worry if we make a coalition with genuine reformist communists, who are not really communists," he said.

A week later, the talks produced a preliminary agreement between the communists and six opposition groups, with the Democratic Forum the most important of the lot, concerning the terms of the elections. Haraszti's Free Democrats and the Alliance of Young Democrats, an ideological ally, denounced the agreement. Their major objection was that it called for an election of a president by popular vote before general parliamentary elections. The communists believed this would give Poszgay, who was better known than any opposition leader, the decided edge—and a power base outside of the new parliament. "This is very dangerous," Haraszti warned, calling for the new parliament to elect the president.

The Free Democrats promptly launched an initiative that forced a referendum on the issue in November, which they won by a slim majority. In the first test of the new politics, the Budapest intellectuals had rallied many of their countrymen by appealing to their disaffection with the communist elite, including the reformers, and thus blocking the deal Poszgay had cut with the Democratic Forum.

By the time Hungary held its first free elections, in March and April 1990, the country's political landscape was populated by a plethora of political parties, among which the former communists were only a secondary element. With its appeals to Hungarian nationalist feelings, particularly the concern many people felt about the plight of the large Hungarian minority in Romania, and its broader base in small towns and villages, the Democratic Forum won as expected, with an impressive 42.9 percent of the votes. But, benefiting from their image as the stauncher anticommunists, the Free Democrats came in a solid second, with 23.8 percent. As a result of an electoral law that required any party to win a minimum of 4 percent of the votes, only six parties emerged from the crowded field with parliamentary representation. They grouped into a government coalition around the Democratic Forum and an opposition coalition led by the Free Democrats.

Despite their mutual suspicions and recriminations that flowed from a bitter campaign, the two main parties quickly reached a consensus on how to produce a functional parliament. They agreed that the parliament would elect Arpad Goncz, an older playwright and member of the Free Democrats, as president; though the post was largely ceremonial, Goncz had enough real powers to serve as a check on Prime Minister Antall on several key decisions. In return the Free Democrats agreed to limit the number of issues that would require the approval of a two-thirds majority in parliament, avoiding legislative paralysis.

Some outsiders had made fun of Hungary's immediate transition to a new kind of politics. Unlike Poland and Czechoslovakia, where the first elections amounted to a straightforward vote against the communists, the Hungarians were already involved in postcommunist politics and postcommunist choices. By establishing sensible rules and agreements, they acknowledged their differences but set the stage for a smoother transition than their neighbors'.

The Hungarians were undoubtedly helped in this process by the fact that the Hungarian communists were so accommodating as they faded from the scene, hoping to salvage what they could of their tattered reputation. Novelist Konrad recalls how, in early 1990, the local police chief visited him, apologizing profusely that there were microphones in Konrad's apartment which he would like to remove. "He could have taken them out when we weren't around, but he asked if this was okay," said Konrad. When two "workers" showed up in American plaid shirts to do the job, Konrad asked them where they had picked up the diagrams showing the locations of the hidden microphones. "We put the mikes here," one of them replied.

The different personal histories of the leaders of the two main parties continued to color postcommunist politics in Hungary. Each group claimed to have had the better record during the communist era. The members of the Democratic Forum maintained that their record of independence, refusing ever to join the Communist Party, was far superior to the record of those who had started out as radical communists and ended up as dissidents; the Free Democrats pointed out that they had fought the battles against the old system while their current opponents sat on the sidelines, and that only their pressure had prevented the Democratic Forum from making a deal with the communists that would have allowed them to maintain at least partial control.

Their disputes also contained an emotional undercurrent, centering on periodic allegations or suggestions of anti-Semitism. The Free Democrats were quick to suspect their opponents of anti-Semitic bias, charging that they were willing to exploit the presence of Jews in their leadership ranks to play to anti-Semitic feelings. The members of the Democratic Forum angrily rebuffed such charges, arguing that their opponents were seeking to caricature their views in order to discredit them as nationalist extremists who had little regard for democratic principles. To that end, they added, the Free Democrats would do anything to pin the anti-Semitic label on them.

Istvan Csurka, a playwright who represented the most militantly nationalist wing of the Democratic Forum, stirred up the acrimonious debate with remarks about a "dwarfish minority" dominating Hungarian life. "The whole Jewish issue is exaggerated and overemphasized," he told me in January 1992, offering what he reminded me was his umpteenth explanation to American journalists, who kept bringing up his remarks. "I was referring to a dwarfish minority. A minority does not necessarily mean an ethnic minority. I was referring to the communists." But in a lengthy manifesto issued the following summer, Csurka largely abandoned such pretenses, charging that Jews, communists, and liberals had frustrated efforts to transform the country. He wrote about "the Paris, New York, and Tel Aviv networks," although he later claimed that he was once again being unfairly branded an anti-Semite. In a barely camouflaged allusion to Hungary's large gypsy minority, he blamed the deterioration of the country on "genetic causes," explaining that among the underprivileged "the harsh laws of natural selection no longer function." He also wrote elliptically about the possibilities of creating a new Hungarian "living space," using the direct translation of the German term *Lebensraum,* that had served as the rationale for Nazi conquests. "Only the older generation remembers *Lebensraum,*" he told me. "I don't see why we can't use this term fifty years later in another context with a different meaning." That meaning was not spelled out, but Hungary's neighbors were quick to fear the worst.

Privately, Democratic Forum officials admitted that they found Csurka's crude style somewhat of an embarrassment, but they agreed with his contention that an attack on a former communist official who happened to have been Jewish would immediately be portrayed unfairly as an attack on Jews. They categorically denied any prejudice, and they were quick to bring up the record of Antall's father, who was commissioner for refugees during the war and has been honored for saving the lives of Poles, French POWs, and Jews.

Even after Csurka's broadside in the summer of 1992, the prime minister only cautiously disassociated himself from Csurka's views, arguing that the whole issue was "overblown." Afraid of losing the support of the right wing of his party, he acted as if this were little more than the inconsequential behavior of a temperamental child, even if that child happened to be one of the Democratic Forum's vice-presidents. "Mr. Csurka is in the first place a writer," Antall told me in September 1992. "He is an enfant terrible, a devilish child in political life who has a fancy for risks."

At heart, Antall must have known better and he was increasingly troubled by the deepening shadow Csurka's pronouncements were casting on Hungary's image abroad. In December 1992, he did away with all six of the party's vice-presidents so that his action would not be seen as directed only at Csurka. But the enfant terrible remained on the party's presidium and mounted a new offensive at the party congress in January 1993. Antall retained his leadership post and kept the party from splitting, but Csurka's faction won five of the twenty seats of the new presidium. The prime minister had once again demonstrated that his primary goal was to avoid a confrontation that might split the party and leave him with a smaller political base.

To the government's opponents, such rationalizations confirmed the prime minister's lack of will to take a decisive stance against intolerance. "Antall is personally not an anti-Semite, but he's cynical enough to tolerate it if he thinks it's useful," said philosopher Gaspar Miklos Tamas, a leading Free Democrat. "In a way, I mind this more than all the oafs and boors who really believe this. He never distances himself." Others did, however. Jozsef Debreczeni, who represented the other end of the political spectrum within the Democratic Forum, charged Csurka's manifesto with "laying the foundations of a Nazi ideology." And seventy thousand people turned out for a rally in Budapest in September 1992 "For a Democracy Without Fear," denouncing such right-wing extremism.

While the debate over anti-Semitism was a frequent undercurrent, the two parties clashed more openly over other issues. Antall's contention that he was the prime minister of fifteen million Hungarians, not limiting himself to the ten million inhabitants of Hungary, prompted protests from the Free Democrats, who are quick to denounce nationalist rhetoric that could arouse the fears of the country's neighbors, where large Hungarian minorities live.

Antall remained unfazed. During an interview in the fall of 1991, I asked Antall about that danger. "I want to put this precisely," he replied. "I said that in a judicial sense I am the prime minister of ten million Hungarian citizens, but in sentiment and in spirit I would like to be the prime minister of fifteen million Hungarians. There have been inquiries from the foreign ministries of neighboring countries, and there was no actual protest, not even one. In the case of any mother nation, it is natural that it feels concerned about its children living elsewhere."

The most bitter disputes often centered on domestic affairs. Government officials regularly lambasted the mass media for their alleged pro-opposition bias, demonstrating a genuine anger that exceeded the normal testiness of leaders in the face of critical reporting. They also reacted sharply to any suggestion that their adherence to democratic principles was less than absolute. Antall was infuriated when his opponents circulated a "Democratic Charter" in the fall of 1991, which claimed that the democratic transformation of the country still had a long way to go and offered a list of criteria to measure future progress. After

George Suranyi, the head of the central bank, signed the appeal, Antall quickly replaced him with a party loyalist. "If someone cries for freedom in a place where there is liberty, then he is the victim of a false idea or not telling the truth," the prime minister said to explain his action. The Free Democrats charged that Antall was behaving like his predecessors by dismissing someone who had dared to sign a statement in favor of greater democracy.

The rhetoric was somewhat overblown on all sides. The Antall team was singularly thin-skinned, and its pronouncements often reinforced the impression that sometimes it found democracy to be a discomfiting habitat. But it could, and did, make the case that under its leadership Hungary had achieved remarkable political progress and stability. Similarly, despite his rhetorical bows to Hungarian nationalist feelings, Antall largely avoided stirring up disputes with the country's neighbors, which was no mean feat at a time when the former Yugoslav republics had plunged into a bloody civil war, and the Slovaks were mounting their nationalist campaign to the north. For all the charges and countercharges, Hungarian Jews did not feel victimized by anything like a popular anti-Semitic campaign. In less politically charged moments, even the Free Democrats conceded that Hungary was ahead of its neighbors in the race to become, as Haraszti had told me, "normal, boring countries."

But that may have also accounted for the widespread disaffection many Hungarians felt from their new political life. Voter turnout was low, even during the first free elections, in 1990. The gradualism of many of the changes meant that there was no sense of a single moment of triumph, and the country quickly slid into the discontent associated with the economic hardships of the transition. These problems were compounded by those of servicing the largest per capita foreign debt in the region.

All that spelled trouble for the major political parties. By mid-1992, the Democratic Forum's popularity in the polls had dropped to about 15 percent. The Free Democrats also watched their popularity drop precipitously. Many of the people who had voted for them because of their strong stance against the communists were disenchanted with their staunch defense of civil liberties after the elections, which meant that they generally opposed any sweeping measure to punish former communists. Their instinctive dislike of nationalist gestures also put them at odds with popular sentiment on several occasions. The kind of highly principled stands that they had taken as dissident intellectuals did not always translate into effective politics in the new system.

The sense of drift within the party prompted an internal unheaval in

November 1991. Peter Tolgyessy, a lawyer in his mid-thirties who had not been active in the dissident movement, was elected to replace outgoing party leader Janos Kis, one of the leading intellectuals of the old opposition. "The former leadership was in danger of being restricted to the intellectuals, and a party only for the intellectuals might not even make it into parliament next time," Tolgyessy told me after his victory. "I want to appeal to a broader spectrum of society, especially to entrepreneurs." He immediately sought to emphasize the party's commitment to free-market policies, which it had espoused from the beginning, and he was willing at least to create the impression that he might be tougher on the former communists. Above all, he vowed to establish better communications with voters, avoiding too abstract internal discussions that could only confuse them.

Although no fundamental policy differences emerged, the former dissidents were startled by their setback within the party. "We were perhaps amateurish," Haraszti conceded. "We didn't think that we had to make politics within our own party." Initially, Tolgyessy's election threatened to trigger an internal split. But the former dissidents gradually accepted the new lineup, although they increasingly talked about the possibility of giving up politics. Haraszti told me that if the party regained its strength, guaranteeing healthy political competition in future electoral contests, he could imagine many of his colleagues deciding that they had accomplished their mission. "If all goes well, us old nasty guys should be able to leave the political scene," he said with a grin.

Some would undoubtedly remain, since they had become as committed to the new politics as to their former dissident activism, but, as elsewhere, their influence was beginning to wane. A new generation of politicians was already starting to take their place.

Political parties rarely break neatly along generational lines, but in Hungary in the early 1990s they came closest to doing so. While the Democratic Forum conveyed the image of somber professorial types in their fifties and sixties, and the Free Democrats were still linked with the maverick intellectuals mostly in their forties, the party that began scoring incredibly high in popularity polls was FIDESZ, the Alliance of Young Democrats, whose membership was by statute limited to people under thirty-five. By mid-1992, the Young Democrats were winning about 50 percent approval ratings, although their leader, Viktor Orban, cautioned that this did not necessarily translate into votes in elections, since many people were wary of actually electing a group of politicians in their twenties.

Like the Free Democrats, with whom they were allied in the opposition, the Young Democrats espoused free-market policies and strongly defended civil liberties. But, by virtue of their younger age and style, they projected a fresher image, less caught up with the battles of the communist period; they also delivered their message in crisper fashion, recognizing that political rhetoric must be simpler than intellectual debates. Unlike most of the leading Free Democrats, Orban had not grown up in the Budapest intellectual milieu. He lived in a small village about forty miles from the capital, where his father worked on a cooperative farm and his mother was a teacher of the mentally retarded. When he arrived in Budapest in the early 1980s to enroll at the university, he sensed the difference between himself and the dissidents he began to meet. "They were intellectuals sitting in Budapest and speaking about the society, and I came from another part of that society," he recalled.

Watching the split between the populist writers and academicians who would launch the Democratic Forum and the dissidents, he was not able to understand the confrontation at first, particularly the constant talk about anti-Semitism. "I had never heard about the Jewish question," he noted. "I arrived in Budapest, and on the first day I encountered this question."

Orban quickly became a political activist himself in the student movement, organizing one of several small independent learning centers called "colleges" which offered courses on subjects that could not be taught in the normal curriculum. The first course he organized was called "Independent Movements in Eastern Europe Under Communist Regimes," and the second one was simply called "Poland." Although the authorities were not pleased with such activism, Orban and his colleagues conducted all their business openly, arguing that they were operating within existing laws. "It was a constant struggle against the Communist Party in a very legal way," he said. "We used legality and regulations as a political weapon. The tactics of the Kadar regime at the time were not to create martyrs. They were not eager to start a confrontation with the quite well organized student movement."

The students invited dissidents like Haraszti and Kis for guest appearances. "I really appreciated them," Orban said. "But they are not the proper persons to organize a political party. They are intellectuals—but politicians and intellectuals are two different things. They have no idea how to run a party."

Orban clearly views himself as a better politician, and he demonstrated considerable political skills both before and after the fall of the old regime. During the reburial of Imre Nagy on June 16, 1989, he voiced the sentiments of many of his countrymen by blasting the communist reformers who attended the ceremony for the executed leader of the 1956 uprising. "We cannot understand that those who were eager to slander the revolution and its prime minister have suddenly changed into great supporters and followers of Imre Nagy," he told the crowd of about a hundred thousand people. "Nor can we understand that the party leaders, who made us study from books that falsified the revolution, now rush to touch the coffins as if they were charms of good luck."

However, Orban and his party unambiguously denounced the Democratic Forum's abortive attempt to waive the statue of limitations for those who perpetuated the crimes of 1956, voting against the measure in parliament. Torn by its own internal crisis, the Free Democrats abstained. The Young Democrats represented a clear-cut position, which was understandable if not always popular. Orban argued that the Hungarian transformation had been evolutionary, and that it could not suddenly adopt revolutionary rules, abolishing normal procedures. To do so in this instance might serve to punish communist criminals, but could also set a precedent for the government to take other extraordinary actions which could jeopardize the democratic nature of the changes. The Constitutional Court's rejection of the law in March 1992 appeared to demonstrate the validity of those arguments.

For all his apparent success, Orban recognized he had problems within his own party. Not yet thirty himself, he argued in 1992 that the party had to eliminate the thirty-five-and-under rule for membership in order to transform itself into a real contender at the polls. He feared that otherwise it would remain popular between elections as a magnet for the discontented but continue to be an also-ran in actual elections. In April 1993, the party abolished the age rule. Orban and his colleagues in FIDESZ looked very much like the prototype of the kind of political leaders who are likely to play increasingly important roles in the years ahead, not just in Hungary but in the region as a whole. They had learned about politics under the old system, but they emerged as real politicians only in the new system, which they were helping to define. Even though the dissidents had played an enormous role in creating the conditions that allowed them to operate, the younger breed often demonstrated more skills in playing the new system than those somewhat weary warriors of an earlier era.

Hungary demonstrated that gradual change—the dominant characteristic of the country, in contrast to the abrupt changes elsewhere—spawned a generally stable system. Despite the disaffection of many voters, new leaders and leadership styles were emerging. Like Poland,

Hungary could hardly boast a rich democratic tradition and had spent much of its history dominated by outside powers, but more recent history and the recognition of the need to establish decent political rules and practices allowed it to avoid the Polish brand of more chaotic postcommunist politics. The process of establishing the rules of the new political game proved to be more complicated and painful not just in Poland but also in Czechoslovakia, where the transition from the old system was also far more abrupt and immensely complicated by the Slovak question. But even in both those cases, democracy did not collapse under the conflicting pressures.

Elemer Hankiss, a political-science professor at the University of Budapest who served as the controversial president of Hungarian television in the early 1990s, argued that all the political conflicts of the new Eastern European democracies should be kept in balanced perspective. "In the coming two to five years, it will be decided in this country who will become the winners and the losers for decades to come, who will control the country and who will be rich or poor," he told me in the spring of 1992. "I am amazed that people do not kill themselves. I am amazed by the calm and discipline of the Poles, Czechs, and Hungarians as they try to manage this transition process."

Despite all the appearances to the contrary, he had a valid point. Compared with the turbulent emergence of Western democracies and their long evolutionary development, the Eastern Europeans had to jam an incredible range of experiences into an incredibly compressed period of time. As Walesa had explained, theirs was an accelerated course in democracy. The results were often less than edifying and accompanied by considerable trauma, but no one had yet failed the course. That in itself was no small accomplishment.

TO MARKET

I N 1989, FOLLOWING the political upheavals in Eastern Europe, the first withdrawal of Soviet troops in the region took place from Kiskunhalas, a southern Hungarian town set among sunflower and cornfields. As Hungarian television aired footage of the troops on their way out, it showed them passing a sign proclaiming "Welcome to Kiskunhalas Levi's." The symbolism could not have been more telling. The old system from the East was in retreat, and the new system from the West was already crowding in. The declining superpower was carting away its tons of weaponry, which had proved in the end to be singularly impotent, while the other superpower was advancing with the most potent firepower in its arsenal: blue jeans.

The parable did not end there. When I visited Kiskunhalas in the fall of 1990, a single factory floor continued the tale of East versus West. On one side of a sprawling plant, Levi Strauss & Co. was already operating its highly successful American-Hungarian joint venture. The company's three hundred workers churned out five thousand pairs of blue jeans a day and three thousand denim jackets a month, and the walls were decorated with motivational messages: "QUALITY NEVER GOES OUT OF STYLE"; "NOTHING IS MORE AMERICAN THAN LEVI'S." The other side of the partitioned factory told a different story. Most of the spinning, dyeing, and sewing machines stood idle, ready to be dismantled or rented out to private entrepreneurs. The large knitwear firm that occupied the premises, a product of state planners of an earlier era, had been reduced to a handful of administrators whose job was to liquidate its assets. "For the moment, I'm the production manager," Kalman Mazan told me when I found him in a forlorn office pecking away at a small red typewriter. "But we have no production."

At a time when Eastern European governments were desperately seeking to transform their economies and overcome the legacy of four decades of subjugation of economics to ideology, the rise of Levi's and the fall of the knitwear factory offered a casebook study of the new and old business practices in the region. It was not just a matter of a new capitalist venture blossoming and a former showcase socialist enterprise withering away; it was also a laboratory offering insights into the psychology of workers suddenly confronted with clear-cut choices that offered both risk and a chance for significant material gain. What drew me to Kiskunhalas soon after I arrived in the region was the opportunity to witness the interplay of two systems before the old gave way completely to the new in that one small testing ground, since this could offer clues to both the pace of and the resistance to change elsewhere.

The man who made the Levi's operation happen was Andras Pinter, whose career demonstrated that a new class of budding entrepreneurs had been developing even under the communist system. Born in 1939, a textile engineer by training, he spent seven years in Egypt in the 1970s as the manager of the Middle East office of the Csepel Steel and Metal Works. He put together deals to sell a broad array of Hungarian products—textiles, food, machinery, and even two complete garment factories—to Egypt and Syria. During that time, he also met and married Maria Neumannova, Czechoslovakia's best women's tennis player until Martina Navratilova came on the scene, reinforcing his own interest in the sport; he had won the Hungarian university-student championship in 1962. Back in Hungary in the early 1980s, he not only continued to work in the garment industry but also began to promote sports events. One of them was a 1983 tennis tournament sponsored by Levi's that turned into an annual event. In 1987, Pinter decided to use that opening to make a far more ambitious pitch to the American company to set up shop in Hungary. The Americans were understandably wary, for two reasons.

The first was that their experience in Hungary had not been encouraging up to that point. In 1977, Levi's acquired a licensing agreement with a Hungarian state company for the production of jeans under its label. The involvement of the American firm was minimal, and the jeans that were manufactured were of generally inferior quality. The state company had produced only three models of jeans in the subsequent ten years, disregarding fashion trends and devoting almost no attention to marketing. The result was that Levi's share of the market was declining, along with its prestige. In 1987, at about the same time that Pinter began pushing his proposal, Levi's discontinued the licensing agreement.

The other reason was the economic climate in the period before the political transformation of the region. Although Hungary was more inviting to foreign investors than its neighbors were, it still did not permit 100 percent foreign ownership, which is the normal Levi's formula when it sets up a production facility abroad. It could have a 51 percent controlling interest, but it would have to work with Hungarian partners. Pinter was persistent, gradually convincing the executives in San Francisco that they should give his idea a try. In 1988, Levi's formally launched the joint venture with a modest investment of $1.5 million and Pinter serving as general manager. "They probably did not believe this would be a success," he explained as we drove together from Budapest to Kiskunhalas. "That accounted for their low investment."

Levi's chose Kiskunhalas because the already troubled knitwear company was eager to rent out more than half its premises at a bargain price. Launched by the Halasi state firm with a $20 million investment, the knitwear factory had been conceived on a grandiose scale. Mazan, the mournful official I found presiding over its liquidation, recalled, with a hint of the kind of pride that planners must have exuded back at its inauguration: "At the time, it was the most advanced in Europe—in West or East Germany, Italy, Belgium, or Spain." The plan was to have up to fifteen hundred workers who would produce over two million wool-acrylic sweaters a year. Although the factory reached that production level briefly in the early 1980s, the seeds of its destruction had been planted long before its workers completed a single sweater.

Its planners, including Mazan, had begun their work in the early 1970s, when the demand for knitwear was high. But as they drew up their blueprints and began building the installation, they failed to take into account the impact of the oil crisis on the price of acrylic fibers, or anticipate the declining market for its products. The result was a continual crisis. By 1983, Halasi had sold the factory at a huge loss to the Skala department-store chain, which renamed it Texcoop, but the situation went from bad to worse. During successive management shake-ups, the workers' morale sagged. They were paid poorly, and absenteeism was 26 percent. Facing losses of up to $2 million a year, Texcoop stopped production in the summer of 1988. Mazan still found it difficult to come to terms with what had happened. "It's the death of a factory—it's very sad," he told me. "I worked here for almost twenty years."

In theory, the knitwear factory's travails should have prompted its workers to rush to look for jobs at Levi's as soon as the American company moved in, with its promises of higher wages. But that was far from the case. Some clung to the hope that the knitwear factory would survive, but most of all they were put off by Levi's no-nonsense approach. Although the company was looking for a relatively small work force, recruitment was initially a major problem. "Many people don't want to work as hard as they have to here," said Ica Kamenyfi, a former chief engineer of Texcoop who became the plant's manager. A mother in her early thirties, she made it clear from day one that she would not tolerate frequent absences by the mostly female workers to care for their children. Aside from a half-hour for lunch, workers get only two ten-minute breaks a day. New workers are put through a trial period, and the company does not hesitate to fire those who do not measure up.

On the factory floor, pop music plays over loudspeakers, and the facilities are clean, well lit, and modern, but there is no disguising the drudgery of the work. "I thought I would never last a month here," admitted Marika Sandor, forty-seven, when I stopped to chat. "But I learned how to work." So did her daughter, who was working only a few yards away. Erzsebet Balla, a young foreman, offered the simplest explanation for such changes in behavior: "They have to work differently, but they also know they will be paid differently."

The company delivered on its promised payoffs. At the time of my visit, sewing-machine operators were making about $270 a month, nearly double the rate for comparable work in the area. The plant's ten administrators—as compared with 150 for Texcoop—also learned from Levi's trainers about other methods of rewarding good work. Every month, the five best workers were invited for a free dinner at a local restaurant; once a year, five workers and their families were awarded a paid vacation abroad—to Yugoslavia at first and, after the fighting started there, to Greece. The combination of discipline and rewards cut absenteeism to only about 7 percent, a remarkable feat in a country where work habits had been slipping for decades. And it ended the recruitment problems that plagued the company in its start-up period; many young women applied straight out of school.

But only about 10 percent of the workers were veterans of Texcoop. As I discovered as I wandered through Texcoop's largely abandoned facilities, most of its workers still had no desire to seek work at Levi's. A small portion of the staff were clinging to jobs in the old factory, working for small companies that had rented the equipment. In one work-shop, the atmosphere was redolent of old times, with the women munching on sausage and bread as they stitched sweaters for $125 a month. They were happy to spell out why they were there. "Money isn't everything," said Ilona Huszti, explaining that she and her friends also could supplement their income by raising pigs or growing paprika. "After Levi's work, you are too tired to work at home. After this work, you can do anything you want. I don't want to work like a robot." From a neighboring table, her friend Piroska Szatmari added: "If I have to leave here, I'll go anywhere—but not to Levi's."

Such statements left little doubt that old attitudes die hard, especially among the more seasoned workers. But Levi's did not need to convert everyone; by recruiting a dedicated if relatively small work force, it had achieved its goals. Producing twenty different styles of jeans that were sold throughout Eastern Europe, the Middle East, and Africa, the Hungarian operation made about $1 million in profits in 1989, $2 million in 1990, and $4 million in 1991. "This shows that it was the system and not the people that was the problem," argued Pinter. San Francisco came to the same conclusion. Encouraged by its Hungarian success story, Levi Strauss opened a considerably larger plant in Poland in 1991.

Like all parables, the Levi Strauss story has its shortcomings. The contrast between the old system and the new was more neatly drawn than in most cases, and it is far from always true that an attractive joint venture with an experienced and highly successful Western partner immediately arrives to offer opportunities to at least a portion of those who are losing their jobs in a collapsing state enterprise. Even in Hungary, foreign investors could not always be counted on to be the solution.

But, as Pinter pointed out, what the Levi's experience demonstrated was that a remarkable change in work habits and performance could be achieved if the right incentives were put in place. The rapidity of the changes in the urban landscapes of Poland—and, once its economic reform was launched a bit later, in Czechoslovakia—demonstrated how fast the drab socialist look could be relegated to the famous dustbin of history with the introduction of fledgling capitalist conditions. New shops, offices, restaurants, and other services sprouted with amazing speed, injecting cities with new life as their proud owners, reviving the almost forgotten notion of care and cleanliness, spruced up dilapidated premises and decked them out with colorful signs and neon lighting.

During the long era of Soviet domination of the region, the concept of *"Homo sovieticus"* had gained widespread currency: a passive personality who had had all initiative and drive beaten out of him by the system, and who no longer would know how to work normally and to seize opportunities even if they should suddenly become available. If some of the workers in Kiskunhalas exhibited such behavior, Levi's found enough of those who did not. The problem of overcoming the psychological scars of the old era proved eminently surmountable in this case.

Such experiences deepened the conviction among the new breed of economic reformers throughout the region that the notion of *Homo sovieticus* was fundamentally wrong. "As a mainstream economist who believes in basic textbook economic thinking, [I believe] we are all *Homo economicus,*" Vaclav Klaus, then Czechoslovakia's finance minister, told me as he was drawing up the plans for his country's economic reforms in 1990. "All of us try to maximize something under the given constraints. And if you change the constraints, if you change the incentives, I am pretty sure that the behavior of people will adapt without starting new management schools or new retraining centers. *Homo sovieticus* never existed here. People are motivated by economic conditions."

Or not motivated at all. It is difficult to exaggerate the extent to which the old system failed to establish or abide by the most basic economic rules, producing prices that did not reflect cost or value, wages that did not reflect real labor, and paper that bore little or no resemblance to real money. If Klaus and other reformers were largely correct in dispelling the myth of *Homo sovieticus,* they went too far in dismissing the psychological disorientation produced by life in such an irrational economic system. While underestimating the legacy of the old system, they also sometimes overestimated the positive impact of capitalist remedies, failing to reconcile their somewhat idealistic, textbook view of capitalism with its modern, far more regulated variety.

A Polish commentator once called socialism "a tremendous waste of time," which was literally true. Under the old system, many people did not have any sense of the value of time, or that there was anything wrong with wasting other people's time by making them stand in endless lines, either to purchase goods or to take care of any bureaucratic formality. That proved to be a behavioral characteristic which was extremely difficult to shed in the new era. Everyone from senior officials to ordinary repairmen still found it distressingly easy to fail to meet appointments altogether, even when such behavior could lead to missed business opportunities.

Especially in areas of work where direct measurement of output is more difficult, the tendency to treat time on the job as an opportunity to run personal errands remained commonplace. When I first arrived in

Warsaw, I was astounded to discover that the worst traffic jams occurred at midday instead of at the beginning and end of the working day; later in my stay, that pattern began to change, but only gradually. Only when the transformation was completed, I concluded, would I believe that the old work habits had been banished along with the system that had produced them.

Another legacy that was particularly deep-rooted was the notion that, since the previous system had failed to reward honest work and was imposed by an alien power, cheating the system for private gain was not only natural but almost a noble activity. Polish communist governments tolerated the emergence of a small class of private entrepreneurs, but the businessmen had to cheat to survive. Central planning, confiscatory taxes, and the totally arbitrary powers of the bureaucrats ensured that the businessmen had to pay off officials with bribes, and routinely to arrange "purchases" of raw materials from state institutions that, according to the laws of the time, amounted to outright theft.

Accounting belonged to the creative arts, not to the domain of cut-and-dried procedures. Some successful businessmen were rumored never to allow their accountants to go on vacation, since they could not possibly allow someone else to see how phony the books were. If the authorities threatened to get serious about examining them, drastic measures were called for. One well-known businessman sprinkled water and sugar on his books and left them in the basement, so that the rats would get to them before the state auditors could.

Given that background it was hardly surprising that the concept of honest, straightforward business practices was slow in catching on in the new era. As governments tried to introduce Western-style income and corporate taxes, most citizens reacted as they always had—with the kind of widespread, flagrant tax-evasion practices more familiar to Italy than to the United States or Great Britain. Landlords continued to demand that tenants sign bogus leases for nominal rents which were reported to the authorities, and many business transactions never showed up on anyone's records. With only a fraction of the staff and none of the modern computer technology of their Western counterparts, Polish tax departments were simply incapable of effectively enforcing the new laws. Perhaps it was inevitable that the next stage after communism would be a highly corrupted form of capitalism, but that is not what the architects of the economic-reform movement had in mind.

Unfortunately, the woefully inadequate infrastructure the reformers inherited from the old system only strengthened those tendencies. In Poland in 1992, after two years of seeking to expand phone availability, there were 9.3 telephones per hundred inhabitants, whereas the corresponding number for a country like France was 58.8 per hundred inhabitants; the normal waiting time to install a new phone was not months but years. The fastest way for a foreign or local businessmen to get a phone installed, or get anything else done, was to distribute payments above and beyond the nominal fees. With the rules and regulations changing almost daily while businessmen were impatiently seeking to expand their operations, bureaucrats also had expanded opportunities to collect bribes. Rumors of much larger under-the-counter transactions accompanied the bidding wars of foreign contractors seeking lucrative contracts to upgrade telecommunications and other services. But at least the range of services began to improve rapidly.

If many of the technical services could be relatively quickly upgraded, financial services were another matter. During four decades of communism, commercial banking had disappeared. Business was normally done strictly with cash, since checks were virtually unknown and credit cards were largely reserved for businesses catering to foreigners. Employers paid their employees with cash, and mail carriers delivered bundles of bills to pensioners each month. Bank transfers were possible but painfully slow, with the result that even suppliers to major factories expected cash on delivery.

Instead of lending to borrowers who could use the money productively, banks did the exact opposite under communism, funneling subsidized loans to state enterprises without worrying about repayment. As Czech economist Miroslav Tucek, a reformer who was purged after the Prague Spring and later became the chairman of the Investment Bank, explained: "Banks were credit-allocation agencies. They had targets from state planners, and they were not guided by any concepts of economic efficiency."

To change that approach radically, all three countries began redefining the role of central banks, splitting off some departments and branches into commercial banks, and issuing licenses to a small but growing number of private, joint-venture, and foreign banks. Poland took the lead in issuing licenses to private banks, although most were small and thinly capitalized, and some quickly found themselves on shaky financial ground after making bad loans.

As in other fields, Hungary had started banking reform the earliest, even before the political upheaval of 1989, and laid the most solid groundwork for change. In 1987, it had become the first country in the region to create commercial banks independent of the central bank. Of the approximately twenty commercial banks in operation by the early 1990s, most were mixed entities, neither completely state nor private institutions. State companies were major shareholders, with privatization envisaged as a gradual process as more shares were made available to private investors. About half of the new banks were partially owned by foreign institutions, which equipped them with spiffier offices and a more competitive management style.

But even Hungary's relatively long experience with banking reform did not ensure good service, particularly for small businessmen, whose success was essential for an economic recovery. As Peter Szirmai of the National Association of Entrepreneurs explained: "The banks are not really interested in working with small firms. They have to do the same amount of work for a small loan as for a big one." Venture capital was still unknown, and banks saw little need to take risks when a virtually unlimited demand for credits existed and they had so few competitors; as a result of the vast lending needs and the extremely limited amount of local capital available, banks were in a sellers' market. "None of the banks, ourselves included, are forced by competition to back start-up ventures," admitted Peter Felcsuti, the managing director of Unicbank, an Austrian-German-Hungarian joint venture. "The banking system is not prepared to do what is needed to help the Hungarian economy."

Aspiring entrepreneurs were often hit with the double whammy of high interest rates and leftover restrictions of the old system. Karoly Olah was a prime example. Following a kidney transplant operation, he drew up a promising plan to build and run a kidney dialysis clinic to serve both Hungarians and visiting foreigners; he eagerly showed me his correspondence with Western European organizations that had expressed interest in using its services. But when he went to Hungarian banks to apply for a loan in 1990, he was told he would have to pay 32 percent interest on whatever he borrowed. Since that interest rate was more than the 20 percent profit that government regulations allowed private medical facilities to earn, the project was going nowhere when I talked to him about it a year later. "Even if I turn over all the profits to the banks, it's less than I would owe," he said.

Throughout the region, capital, management experience, and trained staff were in short supply. New training centers for bankers attempted to prepare managers better, and new technologies started to be introduced to improve banking services. But the development of a modern banking sector continued to lag far behind the demand for its services, creating a situation that concealed numerous dangers and opportunities for dubious practices. Despite the ostensible shortage of credit, a nouveau riche class was rapidly emerging, particularly in Poland, where capitalism was galloping ahead the fastest. The social transformation gathered incredible momentum during the first couple of years of the new political and economic order.

Whereas many normal Polish workers saw their real wages drop sharply during the initial period of economic reforms, the new capitalist class lived in a world apart. They gave dinner parties at which the women were decked out in the kinds of original designer dresses that are featured in *Vogue;* they skied in the Swiss or French Alps instead of in southern Poland or northern Slovakia, and they vacationed in Club Med hotels in more tropical climes; they drove only the priciest Western cars. During the first two days after a Mercedes-Porsche showroom opened in Warsaw in April 1991, twenty cars were sold, several to customers who arrived carrying briefcases stuffed with cash; by the end of the year, the dealer had sold two thousand vehicles, whose prices ranged from about $20,000 to $150,000.

For those kinds of customers, price was no object. On Hunter's Day in 1991, a fall gathering of horseback riding and jumping followed by a cookout organized by stables patronized by wealthy Poles, I rode in a Jeep Cherokee with four members of the new business class. As we drove along the roads in the woods leading to the jump sites, my companions became involved in a discussion of the merits of British versus Swiss boarding schools for their children. The consensus was that British schools were better. "Don't send him to Switzerland, where he'll learn which wine to serve with which course but not how to read," the woman driving advised one of her passengers, who was making up his mind about what to do with his ten-year-old son. When I somewhat sheepishly asked how much British boarding schools cost, I was informed that the bill came to about $15,000 a year.

"It's expensive, but Swiss schools cost about as much," the woman added.

The businessman was hardly put off by that figure: "This is an investment in our children. It'll pay off."

Where did such money come from? Some new Polish entrepreneurs, like the businessman in question, had made their initial capital abroad and then invested wisely upon their return. Given an economy of shortages, opportunities abounded for those who had the means and skill to exploit them. Many did so, paying the inevitable bribes but running what were considered generally legitimate businesses; they relied primarily on hard work and initiative. Others, however, pushed their luck to the limit, seeking to work every angle in a transition period rife with far more questionable practices. It was no accident that Poland rapidly became known as the Wild East of capitalism.

My first encounter with Boguslaw Bagsik was at a dinner party given by friends who lived near us in the Zoliborz section of Warsaw. The evening was a typical gathering of Polish intellectuals, with plenty of good food and liquor and lots of talk of movies, books, and personal intrigues in the artistic and political world, where everyone seemed to have known everyone else for ages, allowing discussions and debates to flow easily, picking up from wherever they had left off at the last dinner party. But Bagsik was the exception in this mix, the one unfamiliar face in a very familiar crowd, who happened to have been invited as a friend of a friend. A small man with a neatly trimmed beard, only twenty-eight at the time, he nursed a drink and initially talked quietly to one or two people in the kitchen, where guests helped themselves to the dishes of Italian cooking our hostess served up.

But Bagsik was too intriguing a figure to be ignored by the rest of the guests for long. According to the rumors, he was a fabulously wealthy businessman from Cieszyn, a town on Poland's southern border, but no one quite knew what his company, mysteriously called Art B, really did. It had first attracted attention when it inexplicably pledged to buy out the entire production of seventy-five hundred tractors from the Ursus tractor factory, a faltering state enterprise that had not been able to sell its tractors anywhere. This was the spring of 1991, and stories about instant millionaires abounded, although sorting out fact from fantasy was next to impossible in many cases.

Other guests made polite conversation with Bagsik as they tried to size him up, but I tried my usual straightforward journalistic approach when I had an opportunity to talk to him alone.

What did Art B stand for?

"Artistic business."

And what kind of business was that?

"Everything," he said, laughing. Then he added, with an ambiguous grin: "We pay newspapers not to write about us."

I found myself somewhat awkwardly trying to express my skepticism that this was possible and my hope that he was only joking, but he merely brushed my opening aside. "If an editor is making a couple of million zlotys a month [about $200], what problem is it to make it worth his while to sit on a story?"

Other guests came up, and we dropped the subject. Instead, the conversation turned to the news that Poland's Western creditors had decided to write off 50 percent of the country's foreign debt as a means of bolstering its economic reform program. Most of the guests were delighted, but when one asked Bagsik what he thought of the decision as a businessman, he, to everyone's surprise, dismissed it as nonsensical.

Asked to explain, he opined that cutting a debt in half benefited no one, neither the creditor nor the debtor. Meeting our somewhat blank stares, he said he would illustrate his point, pulled out a wad of $100 bills, and peeled off one. "Look, if there is one hundred dollars here and I split it . . ."

Before he could tear the bill, a couple of the guests restrained him. "Don't do it," they cried. Bagsik hesitated and then pocketed the bill, making a dismissive gesture to indicate just how inconsequential it was to him. Pulling out a 50,000-zloty note, which was the equivalent of about $5, he shrugged and tore it in half. "If I give you one half and keep one for myself, what do we both have?" he asked. "Nothing."

Then he pocketed both halves of the bill and flashed another grin. "I can always return both halves of a torn bill to the bank and get it replaced."

I was still not sure I understood the point Bagsik had been trying to make, but I knew that I wanted to get beyond such verbal dueling to find out what his business really was and whether he was as wealthy and as much of a rising star as rumor had it. Before we parted that evening, I asked him if we could meet again to talk about his activities; although he continued to express reservations concerning how much he would like to discuss with a journalist, he agreed. During the following weeks, I met repeatedly with him and his partner, Andrzej Gasiorowski, who was thirty-two at the time, as I tried to put together their story. What I did not realize when I initiated those meetings was that I had stepped into a drama that was rapidly building to a climax.

On my first visit to the Art B headquarters on Wspolna Street in downtown Warsaw, the world I was entering confirmed the impression that this was an operation moving in the fast lane. A big blond bouncer in a double-breasted suit checked my business at the entrance to the fifth-floor suite, and the offices themselves had clearly been renovated with a lot of money. The color scheme was black and white: white walls and black desks and black leather couches. The offices were fully computerized and equipped with new televisions; the telephone system boasted nine lines, including five that were direct international satellite lines that bypassed the antiquated Polish phone network. In Gasiorowski's office, where I talked with him and Bagsik, a photo on the wall beamed the message of wealth and success, showing Gasiorowski with his wife and two small children in the driveway of their lavish American-style ranch house in southern Poland in front of a shiny BMW and Pontiac Grand Prix.

As the two partners told it, theirs was a rags-to-riches story, Polish-style. Three years earlier, Gasiorowski had been a doctor in Cieszyn making $30 in month; Bagsik had been an elementary-school music teacher making even less, who supplemented his income with part-time construction jobs. Then they discovered they shared a love of jazz—and capitalist ambition. After playing music together, they began making money together. Starting in 1989, when the economic conditions in the country began changing dramatically, they formed one of the most extraordinary business empires in Eastern Europe. Their newly launched company, Art B, rocketed into the stratosphere of high finance, reporting profits of $30 million on revenues of $300 million in 1990.

Through their firm, which operated as a holding company, Bagsik and Gasiorowski claimed a controlling stake in two thousand widely varied Polish companies and other ventures as far afield as Hong Kong and Mexico. Art B assembled South Korean television sets and VCRs, they told me, and controlled a growing share of Poland's vegetable-oil- and food-processing plants; it also was beginning to produce heart electrodes and irrigation equipment. Aside from its $35 million tractor deal, Bagsik was seeking, through companies Art B controlled abroad, a 50 percent stake in the Israeli oil company Paz, an investment of about $85 million. Art B also owned four Czechoslovak turbo-planes, a Canadian Challenger executive jet, two Soviet helicopters, and a Cadillac stretch limousine. Each of its twenty-five department heads drove a Pontiac Grand Prix, courtesy of the company; in Poland, a flashy American car is often more prestigious than—and as costly as—a modest Mercedes.

Their spectacular record had already spawned any number of conspiracy theories, according to which Art B was a money-laundering operation and front for drug lords, the former communist ruling class, the CIA, KGB, or Mossad; the possibilities were seemingly endless. When I first asked a senior government official dealing with national security what to make of all this, he replied: "There are people in the National Bank who do nothing but try to catch Art B, but they haven't caught them at anything."

Bagsik and Gasiorowski shrugged off the conspiracy theories, arguing that no money-laundering operation would be so open about its "geometric growth." But, although they maintained that they were guilty of nothing but success, their increasing willingness to talk about their money-making methods with the press was clearly intended to counter suspicions. In the process, they offered insights into the rough-

and-tumble business world that was emerging in Poland. As Bagsik proudly boasted: "Some of our deals are completely incomprehensible to the West."

During the transition from communism to capitalism, the rules kept changing, producing any number of tempting financial opportunities. Like many Poles who later went on to bigger things, the pair made their first big score as food importers. From June 1989 to February 1990, the Polish government allowed anyone with hard currency to import food, charging only a 7.5 percent levy on profits. Since the communist economy had created severe shortages, anyone who filled a truck in West Germany or Austria could almost be assured of selling everything, often with a 100 percent profit. Bagsik was in Hamburg as often as three times a week, arranging for ever larger deliveries.

That was only the beginning. "We made money on finance, not trade," Gasiorowski explained. "You can't make our kind of profits on trade." At the start of 1990, Polish inflation was still in triple digits while the government maintained a fixed exchange rate for the Polish zloty against hard currencies, to achieve convertibility. Instead of relying on Polish credits, whose high interest rates reflected inflation, Art B operatives lined up letters of credit through foreign banks to import Asian electronic products; those loans were offered at the normal hard-currency rate of about 12 percent a year. During the 120 days they had to repay their foreign bankers, they imported and sold the goods as fast as possible, at or even below cost, and then recycled the cash into Polish banks that offered monthly yields of as much as 84 percent a year.

When it came time to repay the letters of credit, Art B withdrew its deposit of Polish zlotys, plus interest, and converted it to hard currency at the fixed rate. The difference between the Polish interest rate they earned and the hard-currency interest rate they paid represented a tidy profit. Even when inflation and interest rates began to drop, the company continued to make a killing. Whether the Art B pair was buying tractors or shaky state enterprises, they viewed each acquisition as collateral for their next deal.

Bagsik and Gasiorowski clearly relished their roles as the high rollers of Polish capitalism, particularly the attention they began to attract from major foreign companies seeking to break into the Polish market. In talks with visiting Chrysler executives over blini and caviar at a posh Warsaw restaurant in June, Bagsik left no doubt that Art B could easily set up a network of Chrysler dealerships in Poland. Not only could Art B arrange financing, he told his guests, it also might be able to "lock up" the Polish military market, selling perhaps ten thousand vehicles to the army.

Chrysler International vice-president Patrick Smorra looked impressed. Although he was a bit uneasy about my presence as a journalistic interloper at the dinner and did not want to discuss the specifics of the deal he envisaged, he was happy to speak about his admiration for his hosts. "There's optimism, energy, aggressiveness, and drive," he told me during a lull in his conversation with Bagsik. "How are you going to conquer a country which was communist three years ago without these ingredients? Here you have to be imaginative and risk-taking. If anyone is going to be successful, it's going to be the guy who goes for the brass ring."

As we left the restaurant, Gasiorowski invited me to come along to witness Art B's acquisition of a $14 million majority stake in a major poultry-processing plant near Warsaw a week later. His performance there was every bit as energetic as Bagsik's in front of the Chrysler executives, conveying the same impression that Art B would make things happen. After a brief signing ceremony and a quick tour of the facilities, he was all business over a lunch of chicken breasts, chicken sausages, and other products from the plant. He had learned that, instead of operating at its capacity of seventy thousand chickens a day, it was processing only thirty-five thousand. "I'm thinking about how we can make more money," he told the assembled representatives of management and workers. "We know something about music and economics, but you'll have to figure out how to best produce chickens."

To manager Jacek Mackiewicz's cautious question about new investment, Gasiorowski had a ready answer: "We are specialists in raising other people's money." As for export possibilities, he was equally upbeat. "We know about export mechanisms that, regardless of price, allow us to sell our products," he declared with a wide grin. He was clearly going a bit too fast for his hosts, who wanted to believe him but looked less than completely convinced. Most of the chicken parts had been left uneaten when the slightly dazed gathering bid Gasiorowski farewell and he drove off.

I joined Gasiorowski for the ride back, quickly discovering that his show of optimism hardly reflected his mood. As we raced along to the rented small castle that he and Bagsik used as their home and conference center while in Warsaw, he talked almost compulsively. "We will have problems. If you think that I'm a happy person and full of satisfaction that I succeeded in something like someone in the West, you are wrong," he told me.

What problems? He talked about former communists and other members of the banking establishment who were jealous of their success. He mentioned constant monitoring by banking and internal-security services, which fit in with what I had been told by government officials, and a credit squeeze caused by the refusal of Polish banks to lend them new money. "They're trying to get us, and they don't even know what for. I'll tell all in a book, even if I have to go to prison for it. Those guys piss me off."

He was angry enough to complain that he had given "a lot" to Walesa's presidential campaign and to Solidarity foundations, in a bid to cultivate friends in high places. Art B had also provided three South Korean Korando four-wheel-drive vehicles to the financially strapped Warsaw police free of charge on a trial basis, assuring them of a good deal should they choose to purchase them. But such efforts had not prevented the scrutiny of their activities from growing rather than diminishing.

I prodded him about those activites; after all, what I had seen and heard had far from satisfied me that I knew the full story of what accounted for the huge sums they were throwing around. He hinted at more elaborate deals, talking about making profits of 1,600 percent on some operations, using only six people and two cars. How? Gasiorowski hesitated, then mentioned the possibility of moving money around banks but didn't spell out the specifics. I still felt unenlightened, unsure whether this was some kind of preposterous boast intended as a smokescreen, or a serious clue to how they had parlayed the profits from a successful but small start-up business into a megabusiness. Since I did not understand what exactly he was driving at, I also did not know whether he was talking about something illegal.

Six weeks later, on the morning of August 6, 1991, special antiterrorism forces decked out in bulletproof vests and ostentatiously holding their hands on their holstered pistols raided Art B's headquarters in Warsaw. Ordering all the people present to put their hands in the air, they searched them. For five hours, security officers went through their records. A similar raid was carried out on Bagsik and Gasiorowski's rented castle; when the security forces arrived, the officers ordered the staff inside to open the gate within three seconds. Since the electronic gate takes fifteen seconds to open, a police car crashed through it.

The show of force was deliberate, guaranteeing that the crackdown on Art B would dominate the news. Claiming that Art B's dealings were draining the treasury, the authorities froze the company's accounts. They also arrested six bankers, including Polish National Bank Vice-President Wojciech Prokop, for allegedly issuing unsecured loan guarantees to Art B. The bank's president, Grzegorz Wojtowicz, was suspended the same day, after Walesa demanded his dismissal; he was arrested in September for failing to prevent what was quickly billed as the scandal of the year. Later, both Wojtowicz and Prokop were released, but the investigation continued.

It was only in the aftermath of those spectacular events that the rest of the Art B story came together. Gasiorowski had not been trying to throw me off course with his talk of fast footwork with the banks. Taking advantage of the weaknesses of the banking system, he and Bagsik had indeed accelerated their profit-making to dizzying speeds. According to investigators, they would write checks from an account in one bank for deposit in another; since the banks were not equipped to make electronic transfers, they could take advantage of the long "float" to earn interest in both accounts. Honing this technique to a science, they moved checks or cash—sometimes by car, sometimes by helicopter—through a whole chain of accounts in different banks. As a senior government official put it: "They speeded up the circulation of money, and the system did not keep up with them."

Investigators later claimed that many of these transactions were based on bad checks to begin with. Art B obtained guaranteed checks from banks which amounted to a form of short-term credit extended to good clients. They would pay the checks into another bank, which would issue them a certified check based on their "deposit." Art B would then "repay" the loan from the first bank, and so the cycle continued. The implication of the arrests of the bankers was that they had consciously participated in this shell game. A private bank involved in those transactions went bankrupt in March 1992, becoming the first Polish bank to collapse since the introduction of economic reforms.

Bagsik and Gasiorowski had conveniently slipped out of the country a few days before the raid; later, they claimed they were tipped off by a top government official. They turned up in Israel, from where they denied any wrongdoing. They argued that their banking transactions were perfectly legal and routinely performed by others, if not on so grand a scale. They also claimed that the government had chosen them as scapegoats for political reasons, seeking to counter mounting popular concern about corruption by launching a phony cleanup campaign.

That the government took from August until November 1991 to file charges against them suggested that it had considerable difficulty making its case. They were accused of seizing $382 million from the state treasury through their banking operations; if convicted, they could face up to twenty-five years in jail. Many Polish businessmen were outraged;

they claimed that the loopholes in the system were to blame, not those who had taken advantage of them.

Since Israel and Poland have no extradition treaty, Bagsik and Gasiorowski did not appear in any immediate danger. They had gone there in the first place because Bagsik had been prepared for any eventuality. Claiming that his natural parents were Jewish and that he had been adopted by Polish Baptists of German background, he had managed to hold three passports: Polish, German, and Israeli. Gasiorowski had told me he was a Pentecostalist, but he suddenly claimed Jewish lineage when the scandal broke. Living in the beach town of Herzilya Pituach, north of Tel Aviv, Bagsik continued to indulge his familiar habits, such as the black-and-white color schemes he favored. In his house, he had two grand pianos, one black and one white; he also owned one black and one white Mercedes.

The extent of the legality or illegality of Art B's operations may never be resolved to anyone's satisfaction, but there was no doubt that the scandal dealt a serious blow to public confidence in the new system. At the very least, ethical considerations had hardly been present in Bagsik's and Gasiorowski's calculations.

"With each success, we make more enemies," Gasiorowski had told me during our car ride in June. But their worst enemy was their own ambition.

Art B's meteoric rise and fall demonstrated the perils of the transition period from communism to capitalism. To those who were predisposed to write off most of the new business class, bankers, and other officials as crooks operating in a corrupt society, the Art B affair only confirmed their suspicions. An opinion poll conducted in the summer of 1991 asked the question "Who do you think is the most susceptible to corruption in Poland?" Twenty-two percent of the respondents said "old officials," 11 percent said "new officials," and 53 percent said "everybody." Shortly after the raids on Art B's offices, the leftist weekly *Polityka* published an article entitlted "The Stench of Capitalism." Pointing out that the evidence still did not clarify whether any crime had been committed, it summed up the popular mood about the affair. "You might say something stinks, only no one knows what it is," wrote its author, Jerzy Baczynski. "Could this perhaps be the smell of capitalism?"

Baczynski's suggestions, which raised numerous questions about the scandals that accompanied the new era, were eminently reasonable, focusing on the creation of a code of ethics for state officials and regulations governing the switch from public- to private-sector jobs. In the fledgling new era, the huge stakes involved multiplied the opportunities for bribery and other shady practices. Pointing out that "low-paid civil servants made decisions that can be worth millions to the people concerned" on the sale of property, the awarding of licenses, taxation, and other matters, he argued that the transition to a market economy must have clear-cut regulations and enforceable standards.

But the Art B scandal generated relatively little in the way of such sensible measures. Instead, its main effect was to make Polish officials more hesitant about proceeding with privatization and other measures designed to accelerate the transition to capitalism. Increasingly worried about the backlash to more scandals, the politicians dithered. This raised the question whether a postcommunist society was more threatened by a swift and poorly controlled process or by a slower one, where there was more attempt at regulation, but where the momentum and support for change could be lost as the difficulties mounted. Privatization would prove to be the key test for those alternative strategies, demonstrating that there can be many different roads to capitalism but none is risk-free.

The temperature had dropped and a light snow sprinkled from the gray sky, but that did not prevent Prague's future shareholders from waiting patiently outside in a three-hour line to beat the fast-approaching February 29, 1992, deadline for registering their voucher books for a $35 fee. "I'm doing this for my family, for the younger members," said Jaroslav Jasek, a retired technician. "It's a good investment in the future," added Pavel Chalupa, a young actor. And kindergarten teacher Jana Dlouha radiated wonder and optimism. "I find that it's incredible that they suddenly decided to give people such a chance," she said from the back of the line. "You cannot lose on this."

The object of such unbridled admiration was Czechoslovakia's daring "coupon privatization," which entitled each adult, for that $35 fee, to register a voucher book that would allow him to acquire shares in state companies. To its proponents, led by finance Minister Vaclav Klaus, the scheme was a master stroke which would force the speedy transfer of state property into private hands, catapulting the country ahead of Hungary and Poland, the earlier pacesetters of reform, who were struggling with much slower privatization programs. As officials throughout the region were fond of pointing out, they were forced by circumstances to opt for more radical strategies than anything attempted in the West. Even Margaret Thatcher's much-heralded program privatized on average only about two companies a year during the 1980s; at that pace, privatization in Eastern Europe would literally take centuries. "Perhaps a fast privatization is better than no privatization at all," argued Karel Subert, an official at Czechoslovakia's Investment Bank.

But to its critics, the hastily devised and almost completely unregulated giveaway was a populist vote-getting measure that would trigger major financial scandals and crises that the country could hardly afford. "No one is against privatization," Jan Vanous, a Czech émigré who is president of PlanEcon, a Washington-based investment advisory-and-research group specializing in Eastern Europe, told me as the voucher registration deadline neared. "But some of us are saying that we don't want to see Czechoslovakia butchered by this process." No other privatization program touched off so much controversy.

The irony was that, until the scheme was officially launched, Czechoslovakia had been generally perceived as the laggard in the economic-reform process. This enraged Finance Minister Klaus, who all along had claimed that he was methodically implementing the most ambitious program. But the voucher program took off with a force that startled even its architects, shifting the type of criticism leveled against Klaus, and multiplying warnings about the dangers of going too fast instead of too slow. After a distinctly unenthusiastic response when the voucher books were first made available in November 1991, the registration rate soared off the charts. Of 11.3 million eligible citizens, 8.6 million signed on by the February 29, 1992, deadline. In its most optimistic scenarios, the government had hoped to lure four million people to participate. When I visited Czech Privatization Minister Tomas Jezek near the end of the registration period, he seemed somewhat overwhelmed by those results. "I'm a bit nervous with all these people behind me," he admitted.

The real catalysts of the stampede were more than four hundred investment funds that sprang up to take advantage of the privatization program. Leading the pack was Harvard Capital & Consulting, which had no connection to Harvard University other than the fact that its twenty-eight-year-old president, Viktor Kozeny, took an undergraduate economics degree there and had clearly decided that an "American" image would help his company take off. And take off it did. In an aggressive advertising campaign costing over $1 million, Harvard guaranteed a tenfold return on the $35 registration fee within a year to those willing to assign their voucher books to the fund. Fielding twenty-five thousand agents who worked on a commission basis, the fund accumulated over eight hundred thousand voucher books.

With names like "Quick Profit Fund," "Wealth Fund," and "Golden Gate Fund" (whose motto, printed in English on a mock $1,000 bill, was "In Gold We Trust"), others scrambled to follow suit, providing still higher "guarantees." Even funds organized by the state-owned Investment Bank made similiar pledges, offering $35 loans to those who signed up with them so that their customers did not have to put any money down. With such promises of huge profits, vouchermania took over. In the want ads, people offered to sell their registered voucher books for over $1,000 each; one couple sought to trade their two books for a Skoda Favorit, the popular Czechoslovak car.

Since twelve hundred state companies with a book value of more than $9 billion were due to be privatized in the giveaway scheme, fund managers claimed that they would be able to make good on their commitments. Government officials pointed out that, in a straight mathematical calculation, dividing the total book value by the number of participants in the voucher scheme, each voucher book's worth would come to about $1,000; that figure was lower than their original predictions based on the assumption that fewer people would participate, but it still was incredibly high. The question was: what did book value represent? In a country where realistic accounting was only starting to be introduced and the health of many companies was highly questionable, book value was a dubious measure.

That did not appear to give much pause to either the government or the investment funds. At his bustling offices on the outskirts of Prague, Harvard's Kozeny was exultant about his prospects. "We stand to manage roughly $1.5 billion in assets," he boasted. After studying at Harvard and then briefly working at an investment firm in London, Kozeny had returned to Czechoslovakia in 1990 to cash in on the new opportunities there. He claimed that the small consulting business he had founded proved to be profitable enough to provide the start-up funds for the expensive launching of his investment fund, whose results astounded even him. A big grin spread over his boyish face. "I expected to be a capitalist, but I didn't expect to manage those kinds of assets."

Wasn't he worried that he was getting in over his head? "The size of the investments you are managing has no impact on the quality of your portfolio," he responded. Then he launched into a discourse on his investment strategy, claiming that his company would be an "active investor," bringing in Western managers to improve the performance of companies where it gained a controlling interest.

But even proponents of the privatization plan acknowledged the possibility of things going wrong, especially if the new shareholders became nervous and sought to pull out their returns all at once. In such a situation, the funds could face runs they would not be able to handle. When I had spoken with Privatization Minister Jezek, he had argued that the government would have to impose new rules if that happened. For instance, he explained, the new rules might allow people to sell only a small portion of their shares, or they might suspend sales altogether for up to a year. "We can react and regulate the process," he said.

When I recounted that discussion to Kozeny, he suddenly sounded less sanguine about the entire process. The approach Jezek was proposing, he said, would undercut all confidence in the system and produce "a meltdown." He maintained a 90 percent capital-gains tax would be a better alternative, compelling people to stay in the market. But that suggested that Harvard and the other funds were more worried than they admitted about fulfilling their guarantees. "If everyone would like to sell, you would have a collapse of prices," Kozeny acknowledged. "We are quite eager to discharge our obligations before the market starts to collapse." He hastily corrected himself: " 'Collapse' is kind of a dirty word. Before the market will be under pressure."

The uncertainty was compounded by rumors that dirty money was behind some of the funds. "These rumors are 99 percent not true," Cenek Petak, the chairman of the Association of Investment Funds, assured me. But the market was started without rules—almost nothing on disclosure, conflict of interest, or insider trading to counter the impression that anything goes. Until publicity forced some resignations, scores of government officials were involved in funds, and some persisted in refusing to resign, particularly in Slovakia. Bank funds also continued to boast to potential customers that they had inside information on companies.

Part of the problem was that Finance Minister Klaus and his supporters appeared to have a vision of capitalism that was more closely in tune with Adam Smith than with modern securities markets. Although they finally began drafting new regulations to prevent abuses, they felt more comfortable with Smith's notion of an invisible hand providing the regulation than the strictly controlled process that exists in the West. Daniel Arbess, representing the New York law firm White & Case in Prague, explained: "It's a free market in the Hobbesian sense. There is a tendency to equate a free market with a free-for-all. People in this government are inherently reluctant to regulate: they tend to equate regulation with planning. So what happens is that they don't regulate until a crisis looms."

Arbess put the chances of a large-scale catastrophe at 20 percent. "That's still not bad, considering the scale of the effort here," he said.

The critics were hardly mollified by such reasoning. PlanEcon's Vanous charged that, by conservative estimates, 10 percent of the funds were linked to criminal elements. "In order to set up a restaurant or become a barber, you need to show that you don't have a criminal record,"

he pointed out. "To set up a fund, you don't have to show anything."
The danger in such a permissive approach to the funds, he warned, was
that they would be in a position to do incredible damage. "If I were a
company seeking restructuring, I wouldn't want to be in the hands of a
fund with no experience and in the midst of a liquidity crisis," he said.

But the plan's proponents claimed that the prospect of speedy privatization was already attracting considerable attention among foreign investors, which could lessen the prospects of a cash crunch; Arbess called
the surge in interest "a tidal wave." Along with coupon privatization,
Czechoslovakia was busily selling major stakes in companies directly to
foreign investors, particularly to German firms. In addition, once Czechs
and Slovaks traded their voucher books for actual shares, foreigners
would be free to buy them.

Up to that point, Hungary had led the way in attracting foreign investors, and its initial privatization plan consisted almost exclusively of
straight sales of state firms, usually with foreigners among the buyers.
Foreign investors were seen as providing modern management and marketing, along with an infusion of new capital and technology. "By doing a distributive privatization, you don't get any of these things," said
George Hollo, a Hungarian-born Canadian adviser to the State Privatization Agency. "There's not much point in ownership transformation
unless you get a foreign investor."

But such a program was inevitably slower and more ensnared in bureaucratic wrangling. And it also risked creating a backlash. To avert
criticism at home, the government announced in the spring of 1992
that it would offer preferential treatment to domestic over foreign investors in cases where the bids were similar. Later that year, it began
drawing up plans to give citizens "credit cards" to purchase state assets,
effectively providing them with loans to make it easier for them to participate in privatization. While emphasizing that this was not a giveaway
scheme, officials explained that they hoped it would accelerate the
process.

Poland experimented with various approaches to privatization. Its la-
borious efforts to privatize in the traditional fashion, by public share offers, produced meager results. After two years of that program, the
Warsaw stock exchange listed only a dozen privatized companies. The
government proceeded at a faster pace with "liquidation" deals, whereby
management or investors lease or buy factories and equipment; during
the same period of 1990 and 1991, 950 small and medium-sized factories went that route. It also moved ahead with plans to offer shares in
hundreds of larger state companies, at a nominal charge to the popula-

tion, as part of its own giveaway program. Unlike their counterparts in Czechoslovakia, however, Polish officials emphasized that they were seeking to lay the groundwork carefully for a capital market, inviting Westerners to manage a small number of investment funds. More conscious, from bitter experience, of the danger of financial scandals, they vowed to resist pressure to accelerate their slower timetable to match Czechoslovakia, which they predicted would eventually regret its haste.

The verdict on the alternative approaches will only come once the track records of all three countries over the next few years can be examined. There was no doubt that Czechoslovakia was taking the biggest gamble. But officials contended that delaying privatization was even riskier, allowing popular support for reform to wane and state industries to continue in their old ways. In Poland, some of the delays were caused not just by understandably cautious preparation but also by successive politicial shake-ups, which produced precisely that kind of loss of momentum. And even in Hungary, officials admitted that privatization in the entire region amounted to a race against bankruptcy, which meant that prudent deliberation had to have its limits.

During my time with Czech Privatization Minister Jezek, he freely admitted that his team had made mistakes. "It could have been done better if we had had enough experience," he said, adding with a laugh: "The next time will be better." The joke was that the state can only divest itself of its holdings once—and then it has to live with the consequences. It was easy to second-guess many of the decisions, but those who made them deserved at least some applause for summoning the courage to plunge ahead. No other area of economic policy represented such a leap into the unknown.

Driving from Prague to Bratislava in the winter of 1991, I passed the first billboards I had seen on that main artery. "I AM A BILLBOARD. I SELL YOUR PRODUCTS," they proclaimed, listing a Vienna phone number. An Austrian firm had decided to introduce a new sales technique to Czechoslovakia's market, but first it felt compelled to offer lesson one of Western Economics 101. In the aftermath of the political changes that had swept across Eastern Europe in 1989, Western businessmen, consultants, advisers, and representatives of myriad government and private organizations traveled to the region to participate in the floating seminar about the known areas of capitalist economics, everything from simple billboards to complex securities laws.

The need was certainly there. Sitting in on a marketing class in the newly established International School of Banking and Finance in Katowice, Poland, in early 1991, I watched French instructor Michel Mallet devote an entire lesson to the need to woo customers by providing the best service. But when he asked the Polish bankers whether they could change their traditional scornful view of customers, an older banker replied: "Right now there is no need to, since the competition for customers hasn't really begun." The younger bankers in the room groaned. After the class, Mallet told me: "Before we can talk about marketing, we have to explain basic concepts and change their mentality."

Such examples of outright resistance to change were relatively rare and generally confined to the older generation. The prevailing sentiment was a desire to learn new methods. According to Janos Szaz, the director of education at Budapest's International Training Center for Bankers, which was the first school of its type in the region: "Some students have problems, but they feel they have to learn and they have to change their attitudes." The French staffers at the Katowice school also credited the Poles with a high willingness to learn, despite the occasional recalcitrance of the older bankers. Eric Thomas, who coordinated the teaching program of the instructors sent from France, pointed out that part of the problem was caused by the lack of previous formal training. "In practice, many small businessmen use methods that they don't know how to identify," he said. "They are like Molière's character who doesn't know he speaks in prose."

Westerners could also provide solid practical advice based on their far more extensive experience of dealing in a competitive market. In Blazowa, a small village in southeastern Poland, I watched two American agricultural experts try to suggest sales strategy to the owner of a store selling pesticides to farmers. The Americans were Gregory Vaut, the Warsaw-based executive director of the Foundation for the Development of Polish Agriculture (FDPA), which was backed by American private foundations, and Homer Porter, a retired executive of Land O'Lakes with extensive experience in marketing farm supplies in the Midwest, who was a visiting volunteer. The FDPA was involved in setting up a network of private pesticide distributors to replace the crumbling state monopoly.

Halina Bator, the store owner, was pleased with her first sales efforts. She was deliberately selling a modest selection of pesticides, herbicides, and insecticides at a low mark-up to bring in the local farmers, who had been making their purchases at a larger town nearby where the prices were higher. "We are not seeking high profits," she explained. "If we attract the customers, we'll be in good shape next year."

Porter asked what she would do if her competitor lowered his prices.

"We'll lower our price," she replied, adding that she had already sold some products at a semiwholesale price to keep one customer.

"Offering a full range of products is a good way of competing," Vaut pointed out. "It's better than lowering prices, which anyone can do."

Afterward, both of the Americans had the same worry. "We've put people in business, but they have a long way to go in learning how to maintain profitability and to maintain their business," Vaut told me. "Everyone knows how to cut prices." Porter added: "It's the best way I know how to go bankrupt."

Arguably, many new entrepreneurs would have to learn such lessons for themselves, often the hard way, and they would not necessarily take the tips of outsiders all that seriously. But Vaut and Porter had at least suggested an alternative approach, leaving the seed of an idea behind. That was a significant addition to the practical support FDPA provided by acting as a national distributor which channeled supplies to such local distributors. Successful Western programs often planted ideas that would be perfectly obvious to experienced small businessmen in the West but not necessarily to novices like Bator.

The programs that worked also had to allow for a large amount of improvisation, since Western and Polish expectations did not always mesh. When the Peace Corps responded to the political changes in Eastern Europe by dispatching volunteers there, its initial experience proved mixed. The English teachers in the group generally adapted easily; their task was clear-cut, and the need for their services was enormous. But the more ambitious "small-enterprise development" program in Poland, which dispatched volunteers with business or local-government backgrounds around the country, got off to a shaky start. The volunteers received relatively little language training, forcing them to rely mainly on translators, and some found themselves in small towns with little idea of what to do with them. The resulting sense of frustration on both the Polish and American sides finally led to a shake-up of the local Peace Corps staff.

Thaddeus Kontek, the new man in charge of the business program, promptly began reassigning some volunteers to new sites and sought more actively to match local needs with the skills of incoming volunteers. "Our business volunteers are not content to sit and have a Peace Corps experience," he explained. "There's less of the folksy 'We're here to have a cultural experience' and more of a serious transfer of skills."

But even with the best preparation, the business volunteers, who were generally older and more seasoned than their counterparts in more traditional Peace Corps programs, often discovered that the skill they needed the most was the ability to improvise. Wall Street trader John Wienke's most significant contribution to the town of Jaroslaw (population forty-five thousand) proved to be a spur-of-the-moment idea. "I arrived and asked for a business directory to see where I could get my laundry done," he recalled. "They all looked at me as if I was crazy." With local encouragement and American financing, Wienke produced a directory with a hundred paid ads in the first edition.

Ann Newman, who ran a car rental agency in Texas, discovered that she could not carry out her mission of helping to privatize the state sanitariums in Rymanow because the appropriate legislation had not been passed. Instead, she began lobbying Jewish organizations in New York and Israel to pay for the restoration of the town's synagogue, once considered among the most beautiful in Europe, as a means of promoting tourism. James Cason, a water-treatment specialist from Florida, found that he was not only offering advice on sewage systems and waste disposal but also providing local officials with tips on how to deal with the sudden influx of Western companies seeking to peddle their wares. "With bad times in the West, environmental firms are coming in here and offering what look like high-tech solutions," he said. "I've advised them to stick with more conventional treatment facilities." His message was that the most expensive offerings were not always what Polish towns need.

Local government officials were far from alone in needing advice about how to deal with Westerners, or a bit of honest explanation about the workings of the Western world. A European Community official who served as an adviser to the Polish government was taken aback by how literally some senior officials appeared to accept Western assurances that they were promoting free trade; they only slowly began to wake up to the fact that free trade in the West is anything but fully free. Even when Western imports began flooding the Polish market, Finance Minister Leszek Balcerowicz, the architect of Polish reforms and a firm believer in Western economic theory, long resisted appeals to raise tariffs to protect Polish producers who were rapidly going out of business. When I talked to him as he was about to step down from his post in November 1991, he appeared genuinely disappointed by the "petty reaction" of Western Europe, which had been resisting opening up its markets further to Polish products. He had taken Western free trade rhetoric too much at face value.

There were other sources of disappointment as well. Some Poles began to feel resentful about how much purported Western assistance was funneled to consultants who quickly were dubbed "the Marriott brigade," because they stayed at the posh new Marriott in Warsaw, running up hefty bills for their expenses and day rates. Some provided needed services or technical skills, but others left behind nothing more than a feasibility study or two of dubious value. At least a portion of the blame had to be shared by the Polish authorities, whose inability to sort out their own priorities made it easier for high-priced consulting firms to take advantage of the situation.

Some consultants had little knowledge of local conditions, resulting in less-than-impressive performance of specific tasks. Anna Halustyik, a Hungarian lawyer who received her legal training at the University of Illinois, represents foreign firms in negotiating joint-venture deals with Hungary's State Privatization Agency. She found that Western lawyers and accountants advising the agency were often doing a poor job. They sometimes did not know the most basic local regulations, and they failed to point out obvious drawbacks in the proposals of the foreign company, particularly environmental risks. "When I represent the foreign investor, I see this," she said. She paused briefly before adding, with disarming honesty: "But I won't point it out, because I'm representing the investor."

One dramatic measure of the extent of the problems with Western assistance programs was just how slow the delivery was on many of them. From the time of Poland's political turnaround, the country was offered $7.6 billion in credits by international institutions and foreign governments. As of the beginning of 1992, the Poles had drawn on only 7 percent of those credits. A large part of the problem was that the Poles were poorly prepared to take advantage of the available credits; they often did not know how to prepare proposals that could win approval. Some senior officials also clung to the old habit of never accepting responsibility for a project that might go wrong; they would rather sit on a proposal than sign off on it. In some cases, the Western offers of credits were too restrictive, aimed only at projects that met very narrow specifications.

Both the Poles and the West frequently had reasons to feel frustrated with one another. The government of Prime Minister Jan Olszewski, which took office in December 1991, began to criticize openly Western consultants and the role they had played in the country's economic development. Addressing the Council of Europe in Strasbourg in February 1992, President Walesa castigated Western Europeans for their reluctance to invest more in the East and to open their markets to Eastern European products. Warning that "the fruits of victory have turned sour" and that "democracy is losing its supporters," he asserted: "The West was supposed to help us in getting organized on new principles.

Polish shops have been inundated with waves of your products. It is you who made good business on the Polish revolution."

Westerners involved in serious projects resented the new tone, which lumped them together with the fast-buck artists. "This is not a good time to be a foreign banker, adviser, or consultant," complained a British banker setting up a new investment bank in Warsaw that employed almost an entirely Polish staff. "We're building an institution this country needs. I don't get it." In fact, Polish officials tended to be much less critical in direct discussions with Westerners, where they freely acknowledged their need for the services the West had to offer. Their harsher public rhetoric was often designed to deflect public attention from the shortcomings of their own policies.

But such public rhetoric carried its price. By playing up the negative side of Western involvement in Eastern Europe, the Poles undercut their appeals for more Western investment. Western businessmen initially looked at Poland as a riskier bet than Hungary or even Czechoslovakia. By issuing sweeping warnings, as he did at the Council of Europe, about the perils of the reform process, Walesa left the impression that Poland was shakier than it really was. After his speech, I asked Walesa whether he really believed there was much disillusionment with capitalism in Poland. "It is not disillusionment with capitalism," he replied. "But the Poles want to build their own capitalism rather than spend all their money on the products of foreign capitalism." He was fully justified in calling for more open Western markets and more investment in production facilities inside Poland, but the cumulative effect of such pronouncements was to weaken rather than strengthen the appeal of Poland for Western businessmen during that period. However, many of those businessmen continued to recognize Poland's potential as the largest market in the region. By late 1992, an improved political climate and a number of positive economic trends had begun to undo some of the damage generated by the earlier contradictory signals, generating new interest from previously wary investors.

Perhaps it was inevitable that Poland, which was the first to launch radical economic reforms, was the first to display the most serious doubts about their effects, producing both a sense of disenchantment and drift. But the discontent was not limited to Poland. Though Hungarians may have been lucky to undergo more incremental reforms, the disadvantage was that they did not experience the sense of a clear turning point, which could provide at least a brief moment of inspiration; as a result, they were perpetually short of enthusiasm. Czechoslovakia, which only launched its reforms in early 1991, quickly experienced the kind of pain that Poland was already familiar with. Industrial production dropped 23.1 percent in 1991, and unemployment jumped to 6.6 percent, a figure that masked the far higher rate in Slovakia. Since Czechs and Slovaks had lived better than the Poles under communism, they were less prepared for such jolts.

Public-opinion polls amply documented the pessimistic mood everywhere. According to a poll conducted by the United States Information Agency, 68 percent of Hungarians and 57 percent of Poles declared in early 1992 that "life-in-general" was worse than under communism; in November 1991, 83 percent of the Czechoslovaks polled said that the impact of the changes since 1989 on their standard of living was "bad."

But, at the very least, those figures seemed curious. They did not jibe with the visible transformation of the economic landscape, despite the all-too-apparent difficulties. They did not seem to take into account the rapid growth of small private businesses, as people who had somehow accumulated decent savings or made money as roving traders and guest workers abroad invested their modest private capital into shops and services. They did not fit into an impression that I frequently had when talking to people throughout the region that, though they viewed the overall economic climate as bad, they saw numerous possibilities for themselves.

Some sociologists and pollsters confirmed my impression that there was a discrepancy between the general pessimism and the broader sense of individual potential. In many cases, the same person who described economic conditions as terrible would offer a far different answer about his individual situation, saying that he was coping somehow and, often, even better than before. In a survey of Poles conducted by the CBOS polling organization in the fall of 1992, 59 percent of the respondents described their own material situation as good or average, but only 21 percent were of the opinion that others lived in decent conditions. It was almost as if a secret social compact existed whereby everyone wrung his hands in public and avoided admitting that some things were going right. Even when Poland became the first country in the region to demonstrate signs of an economic turnaround, with industrial output growing by 2 percent in 1992 after three years of sharp decline, the public mood remained decidedly downbeat.

Agnieszka Wroblewska, a commentator for the Polish daily *Zycie Warszawy*, noted in a column on April 4, 1992: "I often hear that nervous people should not be provoked further. When you tell them that things are hopeless, they sleep peacefully and digest well. But when you express doubt that the world is falling apart, you irritate your fellow man, which is a sin. One of the economists in the government warned a couple of months ago against publicizing that consumption in 1991 rose by 8 percent. 'It's true,' he admitted, 'but we should not speak aloud of this, because this irritates people.' "

Along with genuine economic hardship, the positive indicators were indisputable. If privatization of large state industries was often agonizingly slow, Poland demonstrated that it is easier to create conditions that allow entrepreneurs to quickly develop new private businesses from scratch. At the end of 1991, the second year of the economic reforms, the retail trade was almost entirely in private hands, accounting for 80 percent of sales on the domestic market. The private-sector share of total sales was 24 percent, and its share of foreign trade was growing rapidly. Fifty-five percent of the construction industry and 24 percent of transport services were in private hands.

Although the recession put the squeeze on private as well as state firms, people with initiative continued to launch new shops, services, and companies. While some were still hunting for short-term profits and not shrinking from highly dubious means to achieve them, many of the new entrepreneurs were plowing back whatever they made into their businesses and thinking about their long-term prospects, indicating the development of a healthier capitalist mentality. By the end of 1992, 56 percent of the overall labor force worked in the private sector, generating almost half of the country's GDP. Admittedly, this included the country's large private farming sector, but the shift toward private enterprise in almost all fields was unmistakable.

Despite those encouraging developments, the obstacles to overcoming the communist legacy remained tremendous. Even in the former East Germany, the process of overcoming the economic gap was proving far more difficult than anyone had imagined. Despite the massive investments by the German government and private companies, the German Institute for Economic Research estimated in 1992 that it would take another twenty years for living standards in the Eastern part of the country to reach the level of its Western part. The Eastern Europeans, who could only dream about such huge investments, had plenty of reasons to be discouraged by such an example next door.

But a comparison of the early experiences of East Germany and Eastern Europe revealed essential differences in their situations, which at least in part compensated for the financial disparities. One key area was psychological adjustment to change, underscoring the importance of that factor in the economic-transformation process.

On the eve of German unification, most East Germans were convinced that they would make the transition from communism to capitalism more smoothly than their Eastern European neighbors. After all, they had usually lived better than their counterparts in Poland, Czechoslovakia, and Hungary under communism, and the West Germans appeared ready to provide them with means to integrate their economy into the powerful capitalist machine. But the reality of collapsing industries which could not compete and mushrooming unemployment quickly triggered widespread disillusionment that sapped morale more than was the case among its Eastern neighbors. The strikes, demoralization, and passivity of the East Germans left little doubt that they found it harder to adapt psychologically to capitalism.

This was partly because, under communism, the East Germans had believed more in the myths of their propaganda. Though aware that their living standards lagged far behind the West, the East Germans took solace in the notion that their leaders had made communism work more efficiently than anywhere else. Their reasoning was further twisted by their sense of nationalist superiority. The East Germans were encouraged to dismiss the disarray of the *polnische Wirtschaft*, the Polish economy, as the product of the Polish character rather than communism. Their communism was German communism, inevitably more efficient. It rarely occurred to them that much of their relative well-being was the product of hidden subsidies from West Germany in the form of "transit fees," ransoms paid for political prisoners and other funds extorted by the Honecker regime from Bonn.

East Germany's absorption into the paternal embrace of the West allowed many East Germans to continue deceiving themselves that their problems were not their own responsibility—but the responsibility of higher authorities. By contrast, Eastern Europeans were quicker to dismiss such escapism. "We Czechs, Hungarians, or Poles are disappointed because we have made mistakes and wrong choices, but it is we Czechs, Hungarians, or Poles who made those choices," Czech historian Jan Havranek pointed out. "The East Germans feel that *they*—the West Germans—decide." And given the prosperity of West Germany, East Germans did not understand why they should have to suffer economic setbacks on the way to a new system, something that seemed perfectly evident to Eastern Europeans, who had few illusions about the economic mess produced by the old system. If the East Germans felt entitled to a bare minimum under communism, they subsequently felt entitled to a much higher minimum under prosperous capitalism.

That two generations of West Germans had worked hard to achieve that prosperity was only dimly perceived, if at all. The notion of individual work and individual reward never had a chance in the old East Germany. The long history of Polish and Hungarian economic reforms may have produced dismal economic results, but it allowed for the emergence of a small private sector that nurtured the entrepreneurial spirit in a largely hostile environment. Though citing the East German difficulties as a warning for his countrymen not to let their aspirations run too far ahead of their possibilities, Poland's second postcommunist prime minister, Jan Krzysztof Bielecki, was convinced that the early reforms and resistance to communism prepared Poles psychologically for the transition to capitalism better than the East Germans were prepared. "The Poles are entrepreneurs," he declared. "I believe that."

In the waning days of the communist era, when a political breakthrough still seemed out of reach, many Poles were losing hope that their entrepreneurial spirit would ever be allowed to flourish. During my visits to Poland in 1988 and 1989, I found young people, including the most talented university students, despondent about their prospects; many talked of nothing but emigration, or at least of finding ways to live and work abroad for a prolonged period, since they could not envisage how they would support themselves or a family in a collapsing system.

They also knew enough about the world around them to be haunted by the contrasts with their own situation. In a long conversation, Hanna Jagiello, a medical student in Gdansk, came across as a somber young woman with a realistic view of life, with no inclinations toward self-pity, ready to take the daily hardships in stride. But she confessed that, when she heard about Western Europe's growing unity and prosperity, "I just want to cry." Nothing was more discouraging than the notion that Poland and "Europe," the continent of political freedom and economic well-being, were drifting further apart.

One of the greatest achievements of the initial economic reforms in Poland was to convince gifted and talented young people that their country was starting on the journey back to Europe, no matter how long it might take to make headway in narrowing the gap that separated them from the rest of the continent. This led to a major shift in outlook that I first discovered while chatting with a group of third-year law students over beers in a greasy pub in the western Polish city of Wroclaw. It was December 1990, the end of the first year of economic changes, and the students were debating the merits of pursuing legal careers or going into business—but, in either case, in Poland. They no longer felt that they had to go abroad to be successful, and they exuded a confidence and pride in their country that had been sorely missing before.

"I could have stayed in England for a couple of years as a painter or a bricklayer," explained Wojciech Slonczewski, who had spent the previous summer working as a house painter there to pay for his travels. "But I wanted to do something for my country." His friend Radoslaw Rejmoniak added: "I really believe in our society. If you look at the countries of the old socialist bloc, we're the most dynamic."

To be sure, many Poles, especially those who felt stuck in dead-end jobs in collapsing sectors of the economy, hardly shared such optimism. And even the gifted and talented throughout the region grew discouraged by the setbacks that slowed the transformation process, and by the distance their countries had to travel to begin to aspire to a quality of life comparable to that of Western Europe. But Europe no longer seemed to be drifting further away. It was not simply that full membership in the European Community was taken increasingly as an inevitable if still-long-term goal; the Poles, Czechs, and Hungarians felt instinctively that they were regaining their status as Europeans. For all the hardships, failures, and scandals, they sensed that history was now on their side and that, one way or another, they would navigate the passage to a capitalist system. They were still making costly mistakes that often overshadowed their initial accomplishments, but their voyage had definitely begun.

POISONED AIR, POISONED BODIES

ASLEEP WITH HER blond hair spilling through the protective metal bars of her hospital bed, Dorota appeared at peace with the world. She clutched the remnant of a plastic toy dog like any two-year-old, and her pretty face bore a serene expression. But to look at her more closely meant spotting the telling evidence that the world had not been at peace with her. A tube emerged from her throat, the result of surgery that had been performed two months earlier. During the previous year, Dorota has been dispatched to the Children's Hospital in the Silesian city of Chorzow, in southern Poland, eight times because of severe respiratory problems. On her last visit, her larynx was so narrowed that the only way to save her was to perform a tracheotomy, the insertion of a tube directly into the throat to allow her to get air into her lungs. Dr. Henryk Kawalski, the head of the laryngology ward, had no doubt that the operation prevented her from choking to death. He also had no doubt why such an operation was needed by a two-year-old. "This is a result of the catastrophic ecological situation," he said flatly.

Of all the legacies of communism in Eastern Europe, the ecological disaster and its effects on the region's inhabitants, particularly its children, may prove to be the most difficult to overcome. Dorota is only one of many young casualties of the "black triangle"—the region of southern Poland, northern Czechoslovakia, and the southern part of what used to be East Germany, one of the most befouled regions in the world. The results are heightened rates of infant mortality, premature births, congenital defects, and mental retardation. But everything I had heard about the problems still did not prepare me for my visit to the Children's Hospital in Chorzow in March 1991. There the generalizations about pollution and its effects took on a very specific meaning, and the abstract statistics were represented by very real faces like Dorota's.

The hospital is a compound of two-story buildings painted a dark, sickly yellow color. Dr. Jan Gruszczynski, the hospital director, told me that the buildings had been recently renovated, but it was hardly surprising that this was difficult to surmise. Official statistics indicate that thirty-five hundred tons of dust descend on each square kilometer of Chorzow every year. The hospital, whose mission is to rescue the young victims of this onslaught, must receive at least that much: it is located only a few hundred yards from the Kosciuszko steel mill, a sprawling monstrosity jutting out huge smokestacks which spew out dust and gases over the "recovering" children. Gruszczynski pointed out that at the end of every day he has to wipe a film of dust from the windshield of his Polish Fiat, which he parks near his office. He did not have to spell out the implications for his patients.

The director took me to see Dr. Joanna Kasznia-Kocot, the in-house specialist on ecological issues, who combines her medical duties at the hospital with extracurricular membership in a local ecology club. A young mother with two small children of her own, she explained that the poisoning of children's bodies begins long before birth. "The toxins create a completely different placenta," she said. Zinc, lead, cadmium, and other dangerous substances present in the wombs of pregnant women become part of the placenta, leaving less oxygen for the fetus. Miscarriages are commonplace.

In Chorzow, she continued, the infant-mortality rate is twenty-two per thousand live births, as compared with the Polish average of about seventeen, the U.S. rate of ten, and Sweden's rate of six. Her other statistics were equally chilling: whereas the national average for premature births was just under 9 percent, Chorzow's was 14 percent, and in the worst districts of the city the numbers were between 16 and 20 percent. As she pointed out, this translated into more underweight infants, more prone to serious medical problems. A distressingly large number of the expectant mothers, who usually continued working during pregnancy out of economic necessity, made things harder for their children by smoking heavily; 58 percent of the mothers of premature babies were smokers. After childbirth, the parents' destructive smoking habits further endangered their children. "We had a case where a two-year-old fainted while the parents were playing bridge," Kasznia-Kocot recalled. "The child had been poisoned by passive smoking."

The incidence of bronchitis, pneumonia, and other respiratory illnesses was much higher than elsewhere, along with anemia, rickets, and infectious diseases. Mental retardation was on the rise, and teachers were convinced that the increasingly aggressive behavior of some of their pupils was linked to lead poisoning. Kasznia-Kocot showed me a medical study from Zabrze, which, like Chorzow, is one of Silesia's most polluted cities. The study found that 47 percent of four-year-olds, 61 percent of six-year-olds, and 71 percent of ten-year-olds suffered from illnesses or developmental disturbances.

The Children's Hopsital and others like it were poorly equipped to deal with the young environmental casualties. When we left Kasznia-Kocot's office, Gruszczynski took me around the wards, pointing out the deficiencies. His facility was short of intravenous equipment, disposable needles, and oxygen tents; on one ward, a battered oxygen tent was heavily taped up to keep it functional. The hospital had only one respirator and no humidifiers; nurses hung wet towels over the beds of infants. But the worst problem was the hospital's location under the shadow of the steel mill. "The dirt is terrifying. This is our tragedy," nurse Maria Schelenz told me. "I envy people who live elsewhere."

The staff could easily be demoralized for other reasons as well. The basic pay for nurses was less than $100 a month. Doctors who served as department heads and had over twenty years of experience made less than $200; some of them took extra shifts riding in ambulances as emergency pediatricians to earn extra money. "We are still fighting to make the average pay in the health services reach the average wage in the country," Gruszczynski said.

I asked him if that meant that the staff accepted bribes, as had been commonplace in the communist era. "Of course," he replied. "Can you be surprised? It's nothing surprising." In what kinds of situations were bribes paid? "For example, when someone wants to get his child admitted sooner, or to get a doctor to make a house call out of order."

But the dedication of many of the doctors was also evident. After our rounds, I again met with Kasznia-Kocot, who began telling me about one of her more mundane but excruciatingly maddening frustrations. She and her husband, who is a surgeon, had been trying to get a phone for their apartment for eight years. Every six months, they had reapplied, Gruszczynski had signed their request to give it added weight, and still nothing happened. She recalled that a Swedish sociologist had recently visited her and gone away convinced that she could not get a phone because the authorities were punishing her for her ecological activism. "How can you explain the phone situation here to a rational person from the outside?" she asked with a laugh.

When I asked how she felt about watching her own children, who were six or seven at the time, grow up in such an environment, she answered evenly that they looked healthy, they were good-sized, and she and her husband made a point of getting them away from Silesia's environment at regular intervals. "I have not tested them for lead levels, because I don't want to stress myself," she confessed. Then, after a brief pause, she added: "When I am driving on the road where you look straight down at the chimneys of the steel mill, I ask myself why am I doing this when I could live elsewhere." She left the question hanging, but there was no doubt in my mind that the answer was that she was passionate about her concerns, which encompassed both her medical duties and the battle to clean up Silesia's environment.

The environmental and health crises are inextricably intertwined in Eastern Europe. Ecological devastation is only one of many reasons for the alarming health trends, but to most Eastern Europeans, the confluence of negative factors in both fields is no coincidence. If their environment has been ravaged, and demographic statistics indicate that the inhabitants of the region are living shorter lives than their Western counterparts and even, in many cases, than their fellow countrymen born only a few years earlier, the culprit was clearly the communist system.

"The answer seems to be in the politics," Hungarian Health Minister Laszlo Surjan told me, pointing to the changing patterns of life expectancy in Europe. A couple of decades ago, he noted, noncommunist countries like Ireland and Finland were near the bottom on life expectancy, along with some but not all of the communist countries; Hungary, for instance, was not in that lowest category. By the end of the 1980s, Eastern Europe and the Soviet Union were alone at the bottom of the charts. "That is proof that these bad figures belong to the system," he concluded.

In a June 3, 1992, piece in *The New York Times* timed to coincide with the United Nations Conference on Environment and Development in Rio de Janeiro, Vaclav Havel wrote:

> The then ruling regime took the per capita output of cement and steel as evidence of its own indispensability, as a symptom of prosperity and social development. . . .

Natural resources were squandered; investments in efficient, modern technology were lacking, and free discussions on the consequences of such conduct was not allowed. *Aprè nous le déluge* was the underlying principle.

But that is still not the main problem. These are but consequences of something that goes deeper than that—man's attitude toward the world, toward nature, toward other humans, toward being itself.

These are the consequences of Marxist ideology—the consequences of the arrogance of modern man, who believes he understands everything and knows everything, who names himself master of nature and the world (who is the only one who understands them)—for whose sake this planet is in existence. . . .

Nothing but the arrogance of an alleged master of the world and superior proprietor of reason could have produced the erroneous concept that life, the economy—the whole world—can be managed from one single center by one single planner.

The physical evidence fully supported such sweeping conclusions, particularly in areas like the black triangle. Katowice Province, named after the Silesian capital of the Polish sector of that triangle, accounts for just 2 percent of Poland's territory and is home to 11 percent (four million) of the country's population, but it produces between 30 and 40 percent of the country's air pollution. Nearly all of Poland's coal, zinc, lead, and silver are mined there. The province is crammed with ancient steel mills like the one near the Chorzow Children's Hospital, plus coking plants and chemical enterprises. Coal-burning furnaces and old power plants add to the thick, acrid haze that normally hangs over the region. Children play amid the slag heaps and belching chimneys, their faces—like miners'—often coated with grime. The soil is so laced with hazardous substances that growing garden vegetables is considered an act of recklessness.

Across the border, in the Czech and the former East German sectors of the black triangle, the situation was disturbingly similar. Czechoslovakia's communist authorities classified much of the information about the ecological damage as top secret. "According to the official ideology, it held true for a long time that nothing like a polluted environment can exist under socialism," noted a 1990 report of the Czech Ministry of the Environment. But they implicitly acknowledged the scope of the danger by taking such measures as temporarily relocating entire schools from northern Bohemia twice a year to cleaner regions, to try to limit the damage to children's lungs.

The contrast with Western Europe was enormous. According to the Center for Hazardous Materials Research at the University of Pittsburgh, the per capita sulfur dioxide emissions in 1988 amounted to 317 kilograms in East Germany, 179 kilograms in Czechoslovakia, 115 kilograms in Hungary, and 114 kilograms in Poland. The equivalent figure for West Germany was twenty-one kilograms, for France twenty-two.

Much of the pollution was a result of energy-intensive industries with obsolete equipment which squandered natural resources at an incredible rate. The energy efficiency of the Eastern European countries was between about half and a third that of its Western counterparts. A comparison of resource consumption per unit of GNP in 1983 spelled out the specifics: whereas the energy per dollar of GNP, or "megajoules," was 8.6 for France and Sweden, 11.8 for West Germany, and 19.3 for the United States, it was 26.9 for Poland and 30.1 for Czechoslovakia. According to a 1992 study of Czechoslovakia's Federal Committee for the Environment, 32 percent of the country's primary sources of energy in the mid-1980s were lost in the course of transformation, treatment, and distribution before they reached their users.

Water supplies have also suffered steady deterioration. A 1992 report by the Hungarian government noted that pollution had increased or stagnated in thirteen of fourteen water-sampling points during the previous ten years. The Polish environment ministry reported in 1992 that 33 percent of water is discharged completely untreated, 35 percent undergoes inadequate mechanical treatment, and only 32 percent is treated properly.

By any measure, whether poisoned rivers or dead forests, the price for such environmental devastation was incredibly high. And the implications for the inhabitants of the region sometimes sounded like a scenario from a doomsday script. Josef Vavrousek, the chairman of the Federal Committee for the Environment in Czechoslovakia, warned in 1991 that the vast presence of cancer-producing chemicals in the environment might make it necessary to test the milk of mothers before they began breastfeeding. On the most congested streets of Budapest, the lead content found in two- and three-year-olds was barely considered safe for a 155-pound industrial worker.

It was as if an invading army had worked furiously to wreak the greatest ecological damage possible in the shortest time possible. In some cases, it had. When the inhabitants of the southern Hungarian village of Sarmellek began hauling up a black, viscous substance from their water wells in 1991, they were convinced that they had struck oil. The substance burned easily, but it turned out that this was no natural resource that could make them rich but nine hundred tons of jet fuel dumped at an abandoned Soviet air base nearby. In theory, that much fuel could have allowed a fully loaded Boeing 747 to circle the globe; instead, it had soaked the soil and seeped into the water table. At another former Soviet air base—at Tokol, near Budapest—the Hungarian authorities discovered that the water of a small lake was covered with a three-foot-thick layer of jet fuel.

Even after the downfall of communism and the withdrawal of Soviet troops, the old system and a ghostly army was capable of mounting surprise attacks. The Eastern Europeans kept making new, dismaying discoveries about the extent of the price they had paid and were continuing to pay for four decades of communism. The traces of the Soviet Army were merely a small, highly symbolic manifestation of a much bigger problem, whose genuine dimensions were only slowly becoming apparent.

Back in 1980, Christoper Davis and Murray Feshbach wrote a report for the U.S. Census Bureau whose conclusions were nothing short of astounding: the Soviet Union had become the first industrialized country in the world to experience a jump in its infant-mortality rates and a decline in life expectancy. This reversal in what had seemed to be historically irreversible trends, not just in the Soviet Union but in every industrial nation, could not be dismissed as a minor statistical deviation. Their evidence pointed to a 36 percent rise in infant mortality between 1971 and 1976, and a drop in life expectancy for Soviet men from sixty-six to sixty-three years, while the figure for Soviet women had leveled off at seventy-four years.

Those were the days of the late Brezhnev era, and Soviet officials were not about to concede the accuracy of the Davis-Feshbach report and its conclusions about a health crisis of monumental proportions. Instead, they maintained that any apparent rise in the infant-mortality figures was purely the result of improved statistical data from the Central Asian republics. Some Western analysts endorsed that view, dismissing the notion of a major reversal in these key health indicators as a preposterous misinterpretation of the evidence.

But the problem was that neither Soviet officials nor their Western defenders could adequately explain why, if there was nothing to hide, Moscow had failed to publish life-expectancy figures since 1972 and infant-mortality rates since 1974. Those glaring omissions had prompted Davis and Feshbach to make their own calculations based on other data, which, significantly enough, indicated that infant mortality was on the rise in many parts of the Soviet Union, not merely in Central Asia.

Finally, with the progressive revelations of glasnost in the late 1980s, Soviet officials conceded that Davis and Feshback were right in suspecting the worse. In an interview that appeared in *Pravda* on September 16, 1988, Mikhail Korolev of Goskomstat, the government statistics bureau, admitted that the Brezhnev team, when confronted with the unfavorable figures of the 1979 census, had acted to suppress them. Since falsification of such data would be tricky and susceptible to exposure, they decided to delete them altogether from the published census, locking them up in a safe whose combination was known to "only a very small circle of people."

If some Western analysts had been reluctant to accept the evidence up till that point, many Eastern Europeans had been quicker to recognize similar patterns in their own countries. "The health situation is deteriorating all over Eastern Europe," Hungarian sociologist Julia Szalai, the author of a book called *Diseases of the Health Services,* told me in 1988. Eastern Europe's indicators were generally less dramatic than the Soviet Union's, and they remained well above Third World levels, but many of the trends mirrored the ones farther east, as did the catalogue of causes. These included the environment, heavy drinking and smoking, abysmal diets, high levels of stress, the medical system's increasingly poor services, and the tendency of women to resort to multiple abortions rather than use birth-control devices, which were often in short supply. The cumulative impact underscored the correlation between the political system and public health, since no industrialized countries outside of the Soviet bloc had experienced such reversals in key measuring sticks such as life expectancy.

According to Nick Eberstadt's research conducted at the Harvard Center for Population Studies, the gap between average life expectancy in Western and Eastern Europe had narrowed to 2.5 years in the 1960s but widened in the 1980s to nearly five years. The figures for men were particularly disturbing. Life expectancy for Polish men peaked in 1974 at sixty-eight years, and by 1989 it had dropped to sixty-six years. Hungary ranked at the bottom of the list for male life expectancy, which stood at sixty-five years in 1970 and, after some slight fluctuations, remained at the precise same figure in 1990. Czechoslovakia's figures for men stood at 67.7 years in 1989, but that was still significantly behind the Western European average of about seventy-two years. In most cases, women's life expectancy generally did not decrease, but women have also rarely registered any gains in recent years. With the life expectancy of Polish, Hungarian, Czech, and Slovak women about seventy-four or seventy-five years, they lagged behind their Western counterparts by about three years.

Whereas fatal heart-attack and stroke rates were declining in the West in the past two decades, they rose in several Eastern European countries. Hungary's mortality rate soared to one of the highest in the world, rising from 9.6 deaths per thousand inhabitants in 1961 to 14.1 in 1991. The growth in the elderly population was a key factor, but the rate of heart attacks among middle-aged men contributed to the startling difference between Hungary and Western European countries, which also have large graying populations. Combined with the country's low birthrate, this meant that Hungary's population decreased from 10.7 million in 1982 to 10.3 million in 1991.

Some of those grim statistics can be blamed on self-destructive habits. Eastern Europeans are among the world's heaviest drinkers and smokers, and their diet is loaded with fats. But even if those tendencies predate communist times, they were strengthened during the four decades of communist rule. Vodka and cigarettes were cheap for much of that period, easily affordable in large quantities to ordinary workers. Many governments appeared, at least subconsciously, to operate on the assumption that a worker who started drinking vodka at ten in the morning was preferable to a sober worker inclined to express his anger at social and economic conditions. Alcohol and tobacco consumption kept rising in Eastern Europe, contrary to the trends elsewhere. Between the periods 1974–76 and 1984–86, according to the Food and Agricultural Organization, total tobacco consumption rose by 1.2 percent in Eastern Europe while dropping by 0.7 percent in Western Europe and 1.1 percent in North America. Hungarian consumption of pure alcohol increased from about nine liters per person in 1970 to nearly eleven liters in 1986, while the European average dropped from eight liters to less than seven liters in the same period.

As for diet, the bad habits of Eastern Europeans were encouraged by a system in which the average citizen had little choice of which foods to buy. Postcommunist governments published information about the state of livestock and the condition of food that confirmed widespread suspicions about its quality. In 1990, the Czech Ministry of the Environment reported that only 10 percent of domestic animals were kept "under appropriate conditions" and about 60 percent "live miserably, in totally unsuitable conditions." During the first three quarters of 1989, 70.8 percent of calves had to be slaughtered because of health reasons, usually diseases caused by bad breeding conditions. Nearly 75 percent of pig and 80 percent of cattle kidneys, the report added, contained mercury at concentrations exceeding permissible limits.

In some cases, the normal hardships of life under communism combined with new aspirations to produce extremely high stress levels, which doctors believed were major contributors to the sharp rises in cardiovascular problems among middle-aged men. In the 1960s and 1970s, Hungary's Health Minister Surjan pointed out, his country had become relatively open, and many people had had the chance to visit the West, where they acquired the taste for a different life-style. "Despite all the difficulties, they wanted a life that is relatively similar," he said. "The way to do that was to work more." They took second and even third jobs in the black or gray market, working overtime and forgetting about vacations or leisure with their families, he continued, and gradually they achieved "success."

"They changed the bike to a motorbike, the motorbike to a Trabant, the Trabant to a Skoda," Surjan said, referring to the East German- and Czechoslovak-produced automobiles. "But this was not coming from your normal work but from overwork or something related to the black market. The previous system was definitely unable to give possibilities to workers and others to earn more money working on your [regular] job."

The health-care system was ill-prepared to cope with the crisis, and its inadequacy exacerbated the negative trends. While the United States spent about 11 percent of GNP on health care, the equivalent figure for Poland, Czechoslovakia, and Hungary was no more than 4 percent. Western European countries spent something in between the American high figure and the Eastern European low one, but the disparity was of course far greater than the percentage gap, because the GNP of any Western country was so much higher to begin with.

Raw statistics could not begin to convey the suffering and deprivation they represented. Though Eastern Europe had its share of showcase hospitals with the latest in Western technology and well-trained doctors performing transplant and other sophisticated operations, many health facilities were overcrowded, dirty, and lacking everything from disposable hypodermic needles and sanitary napkins to nurses and orderlies. In some Polish hospitals in the 1980s, patients were not admitted unless they brought their own cots, and occasionally routine operations—like tonsillectomies for children—were performed without anesthesia when supplies were short.

The scarcity of resources led inevitably to inequity and corruption. "You do not find any other sphere of social life where inequalities are as great as in health care," maintained Hungarian sociologist Szalai in 1988.

As in the Soviet Union, the political and military elites were treated at special hospitals and clinics, insulating them from the crisis in medical care. Others struggled to pull strings or spend enough money to obtain decent treatment. Bribes were commonplace, offered to doctors and nurses to perform an operation well, and to overworked orderlies to change the sheets or empty bedpans. Those health officials who were candid enough to acknowledge such practices admitted they were powerless to stop them. Malpractice suits might be out of control in the United States, but they were unknown in Eastern Europe. Average patients, too old or too poor to assure themselves special favors, were frequently short-changed in their treatment, or even contemptuously upbraided by doctors or nurses if they were deemed too demanding.

The old system not only destroyed the environment but encouraged a widespread contempt for human life, sometimes even among those whose profession called for its protection. The contempt was not directed merely at others but also inward. If Eastern Europeans seemed less concerned about maintaining healthy habits, if they shrugged off warnings about the dangers of drinking, smoking, and lack of exercise more easily than their Western counterparts, if they seemed to take ecological devastation more fatalistically, this was a natural result of the sense of powerlessness the communist system encouraged at every turn. The question was whether the abolition of that political system, produced by an incredible display of the power of the powerless, would begin to change such attitudes toward the destruction of nature and man.

With a population of ten thousand, Bialobrzegi looks like many small towns in central Poland. Several small stores, restaurants, and beer pubs line the main street, which is on the road from Warsaw to Krakow, thus guaranteeing a steady flow of customers. Besides the through traffic, farmers from the surrounding area drive into town to pick up supplies, sometimes in their own cars, sometimes on traditional horse-drawn carts. When I visited a swampy area on the outskirts of the town on a spring day in 1992, the sights and smells were also typical. Raw sewage flowed sluggishly through a foul-smelling canal into the Pilica River, which connects with the larger Vistula, which eventually dumps its burden into the imperiled Baltic Sea.

But nearby there was something new: a private Polish environmental company was putting the finishing touches on a modern sewage treatment plant, the pride of the town's authorities. After they were voted into office in the first free local elections, in 1990, the officials promptly resolved to commission the plant, which had been long promised—but never delivered—by their communist predecessors. Their motivation was based as much on economic as ecological considerations. "We as a town are looking for investors," Mayor Janusz Malik, a former Solidarity activist, told me. "This town will be more attractive for investors now that we have this facility."

The massive damage to Eastern Europe's environment cannot be quickly or cheaply undone. In May 1992, when approving a loan of $246 million to help Czechoslovakia start modernizing its power plants to reduce emissions, the World Bank estimated that more than $50 billion would be needed to bring pollution down to acceptable levels in Czechoslovakia alone. Nonetheless, the sewage-treatment plant in Bialobrzegi was only one of a growing number of small but significant indicators that the region was beginning to experience an environmental awakening.

Stimulated by imaginative government policies and increasingly competitive business practices, a new consciousness was gradually taking hold. "Up till now, we talked about economic growth," Polish environment minister Stefan Kozlowski told me around the time I visited Bialobrzegi. "We have changed this to sustainable development." Despite the still-meager resources that were available to environmental protection as measured against the dimensions of the problem, such pronouncements constituted more than just a perfunctory nod to currently fashionable rhetoric.

Environmental consciousness did not catch on overnight. During the Communist era, Solidarity and Charter 77 activists produced reports on the ecological and health crisis in Poland and Czechoslovakia, and later many of those activists went on to take government posts, in which they lobbied to promote pro-environmental policies. In Hungary, fervent opposition to a grandiose joint project with Czechoslovakia to build a major dam on the Danube, along the Hungarian-Slovak border, helped spur the growth of dissent in the 1980s. In 1989, Hungary suspended work on the dam project, which environmentalists charged would pollute drinking water supplies and inflict serious damage on the ecology of the Danube basin, and in May 1992 it unilaterally abrogated the 1977 treaty with Czechoslovakia that had initiated the project. Nonetheless, by October the Slovaks had completed construction of a 25-kilometer channel and redirected the Danube's flow toward the controversial Gabcikovo Dam, which immediately was put into operation despite more protests. To the Hungarians, the Danube diversion was a monument to communist folly; to the Slovaks, however, the giant construction project had become a point of national pride.

With communism gone, the ecologically minded activists still had to work hard to keep environmental issues reasonably high on an agenda crammed with seemingly more immediate political and economic concerns, and to prevent backsliding on early commitments to make life hard for polluters. They could hardly propose to spend vast sums that were simply unavailable. But they managed to convince governments that some changes could be produced at relatively low cost or on a self-financing basis.

Hungary introduced strict annual testing of automobiles to determine that they meet emission standards, and in 1992 it imposed a gasoline tax of 2.5 cents a gallon to provide a fund for combating air pollution. The first use of the fund was to be the renovation of the run-down fleet of public buses, with the goal of cutting emissions of the ones used on the most heavily congested urban routes. Unleaded gas was increasingly widely available and cheaper than leaded, and the government slashed import duties and road taxes for cars equipped with catalytic converters. Commercial companies were prohibited from buying belching, two-cylinder vehicles, and no one was allowed to import cars over seven years old.

In Budapest and other cities, East German Trabants, tiny cars that spew tremendous exhaust, were rapidly being replaced by West German and Japanese models. Explaining the children's games she played with her friends, twelve-year-old Anna Haraszti, the daughter of former dissident Miklos Haraszti, told me in 1992: "We used to count the number of Western cars on the street. Now we count the number of Trabants." But the Trabant problem did not disappear so easily. With German junkyards demanding stiff payments to dispose of the problematic vehicles, many East Germans drove their Trabants across the Polish border, abandoned them there, and returned by foot to Germany.

In tackling the larger problem of industrial pollution, Hungary, Czechoslovakia, and Poland were spurred by their desire to meet European Community standards, bolstering their drive for membership. In some cases, earlier communist governments had set fairly reasonable preliminary standards—but largely ignored them. Hungarian environmental officials estimated that almost 80 percent of their country's air pollution was the result of exemptions granted to existing regulations, and they vowed to begin serious enforcement efforts.

In Czechoslovakia, the communists had distributed environmental responsibilities among about sixteen ministries. "Everyone was responsible and no one was responsible," noted Josef Vavrousek, who became chairman of the Federal Committee for the Environment, which, along with separate Czech and Slovak environmental ministries, was launched in 1990. The new environmental bodies pushed through clean-air legislation. In order not to trigger massive unemployment, older plants were given five years to reach the newly established standards, but new factories were required to meet them from the start. As Vavrousek put it: "We want to be tough enough to clean up the air but not so tough as to destroy the economy."

Aside from stepping up efforts to convert heating in private dwellings from coal to natural gas, Poland put eighty of its worst-polluting factories on notice that they were subject to closure if they did not clean up their act, and about twenty hopeless cases in hard-hit Silesia were immediately shut down. The country also aggressively upped the fines imposed on polluters. In the communist period, fines were largely symbolic: they were low to begin with, and they were paid by state firms to the same state budget that subsidized their existence. But that cozy relationship disappeared along with the communist system.

Danuta Plinta, an official at the ecology division of the Katowice government explained: "With this level of fines, enterprises begin to calculate that it will be cheaper to modernize the technology than to keep paying." Officials in major enterprises agreed with that assessment. "The steep increase in fines really made itself felt in the last couple of years," said Jerzy Dobrzanski, an environmental specialist at a giant copper mill in Glogow which has invested heavily in a major cleanup effort. "All modernization investments are now tied to environmental activities."

The emphasis on ecological concerns was dramatically demonstrated in June 1992, when, two days after the official inauguration of a long-awaited $200 million new airport in Warsaw, environmental officials threatened to close it down indefinitely. The facility had still not met the requirements for adequate sewage treatment and monitoring of noise levels. After a brief delay, the airport was allowed to start functioning, but only on strict conditions that required a stepped-up schedule for installing the antipollution devices.

The fines and resource fees imposed by Polish authorities were plowed into national and regional environmental funds, which are not subject to national budget restrictions. The funds were used to establish an ecological bank, which offers low-interest loans to environmental projects. At the local level, new tax laws meant that small towns and cities began to have revenues of their own instead of waiting for allocations from Warsaw. By taking out commercial loans against future tax revenues and drawing upon the environmental funds, Bialobrzegi was able to invest over $500,000 in its water-treatment plant.

All that was good news for a growing number of small private environmental companies, which eagerly bid for contracts. "Until 1990, no one was taking care of the small towns, since most resources were allocated to big investments," said Janusz Kaczmarek, the project manager for Rollstick, the company that built the Bialobrzegi plant. After reeling off a string of other sewage-treatment projects for municipalities or private businesses his small firm was already constructing or was bidding on, he added: "Environmental protection is the field of the future." An enterprising private garbage company in Warsaw distributed brightly colored recycling bins around the city in 1992, making money on the contents they regularly collected. In some cases, new private businesses like food-processing plants were immediately installing equipment to meet ecological standards that they anticipated for the future but that were not yet mandated by law.

Despite a prolonged recession, Poland's share of environmental expenditures, which never had exceeded 0.8 percent of GNP before, jumped to 1.2 percent in 1991. Polish officials estimated that a massive cleanup effort could theoretically require 4 to 5 percent of GNP, but this still represented significant progress. Another source of funding was Western aid. The Nordic countries, the European Community, and the United States provided funds for various pollution-control and research projects in the region. Germany, for instance, provided credits that could only be applied to specific projects, such as municipal sewage treatment. By seeking to bring the Eastern part of Germany up to Western European environmental standards by the year 2000 and drawing up plans to phase out the highly polluting brown-coal power plants on which the region depended, the Germans also were contributing to a reduction of cross-border pollution, particularly in the black triangle.

Another source of funding was debt-for-nature swaps. When the United States decided, in 1991, to write off 70 percent of $3.1 billion in Polish debts, Washington designated that 10 percent should be allocated to environmental projects over a period of eighteen years. Polish officials were subsequently urging their other Western creditors to follow suit, arguing that investments in cleaning up Poland's environment would benefit everyone.

This was not mere self-promotion. According to a research study published in April 1992 by the East-West International Institute for Applied Systems in Vienna, Western countries would find that paying the Eastern Europeans to reduce emissions is quite cost-effective. "Sulfur dioxide and other pollutants from these countries [of the East] cause acid rain throughout Europe," the report noted. It argued that the antipollution equipment needed for the outdated Eastern European industries was significantly cheaper than the highly sophisticated technology required by Western European countries to reduce their own pollution further. The simple lesson of recent progress on environmental issues is that initial reductions of high pollution levels are relatively cheap compared with subsequent marginal reductions of already low levels. Since the Eastern Europeans are still at that first phase, they should be able to make significant progress in the years ahead.

When it comes to discussing the environmental crisis in Eastern Europe, Western and Eastern environmentalists sometimes disagree on both the causes and how to solve it. At a UNICEF-sponsored environmental conference in Florence I attended in March 1991, American environmentalist and "futurist" author Hazel Hendersen lectured the Eastern European participants: "The Cold War between capitalism and communism is over. The whole world now realizes we must give a decent burial to both Karl Marx and Adam Smith." Then, declaring that Eastern Europeans should seek to find a "third way" that avoided a repetition of either the communist or the capitalist development pattern, she added: "You cannot run societies based on greed as we have done in the capitalistic countries."

As far as the Eastern European participants were concerned, Hendersen just didn't get it. Her claim that Marx and Smith had failed equally flew in the face of everything they had experienced, and they were no more eager to discover a "third way" to clean up the environment than to embrace "third way" economic policies. Whereas militant environmentalists in the West are often suspicious of market forces, Eastern European environmentalists consider them, on balance, to be their strongest ally, although they acknowledge the need to impose environmental regulations as Western societies have done in recent times. "Market forces encourage the more efficient allocation of resources," a 1992 Hungarian government report on environmental issues declared. "The wasteful management of state-owned funds is being replaced by cost-effective capital allocation."

Sometimes the Eastern European faith in the market and all things Western left others gaping in disbelief. At a conference on a "tobacco-free new Europe" organized in Poland by the World Health Organization in November 1990, the discussion turned to how to respond to Western tobacco companies moving aggressively into Eastern European markets. To the amazement of many participants, Grazyna Rokicka, an executive of the Polish Consumers' Federation, signaled her support for their efforts. "Poland produces the worst cigarettes in Europe," she told them. "If people have to smoke, it's better they smoke Marlboros."

But such views were attacked within Poland itself. "If American cigarettes are so healthy, why are hundreds of thousands of Americans dying of lung cancer?" demanded Dr. Witold Zatonski, a leader of the country's small but increasingly vocal antismoking lobby. "The question is not the quality of the cigarettes but whether you smoke at all." He argued that the onslaught of advertising for Marlboros, Camels, and other Western brands only glamorized a habit that should be combated, and Eastern Europeans needed to become selective in what they learned from the West. The proper lesson was that antismoking educational efforts should be stepped up. "In America in the 1950s, 70 percent of people smoked, because they didn't know better," Zatonski asserted. "The same is still true here. Health is not treated as a value here."

That, too, was changing, however. There were some attempts to restrict smoking: the southern Polish city of Krakow, for instance, banned smoking in a wide variety of public places—health facilities, schools, sports stadiums, and tram and bus stops—starting in the fall of 1992. In February 1993, the lower house of the Polish parliament voted for a sweeping ban on all advertising of tobacco products, but the Senate then dropped its stiffest provisions. A similar ban had been approved by Czechoslovakia's federal parliament just before it dissolved in December 1992, but cigarette companies were quick to challenge its validity after the breakup of the federation.

It was too soon to detect statistical evidence that the inhabitants of the region were altering their personal habits, but, at least among the more upwardly mobile social groups, changing behavior patterns were visible. Helena Klimova, a former Czech dissident who works as a psychotherapist at a clinic in Prague, observed growing interest in healthier foods, along with other new trends. "I think people drink less because they are less frustrated," she told me. "There were many men who had the habit of going to the pub after work and drinking five or six beers, which was not enough to make them drunk but enough to make them unpleasant. They drank because they were terribly bored. Now they are free to do whatever they want and, for a long time, I haven't heard a woman complain that her husband drinks every afternoon. Now they complain that the men work too much, which is another obsession.

"Women ask: What should I do with my husband who is never at home since he works all the time?" Klimova continued. "People are doing all sorts of new jobs, so they work from morning till the evening. Mothers on maternity leave, who are a large part of our clientele, are not satisfied with this. They are lonely."

Such new work habits are likely to produce new tensions, as Hungary's longer experience with a more open system has already demonstrated. But, on balance, the first signs of more goal-oriented behavior, and, in some cases, less smoking and drinking indicated that the reckless contempt for individual health may begin to diminish somewhat. Another crucial ingredient for change, a major overhaul of the health-care system in each country, was slower in getting started. In Poland, already existing private medical facilities gradually expanded, and Czechoslovakia proposed reforms aimed at allowing doctors to start private practices for the first time and to offer patients a greater sense of choice within the state system. But more ambitious proposals to create national health-insurance schemes modeled on Western European health systems were often put on the back burner. Government officials were more preoccupied with keeping the existing system together in a period of chronic budget crises.

Despite the more tangible signs of progress in the environmental field, dangers existed there also. The sheer size of the ecological problems could scare off foreign investment, which is desperately needed to accelerate the process of upgrading existing industrial plants. After initially listing environmental concerns at the top of their priority lists, many Eastern Europeans began to focus on more immediate worries, like rising unemployment. The recession that hit the region in the early postcommunist era contributed to a modest drop in energy use and pollution, but only healthy, growing economies will generate the money necessary to modernize the region's energy-intensive, heavily polluting industries.

But, for the first time, the ecology and health gap between Eastern and Western Europe may begin to narrow, however slowly, as the importance of the link between maintaining an efficient economy and meeting ecological standards continues to sink in. For previous, communist governments, the environment was a nonproductive sector not worthy of serious investment. The new officials in Eastern Europe are taking a different approach. "It's quite possible to combine both our ecological and economic goals," argued Czechoslovakia's Vavrousek.

Local environmental activists acknowledge the progress this represents. "For this whole period of forty years, there was no real environmental policy," Piotr Poborski, a leader of the Polish Ecological Club in Katowice, told me. "Now a policy is beginning to emerge for the first time." And what is striking about the activists is that their goals look eminently realistic, unlike the more doctrinaire, anti–economic-growth approaches of some ecologists in the West. They argue that the challenges are far too daunting to waste time looking for utopian solutions. "We are not hoping to return to preindustrial levels but to reach the technology and emission levels of the Ruhr Valley or Pittsburgh," said Marek Gregorczuk, a Green Party activist in Katowice. "There you don't feel the pollution level the way you do here."

To Westerners, the Ruhr Valley or Pittsburgh may symbolize the reckless destruction of the environment during an earlier era. But they are far less polluted than before, which is what immensely impresses Eastern Europeans. For them, these sites are symbols of hope. One day, they, too, can imagine looking back at their current environmental catastrophe as a nightmare they have largely put behind them.

LIFE WITHOUT CENSORS

IN THE EARLY fall of 1990, I found Hungarian novelist George Konrad and his wife, Judit, in a singularly downbeat mood. They were pleased with the political transformation their country had just undergone, and they certainly did not mourn the abolition of censorship, but they were troubled about the prospects for cultural life in the new postcommunist order that was emerging. As we shared a bottle of red wine in the kitchen after Judit had tucked the children into bed, they explained their pessimism by contrasting the positive trends that had been associated with the oppressive system and the negative trends that were already emerging in the more open society.

"With the end of communism, there is the end of intellectual snobbism," Judit declared. "Before, it was important for people to have good books on their shelves; now what's important is videos and MTV." In the old days, she continued, the news on television and the newspapers was so boring that people preferred to read good poetry or a serious novel; they took pride in discussing such books with their friends and neighbors.

"Good novels would sell sixty to a hundred thousand copies, and books of poetry would be published and sell out editions of thirty thousand copies," George interjected. "This is extraordinary for a small country." Since Hungary's censors were less draconian than those of its neighbors, many serious books were made available at cheap prices from heavily subsidized state publishing houses, even if the works of dissidents like himself were usually banned and circulated only in samizdat. As the bookpublishing world faced increasing commercial pressures, and subsidies dwindled, all books would inevitably become more expensive.

However, George believed that the most significant factor was not price but changing life-styles and competing attractions that would change reading habits. "Now people have less time. They watch television and read the newspapers, which have become more interesting, and they read commercial literature," he said, referring to the sudden flood of Western best-sellers by the likes of Frederick Forsyth, Stephen King, and Danielle Steel offered in translation by new private publishers seeking to make quick profits. "There will be two cultures now—high culture and mass culture. People will be able to choose between Tolstoy and Forsyth, and they'll choose Forsyth."

Maybe I should not have been surprised by that bleak assessment, which the Konrads delivered in a tone more of resignation than of indignation, but I was somewhat taken aback at how quickly the new worries had replaced any brief sense of triumph as the old system had given way to the new. It was only natural, however, that the same people who had been at the heart of the intellectual ferment that had forced the pace of change were quickly identifying the new threats to intellectual life. In many cases, their own livelihoods were at stake, but their concerns were far broader than those represented by self-interest alone. They were raising fundamental questions about the nature of cultural and intellectual life in new conditions.

Many Western writers and Eastern European émigrés had long marveled at the intensity and scope of intellectual life in Eastern Europe under communism, despite the very real hardships and acts of repression. In his novel *The Engineer of Human Souls,* Czech émigré writer Josef Skvorecky's narrator muses about "the light that seems to shine only in dictatorships, for in democracies it is outdone by the glare of glossy magazines." His character observes further: "The real religion of life, the true idolatry of literature, can never flourish in democracies, in those vague, boring kingdoms of the freedom not to read, not to suffer, not to desire, not to know, not to understand."

In his essay "The High Wall," written several years before the communist system collapsed, Polish émigré poet Adam Zagajewski offered this bit of prescient speculation:

What would happen if one day—one beautiful day—Poland regained the freedom of political life? Would this splendid tautness—

which surely characterizes the entire nation or at least its altogether numerous and quite democratic elite—survive? Would the churches be deserted? Would poetry become—as it does in untroubled countries—food for a bored handful of experts, and film one branch of commercialized entertainment? Would what could be saved in the Polish context protect us from the flood, from destruction, and even rise above the danger, like a high and beautiful wall, or would what arose in response to the dangerous challenge of totalitarianism cease to exist on the same day as the challenge?

Those words were written at a time when the author felt compelled to add quickly: "Of course, put this way the question has something decidedly premature and even extravagant about it." But the political fantasy of liberation had become reality in a shorter time than anyone had anticipated, and it soon became possible to examine the impact on culture in the broadest sense, from the world of films and books to the press, television, and general education.

When Soviet troops invaded Czechoslovakia in 1968, Vlastimil Venclik was a student at the film academy in Prague with dreams of joining the ranks of his country's richly talented directors. But in the aftermath of the invasion, he directed a student film called *The Uninvited Guest,* which changed his life. In the film, a stranger walks into a couple's house while they are making love one night. The husband runs to get help from his neighbors but discovers they all have uninvited guests at home also, which means everyone has to learn to live with the new arrivals. Reacting to the thinly veiled metaphor about the Soviet occupation, the authorities promptly confiscated the film, expelled Venclik from the film academy, and barred him from any movie-making work. "This became my fatal film," he recalled when we met in the Slavia Café, a popular artistic hangout in Prague.

Taking a job as a medical orderly, Venclik kept writing scripts and nurturing his dreams until the seemingly impossible happened: the toppling of the communist government. He was able to retrieve a copy of *The Uninvited Guest* from the Ministry of Interior archives, where it had been locked up for two decades, and he briefly enjoyed success. The movie was shown on Czechoslovak television and at the film festival in Karlovy Vary; later, it even won a prize at a festival in Oberhausen, Germany.

"Always before, I felt that if we got rid of communism I would be fulfilled," he said, a rueful note entering his voice. Although he was elected president of Czechoslovakia's film and television union, FITES, he quickly shed those "illusions," he added. Working in television because he could not find anyone to produce his films, he bemoaned the new commercial dictates of his field and the rapidly dwindling subsidies for the film industry. He was lost and embittered.

"We find ourselves in a situation where the film culture is threatened," he said. "In such a small state as Czechoslovakia, films cannot exist without the support of the state. Now, after twenty years, I can go abroad and see what it's like elsewhere. They seem to be societies of comfort and abundance. But citizens of such societies do not need real culture. I don't mean entertainment. I'm afraid that, sooner or later, better living conditions here will also produce less need for real culture. And I'm afraid that the ideological dictatorship will be replaced by the dictatorship of the market."

Venclik's lament may have been particularly anguished and sweepingly damning in its conclusions because he was convinced that he was cheated by both the old and new systems, but he was far from alone in feeling disoriented. During four decades of communist rule in the region, Eastern European film directors had cursed, confronted, and conspired to outmaneuver their censors—often brilliantly. Despite, or precisely because of, the oppressive political climate, artists like Poland's Andrzej Wajda and Krzysztof Zanussi, Czechoslovakia's Milos Forman and Jiri Menzel, and Hungary's Istvan Szabo and Miklos Jancso electrified audiences with their mix of realism, surrealist metaphor, and piercing, sometimes outrageously funny satire. Movies were both a release and an essential part of the political struggle. But once that struggle was over, many of the victors were curiously adrift. They knew neither what kinds of films to make nor how to get them financed.

In many cases, neither had been a problem before. If Czechoslovakia after 1968 still demonstrated the power of the censors, the state authorities proved much less of an obstacle in Poland and Hungary. "In the old days, it was easy," argued Polish film director Jan Kidawa-Blonski, the president of the Association of Polish Filmmakers. "The communists paid and we made films against them that everyone loved, here and in the West." Allowing for more than a bit of hyperbole in his observation, which overlooked how difficult and costly the battles with the censors really were, he had a point. The state wanted to be able to show that it was permitting famous directors to do their work even as it tried to hem them in, while audiences eagerly flocked to their films to hunt for any political allusions that had slipped past the censors.

This applied to all fields of culture, not just movies. "Life was so gray that people sought refuge in cultural life," explained Maciej Karpinski, another Polish director and screenwriter. "People talked about books, analyzed the latest critical article, movie, or play. It was all taken so seriously, and everyone took themselves so seriously."

After the initial euphoria of the political upheavals of 1989 wore off, that seriousness and passion evaporated, and the filmmakers were confronted with a new realization. "When you can talk about anything, what do you talk about?" asked Karpinski. They recognized that a key ingredient to their earlier successes was no longer there. Making the rounds of film directors in the region, I found that they struck a common note, which was best spelled out by Hungary's Zsolt Kezdi-Kovacs. "The real problem is that we were conditioned by a situation where we knew who the enemy was," he said. "I always had an enemy to track, the goal of showing more and more reality to expose the system. Now the enemy is gone, and you lose your sense of purpose. For many of us, it is frightening."

Part of the problem was purely economic: the new governments were no longer willing or able to underwrite fully an industry that was as bloated as other communist-era institutions. "Barrandov wasn't a studio, it was a factory," Vaclav Marhoul, the thirty-one-year-old newly appointed director of Czechoslovakia's largest film unit, told me when I first met him in 1991. "We want to transform it into a studio." Barrandov has a rich history: the studio was originally built in 1931 by Vaclav Havel's father and uncle, and the famous films of Czechoslovakia's new wave of the 1960s—like Forman's *Loves of a Blonde* and Menzel's *Closely Watched Trains*—were shot there. But when the government decided to end direct subsidies to studios on January 1, 1991, and only to contribute to specific film projects, Marhoul began slashing staff. By the summer of 1992, when the studio was transformed into a private company owned by a group of Czech investors headed by Marhoul, he had trimmed the staff from twenty-three hundred full-time employees to six hundred, although some former employees continued to be hired for specific projects.

Older directors like Menzel and Vera Chytilova, who had been part of the 1960s new wave, had protested against the privatization of Barrandov. They had argued that at least 34 percent of the shares should remain in state hands to protect the tradition of Czech films, which they feared would not be the case under purely commercial conditions. But to no avail. In the old days, Barrandov had produced about thirty-five films a year. In 1991, it produced fifteen feature films, of which nine were Czech films and the six others were foreign productions that made use of the studio's facilities. In 1992, the overall number was about the same, but only four Czech films were in the mix. Despite protests that this was far too little for the country's major studio, Marhoul asserted flatly that he did not expect the Czech component to rise. "Four Czech features a year would be good," he told me.

The Polish and Hungarian governments maintained a higher level of subsidies, but they, too, eliminated direct financing of studios. Both state and private studios could compete for partial funding for specific projects, with the state subsidy often as high as about 80 percent of a film budget in Hungary, while in Poland the average was about 50 percent. As a result, state studios there were also trimming staffs, and some were expected to fold long before they could be privatized.

If an Eastern European director managed to produce a film, his troubles were far from over. With the disintegration of state control over distribution and movie theaters, new private distributors were pushing Hollywood's hottest properties, which offered the best chance of drawing big audiences. As in the West, overall movie attendance had plunged, partly because tickets became more expensive during a period of economic hard times, but also because of the proliferation of VCRs. Promotions of American films was no challenge, since they had achieved advance billing in the United States, and hits like *Dances with Wolves, Silence of the Lambs,* and *Basic Instinct* continued to do well. As Barrandov's Marhoul put it, "The American films are king—that's a fact." In Polish cinemas, American films accounted for an estimated 95 percent of the showings.

That was bad news for local films, even when they dealt with subjects that in an earlier period would have guaranteed them instant success. *Magyar Requiem,* a Hungarian film about the 1956 revolution, was seen by a mere ten thousand viewers; any Hungarian film that drew as few as twenty thousand viewers in the postcommunist era was considered a moderate success. Before the political changes, almost any Wajda film was a certain hit. But *Korczak,* his first film of the new era, which told the story of the legendary Jewish doctor who would not abandon his orphans in the Warsaw ghetto, drew only a fraction of his usual mass audience. Directors without Wajda's star quality often could not get anything approaching a decent run for their films. Jan Lomnicki's *Beyond the Forest,* a sensitive exploration of the relations between Polish Catholics and Jews during World War II, was shown in classrooms but only fleetingly in a couple of theaters, with virtually no notice.

In both cases, the Jewish themes had nothing to do with the problem, as the two directors were quick to point out. A Polish film like

Grievance, a lugubrious account of the efforts of the parents of a teenager who was killed during the 1970 unrest in Szczecin to organize a proper burial for him, also played briefly to practically empty houses. "The public has changed," Wajda explained. "There are younger viewers, for whom the problems of the war, the occupation, and even Solidarity are only history." He also warned against portraying the former period as a golden age of film, pointing out that the quantity of films was often more impressive than the quality. "In the communist period, a huge number of films were made for no one, not for the viewers or the critics," he noted. Since the choices for the viewers of films were limited, they often went to see the dismal films along with the good ones.

The adjustment to the new demands of a new period does not come easily. Hungary's Pal Sandor confessed: "I have to rethink a thirty-year career. I know that the reflexes with which I made films are no longer suited to this period." Though no one was arguing that Eastern European films should try to duplicate Hollywood fare, they had to begin taking into account new expectations. "We have to find something more attractive in action and form," said Polish producer Janusz Morgenstern. Then he added: "I'm not getting proposals of that kind." Disorientation and frustration in the film world were the norm in the first couple of years after the political upheavals, with only rare exceptions.

Martin Kratochvil was one of those exceptions. As the head of Bonton, a highly successful entertainment company that produces records and runs a popular private radio station, Kratochvil loves preaching the gospel of free enterprise—and living the life of a rising capitalist star. He claimed to be the first person in Czechoslovakia to own a private plane, a Cessna 172 four-seater. "I learned to fly because I'm fed up with driving cars," he told me with a mischievous grin. "Music and flying keep me alive."

But Kartochvil's greatest flight of fancy was his determination to prove that a Czech film could be profitable, although he had never produced a film before. "I'm a Milton Friedman freak," he proclaimed. "I believe the business has to provide its own resources." He simply refused to buy the argument that economic hard times or the political changes made that impossible. "Once the emotions of the revolution are gone, what will people do?" he asked rhetorically. "They will go to the movies and buy records. Look at Hollywood in the 1930s: it was blossoming."

He tested the movie market by pumping over $500,000 into the production of *The Tank Battalion,* a ribald account of army life in 1953 based on a Skvorecky novel. As the first privately produced film in

Czechoslovakia, it was launched in May 1991 with an imaginative, all-out promotion campaign: Bonton scattered army uniforms, mock soldiers, and tanks around Prague and distributed camouflage-colored condoms. The film, which mixes satire, sex, and a touch of more somber drama reflecting the end of the Stalinist era, went on to become a box-office smash, drawing over three million viewers in Czechoslovakia and receiving modest but respectable distribution abroad. "We really hit it with the common man," Kratochvil declared later. "We can't repeat this easily, but I'm optimistic about Czech films."

There were also other signs that the prospects might not be all that dismal. To keep themselves in business, both state and a growing number of private film companies began luring Western filmmakers, who discovered they could shoot their films in Eastern Europe at bargain prices. Increasingly, Eastern European directors put together coproductions, which provided them not only with financial backing but also with the chance of reaching a broader audience. "We want to make films for viewers in Paris, New York, and Tokyo," Waldemar Dziki, a Polish director who founded a private company called Pleograf, told me. "We cannot make films only for Poland."

In Poland, the new forms of cooperation produced impressive results. During the communist era, the country had churned out about forty films a year, with the number dropping to twenty-four in 1991, as the state became less forthcoming in providing funding. In 1992, the state contributed a bit less money than in 1991, but about thirty-five films were made. With greater input from domestic and foreign backers, the state subsidies were made to go a longer way. The majority of the films were coproductions, which meant that Polish input varied greatly. Zanussi's *The Touch* was typical of the form—it was an English-Danish-Polish coproduction starring Max von Sydow and Sarah Miles. The famed Polish director offered his characterization of his product after an early screening: "This is real Europudding."

Some Polish directors worried about the implications of the trend. Noting that he was writing a script about a German's love affair with a Pole for a German-Polish coproduction, Feliks Falk argued that he was uncomfortable with the conditions imposed by foreign partners. "The French don't want politics, for instance," he told me, adding that they were searching for more universal themes.

I asked him what was wrong with that, since Polish films needed to have a broader appeal. "I'm afraid we'll lose the ability to make Polish films," he replied. "Our strength was in political and historical films. That tradition may disappear."

The concern to maintain a certain national tradition may be perfectly legitimate, but there is the danger of not recognizing that some of what passed for the Polishness of Polish films was tied up with the peculiar conditions of a bygone era. As Polish poet Zagajewski wrote: "If politics is forbidden it is sought everywhere." That was the secret of many artistic-political successes under the old regime. It could not be the source of success in democratic conditions.

Within the film industry, there was growing recognition of that fact, although younger members tended to catch on faster. "For me, political films are boring," said Barrandov's Marhoul in Prague. "The older generation is writing scripts about how bad communism was. We know that. I trust young people to make films about universal themes." When I talked to Marhoul in the summer of 1992, the three Czech films in the making in his studio were all by young directors; they included a comedy, a musical, and a horror story.

One of the best new Polish films—and one of the first to have a decent if modest run in the new era—was *Kroll*, which marked the debut of Wladyslaw Pasikowski, a promising young director. The film is set in the communist era, but it is not political. Though the main character is a Polish soldier who deserts his unit to escape the brutality of army life, his real drama revolves around human relationships once he is "free," how he is confronted with the betrayal of his wife and best friend. With an arresting opening scene, a surprising twist at the end, and a brisk pace throughout, the film displayed Pasikowski's considerable talents and proved that some directors were able to respond to new challenges.

As in Western Europe, however, even talented filmmakers needed continuing state support in order to survive. The industry could not be left completely on its own. Aside from providing partial subsidies for specific film projects, the governments in the region slowly began taking other measures to prevent total domination of local screens by Hollywood productions. Poland introduced tax breaks to encourage distributors to show more Polish and European "art" films, and Hungary set up a network of "art cinemas." Filmmakers maintained that more needed to be done, but at least some of them began to revise their earlier gloomy predictions.

The same was true in other fields as well. When I saw Hungarian novelist Konrad in early 1992, he pointed out with satisfaction that the publishing world was continuing to offer more variety than he had expected. While some publishers had collapsed, others had taken their place in an increasingly crowded field; small literary reviews proliferated, along with small publishing houses that published serious books, which had far from completely disappeared in the tide of schlock best-sellers. In some cases, private foundations stepped in to help small publications that could not otherwise survive. "It is not so black as it first seemed," he noted. "If someone is smart and energetic enough, you can do a lot." The first rush to churn out Harlequin romances or pornography was gradually being balanced somewhat by publishers who recognized that readers still wanted books that counted.

At a dinner party in Warsaw a short time later, Polish writer Ryszard Kapuscinski echoed those sentiments. The bookstores were carrying a new collection of Proust, along with new editions of Bruno Schulz, Czeslaw Milosz, and Nietzsche, he noted, adding: "When I go to a bookstore these days, I have trouble with my pocket [covering expenses], because there are so many good books I want to buy."

None of this was to downplay the very real problems the cultural world was facing. Publishers were fighting for survival, as were film studios and theaters. A shaking-out process in all these fields was already taking place, often leaving the old hands stunned and angry. But others recognized that a true "normalization," not the infamous normalization of the post-1968 period in Czechoslovakia, was taking place in the arts, bringing the region closer to a broader European experience. It was easy to mock "Europudding" in films, but its virtue was that it was genuinely European.

In an interview for the August 1991 issue of *Prognosis,* an English-language publication in Prague, émigré novelist Skvorecky sounded considerably different from his narrator in *The Engineer of Human Souls,* who talked about "the light that seems to shine only in dictatorships." The elevated status of literature and the arts under communism was a product of an unhealthy situation in which writers had to make up for the lack of real journalism, he declared. "Under totalitarian rule, papers are extremely boring. . . . Now there is no censorship; you can read about the problems of daily life. Therefore people have stopped buying so many books and going to the theater—they prefer reading papers. I think this is quite normal. Under censorship, books are the only source of some sort of information about life."

He predicted that Czech literature will finally "be normal. As it is in the West. The importance of literature in these countries was very much overblown. Writers had to substitute for many other things. They were public figures, spokesmen for the nation. . . . Now they will have to be just writers, and that's healthy."

That was a conclusion others had reached also, not just in the writing field. "Now art is art. We have to deal with normal human affairs,"

Polish film director Zanussi told me. He was not bemoaning the somewhat reduced role of his profession. "I have made my peace with this. I know things for me will never be as good as they were earlier." He paused a moment and added: "A society which is unjust needs artists more, but that doesn't mean you wish for more injustice. Just as a doctor doesn't wish for more illness."

In the days when the Communist Party still ruled Czechoslovakia, the white phone on the desk of the editor-in-chief of *Mlada Fronta* was known as "the yes line." Linked through a special network to top party and government offices, the phone rang frequently as officials provided "advice" on what to publish; the editor's role was simply to assent. But then the Velvet Revolution toppled the communists, and Libor Sevcik took over as editor-in-chief of the daily, which still formally belonged to the Socialist Federation of Youth. "It was interesting that some people in the new government who learned of this line tried to use it," Sevcik told me, gesturing to the white phone that was still planted on his desk. "After I said 'no' several times, the phone stopped ringing." Since the white phone with its special four-digit number is far more reliable than those hooked into the regular phone network, Sevcik decided to keep it. Only its role is different. "I am the one who calls the others now," he said with quiet satisfaction.

If art was becoming art in the aftermath of the revolutions that swept across Eastern Europe in 1989, journalism was finally free to become journalism. The immediate result of the political upheavals was the liberation of the press and a heady new sense of freedom. Censors disappeared, newspapers and magazines multiplied, and old publications discovered they were capable of recasting themselves in a new, more exciting image. Released from the old controls and not yet constrained by the discipline of the market, journalists felt free to experiment, to provoke, to prod. But it is one thing to oust a communist government and introduce the rudiments of democracy; it is another to build a healthy independent press after four decades of dependence on totalitarian institutions—and to banish the mentality associated with the old era. Though the press was faster to change than most other institutions, editors and reporters quickly recognized that they had embarked on a process that was far from complete. They were learning to be free.

Sometimes painfully. The elimination of government control also meant the end of subsidies. At the same time, a growing number of publications were struggling for survival in an increasingly competitive market. In 1988, when the communist government was still in power,

Hungary had about eighteen hundred publications; in 1991, the number had leapt to thirty-two hundred. The market had spawned everything from porn magazines to specialty publications and a host of new dailies, including racy afternoon tabloids, seeking to elbow their way into an already crowded field. "It's like swimming through seaweed that can pull you down—and you have to make it to open water. We hope not to drown," explained Peter Nemeth, the editor-in-chief of *Magyar Hirlap*, the former Hungarian government daily, which was bought by British media tycoon Robert Maxwell and, after his death, was purchased by a Swiss company. The task was complicated by obstacles in printing and distribution, where old state monopolies were crumbling but a private sector was only beginning to emerge.

The problems were more than just economic. With television still in state hands, the print media offered the best forum for the ideas and debates that were vitally needed to energize the processes of further democratization and economic reforms. But many Eastern Europeans questioned whether the press was up to that task. Most journalists served a political cause under the old system, whether they wrote for the official press or the underground dissident press. After the change in regimes, many still felt they were working for a cause as much as for their individual publications. Balanced reporting was difficult to come by. As Kazimierz Woycicki, the editor of the Polish daily *Zycie Warszawy*, put it: "The danger for a journalist here is the mixing of politics and journalism."

Almost all the choices proved more difficult than the journalists had imagined when they first tasted freedom. What should their relationship be to the new breed of politicians, many of whom were old friends? How should they react when those old friends turned hostile, since some post-communist leaders were deeply suspicious of the free press they helped create? In the search for financial support, is it risky to rely on foreign investors, whose interests may conflict with those of the new editors? Should journalists who made their careers under the old regime be retrained or fired? How do the media achieve the kind of influence that has transformed the Western press into the Fourth Estate?

Take the case of Poland's *Gazeta Wyborcza*. The 1989 round-table negotiations between the communists and Solidarity produced an agreement that the opposition would be allowed to publish this daily newspaper. Adam Michnik became its editor, and he claimed that his years of writing for the underground press were "a good school" for the job. "Because I wrote for the underground press without censorship, I did not have to learn writing from the beginning," he said. When I asked him about his weaknesses, he replied that he was ill-prepared for the business side of his new venture. "After all, the underground press never had to earn its way," he said, referring to the funding it had received from domestic and foreign political supporters. "And now, if you don't make a profit, you fail."

As it turned out, the business side of the operation went very well: starting from scratch, *Gazeta Wyborcza* became the country's largest daily, with a circulation of about five hundred thousand in 1992 and hefty advertising sections. After first setting up a makeshift news operation in a former day-care center, the newspaper moved in the fall of 1991 to spiffy new facilities, with the look and feel of an up-to-date newsroom in the West. Initially, it was the only new daily newspaper in the region to become such a tremendous commercial success.

But critics denounced the paper's lively reporting as too heavily partisan. "They specialized in blurring the line between reporting and opinion," charged Maciej Lukasiewicz, the deputy editor of the government daily *Rzeczpospolita*. That tendency became particularly pronounced during the presidential election campaign of 1990, when Michnik used his paper as the forum for his strident attacks on Walesa and his promotion of Mazowiecki's candidacy. By the time dark-horse candidate Stanislaw Tyminski mounted his surprisingly strong challenge, *Gazeta's* credibility had sunk to the point where its damning articles about the Polish-Canadian businessman, along with those of other dailies and Polish television, were dismissed as mere propaganda—and Tyminski beat out Mazowiecki for second place.

Though he defends his paper's overall record, Michnik conceded that his open partisanship had hurt the paper's reputation. "That's happened for the last time," he told me, when we talked in the aftermath of the campaign. He subsequently chose not to run for re-election for parliament in the 1991 fall elections or to formally join the Democratic Union party of Mazowiecki, although he clearly sympathized with its policies. "I had to decide whether I wanted to be in one of ten political parties or the editor of an independent newspaper," he said later.

Michnik was too much of a political personality, accomplished polemicist, and thinker in his own right ever to be taken for a dispassionate editor, but his newspaper lost some of its overtly partisan edge and rode out the controversy about its role in the presidential campaign. He could claim justifiably: "We are a triple success—as a newspaper, as an institution of civil society, and as a business."

All three functions were linked, but many journalists still measured their success primarily by their ability to influence public opinion or government policy. And in terms of influence, they were often far from sure they were doing so well. In Czechoslovakia, the one clear-cut victory of the press was in defense of its immediate interests: through editorials and direct appeals, it pressured the government to reduce by half a 22 percent special tax on newspapers in 1991. But the press rarely produced such immediate results. After writing extensively about *"nomenklatura* companies," firms in which ex–communist officials appropriated state assets to set themselves up in private business, Polish reporters felt frustrated by the lack of government action. It was almost as if the public had lost its capacity for outrage.

"Now that everyone writes what they want, no one is terribly concerned with the criticism of the press," complained Wanda Falkowska, a seasoned law reporter at *Gazeta Wyborcza.* In the old days, when lies were commonplace, a small dose of truth in any publication tended to have a greater impact.

Credibility and influence had to be accumulated in ways that could run counter to the instincts of the former dissidents. "The underground press does not prepare you for today's journalism," said Konstanty Gebert, a Polish political commentator who wrote for the underground press using the pen name David Warszawski, which he continued to use in the new era. "We were excellent, honest propagandists. We wrote honestly, checking our facts. But we never wrote as critically about our own side as we did about the other side." *Gazeta Wyborcza* survived its setbacks and continued to flourish primarily because its mostly young staff exuded journalistic vitality, but it was also helped by its growing ability to look critically at the entire political scene, not just at those parties and movements for whom its editors had little sympathy.

Other publications rooted in the dissident movement fared much worse. Czechoslovakia's *Lidove Noviny,* a former underground paper transformed into a daily, saw its circulation shrink from 280,000 in the first months after the revolution to about a third of that number in 1992. Part of the problem was that the paper was viewed as too closely aligned with President Havel and other dissidents-turned-politicians. "Bad tongues call us the Castle News," said editor and former dissident Rudolf Zeman. "But we are really independent of any political movement or state institution." A bigger problem may have been one of temperament: since dissent was led in Czechoslovakia primarily by intellectuals, far more so than in Poland, *Lidove Noviny* continued to reflect their elevated style. Despite successive editorial shake-ups, the newspaper failed to reach out to a broader readership.

Critics like Vladimir Matejovsky, a young economics commentator for the popular daily *Mlada Fronta,* argued that much of the staff was incapable of writing in a simpler, more accessible and interesting fashion. "They are too sophisticated," he said. "If you were a dissident for twenty years, it's hard to change your way of thinking and writing." The editors and reporters at Poland's *Gazeta Wyborcza* displayed more of an instinct for journalism as a business. "We didn't only want to write nobly but also to sell our product," noted Michnik. At *Lidove Noviny,* the competitive instinct never seemed as strong, nor was there as much understanding of what the market demanded.

Somewhat surprisingly, those competitive instincts and the understanding of the market proved stronger in some of the old newspapers, which managed to regenerate themselves in the new era. *Mlada Fronta* was a prime example. Editor Libor Sevcik belonged neither to the Communist Party nor to the dissident movement, although, as one of the middle-ranking editors in the old days, he had been subject to the dictates of the censors, like all his colleagues. Nonetheless, he defends the paper's record and argues that many good journalists worked on its staff. "Within the narrow framework of that time, *Mlada Fronta* tried to stretch the limits," he said. "We put together a good staff." Following his election as editor in November 1989, he presided over the removal of about one-fifth of that staff, those who were occupying posts because of their political loyalties to the old regime rather than their journalistic skills.

"After the revolution, we did not have to make huge changes," he continued. "We only had to fire the political leadership and let the skilled people do their work." Organized as a new company in 1990, the editors renamed the paper *Mlada Fronta Dnes* (*Youth Front Today*) to sever its ties with the Socialist Federation of Youth, which had rights to the name *Mlada Fronta.* More important, they convinced their readers that they were serious about reporting in a nonpartisan manner, and they earned a reputation for fairness even when they were critical. "The experience of the United States and Western Europe shows that it does not make sense to be associated with a political party, particularly since there is a rejection of partisanship by the Czech public," said Sevcik.

Although the paper's pro–economic-reform editorial line favored Vaclav Klaus and the right-wing parties in the spring 1992 parliamentary elections, its news reporting continued to reflect an independent standpoint. Unlike all the other major dailies, *Mlada Fronta Dnes* refused to accept paid political advertisements from the competing parties during the election campaign. The editors figured that it was more important to nurture the newspaper's reputation for independence than to collect the extra advertising revenue. They were probably right. Despite strong competition, it maintained its position as the highest-circulation daily.

Partisanship hardly disappeared. When the Polish government set up a commission to auction off publications by the former communist press monopoly, political parties clamored for control of the old publications, whose name recognition made them valuable acquisitions in a crowded market. Charges of favoritism abounded as publications were sold for anything from $10 to $4 million. The commission freely conceded that it chose winning bids not on the basis of price alone but with an eye to other factors as well—the intention was to promote a "pluralistic" press. But if the process left few bidders completely satisfied, and bitter recriminations abounded about the alleged failure to wrest control of key publications from people who had served the old system, there was little doubt that the government achieved its aim of destroying "the pyramid of lies" inherited from the former regime. The new press was anything but monolithic.

The independence of the press often displeased the political leaders who had engineered the changes in the first place. After Walesa became president, his aides barred a *Gazeta Wyborcza* reporter from covering his meeting with the diplomatic corps, arguing that the paper was too "critical." During the brief but turbulent existence of the right-wing government of Prime Minister Jan Olszewski in 1992, officials repeatedly attacked the daily *Rzeczpospolita* for what it viewed as negative coverage. The government still controlled 51 percent of the paper's shares, but it had been taking an increasingly independent line for some time; after 49 percent of the shares were sold to French publisher Robert Hersant, that tendency was visibly strengthened. Passions subsequently cooled in Poland, however, and neither *Gazeta Wyborcza* nor *Rzeczpospolita* suffered any serious consequences.

But in Hungary, press relations remained clouded by suspicion. When Hungarian newspapers rushed to round up foreign investors, Prime Minister Antall's government intervened in one highly publicized case. It blocked a prospective joint venture between the daily *Magyar Nemzet* and the liberal Swedish daily *Dagens Nyheter* in favor of a deal with Hersant, whose politics are more conservative. Hersant's participation in the Polish daily *Rzeczpospolita* enhanced the paper's reputation, but here quite the opposite was the case. The government move sparked charges of political manipulation and undermined the newspaper's credibility with the public.

Government officials, in turn, sought to undermine the credibility of most of the remaining press, which it viewed as singularly hostile. "There has been no paper that will publish an article about the government without one bad comment," complained Ferenc Kulin, the chairman of the parliament's cultural committee and a member of the ruling Democratic Forum. Though similar complaints can be heard from Western governments, the dispute in Hungary had an added edge because of the country's recent history. According to Kulin and other members of the Antall camp, most of their journalistic critics had loyally served the old communist system. "They are being so critical now to make people forget their past compromises," he said.

Gabor Bencsik, the secretary general of the Association of Hungarian Journalists, countered that it was the government that was exhibiting antidemocratic instincts in its dealings with the press. "These people feel that democracy is working against them," he told me. "They thought that democracy means getting elected, and then governing as in the old days." The government's charges of journalistic collaboration with the old regime overlooked the fact that, despite the undeniable conformity of many journalists, there were dramatic changes within the Hungarian press before the change in government. Although he is a former dissident who wrote only for the underground press, Miklos Haraszti, of the opposition Free Democrats, is convinced that the press played a vital role in the peaceful political transformation of the country. "The secret of the transition was that the press liberated itself," he argued.

The real source of government-press tension was that many journalists were openly sympathetic with the liberal Free Democrats, which irritated the more conservative Democratic Forum. "The criterion for a free press is not that it should not be under government influence but that it should not be under political influence," Kulin argued. The Antall government viewed liberal journalists with the same sort of intense hostility that the Nixon-Agnew administration once did, but the difference was that the emerging new press market gave it more opportunities for direct intervention. After giving up control of the old government paper *Magyar Hirlap,* some officials began wondering if they hadn't made a mistake. To try to rectify the situation, Democratic Forum supporters launched a new progovernment daily, *Uj Magyarorszag,* in April 1991. After Robert Maxwell's death and the collapse of his media empire in late 1991, the state publishing house actually bought back his shares in *Esti Hirlap,* an afternoon daily.

Some opposition politicians, like Haraszti, charged that this was an attempt to "renationalize" part of the press. Kulin countered that only 7.5 percent of the press was in government hands in 1992, as compared with nearly 100 percent only a couple of years earlier. Haraszti conceded the validity of this point, but refused to give the government credit for the positive and largely irreversible broad developments. "In historical terms, the government has lost this game," he argued, referring to its efforts to regain direct influence. "There will be a free press in spite of the government."

More important, openly partisan publications like *Uj Magyarorszag* fared poorly: despite vigorous efforts by government supporters to promote it, the daily only had a circulation of about fifty thousand after its first year in operation. The experience of openly partisan new publications elsewhere was similar. *Nowy Swiat,* a virulently propagandistic daily launched by supporters of Poland's right-wing Olszewski government, quickly found itself in financial trouble, since it could only appeal to a narrow audience. The Czech daily *Telegraf,* which was launched in January 1992 by members of Vaclav Klaus' Civic Democratic Party, also found itself struggling to attract a respectable number of readers, even though Klaus was riding a political wave; its circulation in mid-1992 stood at about fifty thousand and it merged with another struggling daily, *Metropolitan,* in an effort to stay afloat. The secret of a newspaper's success in the new age, it turned out, was not only good journalism but independent journalism, regardless of its past affiliation.

The extent to which nonpartisanship was considered a virtue was demonstrated in Hungary, oddly enough, by *Nepszabadsag,* the only former communist daily in the region to retain its position as its nation's highest-circulation newspaper. It succeeded in doing so because its editors decided to strip away the paper's communist label, and did so convincingly.

Andras Kereszty returned from a five-year stint as the Washington correspondent for *Nepszabadsag* in 1989 to take up the position of managing editor. Like many of his colleagues, he had taken his party membership for granted, only recognizing during the political upheavals of that year that there were other realistic options. "I always thought you could only change this system from within," he told me in a break between editorial meetings. "I was wrong."

The political changes that coincided with his elevation to the top job at the paper made him reconsider the implications of the lesson he had learned when he started his journalistic career as a sports reporter. At that time, he quickly learned not to root for any particular team. As editor, he realized that his party affiliation was a liability. "It was like being a sports reporter and a fan of a team," he said. "It was impossible."

Kereszty not only resigned from the party but also badgered the reluctant party into giving up its hold on the paper. He kept the communists from acquiring any shares in the company when it was reorganized in 1990, while 41 percent of the shares were purchased by the German publishing firm Bertelsmann. His editorial philosophy could have come from any American journalism textbook. "We separate news and commentary," he declared. The paper's ability to maintain its leading position was due to its track record during the first year of its new operations, when it took great pains to distance itself from its former identification. "It was crystal-clear that we did not print the party's opinions," he said.

Kereszty freely borrowed journalistic and marketing techniques from the American press: boxed commentaries set off visually from news stories; special supplements like a radio-and-television-program guide, and a "Home" section with consumer, health, and beauty tips; even the first cutout discount coupons. The paper's commentaries were still considered vaguely leftist: before the outbreak of the Gulf War, for example, it argued against military intervention, and before the Soviet Union collapsed, it castigated the government for not maintaining closer ties with Moscow. But Kereszty claimed that his paper was "no more leftist than *The New York Times* or *The Washington Post*." Above all, the newspaper had convinced readers that it was not promoting anything but itself. "We are not an opposition or a government newspaper," Kereszty said proudly. "We are just a newspaper."

Czechoslovakia's former Communist Party daily *Rude Pravo* had similar aspirations—and its editor, Zdenek Porybny, a former Washington correspondent, had a similar background. "From my American experience, I learned that you can sell a good newspaper without being connected to a party," he said. Conceding that *Rude Pravo* was "discredited" by its association with a hard-line regime, he not only broke off its formal ties with the party but also dismissed about 40 percent of its old staff—unlike Kereszty at *Nepszabadsag*, who made only a small number of personnel changes. *Rude Pravo's* editorial policy remained more openly leftist, but its reporting won praise even from rival publications. It led the field in its coverage of such stories as Washington's attempts to pressure Prague to stop the sale of tanks to Syria, Czechoslovakia's tensions with Germany over the friendship treaty that was finally signed in February 1992, and the revelations about the high number of government officials who were involved in the investment funds that dominated the "coupon-privatization" process, producing clear conflict-of-interest situations. It also added special supplements on health, entertainment, business, and style.

If such reporting allowed the paper to remain highly competitive, second only to *Mlada Fronta Dnes* in daily circulation and number one in its weekend edition, Czech communists were hardly pleased by its increasing independence. In June 1991, they launched a new daily for their members. But its circulation remained limited to about fifty thousand, representing the party's hard core, not making a serious dent in *Rude Pravo*'s daily circulation, which remained steady at almost four hundred thousand.

The paper's success angered more than just its former owners. In March 1992, federal authorities staged a dramatic arrest of Porybny at his home, handcuffing him before taking him to prison. Held for four days before he was released on bail, he was charged with swindling the state out of an estimated $857,000 when he transferred the publishing rights for *Rude Pravo* from a state publishing house to a joint-stock company he formed in 1990. Porybny argued that this maneuver was executed to wrest control from the Communist Party and in no way entailed any losses to the state. "My prosecution is linked with an attempt to publish a paper independent of any political influences whatsoever," he declared. "The real motivation is clear: we became too successful."

In fact, other publications had changed hands during that early period in similar circumstances, and editorial writers at rival publications denounced the action taken against Porybny, agreeing that it was politically motivated. The government's case quickly began to unravel and, in December 1992, all charges against Porybny were dropped. If anything, his paper emerged even stronger after his ordeal. "I could hardly imagine a better advertisement for *Rude Pravo*," wrote *Mlada Fronta Dnes* editor Sevcik in a commentary. Renounced by its former owners and attacked by what were viewed as right-wing zealots in the Federal Interior Ministry, *Rude Pravo* was in the enviable position of looking defiantly independent.

It was no accident that the one old communist daily that maintained its party affiliation, Poland's *Trybuna*, was the least successful. Poland's communists formally renamed themselves Social Democrats, and *Trybuna* hoped to cash in on popular discontent with postcommunist governments by offering what it billed as a moderate-leftist alternative to the new establishment. But its claims that it was the only true opposition paper did not prevent circulation from sinking, until it finally appeared to stabilize at around seventy thousand. By charging a relatively high price per copy and drastically reducing is staff, its editors claimed they finally stopped having to take subsidies from the party in 1992. But no one had any illusions that it was truly independent, and at best it could only hope to keep scraping by as a fairly marginal publication.

Whether it was of the left or the right, ideology did not sell daily newspapers. But at least one veteran Polish communist ideologist was having a field day. In late 1990, when I visited Jerzy Urban for the first time since the communists had lost power, he exuded the same smug contempt for his political opponents that had made him one of the country's most despised figures when he served as government spokesman throughout the turbulent 1980s. He had just launched his satirical weekly *Nie* (*No*), which proved to be an immediate commercial success, tripling its original run from one hundred thousand to three hundred thousand in the first few weeks. He had also just published *Urban's Alphabet,* a best-seller ridiculing, in alphabetical order, the country's political and cultural elite. "From the financial point of view, I'm living much better now," he told me, puffing on his pipe in his new office and reflecting on the difference between life under socialism and under capitalism. Then, acknowledging the anger many Poles felt about his good fortune, he added: "If I said publicly how much I expect to earn next year, they'd burn this office down."

Since *Nie* was produced by a staff of only about a dozen full-timers and a few stringers, and its circulation had reached six hundred thousand by 1992, it proved to be every bit the money machine Urban had hoped it would be. "A publication that is light and satirical fills a need," he said, to explain its appeal. "We are in tune with social attitudes." "Light and satirical" was his description; more accurately, *Nie*—along with Urban's books—offered a mixture of heavy-handed humor about Poland's new rulers and the Roman Catholic Church, lewd drawings and photos, and anything that smacked of scandal. When he was charged with pornography for publishing a particularly vivid photo of a woman's private parts, Urban responded with a front-page caricature of himself, his legs spread apart to expose female genitalia. Apparently recognizing that any legal action would only provide more publicity that Urban could exploit, a Warsaw court dropped the charges against him, ruling that he was "a negligible social danger." But in the new media competition, he was a major winner.

Urban's unexpected success could be dismissed as simply the product of his ability to tap into the most negative sentiments of the disaffected portion of the population, which was delighted by his willingness to violate any taboo. But it also could be seen as a warning to more serious publications to develop their own voices. "People have had a certain conformism programmed into them for years—that there are authorities you should listen to, even if they were underground authorities," said Michnik of *Gazeta Wyborcza*. Independence, skepticism, even irreverence often did not come naturally to journalists in the region. But Polish writer Hanna Krall, who held informal journalism seminars for young staffers at *Gazeta Wyborcza*, believed that her pupils represented a new generation with new attitudes. "There is already a group of young journalists who are emotionally independent," she maintained. "They are not tied to the church, Walesa, or Solidarity. They think critically."

Some journalists had worried that foreign investors would impose new dictates, although they needed these foreigners' financial backing to modernize printing operations and keep pace with the rising expectations of readers who often had about ten dailies to choose from. When Maxwell moved into Eastern Europe, the British tycoon appeared to demonstrate the legitimacy of those fears. After buying a 40 percent share in the Hungarian daily *Magyar Hirlap* and 100 percent of a new printing plant in Budapest, he immediately began pressuring Peter Nemeth, the editor-in-chief of *Magyar Hirlap*, to make more drastic cuts in staff than he felt were justified. In an outright power play, he pressured stockholders to up his share of the daily to 51 percent, threatening to stop publishing the paper at his printing plant if they did not accede to his demands. Such actions prompted other Eastern Europeans to become more choosy about their partners. In Poland, Maxwell lost a bid for a major stake in the Polish daily *Zycie Warszawy* to an Italian media company.

Nonetheless, fears of editorial meddling by foreign investors proved largely unfounded; these investors were more interested in encouraging solid business practices and providing the resources for new computer systems, printing operations, and redesigns that gave formerly gray, old-fashioned newspapers like *Zycie Warszawy* a clean, modern, new look. When Rupert Murdoch bought 50 percent of the Hungarian tabloid *Mai Nap* in 1990, he had to teach the staff a few simple ways to stay in the black. "Before Murdoch came, we were not very insistent on getting prompt payment from advertisers," admitted deputy editor Ferenc Szollosi. "Now we are quite insistent." But from the vantage point of most editors, the best contribution of a foreign investor was not to interfere in editorial operations; such was the case with Hungary's former communist daily *Nepszabadsag* after Bertelsmann bought a 41 percent stake. "We are like an illegitimate child for Bertelsmann," said editor Kereszty, expressing his delight. "They came, conceived us, and left us alone."

Editors and reporters were more likely to learn about Western editorial practices in other ways. American universities and news organizations set up media centers in Prague and Warsaw, which offered seminars and resources on a broad array of topics. On sponsored trips to the United States, Eastern European journalists picked up tips on everything from phone reporting—even with poor phone lines, this saves time—to the merits of launching regional editions. Not all American practices were welcome: some reporters complained that their editors had picked up the disturbing habit of rewriting their copy too much. But there was an undeniable need to drum in some of the basics of writing, since articles in the Polish, Czech, and Hungarian press often still failed to encapsulate enough basic information to make them understandable to readers who might have missed the previous day's coverage.

There is one dilemma the Eastern European journalists cannot avoid: on the one hand, they are eager to establish their independence of government; on the other, they recognize that they are very much part of the societies in which they live. They are both critics and participants, outsiders and insiders. That is true in other societies as well, but it is a particularly important consideration for journalists when they are operating in societies undergoing such a sweeping transition from old system to new.

Some journalists believe that this fact imposes special obligations. "There is enough disenchantment in Poland," argued *Zycie Warszawy* editor Woycicki. "The role of the press is to explain the difficulties and not to turn people off to politics altogether." As Woycicki sees it, his paper should encourage hard-hitting reporting, but it should remain scrupulously fair in its criticism. Alluding to his efforts to revamp his daily and to retrain its staff over the next few years, he added: "If I need so much time to transform the paper, how much time will be needed to transform the country?" Like the new political institutions growing up around it, Eastern Europe's newly liberated press is defining itself and its goals day by day. But, unlike some other institutions, it has already progressed a very long way in a very short time.

In the 1970s, Polish dissident activist Miroslaw Chojecki helped organize the underground press that gave many of his countrymen access to uncensored news for the first time. In the 1980s, as an exile in Paris, Chojecki expanded into television, churning out documentaries and news shows that were smuggled into Poland on video cassettes or broadcast by satellite. In the aftermath of the political upheaval in Poland, Chojecki returned home, convinced that his dissident days were over and that in the 1990s he would be able to work openly and legally in a new kind of Polish television. But he quickly learned otherwise—and reverted to his old subversive role. Exasperated by the Polish parliament's failure to pass a law opening the airwaves to commercial TV, he decided to launch his New Television Warsaw without a government license.

"We are convinced that we have to start from the beginning and return to the underground," Chojecki told me in the summer of 1992. Then, referring to his former colleagues from the underground who occupied top government posts, he added: "It will be interesting to see how they react."

Chojecki found that launching a new station was more complicated than it first appeared, and it did not go on the air until December 1992, shortly before parliament finally passed a broadcasting law. But his still unlicensed transmissions served to demonstrate how far television lagged behind other institutions in changing with the times in Eastern Europe. While new newspapers and magazines proliferated and private radio stations began to pop up all over, TV remained largely a state monopoly as politicians angrily squabbled over what to do about it. For the new governments, television was still the most influential—and controversial—medium. The long battles over its future demonstrated that, regardless of their protestations to the contrary, many politicians were frightened of letting control of television slip from their hands.

Eastern Europeans are voracious television consumers, with color sets in most households. As of the early 1990s, most could tune in to only two state channels, but almost one million Hungarian families were already hooked up for cable, and one million Poles had put up satellite dishes that provided them with even broader access to foreign channels, from Germany's SAT 1 to CNN and MTV. A demand for more local channels indisputably existed. State-television executives warned that current facilities allowed only for the addition of one or two national channels, but commercial stations could also be launched on a regional basis; if they took off, they could later invest in expanded networks.

In theory, almost everyone favored increased competition and a loosening of state control over the airwaves. The bosses of state television were particularly emphatic about the need for sweeping changes, including the introduction of competitive stations. "We are constantly criticized," said Jiri Kanturek, the director of Czechoslovak television. "To be the director of Czechoslovak television is like sitting permanently in an electric chair." The nervousness of the television bosses was particularly evident during election campaigns. Instead of organizing programs in which candidates would have to face aggressive questioning, or even providing much of their own coverage during regular news broadcasts, the bosses usually opted for allocating free blocks of time to each political party, allowing them, in effect, to do extended commercials. That kind of uncritical nightly exposure, for example, helped launch the candidacy of Stanislaw Tyminski for the Polish presidency in 1990, allowing an unknown émigré suddenly to emerge as a major contender. Though television did sometimes provide a platform for genuinely informative discussions and debates, it too often abrogated its responsibilities or simply failed to live up to its potential.

In practice, reforms ran into opposition at almost every turn. In Czechoslovakia, the debate about television's future was less acrimonious than in Poland or Hungary, but a law on establishing a licensing board for commercial TV stations still went through eight drafts before it finally passed in October 1991; no licenses were issued before the Czech-Slovak split set back the timetable further. The federal parliament was not able to pass a separate law on the reorganization of state television before it went out of existence, leaving that task to the new Czech and Slovak parliaments.

In Hungary, Prime Minister Antall and the opposition Free Democrats fought a running battle over state television, leading to their failure to pass a new media law at the end of 1992 after two years of angry debate. The government claimed its version of the law provided for independent broadcasting on the British model, but the opposition contended that the draft would have still given the government too much control. Since passage of the measure required a two-thirds majority, only a compromise could have saved the bill, but neither side was in a mood to give ground.

Throughout the debate, Antall repeatedly tried to fire state television president Elemer Hankiss, charging that he was not fulfilling his duties. President Arpad Goncz, an opposition Free Democrat, blocked those bids along with the government's efforts to oust Csaba Gombar, the head of state radio, arguing that he was seeking to uphold freedom of the press and the principles of balanced reporting. But in December 1992, Antall suspended Hankiss, charging that he had signed contracts that harmed the broadcasting service, and in January 1993 both Hankiss and Gombar resigned in protest.

Opposition politicians had long claimed that Hankiss' only sin was his independence and his determination to rid news coverage of its progovernment slant. For his part, Hankiss, who normally teaches political science, was quick to fire back at the government that wanted him out. "The government may believe it wants an independent television, but it's not doing anything to create one," he told me in mid-1992. "They believe they represent the interests of the Hungarian nation, and they would like Hungarian TV to radiate the ideology of the ruling parties." In fact, Hankiss was vulnerable to criticism that he was less than a convincing administrator; in early 1992, he actually attempted to fulfill a commitment to be a visiting professor at Stanford University for a semester, commuting back and forth between Palo Alto and Budapest, until the government's efforts to institute changes in his absence forced him to return full-time. But there was little doubt that politics, not competence, was the primary issue.

That was also the case in Poland, where any pretense that television was seen as "public" rather than an instrument of power disappeared during the tenure of Prime Minister Olszewski's right-wing government in 1992. As the split between Walesa and Olszewski turned into open warfare, television became a major battlefield. The government, which blamed adverse media coverage for its repeated setbacks, canceled programs it disliked and replaced key network executives with partisan zealots. "This television will certainly not be antigovernment," vowed Robert Terentiew, who was appointed head of the news division in March. "From the very first day, this government was attacked by the press. This is a result of a sick information system."

He wasted no time in warning young reporters not to ask "aggressive" questions, and began a shakeout of the staff. "I have to clean out the people tied to the old establishment," he told me. "Without that, I won't be able to do anything." To the Olszewski government, the old establishment included not only former communists but also supporters of the Democratic Union, the party of former Prime Minister Mazowiecki, and those considered in the pro-Walesa camp. The president's supporters accused the government of using "decommunization" as a pretext for purges aimed at giving control to its partisans.

The ensuing firings and counterfirings looked almost like a slapstick routine, except for the sorry fact that it reflected the total politicization of television. As the Olszewski government began to crumble in May, the Walesa camp prevailed on Janusz Zaorski, the chairman of the State Broadcasting Authority, to fire Terentiew. Then Olszewski responded by firing Zaorski and reinstating Terentiew. The prime minister's spokesman claimed that the government was only exercising its "ownership rights" over television. As soon as the Olszewski government collapsed in June, Zaorski was reinstated and Terentiew was dismissed a second time.

The blame for the degeneration of the situation to that point could be spread around. The Mazowiecki government, the first postcommunist team, initially introduced a liberal broadcasting law that would have created a more independent public-television structure and allowed for commercial stations. But later, faced with a crowded legislative agenda, the government largely abandoned its efforts to push the measure through parliament. "The importance of this issue was underestimated; it was treated as a secondary matter," Juliusz Braun, a Mazowiecki supporter who chaired the parliamentary subcommittee dealing with radio and television, told me. However, critics charged that the Mazowiecki team had also succumbed to the temptation of trying to manipulate television coverage, losing its appetite for reforms designed to prevent such manipulation. Walesa had meddled even more blatantly in television, blocking the passage of a new broadcasting law in late 1991.

In effect, television reform became a hostage to three competing power centers. "The president, the government, and parliament all want political influence over whoever controls television," explained State Broadcasting Authority chairman Zaorski, when I discussed the issue with him during the turbulent spring of 1992. "If they don't come to terms, we won't have a law."

But gradually the consensus grew that a broader solution, not successive firings by whatever political camp was stronger at any given moment, was needed. The authorities also recognized that they could not merely slap down those who were eager to start up new broadcasting ventures. Walesa himself signaled an understanding for challenges to existing restrictions in May 1992, when he told a reporter for radio WAWA, an unlicensed radio station in Warsaw: "Were it not for pirate stations, I would not be at the Belvedere [the presidential palace] today." When Chojecki's New Television Warsaw and another unlicensed station went on the air later that year, government officials often participated in their programs; the earlier fears of a crackdown proved unfounded. In December 1992, the Polish parliament finally passed a broadcasting law, establishing new guidelines for state television and opening the way for the licensing of private stations. While such legislation was long overdue, it, too, reflected the political pressures of the time, since right-wing parliamentarians succeeded in inserting a controversial clause requiring broadcasters to respect "Christian values."

Even with new legislation, the commercial viability of nongovernment channels remained an open question. When I visited Nap TV in Budapest in the spring of 1992, a commercial morning show that was buying unused time on Hungarian TV, executives spoke openly about their problems in drumming up advertising. "I don't think a twenty-four-hour commercial channel will survive," said deputy editor Tibor

Udvarhelyi. In Czechoslovakia, OK3, the former Soviet armed-forces channel that broadcast foreign programming, was experiencing similar troubles. Petr Kubanek, the station's programming director, predicted that "it will be very difficult for private broadcasters here." One solution under consideration was for the government to offer commercial stations a time-sharing arrangement on OK3, instead of opting for one station to take over a full-time channel.

Foreign investors looked far from eager to pour money into the region. "Commercial television means big money, so we are a bit wary of investing before the market warrants it," said Paolo Brera, a spokesman for Italian television mogul Silvio Berlusconi. They were also nervous as parliaments debated local-content requirements designed to limit the "Americanization" of the market, with new commercial stations only running American programs which could be acquired cheaply. Sometimes such concerns went even further. "I am horrified by commercial TV, which lowers standards in order to get more and more viewers," Hungarian super-nationalist parliamentarian Istvan Csurka told me. But he conceded that he was isolated on this issue even within his own party, the ruling Democratic Forum: "I'm alone in opposition to all commercial TV."

Most politicians recognized that, whatever their reservations about commercial television, such stations would introduce an element of badly needed competition. TV producers and reporters were convinced that, without competitors, state television would never reform itself. In the long run, competition could also restore the credibility of news programming, which would always remain suspect as long as it emanated from a single source. There were other considerations, too. Local filmmakers hoped that the advent of commercial television would give them an additional outlet that their counterparts in the West routinely benefited from.

Given the political and economic hurdles, some officials argued that their countries should not be judged too harshly for the delays in implementing television reforms. They pointed out that Spain and Portugal had taken several years to introduce new broadcasting laws after they abandoned authoritarian rule. But Chojecki, the former underground activist and the initiator of New Television Warsaw, found such comparisons misleading. "Those countries had dictatorships, but they already had a market economy," he said. "We don't have a full market economy yet. Television could play a huge role in its development." Although that was true, it was perhaps not the main difference. In Eastern Europe, the new governments needed to bolster their own political stature by demonstrating they did not fear competing sources of news and other programming on the airwaves. By dragging their feet on reforms for so long, they proved to be their own worst enemies.

In another field where the state had once exercised extremely strict control, Eastern European governments moved much more quickly to allow competition. This field was educaton, and the evidence of the sudden change was the dramatic appearance of private schools. Within an astonishingly short period of time, education began to take on the pluralistic forms and sharp contrasts it has in free-market economies. On a series of visits to schools in Warsaw, Budapest, and Prague during the first semester of the 1991–92 school year, I found a far greater range of choices for parents and students than I had anticipated. The political revolution may have been far from complete, but an educational revolution had already begun.

The contrast between the most expensive new private schools and the state schools was particularly jarring. At the Baccalarius elementary school in Warsaw, pupils entered a privileged world as soon as they opened the door with their magnetic cards, which registered their attendance in the office computer. Class size rarely exceeded about a dozen students. There was particular emphasis on a language program that provided daily English lessons for everyone from kindergarten on up. By the fourth grade, pupils were also studying French or German. Aside from taking the normal required subjects, students used a well-appointed computer room, rode horseback, and took field trips to France and Italy. Teachers, who earned about twice as much as their counterparts in the state system, were expected to be accessible in and out of class. "Our school is the best," boasted founder and owner Andrzej Liszka. "The children do not have a chance to be bored here." Many wealthy Polish parents seemed to agree. Despite an enrollment fee of $1,800 and annual tuition of over $3,000, the year-old school had 108 students—and a waiting list of three hundred.

Across town, at State Elementary School Number 34, principal Krystyna Sawicka was struggling to provide a good education to her 770 students, from kindergarten to the eighth grade. The odds were stacked against her. Teachers had to contend with an average class size of about thirty, and their salaries were often less than $100 a month. "Teachers are disillusioned, because they can't make it from payday to payday," said Sawicka, who fretted about their sinking morale. English instruction was only offered to the fifth and sixth grades, since the school had only one qualified English teacher; even those classes had just lost an hour of instruction a week, thanks to cutbacks in teaching hours mandated by the Ministry of Education, for budgetary reasons. The seventh- and eighth-graders had to continue with Russian instruction, a language most Poles had no interest in learning. Sawicka pointed out that five computers had been donated to the school, but they were stashed away in a storage room; the school could not afford to pay anyone to show the kids how to use them, since computer specialists had far more attractive options. "You can't get anyone to teach computers for a normal salary," she said.

While the pressure of shrinking budgets was putting the squeeze on state schools, an increasing number of educators and parents were organizing new alternatives, reviving the traditions of private and religious schools that had flourished in Poland, Czechoslovakia, and Hungary before World War II. Some of those new institutions, like Baccalarius, were for the children of the nouveaux riches, but most were far more modest, received some form of state subsidy, and attracted a much broader clientele. "Private schools here are not for rich people," Ondrej Steffl, the director of the First Independent High School in Prague, told me. "They are for people who aren't satisfied with the state system."

That system had combined a traditional authoritarian approach to education with communist ideology, prompting some educators to dream of alternative schooling even before the political changes. But it was only after communism crumbled that they were able to act, and they leapt at the new opportunities. In Poland, the movement had grown the fastest, with about thirty thousand students studying in about four hundred independent schools during the 1991–92 academic year. Hungary and Czechoslovakia were a bit slower getting started, but the same process was also well under way. Education Ministry officials approved almost every project submitted to them, working on the theory that such private initiatives should be encouraged.

Some of the new schools were geared toward putting precocious children on the fast track. After spending a year at the Genius Elementary School in Budapest, students were already one year ahead of their counterparts in state schools in math. And as in almost all the new schools, they started English and other foreign languages much earlier and studied them more intensively; despite the general shortage of English teachers, many private schools ensured adequate staffing by offering them higher salaries. Some schools also experimented with novel curriculums. At the First Communal High School in Warsaw, subjects were taught in clusters: in the humanities cluster, for example, students studied the Middle Ages at the same time in their history, literature, and philosophy classes.

But the most common distinctive feature of the new schools was their looser atmosphere, with far more relaxed relations between teachers and students than in state schools. "When we have problems, we can talk to the teachers and be sure that they'll listen," said Katerina Benoniova, a student at the First Indpendent High School in Prague. Dominika Janocha, a student at Warsaw's First Communal High School, told me: "It's somewhat chaotic, but we like it very much. The school assumes you want to learn something for yourself." Administrators at the school admitted that, in strict academic terms, their students may not cover as much ground as at a top state high school, but argued that they learned to think more for themselves. None of this meant anything approaching anarchy or even 1960s-style alternative schools in the West. In the schools that were off to a good start, the atmosphere was more often comparable to that of a well-run public school in the United States, but this represented a radical departure from the traditional Eastern European model.

Religious schools were another matter, since they often represented a return to past practices. When they had seized power in Hungary, the communists nationalized the extensive network of religious schools; after the change of government, those schools began reclaiming their old buildings, often pushing out the state schools that had taken their place. Acknowledging the mixed feelings of many Hungarians about this process, Oszkar Nikowitz, the director of a Roman Catholic high school on the outskirts of Budapest, was careful to frame his goals in ecumenical terms, emphasizing the need to undo the moral damage of the communist period. "We are trying to rebuild the old Christian values—discipline, the family, tolerance," he said. "We want to bring up civilized children. Making them into believers comes second."

Whatever their orientation, many schools had an extremely difficult start. They often lacked common facilities, forcing them to rent out classrooms in different locations. Most were continually strapped for cash, since they attempted to keep their fees affordable and even to offer scholarships to needy but talented applicants. "The existence of very rich schools is not good," argued Krystyna Starczewska, the director of the First Communal High School in Warsaw, where the annual fee was about $550 and a quarter of the students received some financial assistance. "There's still an egalitarian ethos here." Only Polish private schools received no funding from the state, while "communal" schools received subsidies of 50 percent of what the state paid for each pupil in its schools. In Czechoslovakia and Hungary, the subsidies were higher, but the smaller class size meant that parents still often had to pay the equivalent of two months' average salary in annual tuition.

Some schools quickly closed their doors. Baccalarius, the elementary school for Poland's new wealthy business class which had appeared to be off to such a promising start, turned into the most tragic case. During the spring semester of 1992, owner Liszka announced a big increase in the already hefty monthly fees, ignoring an earlier pledge that tuition would not be raised further that year. The parents, many of whom felt that the school had not lived up to their initial high expectations, were enraged. A bitter confrontation ensued, with parents refusing to pay the extra fees and charging that Liszka was not able to account for nearly $100,000 of the fees that he had already collected.

Liszka alternately threatened the parents and tried to placate them, but he refused to provide a detailed accounting of the school's finances. Though he still talked about establishing a network of similar schools around Poland, he was faced with the prospect of a mass exodus from his Warsaw school at the end of the year. When I spoke with him briefly in April, he blamed the crisis on "bad information" and admitted that a group of parents were planning to try to organize their own school, which they believed would be both cheaper and better. "But they are doing what always happens in socialism," he said. "They are trying to destroy us first." At the end of May, Liszka was found hanging from a belt in his apartment, an apparent suicide, and his wife, who served as the school's director, was also found dead; the police speculated that she may have been killed by her husband. Prosecutors were left to sift through the evidence to determine what had really happened and what the true state of the school's finances had been.

For all the setbacks, there was little doubt that many private schools would survive and others would be launched, since the notion of broader educational choices was appealing to a growing number of parents and pupils. Although the higher pay and more flexible work environment at private schools may make it harder for state schools to attract good teachers, many educators in the public sector said they welcomed the competition. The newcomers, they maintained, may force state schools to improve their methods; a few have already adopted programs developed at private institutions. "The existence of private schools will improve the quality of state schools," predicted Polish Education Ministry official Krzysztof Skolimowski.

The level of experimentation and initiative taking place demonstrated

that more and more areas of life were undergoing a process of diversi-
fication. Pluralism was far from limited to politics; it had spread to cultural life, much of the media, and the most basic function of any society,
the education of its children. The personal adjustments to the changing situation—particularly to the new forms of competition in all fields—
were often more difficult than anyone expected, producing bitter
disappointments along with new triumphs. But more and more inhabitants of the region were learning to create their own opportunities, instead of simply assuming that they had to fit into an existing framework
imposed from on high. Judging by the early results, new patterns of
thinking were emerging along with new institutions.

GOD AND
THE DEVIL

Dressed in a brown habit, Sister Semeona placed a crucifix and a lighted candle on her desk and drilled her first-grade class at Izabelin, a village near Warsaw, in a friendly but authoritative manner.

"Who created you and me?" she asked.

"Our Father, the Lord," the class responded in unison.

"How can you praise God?"

"By loving everyone," "By praying, "By singing," different voices responded.

"Is God among us?"

"Yes," everyone replied.

"Can we see him?"

The class hesitated, and Sister Semeona supplied the answer. "No, because God is invisible."

In the fall of 1990, priests, nuns, and lay teachers started conducting similar drills in the classrooms of public schools all over Poland. The new Polish government had just authorized voluntary religious instruction in public schools, a practice that had been banned for nearly three decades by the communists. Even though an overwhelming majority of the children in villages like Izabelin had attended religious-instruction classes conducted in parish houses and other church facilities during that period, local pastors were delighted by the change to what they viewed as the normal state of things. "For us this is a return to something we already had," said Father Jozef Podstawa, the portly, balding parish priest in Izabelin. Until recently, he told me, children could have been confused by the conflict between what they were taught in schools and at church. "Now," he said with satisfaction, "there is one direction, there is one voice."

But that was hardly the case. If the Catholic Church in Poland was under the impression that the political transformation of the country would lead to a one-voice approach to social and religious issues, it was grievously mistaken. The church's own assertive new stance in the public arena, epitomized by its ability to force the hasty decision to allow religious instruction in public schools, triggered an immediate popular backlash. Besides ending government policies aimed at curbing the influence of the church, the new freedoms opened the doors to other conflicting values and patterns of behavior. In the early 1990s, the newly liberated Eastern European nations were speaking with many voices, demonstrating that the issues of morality and conscience were among the hardest, not the easiest, to tackle. After the first grade, unanimous responses were few and far between.

The evidence of moral confusion, or at least of moral crosscurrents, was everywhere. The introduction of Western-style mass culture included a proliferation of pornographic magazines, and the region's first sex shops. Although prostitution had always existed, particularly in the high-priced hotels where foreigners stayed, it was out in the open as never before. Sex clubs sprang up in Budapest, and young prostitutes, some only in their early teens, accosted visitors strolling through Prague's historic center. The Catholic Church in Poland obtained unprecedented access to state television, but the same channels aired films with sexually explicit scenes that would never be shown by the major American networks. The result could be a priest's homily followed by a good deal of heavy breathing.

One evening only a few months after the downfall of the communist regime, I switched on the TV and watched a rather arresting scene of an intertwined couple; this was followed by an abrupt transition to another couple in a different setting, but similarly engaged; then another panting couple appeared. Like any conscientious reporter faced with an inexplicable chain of events, I dutifully kept watching scene after scene, waiting for some kind of indication of what all this was supposed to represent. Finally, the credits rolled around and a voice explained: "You have been watching a history of sex in Polish cinema." That was it: someone had strung together the most graphic scenes from Polish movies and run them on prime time.

Little wonder that some religious activists who had fought communist repression were refocusing on the dangers of "Western morality." I revisited Jiri Kaplan, a Catholic activist in Prague who had conducted prayer groups for young people in the days when the church was persecuted; he promptly informed me that he had decided to continue with the weekly meetings of the group, although persecution was no longer a problem. "We dreamed about the arrival of democracy. We thought it would be a panacea," he said. "No. We are at the beginning of a very difficult period."

Far more disturbing to most Poles, Czechs, and Hungarians was the sudden crime wave that accompanied the changeover to a new political and economic system. Car thefts, robberies, and break-ins became disturbingly commonplace, and even violent crimes became more frequent, although the rates were still low compared with those of many Western European, not to mention American, cities.

The problem was partly caused by the sudden disappearance of the police state. Many policemen were initially demoralized and confused by their abrupt change in status. If they had felt empowered by the old system to intimidate anyone they pleased and focused much of their efforts on political enemies, they now were charged with the more mundane task of protecting citizens who still instinctively distrusted them, and they were uncertain what authority they still possessed as their new bosses vowed to put a stop to past abuses. In 1990, I met Jaroslaw Kosciuszko, a former police captain who had quit the force to set up a successful private security service and a chain of stores selling tear gas and mace guns. "Everyone knows that the policeman does not know what he is allowed to do anymore," he asserted.

But the police problem went deeper than that. Krzysztof Kozlowski, Poland's first postcommunist interior minister, told me that when he took on his new job he discovered that the police had eighty-five hundred heavy machine guns and massive chemical arsenals, but the force did not own a single fax machine. "The police were armed to fight the society, but not to do police work," he said.

Criminals were motivated not simply by the lack of adequate preventive measures or the softness of the new authorities. Many Czechs, for example, complained that President Havel had made a mistake in letting too many criminals out of jail shortly after taking office as part of a broad amnesty. Prague psychotherapist Helena Klimova noted that "heightened aggression" was hardly surprising, given the abrupt shifts in people's lives. "When people undergo a transition, they undergo an emotional regression connected to their sense of insecurity," she explained. "When a person is afraid, he is more prone to be aggressive."

In his book *Summer Meditations,* Havel wrote:

> The return of freedom to a society that was morally unhinged has produced something it clearly had to produce, and something we therefore might have expected, but which has turned out to be far more serious than anyone could have predicted: an enormous and dazzling explosion of every imaginable human vice. A wide range of questionable or at least morally ambiguous human tendencies, subtly encouraged over the years and, at the same time, subtly pressed to serve the daily operaton of the totalitarian system, have suddenly been liberated, as it were, from their straitjacket and given freedom at last. The authoritarian regime imposed a certain order—if that is the right expression for it—on these vices (and in doing so "legitimized" them, in a sense). This order has now been shattered, but a new order that would limit rather than exploit these vices, an order based on freely accepted responsibility to and for the whole of society, has not yet been built—nor could it have been, for such an order takes years to develop and cultivate.
>
> Thus we are witnesses to a bizarre state of affairs: society has freed itself, true, but in some ways it behaves worse than when it was in chains. . . .

Havel and other former dissidents in the region were particularly concerned about incidents of racial and ethnic violence. Skinheads attacked anyone who looked different—gypsies, and Asian or African visitors. The nationalism that helped fuel the drive for freedom was sometimes transformed into outright chauvinism, with old familiar demons like anti-Semitism and an instinctive distrust of all outsiders not just lurking in the shadows but openly on display. The suppression of free speech for so long meant that the ensuing debates threatened to become a deafening roar in which rational voices would find it difficult to make themselves heard.

In his 1977 novel *The Polish Complex,* Tadeusz Konwicki made a grim prediction. "Previously, when a captive nation regained its freedom, it was not hindered in joining the great family of free nations," he wrote. "Today, if by chance it is set free, it will no longer be fit for life and will perish from the poisons accumulated during the dark night of captivity."

That day of freedom had come. The question was whether the poisons could be neutralized, or at least kept at bay, and how the newly freed societies would go about the business of trying to construct a new moral order.

In June 1991, Pope John Paul II made his first visit to Poland since the collapse of the communist government. On his three previous pilgrimages to his homeland following his election to the papacy, John Paul had electrified his countrymen with his defense of human rights and his espousal of ideals that were clearly in conflict with the ideology and politics of the embattled and frightened ruling elite. This time, Poland's new rulers were eager to embrace and applaud him for his role in the transformation of the nation. Welcoming the pontiff in a drizzling rain, President Walesa greeted him as "a symbol of the spirit of this nation, of a nation that never accepted a system of enslavement." "A free homeland is the fruit of the seed that you, too, have sown," Walesa declared. "Without your work and prayer to 'renew the face of this earth,' there would be no 'Solidarity.' There would have been no Polish August and no victory of freedom."

John Paul acknowledged the "new voice . . . of a sovereign nation and society," but his nine-day visit was less a celebration of the new era than a stern series of lectures, with each mass focused on one of the Ten Commandments, about the perils of the new era. He almost seemed to have felt more comfortable with his countrymen when they were still oppressed by communist governments than with the newly liberated Poles, many of whom were visibly troubled by what they saw as the church's heavy-handed efforts to dictate morality. He warned against "an easy and mechanistic copying" of Western hedonistic values, and berated Poles for their failure to end the widespread practice of abortion. "Understand, all you who are careless in these matters, understand that you cannot fail to concern me and cannot fail to hurt me," he told a rain-soaked crowd at a mass in Kielce. His voice rising with emotion as the skies dumped more rain, he added: "And it should hurt you as well."

As the pope traveled to parts of the country that he had not been able to visit before—along the border with the disintegrating Soviet Union—his visit took on an oddly schizophrenic tone. When he was addressing the Lithuanians, Byelorussians, and Ukrainians who were able to cross over to see him, he received the kind of wildly enthusiastic response that the Poles had awarded him in the 1980s. For those former Soviet nationalities, the pope was still primarily a symbol of hope in their not-yet-completed drive for independence; his mission was to reinforce, as he had done earlier in Poland, the efforts to dismantle totalitarianism. The simple fact that the visitors could see him in person for the first time was part of that process. "The closer he is to Lithuania, the closer we are to our goal," said Vitas Radzavicius, a Lithuanian construction worker who had traveled to the northeastern town of Lomza, where the pope greeted the visitors in Lithuanian.

But the pope excited his countrymen less than the visitors. Part of the reason may have been that Poles had grown accustomed to his visits, even if the inhabitants of smaller cities like Lomza were hosting him for the first time. He continued to draw large crowds, and the respect he commanded was beyond dispute, but even the faithful often had doubts about the role the church was playing in Polish society, and about the pope's stern dictates.

Waiting for the pope's arrival in Lomza, Barbara Szwarc, a twenty-three-year-old schoolteacher and mother of two, explained: "I would never have an abortion, but I am against a ban. Everyone should act according to their own consciences." The effort to legislate morality, she said, referring to the efforts of the church to promote a tough antiabortion law, was "a return to the Middle Ages." And she had no doubts that the church was wrong in its opposition to teaching children about contraception. "We should have education about birth control," she told me, as her children played in a sandbox nearby. "Kids start sex early but know nothing about birth control."

For the first time, the pope's relations with his own people lacked the kind of uncritical glow that still hovered around his meetings with the visitors from across the border. On both sides, there were signs of disenchantment. Later, in its November 1991 issue, the respected Polish Catholic monthly *Znak* carried the cover question: "Have we failed the pope?" But for many Poles, the more apt question was: "Has the church failed to understand our new conditions?"

On one level, the increasingly heated debate about the role of the church was the natural product of a period in which all doctrines could be questioned and a search for new standards of behavior was under way. On another, it reflected old contradictory strains in Polish society as much as new ones, since Poles had long expressed ambivalent feelings about the church that was so much a part of their cultural identity. The power of faith was tremendous. On my first visits to Poland, in the 1960s and later in the 1970s and 1980s, I was struck not just by the crowds spilling out of churches every Sunday but by the contrast between attending a mass in a Polish church and a mass in an American church. The priest on the altar in Poland was usually a more remote figure than his American counterpart, but the Polish worshippers seemed to radiate a singular intensity—call it a genuine spirituality—during the service that I could not recall feeling in American churches. Yet, at the same time, a strong streak of anticlericalism had long coexisted with deep religious commitment.

Those contradictions were often not apparent to the casual observer during the forty-five years of communist rule. The repeated attempts by the early communist governments to intimidate church leaders and to diminish their influence produced the exact opposite effect. Attending mass and praying for someone like Cardinal Stefan Wyszynski, the Polish primate who was imprisoned from 1953 to 1956, constituted an act of patriotism and defiance against a hated regime, attracting both the faithful and those who in more normal circumstances would be far less conscientious about going to church on a Sunday morning. Wyszynski's ability to outmaneuver successive communist regimes, winning more freedom for the church in Poland than it enjoyed anywhere else in Eastern Europe, only increased his standing among his people.

After Wyszynski's death in 1981, his successor, Cardinal Jozef Glemp, could not come close to matching him in moral courage, diplomatic skill, or popularity. Although he worked hard for the release of political prisoners, he sometimes appeared ready to write off Solidarity, and he was genuinely alarmed by the more militant stance of some of his priests, like Father Jerzy Popieluszko, the young pastor who was murdered by the secret police in 1984. But if Glemp sent out ambiguous signals, other bishops and priests across the country provided practical support that proved indispensable to the opposition's sustained resistance. Parish houses offered a venue for speeches, meetings, theatrical productions, and video showings; as the one legal national institution free of government control, the church was a haven for independent activity.

During the 1980s, when the Jaruzelski regime launched its crackdown on Solidarity, the church flourished as never before. The combination of the presence of a Polish pope in the Vatican and the high moral prestige of the church as the defender of human rights prompted record numbers of young men to enter seminaries. While the number of new priests was dropping steadily in the West, Polish seminaries were expanding at an astonishing pace. In 1980, 6,285 men were studying for the priesthood, which already represented a dramatic increase over previous periods; by 1987, the number peaked at 9,038. In the next few years, the figures gradually declined but still remained at impressive levels.

Somewhat paradoxically, the church benefited in other ways from the period of repression. Despite the murder of Popieluszko, the suspicious deaths of other priests, and the harassment of both clerics and lay activists, the government often seemed eager to ingratiate itself with the church hierarchy. Bishop Alojzy Orszulik, who served as a spokesman for the episcopate, suggested that the authorities may have believed that they could avoid waging a simultaneous two-front war against both the society and the church. While fighting with the society, the authorities sought to placate the church by issuing record numbers of building permits for new churches and chapels; in the 1980s, about a thousand new places of worship were built all over the country in an unprecedented building boom. After helping to pressure the authorities into sitting down with the opposition at the round table in 1989, the church looked singularly well placed to promote its message of a renewal of Christian values. It had won on all fronts and seemed invincible; it was indisputably the most respected national institution. In the fall of 1990, I heard a news report that seemed indicative of the times: in a volleyball match between priests and the police, an event that would have been inconceivable in the old era, the clerics trounced their opponents, three to nothing.

But within a brief period, the church's standing declined dramatically in this overwhelmingly Catholic nation. Its approval rating at first slipped behind that of the army, and then even behind that of the police, who only a few years earlier had been despised by the population. In a poll published in June 1992, the army's approval rating was 68 percent, the police scored 66 percent, and the church only 48 percent. Among young people, the negative trend was particularly pronounced. In 1990, 70 percent of young people approved of the church's activities, while 14 percent disapproved; in 1992, 34 percent approved, and 45 percent disapproved. Something had gone wrong, very wrong, with the institution that had seemed best prepared to provide moral guidance during the transition from the old system to the new.

In the fall of 1989, only one month after the first postcommunist government had come to power in Poland, I chatted with Father Jacek Pleskaczynski of the Holy Name of Jesus Church in the industrial city of Lodz. A middle-aged priest who worked closely with young people, he instinctively sensed that the church should be wary of misplaying its hand during the rapid political and economic transformation taking place. There were few danger signals yet, but he answered warily when I asked him about the position of the church in the changed environment. "Different, difficult," he replied. "Very few priests know how to articulate what our new role should be."

He was careful not to criticize the church leadership, but he offered other cautionary observations, alluding to the prewar drive of Catholic right-wingers to impose a narrow, intolerant brand of Catholicism on the nation. "It would be archaic to push in the direction of national Christianity," he said. And he warned against self-congratulation. "When the [economic and political] crisis ends and life gets better, everything that pushed people to the church may disappear, and some of our weaknesses will be apparent. In Poland, you have people who are practicing Catholics but not believers. That's hard to imagine elsewhere. If their motivation was political, they may find new places for themselves."

Most of the church hierarchy and many of Pleskaczynski's fellow priests ignored such warnings, however. After years of wrestling with a hostile regime, they were delighted with the increasingly blurred boundaries between church and state: the sight of Walesa, Mazowiecki, and other new leaders attending church ceremonies, or of soldiers marching in pilgrimages to the shrine of the Black Madonna in Czestochowa; the opportunity to transmit religious programming on state television; the requests for local bishops to bestow their blessings on new premises of state and private offices and institutions. Instead of anticipating dangers, they saw the chance to consolidate their gains and to expand their influence further.

The first indication of trouble was the uneasy reaction of many Poles to the introduction of religious education into public schools. Church officials pointed out that moving religious education from church facilities to schools was a convenience for many parents and pupils, and there was ample precedent for such action in several Western European countries. But the decision was made hastily during the summer of 1990, without parliamentary approval, prompting a protest from Poland's ombudsman that this violated constitutional procedures. Church officials had rammed the measure through, taking advantage of their political clout. Wiktor Kulerski, the state secretary of the Ministry of National Education, conceded that the government moved quickly because it "could not allow itself to have a confrontation with the church."

Critics charged that pupils would feel pressured to enroll, and that few schools provided alternative activities for those who opted not to. "This is going from one form of indoctrination to another," said Iwona Osuch, whose fourteen-year-old son sat outside in the corridor while the rest of his class had religious instruction. Despite protests and even catechism burnings, the right-wing Olszewski government introduced a measure in the spring of 1992 requiring that grades for religion or alternative ethic classes appear on each student's regular report card instead of as a separate grade, as it had up till that point; if a student opted not to take either class, the space for the grade would remain blank. The voluntary nature of such classes seemed increasingly at risk. High-school students in cities did not seem to hesitate to refuse to take religion if they were so inclined, but in smaller communities the social pressure to conform could be far more intense. "The church may have a monopoly on morality, because the only lay morality here was associated with communism," noted writer Marek Nowakowski. "But this can lead to intolerance."

The criticism of the church escalated during the abortion debate. Church leaders lobbied hard for an end to a 1956 law that permitted abortion on demand and an estimated five to six hundred thousand abortions a year, approximately equaling the number of births. As elsewhere in Eastern Europe and the Soviet Union, abortion had often served as a substitute for contraception in Poland; women resorted to multiple abortions, largely oblivious to any ethical, religious, or even medical considerations. They casually referred to their *skrobanki*, or "scrubbings." A backlash was almost inevitable. The antiabortion advocates in parliament proposed a bill banning all abortions, even in cases of rape or incest, and imposing prison terms on doctors who performed them.

After repeated stalling tactics by opponents of the measure and prolonged debates, parliament finally passed a considerably weaker antiabortion law in January 1993. Under its provisions, abortions are allowed in cases of rape or incest, when prenatal tests show that the fetus is seriously damaged, and when a mother's health is in danger; but pro-choice activists lost in their bid to include another provision taking into account the social circumstances of the mother. Ignoring church objections, parliament also voted to require schools to teach sex education and to ensure free access to birth control for the public. While a provision for criminal penalties for self-abortion was dropped, doctors who perform illegal abortions could still face prison terms. Neither side was fully satisfied with the result, which suggested that the issue had hardly been put to rest.

Church officials denied that they were mixing in politics, although they defended their right to espouse long-held principles. "The church does not seek power," Bishop Orszulik told me. "But the church will always declare its moral judgment of political actions and social behavior." The bishops did admonish priests not to embrace particular political parties, but stories still circulated of parish priests who left no doubt that they supported Catholic right-wing parties. This confirmed the worst fears of those who distrusted the church—that the church was attempting to dictate the political agenda and influence the outcome of elections. "The church today is triumphant, expansive, and intolerant," charged Barbara Labuda, a former Solidarity activist and the leader of the women's caucus in the Polish parliament. "Supporting such a church means playing the toady. It is not the same as supporting the church at the time it was subject to persecution."

Cardinal Glemp countered that such critics were no more than "barking mongrels." He blamed the scattered protests, by a "very noisy minority," against religious instruction in public schools, on the legacy of the communist system, which encouraged "an aversion to God." Church officials spun their own conspiracy theories, blaming the mounting criticism of the church on left-leaning intellectuals both from the old Solidarity and the communist camps. Orszulik charged that "aggression against the church was whipped up by leftist lay forces" and that the mass media, in particular, were dominated by "people educated on the basis of Marxist social teachings." The most bitter attacks were often directed at former allies from Solidarity. "Communism was an external threat," said Father Stanislaw Malkowski, a pro-life activist. "The current threat is an internal one: it is more intelligent and perfidious."

Polish intellectuals, including prominent Catholic activists, did articulate views that aroused suspicion among more conservative clerics. "The basic question, as we are returning to Europe, democracy, and pluralism, is what is to be the role of the church," said Jerzy Turowicz, the editor of *Tygodnik Powszechny,* the Krakow-based Catholic weekly that serves as the leading forum for Catholic intellectual debate. "After forty-five years of communism, we don't want to substitute for a false ideology another ideology, even if it is a correct one." In speaking of the backlash against the church, he added: "The church is itself somewhat to blame for this anticlericalism."

It was not just the new signs of the church's more assertive role in public life that troubled many ordinary Poles, but also the accumulated grievances against a clergy whose practices seemed at least anachronistic and, in some cases, plain offensive. While making the rounds to bless homes and collect contributions after Christmas, some priests used the opportunity to reprimand parishioners who had not been to confession. In those parishes, the priests kept track by handing out cards to everyone who went to confession before Easter; the person was then supposed to fill in his name and drop it in a box, to establish his record.

Across the country, I often heard Poles exchanging stories about the arrogance of their local priests. Many concerned money, such as the tales of priests in Czestochowa who read out the addresses of buildings whose inhabitants had not contributed enough to parish fund-raising drives. In Lodz, a priest reprimanded an eleven-year-old girl who dropped two hundred zlotys of her own money, about two cents, into his collection basket. "These days, that doesn't count as money," he reportedly told her. "You can't even take a bus ride for that." The girl was humiliated, and her deeply religious father, who had just dropped in his own, larger contribution, was stunned and outraged.

Other stories circulated that always seemed to be told secondhand and sounded suspiciously apocryphal, raising the possibility that they were no more than the product of virulently anticlerical imaginations. But, true or not, they were another sign of the level of popular distrust and resentment of the church's stance. According to one such tale, the priest in a rural parish asked the children in his first communion class to indicate who was an only child; he attached black ribbons to the shirts of those who raised their hands, as a sign of mourning for their "murdered"—aborted—brothers and sisters. In another story, a priest refused to perform a wedding ceremony until the bride and groom promised not to use contraceptives.

If such stories often seemed hard to believe, there was plenty of evidence that many Polish priests saw themselves as having enforcement duties. In discussing religious education in public schools with Bishop Orszulik, I was taken aback by his casual remark about the consequences for any Catholic who does not attend or does badly in such courses. "They'll be angry when the priest asks for their report card before a church wedding and they'll have to make up courses," he told me.

Such attitudes also prompted the kind of biting humor that had once been aimed at the communist authorities. Alluding to the practice of conductors' spot checks on trams to see if passengers have valid tickets, one joke making the rounds in Warsaw was about a nun who gets on a tram and announces: "Show me your crucifixes." Another joke was aimed at the alleged hypocrisy of the clergy. It recounted the results of a poll on celibacy: 10 percent of the priests voiced their support for celibacy, 10 percent were opposed, and the remaining 80 percent declared their support for keeping things the way they are now.

The growing polarization over the church's role prompted some dire assessments and predictions. In an essay published in the daily *Gazeta Wyborcza* on May 11, 1991, émigré poet Czeslaw Milosz wrote:

> The striking thing about present-day Poland is the reappearance
> of two languages, except that the Marxist idiom has now been re-

placed by the Catholic language. One could only hope that the universal consent to the leading role of Catholicism does not make priests oblivious of a slightly different truth, the one that is revealed in conversations that abruptly end when a clergyman appears. . . .

It may so happen that the clergy will be celebrating national anniversaries, consecrating and exorcising this or that, at the same time making a fool of themselves by suppressing sex, while religion will be eroding from within and in a few decades Poland could become a country with as low a level of religiosity as Britain or France and, on top of that, with the addition of anticlericalism, whose bitterness will be proportional to the influence of the clergy and its program of a religious state.

Milosz's warning was emotionally on target, but it could be disputed on both points. The willingness of many Poles, including the faithful, to debate the role of the church suggested that the notion that the Marxist idiom had been replaced by the Catholic language was more of a facile analogy than an accurate reflection of reality. And Milosz completely overlooked the debates within the church itself. To an outsider, the Polish church might look unchanging and monolithic, but that was hardly the case. In the wake of the political transformation of the country, many priests quietly attempted to work in a different style from their more aggressive colleagues and voiced radically different views.

To a large extent, the differences within clerical ranks reflected the changes produced by the influx of seminarians over the last decade or two. Unlike the older generation of priests, who came largely from the countryside, about half of the new candidates came from urban areas, bringing new attitudes. "We should not be a conquering, dominating church," Maciej Zieba, a young activist who runs the Dominican Brothers' publishing house in Poznan, told me, echoing a view I heard often from other young clerics. The church's main mission, he argued, was to teach tolerance. "This society is not very tolerant. It can't be after fifty years of totalitarianism."

In conversations with other priests, I found them privately critical of their more conservative bishops, and of the politicians who, allegedly in the name of Catholicism, were dividing the nation with their aggressive crusade for sweeping antiabortion legislation. "The politicians who are shouting the loudest about abortion are manipulating the issue and deliberately blow it up," said one priest.

Even some older priests were saddened and frustrated by what they saw as counterproductive tactics. "Why is the church allowing itself to become involved, to become partisan? Why did it get into this abortion issue?" one asked. "It should make its moral stance clear, but it should not be in the business of dictating laws and punishment." He paused and smiled wryly. "I know of only one place where antiabortion legislation was effective: Ceausescu's Romania. When I ask my colleagues if that is what they want, they get angry at me. I try to tell them that anticlericalism is not the result of [the liberal newspaper] *Gazeta Wyborcza*. We should look at the reasons why it exists."

Although the pope left no doubt that he supported extremely tough anti-abortion legislation, he began to demonstrate a sensitivity to at least some of those concerns by trying to put a bit of distance between the church and the right-wing Christian National Union (ZChN). That party embraced absolutist stands against abortion, birth control, and anything else deemed offensive to the church; it also spearheaded the successful effort to insert the clause in the radio and television law passed in December 1992, demanding that broadcasters respect "Christian values." ZChN activists bristled at the label *fundamentalists,* but they left no doubt that they would not balk at censorship if they could get away with it: they even called for a ban on sales of the Polish translation of Salman Rushdie's *Satanic Verses.* Those who rejected their ideas were written off as "phony Catholics." Speaking to Polish bishops in Rome in January 1993, the pope pointedly declared: "No party can usurp the right to represent the Catholic Church."

That was still far from enough to dispel the atmosphere of distrust which had emerged between the church and its critics, including its former allies from the old ranks of the Solidarity movement. "The church is acting stupidly and the opposition is acting stupidly, but they are learning," a young priest asserted, taking a somewhat more detached view. "It was obvious that the church should not get involved directly with politics, and now it is starting to realize that. There is a bit of hysteria: some clergy and believers are convinced that the Democratic Union [Mazowiecki's party, which includes many Solidarity intellectuals] and others want to push the church out of all areas of life, and some in the opposition are convinced that the church wants to make Poland into another Iran. Neither is possible."

Polish Catholicism was showing signs of greater flexibility—if not always among its leaders, then among the lower ranks of the clergy and faithful. And, despite their disagreements with particular aspects of church teaching, I still found many young Poles who considered the faith to be an important part of their lives. They eagerly took part in such church-sponsored events as the Annual World Youth Day which, in the summer of 1991, was held at Poland's holiest shrine, the monastery with the painting of the Black Madonna of Czestochowa, and brought the pope back for a second, quick visit to his homeland within the space of a couple of months.

Working the crowd at a World Youth Day rock concert whose star attraction was Donna Summer, I found attitudes of the young Poles on the most controversial issues to reflect those of their Western counterparts. "I'm for the widest possible distribution of birth control," Krzysztof Soja, a vocational-school student from Olkusz, told me. "There is a lot of ignorance when it comes to sex education, and a lot of fast marriages and early divorces." Katarzyna Krawczyk, a theology student who planned to teach religion, expressed her understanding of the church's opposition to abortion but not of its efforts to outlaw it. "I'm against abortion, but this is an issue that should be left to each person's conscience." Father Andrzej Mulka, a young guitar-toting priest who led a pilgrimage from southern Poland, conceded that the church could not respond to such concerns by merely trying to dictate behavior. "People don't like it when something is imposed on them," he told me. "You have to choose a different road, more in partnership with your parishioners."

Rightly or wrongly, many young Poles still saw the pope, *their* pope, as the advocate of this more open approach, blaming local church leaders for contrary behavior. I talked to Agnieszka Borkowska, a seventeen-year-old who openly challenged the values of her Catholic upbringing. In religion class, she told me, she regularly sparred with the priest about the church's teachings on sexual issues and criticized the church for meddling too much in politics. Nonetheless, she pointed out that she had walked for four days with a pilgrimage from Krakow to Czestochowa, a distance of almost a hundred miles, to see John Paul. "The pope is wonderful," she proclaimed. "The pope is what we would like the church to be. He astounds me."

In the face of such enthusiasm, the pope demonstrated his appreciation by avoiding the kind of chastising tone of his previous visit in June. He did repeat his warnings about the dangers of capitalism, but he stressed to his audience, which was composed not just of Poles but also of a record number of young people from the former Soviet republics, the need to keep the faith and to continue the work of building Europe's "common house." He, too, seemed to have sensed that a church that wanted to appeal to the newly liberated young people of the region had to offer more hope than admonishment.

For all the controversy about the church's current role, I also encountered a deep-seated appreciation for what it represents, sometimes in surprising settings. At a Christmas party for journalists in a private apartment in Warsaw in 1991, this allegedly cynical group took part in the traditional sharing of the Christmas wafer, a local Catholic custom. In one corner of the room where I was standing, a woman journalist started to speak of her profoundly personal experience of joining a pilgrimage to Czestochowa a couple of years earlier, and added, "I'm uncomfortable with all these attacks on the church. I separate the institution, with all its human failings, and the idea. The church is on to something."

"Of course it is," another colleague interjected. "Otherwise, it would not have surived all these centuries."

As Poland becomes truly a part of Europe's "common house," the church will continue to survive. It will become more European, meaning that some of the faithful may lose a degree of the spiritual intensity that sustained them through not just decades but centuries of adversity. It will have to learn to live with more open ambivalence about its teachings, although the ambivalence itself is hardly new.

If it manages to do so, and to restrain some of its more self-destructive instincts, the church will be able to play the role it seeks in helping to shape the morality of the new era, even if the pope's warnings, like Havel's, about the spiritual dangers of Western-style consumer societies initially will fall largely on deaf areas; little else can be expected when for decades the Poles dreamed of having something, almost anything, to consume. The church will have to learn to accommodate diversity better than it has, while still maintaining the principles that have given the institution so much strength. That may be the overriding challenge for the Catholic Church everywhere in the world, but it is particularly true for the Polish church. In a country where the church has played such a special role, it will have to work doubly hard to maintain it.

Dressed in his green vestments, Vaclav Maly celebrated mass at St. Gabriel's, a high-ceilinged, neo-Romanesque church built by the Benedictines at the end of the last century on a hill in the Smihova district of Prague. Despite the Czechs' reputation as a nonreligious people, the church was full, on this particular Sunday morning during the summer of 1991, with a mixture of worshippers of all ages, and an assortment of baby carriages stood in the back. The high point of the mass was the baptism of eight young people, who ranged in age from late teens to early thirties. "Jesus Christ has made you into new people," Maly said simply as he concluded the ceremony. After mass, in front of the altar, the newly baptized and other parishioners shared cucumber sandwiches and pastries in a convivial, relaxed atmosphere. Having changed into a sweatshirt and loose pants, Maly received a steady stream of parishioners and visitors in the sacristy. He looked as modest and unpretentious as I had remembered him, but he also looked pleased, genuinely so, with the opportunity he felt had been granted to him to serve openly once again as a priest.

When I had known Maly in the 1980s, he had led quite a different life. As a young priest, he had become involved in the dissident movement, working with Havel and others to expose human-rights abuses; in response, the regime had formally defrocked him, forcing him to continue whatever priestly duties he could surreptitiously, while he took jobs such as cleaning latrines in the Prague metro to support himself. During the Velvet Revolution of 1989, he served as the popular spokesman of the Civic Forum, the movement that brought down the communist government. But he was not tempted to enter the world of politics, although he continued to maintain close personal ties with Havel and other members of the old dissident movement. Instead, he was eager to resume his calling, first serving as the pastor of St. Gabriel's in the largely working-class Smihova district, and later moving to St. Antonin's, Prague's largest parish.

His goal was to promote "a revival of Christianity," he told me, but he was under no illusions about the difficulties the church faced. First, there was the historical legacy to overcome. "Bohemian society is an atheistic society," he pointed out. Nominally, over a third of Czechs call themselves Catholics, making Catholicism the largest religion, but it is not considered part of the national identity as it is in Poland or, to a somewhat lesser extent, Slovakia. Since Jan Hus was branded a heretic and burned at the stake in 1415, Catholicism had more often been the religion of the conquering power. During the Hapsburg empire, Catholic bishops often spoke only German, not Czech, just as in Slovakia they usually spoke Hungarian, not Slovak. In the communist era, some priests, like Maly, fought the system, and an underground church existed, but others collaborated, joining the government-organized Pacem inTerris movement, which endorsed Prague's policies and sought to limit the influence of the Vatican. Even though a strong movement to liberate the church helped set the stage for the Velvet Revolution, the number of practicing Catholics remained small, particularly in Prague. Maly estimated that only about 1 percent of the city's population could be put in that category.

Maly conceded that the end of the communist era had produced a renewal of interest in religion, but he was careful not to overestimate its importance or hastily accept converts. He was wary of those proclaiming instant new faith. "You have to distinguish between people who are simply seeking new ideas and those who believe," he said. Referring to the eight people he had baptized at St. Gabriel's, he pointed out that he had prepared them by conducting classes for them for a full year. "You have to explain that this is a lifelong commitment. When someone is baptized, he should know what he believes in. I don't like fanaticism, but people should know what the Gospel is."

The church must also face a period of reassessment, he added. Although it is now free and seminaries have reopened, the priest shortage will continue for a long time. While rebuilding its structures and organization, it should focus on its broader spiritual mission of finding ways to contribute to the strengthening of positive trends in the society, not focusing merely on winning converts or on a narrow agenda. "Here certain words have been forgotten—forgiveness, love, trust," Maly said. "People had forty years of hatred of the class enemy. We have to renew the content of certain words, even reintroduce them into the vocabulary." He praised Havel for putting such emphasis on the honest use of words, reversing the process of their debasement. Such tasks, and the addressing of the problems of ordinary life, he argued, were more important than "just saying how people should live sexually, although that is important, too." Or than pushing for antiabortion legislation. "I am a priest and I am against abortion, but it would not be good to have a law against abortion. Society is not ready for it. It must be educated."

Dealing from a position of relative weakness, the church in Czechoslovakia demonstrated far more restraint in trying to rebuild its position than its counterpart in Poland. In Hungary, the church has demonstrated similar restraint. It is theoretically stronger, but may in reality suffer from some of the same weaknesses. Although the majority of the population is Catholic, the church has not played the kind of dominant role it has in Poland, and Hungarian society has been far more secularized. Despite the persecution of the church in the 1950s, which culminated in Cardinal Jozsef Mindszenty's seeking refuge at the United States Embassy when the 1956 revolution was crushed, and more recent conflicts with Catholic activists organized in "basic" communities who advocated conscientious objection to military service, the church was relatively free in the later communist period and suffered more traditional Western ills: a drop in vocations and a general loss of interest, particularly among the young.

The Hungarian churches, including the fairly large Protestant churches, did regain properties confiscated by the communists and, most significantly, many of their old schools. But there was a sense not so much of educators' trying to promote a specific creed as of their promoting broader values. As Oszkar Nikowitz, the director of a Catholic high school on the outskirts of Budapest, had told me, he was pushing not for converts but for the teaching of new behavior by example. "If we succeed in offering children attractive young teachers who are believers, this is something they can take seriously," he said. Istvan Bibo, the director at a Presbyterian high school in Budapest, was hesitant to describe promoting Christian values as his goal, since he felt that the word "Christian" was so overused and devalued. "In Hungary, there is even an organization of Christian stamp collectors," he pointed out. Instead, he defined his school's goal as "raising children to become people of integrity and responsibility."

The implicit assumption was that those qualities had been eroded during the previous decades, if not eradicated completely. Sorting out which behavior was a result of the communist system and which demanded a broader cultural, historical, or sociological explanation is nearly impossible, but there was a widespread conviction that communism had greatly contributed to the more negative tendencies, particularly undermining any sense of personal integrity and mutual responsibility. The concept of individuality had been progressively devalued, and with it individual self-esteem.

The consequences were felt in every area of life, including the most personal: patterns of sexual behavior. It was not that communist leaders openly espoused libertine practices, although some of Stalin's henchmen felt free to kidnap and rape at will, and the Brezhnev era was replete with tales of sexual entertainment organized for the elite. Whatever their personal behavior, most communist leaders quickly disassociated themselves from those early activists who had linked their goals of alleged political liberation with sexual liberation. As recounted by the German revolutionary Clara Zetkin, Lenin appeared genuinely disgusted when he met her to discuss "revolutionary" ideas about sexual behavior. "No doubt you have heard about the famous theory that in communist society satisfying sexual behavior and the craving for love is as simple and trivial as 'drinking a glass of water,' " he told her. "A section of our youth has gone mad, absolutely mad, over this 'glass of water theory.' It has been absolutely fatal to many a young boy and girl. . . . To be sure, thirst has to be quenched. But would a normal person normally lie down in the gutter and drink from a puddle? Or even from a glass whose edge has been greased by many lips? The drinking of water is really an individual matter. But it takes two people to make love, and a third person is likely to come into being. This deed has a social complexion and constitutes a duty to the community."

But if communist leaders could sound positively prudish at times, the system they created—through its utter contempt for human life and, on a more mundane level, the tedious daily existence it produced—encouraged a casual approach to sexual behavior that sometimes verged on the "glass of water" theory long after the theory itself had been virtually forgotten. When I talked to psychotherapist Helena Klimova at her clinic in Prague in June 1992, she offered an intriguing analysis of past and present sexual behavior based on the patients she saw. In the old system, she pointed out, "the opportunities for people to experience some adventure—to explore, to be creative, to do something new— were rather limited; they had no opportunities to start a business, for example. So they turned to the sexual sphere. There was a lot of promiscuity, because promiscuity had its creative and adventurous side. Now we do not see people turning to extramarital sex just because they have no other way of being adventurous."

I asked her if extramarital sex had really decreased. "Morals do not change so quickly," she responded. "But there are alternatives that did not exist before, including spirituality. There is not only the spirituality of churches which support family life and fidelity. Bohemian society is not very religious; we are more atheists. But even atheists can be spiritual, with a new value system that emphasizes the importance of the individual." She spoke of the impact of the writings of Czech philosophers like Jan Patocka and Ladislav Hejdanek, which appeared in samizdat, along with translations of Martin Buber, Freudian works, and Indian philosophers, not just on the dissident community but on many other Czechs who had sought an escape from the oppressive and demeaning official collective ideology. "If you take the individual as unique, as someone who cannot be traded for someone else, then it means more loyalty in sexual relations," she said. Unlike in the West, she concluded, the fear of contacting AIDS through casual sex was not particularly high, so any change in attitudes or behavior had to be ascribed to other causes.

Other social attitudes were also showing the first signs of change. In the communist system, where, even under relatively enlightened regimes, it was impossible to talk about the rule of law, crime was socially acceptable. The state was the number-one criminal, and many people felt that stealing or deceiving the state was perfectly normal behavior. In Poland, where the tradition of resistance against foreign oppressors was strongest, it was practically a patriotic duty. The police were natural enemies, certainly not protectors of the common good. But as open crime increased following the downfall of the old system and the discrediting of the old authorities, the police began to be seen in another light. The opinion polls indicating a higher approval rate for the police than for the church in Poland were not simply a product of the church's declining authority; they reflected a rise in respect for the police.

I noticed a change in my own attitude on the first day of spring in 1991, when I looked out of my office window overlooking Warsaw's Castle Square. Nearly three years before, I had witnessed from the same window the beating of worshippers leaving mass by a police force seeking to intimidate through sheer brutality. It had been an appalling spectacle. This time, groups of teenagers, including a scattering of skinheads, provoked and taunted the police, throwing rocks and engaging in the kind of mindless skirmishes that occur periodically in the West. My sympathy was entirely with the cops who were attempting to uphold public order.

The police will need more time to completely overcome their legacy as the political arm of a hated regime, and more training and equipment to be transformed into an effective fighter against ordinary crime. But the police force seems to be losing some of its hesitation about its new role. Piotr Kochanski, a young Polish lawyer who works for the Warsaw branch of the American law firm Hogan & Hartson, found encouraging signs in his dealings with policemen and prosecuters. They were beginning to understand that, under the new rules, the law was no longer simply something to be manipulated by higher political authorities at will. "For the first time, they are beginning to see that the law is a powerful instrument in their hands," he said, alluding to his firm's efforts to get them to enforce laws against counterfeiting popular products like Johnnie Walker whiskey. He left open the question how long it would take for people to feel that they were living in "a state of law" where the norms of acceptable behavior were clearly established for both ordinary citizens and the authorities, but that day no longer seems impossibly remote.

The most important ingredient in that process is the extent to which people begin to accept that they are themselves responsible for contributing to new standards of behavior. Psychotherapist Klimova was relatively optimistic on that subject as well. She acknowledged the crime wave caused by "heightened aggression" in the new era and the abandonment of more repressive policies that had kept large numbers of people in prison or in fear of punishment. "There certainly are people who needed this authority, and when it disappeared they went astray," she told me. "At the same time, many people are in the process of internalizing authority. They realize that we must make decisions for ourselves and nobody will do this for us. And that is a very good thing."

Whereas the changing attitudes toward sexual relations and criminal behavior were indicative of the deeper transformations taking palce, the real psychological test for the society at large, I felt, was somewhat different: how it would grapple with the issues of intolerance, to what extent it would be able to come to terms with its past and present phobias. If these new societies were to be based on the rule of law and sound moral values rooted in respect for the individual, they would have to, as Father Zieba had put it, learn to be tolerant. Given the history of the region, this did not come naturally or easily. The poisons and demons of the past still lurked within.

On a warm, sunny day in February 1992, I picked up Henryk Grynberg and we headed to a rural area only a short drive northeast of Warsaw but a world apart. In the towns and villages of what is known as the Eastern Mazowsze region, new prosperous-looking homes have cropped up, and their owners drive Polish Fiats and watch television programs beamed in by their satellite dishes, but much of the countryside looks not all that different from the way it did in an earlier era, when a peasant's world was severely circumscribed and only city folks seemed to have broader aspirations. Poorer farmers continue to live in tumbledown cottages and drive horse-drawn carts to market; they work hard, drink hard, and, when they open their mouths, reveal rotting teeth or no teeth at all.

The one really big difference is in the small towns of the region, where an entire sector of the old population has disappeared: almost all of the Jews who once lived in the houses on the main squares and worked as merchants or craftsmen perished in the Holocaust. There was only the occasional survivor like Henryk who wandered back for a brief visit.

I had first met Henryk, who by then was a well-known émigré poet, in Washington a few years earlier. Born in 1936, he had survived the war, studied journalism at Warsaw University, and worked as an actor in the State Jewish Theater until 1967, when the first signs of an officially inspired anti-Semitic campaign prompted him to take advantage of a theatrical visit to the United States to settle there; he had never returned to Poland until this visit in 1992. "For me, ages have passed since I left here," he told me as we drove out of Warsaw. "I wondered if I would ever return." At his home in suburban Virginia, he had become, in his own words, "the writer of the dead," recalling the Jewish lives that had vanished, and he had always been elusive on the queston whether he would ever visit Poland, whether he could confront the memories.

But a Polish television team had called him and requested that he retrace his personal odyssey for a documentary film, and he had agreed. He had already visited the rural area where his family had lived and then hidden during the war, with the film crew chronicling his journey and its most startling discoveries. On this particular day, he was returning without the cameras to try to follow up and see if he could learn more.

As we drove from village to village, checking on rumors or searching for mass graves where executed Jews had been dumped, Henryk recounted his family's story. His father had worked as a dairy middleman, traveling around the region purchasing milk from peasants, processing it himself, and then selling his products to retailers. His mother's father had been a Hasidic butcher, so he also traveled the region, buying calves. This meant that the family knew the peasants of the area well, which proved important for their chances once the deportations to Treblinka started in 1942, and they began a life literally on the run. Henryk was six, and his younger brother only about a year and a half, when they found themselves "running across fields," although in reality his father was carrying Henryk and his mother was carrying his younger brother.

Finding it difficult to carry the baby and fearing that its cries could cause them to be captured, Henryk's mother decided to stop at a farmhouse while her husband continued with Henryk to a peasant's cottage farther away. "A few days later, my mother joined us, but without my little brother," Henryk recalled, his face impassive. "My little brother couldn't be with her because he would cry, so he was left with the farmer's children."

In the following period, Henryk, his parents, and several other members of the family hid in the barn of a peasant named Gryz, who offered temporary refuge to many Jews and somehow managed to convince the Germans, when they questioned him, that he had no idea who had been camping out there. After one close call too many, Henryk's family spent almost the entire winter of 1942–43 in the woods, occasionally hiding in someone's cottage for a few nights, but mostly living in a dugout while his father made the rounds of the neighboring farms at night, scrounging for food. During his earlier return trip to the area, Henryk had even met a peasant woman who remembered her mother taking food into the forest to them. "I remember that food, too," Henryk recalled. "We were in a coniferous forest, and the needles from the trees were dropping into the pot."

The Germans caught several of Henryk's relatives, and that was not the only danger his family faced. Henryk's father knew the peasants well and tried to deal only with those he considered friendly and to avoid the others, but there were also roving bandits of various nationalities. Russian POWs who had escaped from a nearby camp robbed his father and left him naked. At that, he was lucky. Another group of escaped POWs caught his mother's youngest sister in the woods; when she began screaming, Henryk's grandfather ran out, and they shot him dead on the spot. Then, too, there were the more prosaic dangers of trying to survive in a lice-infested dugout in the winter.

Henryk's mother decided that she had to get him to Warsaw; otherwise, she felt, her son would not survive. She traveled ahead to the capital, obtaining fake IDs, and then sent her brother and a Polish woman, who posed as a couple, to pick up Henryk. When Henryk first saw his mother at the train station in Warsaw, he did not recognize her: she had dyed her hair blond, dressed elegantly, and wore a hat veil over her face. For two months, mother and son lived in the Praga section of Warsaw with the daughter of a Polish family from their town. During that time, the Warsaw ghetto uprising took place, and Henryk recalls driving by on occasion and seeing the smoke from the burning buildings. The hunt for Jews in hiding in other parts of the city intensified.

Suspecting that Henryk and his mother were Jewish, one of the neighbors told his mother to leave. "They didn't want to denounce us, but they wanted to get rid of us," Henryk said. "They were probably scared that the news would get out." With nowhere to go, they left and began riding the tram; his mother had thoughts of jumping with Henryk into the Vistula River, ending it all. Then she recalled the address of another woman who had relatives in her village. They found lodging there for two weeks, until the woman passed them on to another apartment. A *szmalcownik,* a blackmailer, spotted Henryk's mother on the street; he told her that he recognized her from her hometown and demanded she pay him the next day to keep quiet. Terrified, she pretended it was all a misunderstanding, but she immediately took up an earlier offer she had received for the two of them to be smuggled into the Polish territories incorporated into the Third Reich, to teach Polish village children illegally. She taught them both Polish and catechism, and she and Henryk regularly attended church, so as not to arouse suspicion. They were afraid not only of the Germans but also of right-wing Polish resistance units in the area who targeted Jews and communists along with the Nazi occupiers. Henryk went to confession and communion with the other children.

In 1944, as Soviet troops took the offensive in Poland, Henryk and his mother returned to their newly liberated region. They learned that several members of the family had died in the forest or been deported to Treblinka. Henryk's father had eluded the Germans, only to be murdered by "bandits" who had stripped him of his clothes, apparently thinking he might have money or valuables, and left his naked body lying in a pit by the road. There was no news of Henryk's baby brother.

During Henryk's visits to the area with the film crew, he learned more about the fate of both his father and brother. From fragmentary evidence he had obtained previously, he had long suspected that his father was murdered by a Polish peasant who had quarreled with him earlier and demanded his personal belongings, arguing that the Germans would take them anyway. Though the peasant had died a decade earlier, his younger brother, who was rumored to have at least witnessed the murder and perhaps even taken part in it, was alive; Henryk visited him. He neither confirmed nor denied the story, but his grandson quickly broke up the conversation and kicked Henryk and the film crew off their land.

A team of diggers began searching for the remains of Henryk's father in the general area where local inhabitants claimed he had been buried. At first, the search seemed futile, but, during the digging, a man of about Henryk's age came by and told him that he knew the precise location. He vividly recalled how, on the way to school one day, he had seen Henryk's father being buried; after the body was lowered into the ground, someone had kicked an empty milk bottle in with it. For Henryk, that detail removed all doubt: he remembered that his father had always carried the bottle with him during the war, hoping to fill it on his nightly rounds.

As the cameras rolled, the diggers began working at that spot. Soon one cried: "The bottle is here." Henryk descended into the pit and dug out his father's remains with his own hands. He subsequently reburied them in a proper grave at the Jewish cemetery in Warsaw. "I feel a relief at having discharged my duty, for burying my father was my duty," Henryk said. He took the milk bottle, which he termed his most treasured inheritance, back home with him to suburban Virginia.

During the filming, Henryk also heard a story about a child that fit his brother's description. The boy had been abandoned near a mill, and a woman had taken him home. But everyone knew the child was Jewish, and soon the locals decided that he had to be handed over to the mayor in the nearby town of Jadow. One of the local farmers told Henryk that he had later heard people at the market saying that a German officer named Stein, who was known for his brutality, was "leading the son of Abraham"; Abraham was Henryk's father. The farmer said he had seen Stein take the boy out near a garbage heap and shoot him. But Henryk was not entirely sure this was his brother; he hoped against hope that another boy he heard about—Jewish, of about the same age, hidden and then adopted by a peasant family—was his brother.

One purpose of our trip was to try to pin this down. However, when we found some relatives of the family that had adopted the Jewish boy, who had indeed survived the war but died in an accident a few years ago, their descriptions left no doubt that this was not Henryk's brother. We drove to Jadow and, with the help of some locals, found the place where Stein had shot his victims. Lucjan Plonski, a man born in 1933, remembered Stein, the other Germans, and their victims, and told us, "I saw children with broken skulls lying in the street—it was terrible."

Plonski led us out of the town to a forest of birch and pine trees where the murdered Jews were buried. The earth was sunken in several places, suggesting mass graves, and tombstones were scattered about in disarray. One, still standing amid the overgrown memorial, read: "Berta and Rubin Berenstein, to parents murdered in 1942 by the Hitlerites." Up till that point, Henryk had not explained to Plonski what exactly he was looking for. When Plonski asked, he replied: "My brother is probably buried here." As the last rays of afternoon sunshine filtered through the trees, Plonski and I left Henry alone with his thoughts.

"I've completed my pilgrimage," Henryk said as he climbed back into my car for the return trip to Warsaw. "Only now."

At first he was silent on the way back, but then began to share some reflections about his return to Poland and the complicated, painful history of Poles and Jews. He found the designation "Poles and Jews" perfectly natural, not offensive, since the country's Jewish community, the largest in the world, had never really assimilated, although there had been intermarriages and many people could find traces of both cultures in their family history. It was part of "a bilateral process," he pointed out. "Jews were isolated, and Jews isolated themselves," he said, referring to the fact that many did not even speak Polish.

He was grateful for the reception he had received from an enthusiastic audience when he held readings in Warsaw and other cities. "As a writer, I was received in such a moving and friendly way that I was deeply surprised. That moved me deeply and convinced me that I was their writer, a Polish writer who has his readers in Poland, and that, at least in that respect, I did not make a mistake in my life," he said, alluding to his decision to keep writing in Polish abroad. "And that my toil—my work, which may have seemed suspended in a vacuum—was not in fact wasted, that it was reaching someone."

As for the broader implications of his personal experience, his family's range of encounters with Poles—from those like the peasant Gryz who had risked his and his family's lives to shelter Jews, to those who turned them away or, in his father's case, resorted to murder—he began on a cautious note. "I remain convinced, as I have been for a long time, that Poland is a very pluralistic society, where you meet people with highly differing views and contrasting moral and intellectual levels," he said. "There was great heroism, much more than could have been expected in those particular conditions from anyone. Those [who sheltered Jews] were not average or normal people." But he also denounced the "shared guilt of all those who created anti-Semitism in European Christian culture," and the lingering, primitive anti-Semitism that continued even when most of the Jewish community had vanished.

He was still understandably bitter about the official revival of anti-Semitism in 1967 and 1968, when a communist hard-line faction had launched an "anti-Zionist" campaign as a pretext for orchestrating new purges. It was not enough simply to write this off as a product of the communist era, he argued; the new Polish government had to "cleanse itself." He found the statements to date on that subject woefully inadequate.

But the subject of Polish behavior during the war remained his central preoccupation. The heroism of those who hid Jews, he suggested, was not enough to balance the behavior of others. "I'd stress that their heroism consisted not only in resistance to the Nazis but also in resistance to their fellow countrymen, whom they often had to fear more than the Nazis. Because the Nazis by themselves would be hard put to find traces of Jews in hiding, while evil, resentful, or envious neighbors were much more dangerous. Jews were first concealed from neighbors and only in the second instance from the Nazis. And that's perhaps the most tragic thing of all."

As we approached Warsaw, he continued in that vein. "I know many instances of people who had hidden Jews throughout the whole war and then asked that no one be told. The pressure was so strong that even after the war it was very awkward, especially in a small community, to be seen as someone who had helped the Jews during the occupation." Both during and after the war, he concluded, people took pride in identifying themselves as resistance fighters, but not those whose heroism had consisted of quietly sheltering Jews.

For better or worse, history lives with a singular intensity in Poland. The debate over what happened during the war continues to color not only Jewish-Polish relations today but also how the Poles see themselves and how they are seen by others. If Henryk's harsh assessments of Polish attitudes flowed from personal experiences that could not be denied, his personal conclusions are wide open to dispute. Other personal experiences suggest different conclusions, or at least serious modifications in them. To achieve consensus on such issues is neither possible nor necessarily desirable, but a variety of perspectives need to be considered, or at least allowed to coexist, if Poland is to come to terms with its past and manage to keep prejudice and intolerance in check, now and in the future.

The broader backdrop of Polish-Jewish relations, with widely disparate interpretations of their shared history, fuels the debate about the war years. In extremely simplified, generalized form, two major opposing interpretations exist. What can be termed the Polish Catholic viewpoint emphasizes Poland's long record as a land of refuge for Jews, beginning with the great migration of Jews from Western Europe in the thirteenth century, and a land of tolerance, where Jews were sometimes granted special privileges by Polish monarchs and nobles. What can be termed the Jewish viewpoint emphasizes the steady growth of anti-Semitism in Polish society, especially when Poland re-emerged as an independent state between the two world wars. In their most extreme manifestations, often triggered by the debate over the war years, those interpretations produced the conviction among some Poles that Jews are virulently anti-Polish, seeking to besmirch their entire history, while reinforcing the view among some Jews that the Poles are virulent anti-Semites intent on whitewashing that history.

In fact, the two interpretations are not necessarily so much at odds with each other as their proponents contend. For centuries, Poland was a haven for Jews, but anti-Semitism was always present, and grew especially in modern times. In earlier periods, the Jews were often seen as allies of the nobility, and suffered accordingly during the Cossack uprising of 1648. From the late eighteenth century, when Poland was partitioned by its neighbors, Polish nationalism inevitably grew narrower in focus as it struggled to preserve the concept of a Polish nation that had been declared extinct. Their Catholicism was a key ingredient of their identity, and Polish Catholicism tended to view Jews as, at the very least, suspect in their loyalties.

Although Poland's Marshal Jozef Pilsudski, the leader of the newly independent Poland for most of the period between the two world wars, envisaged a multinational state and rejected chauvinist doctrines, the clamor from the extreme right kept growing. The National Democratic

Party of Roman Dmowski led the way in propounding racist theories, which helped create the climate for openly anti-Semitic policies, like separate benches for Jewish students at universities, that emerged after Pilsudski's death in 1935. A plaque commemorating Dmowski that still hangs in St. John's Cathedral in Warsaw offers his narrow definition of "Polishness," which was at the core of his beliefs: "Catholicism is not an addition to Polishness but is embedded in its essence. An attempt to separate Catholicism from Polishness . . . constitutes the destruction of the very essence of the nation." Nonetheless, as Aleksander Smolar, a Jewish political scientist who emigrated from Poland in the aftermath of the anti-Semitic campaign of 1968, wrote: "The prewar history of the Jews in Poland was not very different from the history of Jews among many other nations."

The distrust between the two communities grew during the war, particularly in eastern Poland, which was occupied by the Soviet Union from 1939 to 1941 as a consequence of the Molotov-Ribbentrop Pact. Although Jews were among the victims of the Soviet occupiers, the primary target for massive deportations to labor camps inside the Soviet Union were Polish Catholics; in some cases, local Jews embraced the communist cause and were seen as collaborators in this process. The high-profile presence of Jews in the puppet regime installed by Stalin near the end of the war, especially their prominent role in key positions of the secret police, only reinforced the charge of anti-Semitic Poles that "Jewish communists" were responsible for their fate.

Such theories were self-serving and specious. Poles, for instance, were not about to embrace the extreme Russian nationalist view that, because Felix Dzerzhinsky, the founder of the Cheka, the original Bolshevik secret police, was a Polish nobleman, Poles and other outsiders, not Russians, were responsible for communist crimes in their country. This double standard, Polish-born historian Wladyslaw Bartoszewski points out, conveniently ignored the fact that the majority of secret policemen of the new Polish regime were Polish gentiles, and "enabled Poles to ignore their own participation in Stalinist crimes." But reason and fairness are often in short supply when Polish-Jewish relations are debated, particularly the wartime record.

Still, there were extraordinary acts of courage that transcended those recriminations. Walking through Jerusalem's Yad Vashem, the memorial to the Holocaust victims, a visitor cannot help being struck by the large number of trees planted in tribute to Poles who risked their lives to save Jews. In the summer of 1992, I met Helena Sleszynska, the manager of a butcher shop in Czestochowa, whose name, along with that of her deceased father, figures on one of the plaques in front of a tree there. Born in 1930, she was only twelve when her father, who was active in the Home Army resistance movement, decided to try to save Sonia Broder, the six-year-old daughter of a Jew he knew from the prewar days who had appealed for his help. He sent Helena into the ghetto in Czestochowa before it was closed, since she could more easily lead Sonia out without arousing suspicion. "My father asked me if I wanted a sister," Helena recalls. "It was a horrible situation: we all knew what the penalty was." The penalty for hiding Jews was death.

As she fondly brought out snapshots of her visit to Tel Aviv, where she had been invited by Sonia in 1986, Helena recalled the arguments her father's decision had prompted. Her mother had opposed the move, fearing for the family's survival; she was so frightened that initially, after Sonia started living with them, she spent a good deal of time in the countryside; one of Helena's brothers left altogether. Her father remained unmoved; he had vowed to Sonia's father to try to save her. "If God permits, we will live through this," he told the family. Helena remembers living in constant fear, often praying on the way back from school that she would find her house and its inhabitants still intact. They heard about other people in Czestochowa who had been executed for hiding Jews. One night, it looked as if everyone would perish. German soldiers burst in before Sonia could be awakened to take up her customary hiding place behind a closet; but they were only looking for an escaped Russian POW, and they ignored the black-haired child asleep in bed.

Helena knew that, as Henryk Grynberg had pointed out, dangers lurked everywhere, including from Poles who might denounce them. But her experience with Sonia indicated that neighbors could also be allies. "All our neighbors knew about Sonia," she recalls. But no one informed. When the war ended, Sonia was reunited with her parents, who had also miraculously survived. But Helena does not have an idealized vision of her fellow countrymen. Though some were brave and decent, she says, others tried to ingratiate themselves with the German occupiers by denouncing those who hid Jews. She also still shakes her head sadly when contemplating an event like the Kielce pogrom of 1946, when a Polish mob killed forty-two Jews. She is trying to fathom the source of such hatred, and admits that she had not even heard of that tragedy until her trip to Israel.

Marek Edelman, the last surviving leader of the Warsaw ghetto uprising of 1943, has often spoken out about what he terms are the unfair characterizations of Polish behavior during the war. "Take a city like

Warsaw, where on the Aryan side twelve thousand Jews found refuge," he told me, and calculated that on average several people had to be involved in the hiding of a single Jew. "That meant a hundred thousand Poles were involved in that. So one-seventh of the community took a risk to save somebody. Now, that is a very good proportion, very good."

Edelman, who had resolutely stayed on in Poland, is often attacked by fellow Jews and accused of presenting the Poles in too favorable a light. But his views are hardly one-dimensional. "The majority of Poles were indifferent," he said. "You also had the bandits who made money out of that, scoundrels who denounced people, killed them. Naturally, there were scum and bandits—but there were also a large group of society that helped. And, anyway, you had people like that in every country." To those who criticize the Polish Home Army, the resistance, for not doing enough to help the ghetto fighters, he countered that it provided the only significant arms shipment to them. "If it wasn't for the Home Army, there couldn't have been an uprising," he said.

The Home Army issued orders that *szmalcownicy,* those who blackmailed or denounced Jews, should be executed, and it desperately sought to convince the Western powers of what was happening in the death camps, but commanders of some units would not accept Jews into their units. Edelman also pointed out that right-wing extremists formed their own units which killed Jews. Along with the acts of courage, this was a part of the Polish wartime history that had to be acknowledged. Nonetheless, he warned against seeing everything that had happened in the chaotic wartime conditions, when killing was commonplace, as solely a plot against Jews; sometimes the violence was for no discernible reason, or at least no reason that could be neatly categorized as having to do with ethnic or political motives. "It was war, and human life had little value," he said.

Even when killing was part of a larger strategy, the motives could be disputed. On a visit to the small Jewish museum in the Lithuanian capital of Vilnius, I met Rachel Margolis, who was born in that city in 1921 and grew up there during the period between the wars when it was part of Poland. She was Jewish, and had joined a unit of Russian partisans during the Nazi occupation. She accused the Polish Home Army units in the area of killing Jews. "They would shoot at us because we were Russians and Jews," she told me. But Home Army units were fighting a two-front war, trying to liberate Poland from its Nazi occupiers and to prevent their replacement by Soviet occupiers. Whatever the attitudes of individual commanders toward Jews, they were exchanging fire with Soviet units because they saw them as the enemy, the vanguard of a force that was seeking to crush them, and would eventually succeed in that task. In this particular case, they probably neither knew nor cared about the ethnic composition of the units.

The Poles, Edelman argued, are "as xenophobic as any other nation. And, just as any other nationality that is subjugated and has to prove its existence through nationalism, they could not be tolerant." Or, putting it in somewhat different terms, he added: "The Polish people are as tolerant as any other people." But he claimed that the Polish record was no worse and, in many cases, better than that of other nations. Baltic and Russian units had been formed to serve the German cause, but no comparable Polish force of collaborators was ever assembled. Unlike in France or Slovakia, there was no puppet regime that carried out German orders. This does not mean there were no cases of individual collaboration or, as in the case of the murder of Henryk Grynberg's father, numerous crimes committed by Poles against Jews. The record is mixed, neither the glorious tale of uniform resistance that is sometimes presented by the Poles, nor the tale of unrelenting hostility toward the Jews that is sometimes presented by their harshest critics.

I asked Edelman whether he thought that, if their roles had somehow been reversed, a greater proportion of Jews would have risked their lives to save Poles than had been the case with Poles helping Jews. "No, men are men," he said.

Even historians like Bartoszewski, who are scrupulously fair in illuminating the darker side of Polish behavior, point out that Jews who present indictments of the Poles are also guilty of applying double standards. They are far less harsh in their treatment of Jewish leaders and members of the Jewish police who cooperated with the Germans in providing Jews for deportation in the hopes of saving others. "Jews of the ghetto, come to your senses. Volunteer for the transports," implored Mordechai Chaim Rumkowski, the controversial leader of the Lodz ghetto, who was the most avid practitioner of this policy. Adam Czerniakow, his counterpart in the Warsaw ghetto, committed suicide rather than follow a similar course.

Nonetheless, many Poles remain painfully aware of the callous indifference with which many of their countrymen dismissed the fate of the Jews. It was not that the Poles, as they themselves perished by the millions, could have saved the Jews. But the gnawing sense of unease remains, reflected in Czeslaw Milosz's evocative poem "Campo dei Fiori." Comparing the continuation of daily life in Rome as people were burned at the stake to life in Warsaw during the ghetto uprising, he wrote:

I thought of the Campo dei Fiori
in Warsaw by the carousel
one clear spring evening
to the strains of a carnival tune.
The bright melody drowned
the salvos from the ghetto wall,
and couples were flying
high in the cloudless sky.

At times wind from the burning
would drift dark kites along
and riders in the carousel
caught petals in midair.
That same hot wind
blew open the skirts of the girls
and the crowds were laughing
on that beautiful Warsaw Sunday.

And that indifference continued in the postwar years, encouraged by communist authorities who deliberately downplayed Jewish suffering and, at times, stirred up anti-Semitism in a country where most of those Jews who had survived eventually emigrated, leaving only a tiny community of a few thousand. The war years continued to leave their mark, erupting, for instance, in the dispute over the Carmelite convent bordering the Auschwitz camp in the late 1980s. The specific dispute about the convent reflected much deeper divisions. Jews resented Polish tendencies to "Polonize" the Holocaust, blurring the difference between the Nazi treatment of Jews and Poles. While Jews were marked for annihilation, Poles were destined for enslavement—with deadly results, but there was no policy of total extermination. Poles resented what they saw as Jewish efforts to present themselves as the sole victims. Reasonable Jews and Catholics, who acknowledged legitimate concerns on both sides, had a hard time making themselves heard in such debates.

In the communist era, Polish-Jewish relations were only one of many areas of vast falsification and glaring omissions. The Home Army veterans, for example, often had to conceal their wartime records and listen to myths about how the "People's Army," the far smaller communist-organized resistance, had allegedly led the fight against the Nazi occupiers. In that climate, it was easy for counterconspiracy theories to emerge, like the notion that Jewish communists were practically alone responsible for the repression of the postwar era. The moral confusion of those times helped create a climate in which, as Polish historian Andrzej Bryk has written, "anti-Semitism became a matter of opinion, not a moral crime." That probably was the greatest crime of all, allowing the poison of anti-Semitism to continue to infect the minds of too many Poles for far too long.

During the presidential election campaign that pitted Lech Walesa against Tadeusz Mazowiecki in the fall of 1990, my wife, Christina, was driving from her hometown of Czestochowa back to Warsaw and offered a ride to a student hitchhiker. He was attending his final year of law school in the eastern Polish city of Bialystok, and he soon announced that he was an avid supporter of Walesa. "Poland should be governed by a Pole," he said.

"Who is a Pole?" my wife asked, her radar instantly up to the insinuation that Mazowiecki did not qualify on that score, since a widespread rumor campaign had identified him as Jewish. The student's definition of a Pole was someone who was born in Poland, whose allegiance is to Poland, and who is a Catholic. He quickly explained that he considered himself a prime example: he fought against the communists, he was beaten by the police, and he attended mass regularly.

And what about those whose origins might not fit that profile? The student volunteered that a friend whose family comes from Byelorussia was afraid to join the student organization at his university because his name didn't sound Polish. "I feel sorry for him, but, on the other hand, I understand if people don't take him for a real, pure Pole," he said.

My wife pointed out that there had already been a European leader in this century who had insisted on racial purity. "Yes, you are right," he replied. "But the Germans and the Russians couldn't conquer our sense of Polishness; we were such proud Poles that we preserved our language and our culture under the threat of prison and exile to Siberia; so you have to understand that a Pole wants to be a Pole."

He was convinced that questions about people's "origins" were perfectly legitimate, and he criticized Adam Michnik, the editor of *Gazeta Wyborcza* and a Mazowiecki supporter, for calling questions about his family origins "anti-Semitic." "His father's name was Szechter, but his name is Michnik," he said, as if that automatically overruled the objections. Although he used his mother's name, Michnik had never hid his mixed Catholic-Jewish family background—but anti-Semites were constantly "discovering" the Jewish origins of their opponents.

The conversation seemed not only depressing but predictable—that is, until the student prepared to get out of the car. Before doing so, he wrote down his name and phone number, suggesting to Christina that I look him up in Bialystok. His name, which he had not mentioned before, was Szymon Zyberyng. "You think that your name is pure Polish?" Christina asked.

"You know, I have some problems with my name," he admitted. "Some people take me for a German, some take me for a Jew, but I'm Polish. My father says that we don't have anything Jewish in us, but someone from my family told me that I should go to Israel and look for my roots. But, no matter what, I know that I'm Polish."

Like many Polish-Americans, I had wanted to believe that many of the stories about Polish anti-Semitism were exaggerated, that the disease had largely disappeared from the Polish soul. But seeing how easily conspiracy theories could be aroused during the presidential campaign, and how even someone named Szymon Zyberyng could talk about "real Poles," I reluctantly concluded that the poison was stronger than I had anticipated. Mazowiecki and his supporters had no real way of countering the rumors that he was Jewish. If they accurately denied those rumors, it would sound as if they were admitting that it would be bad if he were in fact Jewish. Since they largely remained silent, the whispering campaign grew louder and louder. Nor was there any way for them to convince people that it should not make a difference to them if Mazowiecki were Jewish. The voters who believed the rumors were the ones for whom it did make a difference. Mazowiecki would have been defeated even without this phony issue, but after talking to people around the country, I was convinced that it had contributed to the size of his defeat.

Although anti-Semitism subsided as an issue after the campaign, opinion polls indicated that during the subsequent two years the number of Poles who believed that Jews were too influential in Polish political and economic life actually grew. The phenomenon of "anti-Semitism without Jews" persisted. This was not unique to Poland. In Slovakia, anti-Semitic feelings were expressed by an even larger proportion of the population. In Hungary, where about a hundred thousand Jews still live, anti-Semitism was less evident, despite the periodic charges and countercharges in the political debate. Unlike their counterparts in Slavic countries, Hungarian Jews had been much more assimilated into the society, speaking Hungarian instead of Yiddish in modern times. This meant that anti-Semitism, though by no means completely absent, did not resonate so strongly. "People do not say that Hungarian Jews are not Hungarians," noted philosopher Gaspar Mikos Tamas, a Hungarian Jew and prominent member of the Alliance of Free Democrats, the country's main opposition party. "That would be manifestly absurd in this country."

But neither the Hungarians nor the Czechs, who demonstrated less anti-Semitism than the Slovaks, were free of other forms of racism. In Budapest, the police recorded twenty-two attacks by skinheads against dark-skinned foreign students and gypsies during the first six months of 1992, which they admitted probably constituted only about half or as little as a third of all attacks. During the previous two years, such attacks had become increasingly commonplace, with African and other Third World students forming a Martin Luther King Society to try to report them and pressure the authorities for more effective countermeasures. President Arpad Goncz apologized to the students "in the name of the Hungarian people" and even became the honorary president of the society, but many politicians continued to dismiss the violence as isolated incidents, and the police claimed they were powerless to do anything about them. It was not until March 1992 that the parliamentary commission on human rights provided the students with a forum for their grievances.

Skinheads behaved in similar fashion in Prague and other Czech cities. During a flurry of incidents in late 1991, some young Asian-Americans, who were among the many Americans who had flocked to Prague to teach English or find jobs in new businesses, expressed fears about riding the subway or going to bars. Complaining that he had to spend his weekends "in my flat-turned-prison," Mark Yamamoto, a Japanese-American working for an Austrian company, pleaded in a piece in the English-language weekly *The Prague Post:* "In a corner of the world which so recently liberated itself from the constricton of a conformist system, do the natives really wish to expel those of us who are different?" Some Asian-Americans claimed that the fears were exaggerated and that they felt free to go where they pleased, but they admitted that they were conscious that they could be targeted.

In Poland, the plight of a small but growing number of AIDS victims provided a different kind of demonstration of intolerance. When an antidrugs organization attempted to open shelters for children infected with AIDS in small towns in 1992, local residents staged violent protests, vandalizing the houses that were to have been used as shelters. With no knowledge of the disease, they expressed a variety of fears, ranging from a drop in real-estate values to the contamination of the local water supply.

Arguably, Western societies manifest many of the same symptoms of intolerance, sometimes including violence on a larger scale. Skinheads are a transplant of a Western phenomenon, and AIDS victims have had to fight hard to win acceptance in American and Western European communities. Nor has anti-Semitism been eliminated. The case can be made that the level of overt anti-Semitism in Poland, which is visible in a significant minority of the population, is on an approximate par with the level of anti-Semitism in France, a country that has long been infected with similar prejudices.

But there is a significant difference. In France, political and religious leaders immediately mobilize to denounce anti-Semitic incidents. Under the old regimes, Eastern European nations neither acknowledged nor attempted to combat their basest instincts; in many cases, they did exactly the opposite, deliberately stirring up anti-Semitism. Thus, no natural defense mechanisms developed to counter manifestations of racism or other forms of intolerance. The one institution in Poland that could have filled that role, the Catholic Church, has largely failed to do so—or even to make a sharp break with its own xenophobic traditions. If many Polish clerics have contributed to the Jewish-Christian dialogue and attempted to promote genuine understanding, some continue to manifest old attitudes. During the presidential election campaign, the church did not speak up forcefully against the anti-Semitic rumblings. The Polish bishops issued a strong pastoral letter denouncing anti-Semitism in January 1991, but the tardiness of the response meant that it could not undo the damage.

As an institution, the church demonstrated a similar failure in its response to the issue of shelters for AIDS children. Some individual priests, like Father Arkadiusz Nowak, responded magnificently to the challenge, taking charge of an AIDS shelter and working to promote acceptance of the victims and to dispel popular myths. But, speaking to the pilgrims assembled at Czestochowa in August 1992, Cardinal Glemp demonstrated as much insensitivity on the subject as he had in dealing with Jewish protests about the presence of the Carmelite convent at Auschwitz a few years earlier. "AIDS is a disease that is spread because of the lack of moral values," he declared, and offered his backing to those who opposed the location of shelters in populated areas. Though he talked vaguely about a need to develop a general strategy to deal with the disease, he concentrated on his call for stricter norms of sexual behavior, failing to demonstrate any compassion for the victims, including the infected infants.

After his homily evoked sharply negative coverage in the Polish press, Glemp tried to repair the damage by saying that it would be a "gross simplification to maintain that AIDS is God's punishment for sin," and that its victims deserve "not only tolerance but love." However, this was hardly enough to counter the contrary impression left by his earlier message.

Others proved more responsive. Government officials like veteran Solidarity activist Jacek Kuron, along with famous actors and other public figures, made televised appeals for new understanding, seeking to dispel the more egregious myths about how the disease is spread. Rock groups from around the country staged a giant benefit for AIDS victims on the same weekend Glemp delivered his homily on the subject.

The danger exists that intolerance could gain momentum. In the case of anti-Semitism, Edelman points out, the threat is to the Poles, not the Jews, since there are so few of the latter left in Poland. "It's the Poles who are threatened," he told me. "The threat is that they could isolate themselves from the European world and create a 'bulwark of Christianity' here. They'd close themselves off from Europe." But Edelman and many other Poles who shared his concerns were inclined to believe that this would not happen, that the poison of intolerance could be contained.

The society was beginning the process of developing countermeasures, and many Poles demonstrated an eagerness to learn more about a part of their history that had been ignored or falsified during the communist era. In 1992, the Jewish Historical Institute in Warsaw began running special classes for schoolteachers from around the country about Jewish history and culture, eliciting an enthusiastic response. In early 1993, the Polish episcopate asked the institute to organize similar classes for its religious instruction teachers. There was also an outpouring of new publications on Judaism and an upsurge of Polish-Israeli exchanges. As the immediate crisis atmosphere of the political and economic transition receded, the more positive trends gained momentum.

In their struggle to overthrow the old system, the Poles and other nationalities had insisted on the need for historical truth. I still found many of them willing to try to confront truths that were less flattering and more painful for the society as a whole than the tradition of resistance to foreign and domestic tyrants. In order to develop healthy societies, old poisons must be acknowledged so they can be neutralized—or at least kept in check, as they normally are in Western societies. By that measure, a gradual healing looked possible, even probable, although nothing about the process was inevitable or necessarily irreversible.

NEIGHBORS

WHEN I LANDED for the first time at Warsaw Airport in 1964, I was startled to see a plane emblazoned with the lettering "UNITED STATES OF AMERICA" on the tarmac. It turned out that I had arrived on the same day as Robert Kennedy, who had dropped in for a short visit. Although the Polish authorities had carefully avoided publicizing his arrival and itinerary, Radio Free Europe and the Voice of America had not been so circumspect. On the next day, I followed the crowds to Warsaw's huge Old Market Square in the reconstructed old town, which was packed from end to end with people. As Kennedy emerged from St. John's Cathedral, where he had attended mass, I found myself literally lifted off my feet by the surging crowd chanting "Kennedy, Kennedy." Twice I dangled above the ground, both exhilarated and frightened. Ever since, I have been drawn to the edge of excited crowds but instinctively hesitate to be drawn in.

This was my introduction to a lesson that still strikes me as a good starting point for any examination of how Poles and other Eastern Europeans see the world, their neighbors near and far. The lesson is simple: the Poles have a long-standing love affair with *Ameryka*. As a seventeen-year-old discovering the land of his parents, I was initially somewhat reluctant to understand what I was experiencing during the rest of my visit that summer. I was not eager to admit that I was the beneficiary not just of the magic of the Kennedy name, which possessed an intense emotional resonance in the wake of JFK's assassination, but also of the deeper magic of the word *Ameryka*. When Poles would solemnly declare that I had the "Kennedy look," something that no one had ever noticed back home, I chalked it up to their perspicacity. When young women flashed dazzling smiles after they heard me described as an *Amerykanin*, I simply figured that Polish women had much better taste than American high-school girls.

But soon I had, somewhat sorrowfully, to concede that other factors were at work, since the evidence was just too overwhelming. No country in the world was as unabashedly pro-American as the Polish People's Republic, and the only ones that came close were the neighboring people's republics. The communist era elevated the myth of *Ameryka* to the status of supermyth, a blind faith and set of common assumptions that are only just beginning to undergo some mildly critical scrutiny now that people's democracies are no more. The legacy of that period is that *Ameryka* is associated with everything positive and far away, and considered the antithesis of all that is sinister and nearby.

Ameryka means wealth and success. Meeting someone who is turned out in fancy clothes or drives a new car, a Pole would say: "I see that *Ameryka* has opened up to you." A relative of mine went to a wedding in the countryside durng the communist era, when shortages were still the norm. As the guests heaped on huge helpings of food, the bride's father muttered: "Where do they think they are—in *Ameryka?*"

Ameryka also means a state of mind, embracing not just freedom but also civility, in a society based on constitutional rights. If under the old regime a Pole demanded to be treated with respect and talked back to a petty bureaucrat, the bureaucrat was likely to bark: "What do you think, that this is *Ameryka?*" The assumption about the meaning of *Ameryka* was shared by both parties in such an exchange.

The more that communist governments would attempt to counteract such thinking by talking about the horrors of American life, the less they were believed. Polish writer Ryszard Kapuscinski recalls how a friend, a Polish journalist, arrived in New York for his first visit to the United States in 1980 thoroughly convinced that all the reports in the Polish press about the crime rate there were "communist lies." The first thing he did to disprove those "lies" was to take the subway to the South Bronx. Before he even reached his destination, he was mugged and beaten in the train. "Those are the ironies of communist propaganda," Kapuscinski observed.

Successive attempts by communist officials to discredit their opponents as American puppets or agents also backfired. Solidarity's support of American economic sanctions against Poland in the wake of the imposition of martial law in 1981 was widely applauded, despite the government's efforts to portray Washington as the cause of the country's economic disarray. Anti-American posters had to be displayed on the inside of shop windows; otherwise, they were immediately torn down. By the time of the first partially free elections, in 1989, communist officials were tacitly acknowledging reality and doing everything to obscure their true affiliation. One communist, an author of several books about the United States that reflected the norms of political correctness of an earlier era, promoted his candidacy by posing against a backdrop of American flags.

Above all, *Ameryka* represented the forces of good versus the all-too-familiar forces of evil at home and across the Soviet border. When Ronald Reagan began speaking of "the evil empire," Poles were ecstatic that finally an American president was echoing what they had been saying all along. Every East-West confrontation was seen through that prism. In the early 1980s, when West Germans took to the streets to protest the deployment of American medium-range missiles in their country, Poles contemptuously dismissed their concerns. "Better a Pershing than a Soviet soldier in your back yard," they were fond of saying.

Poles were far from alone in equating America with freedom. Hungarian film director Zsolt Kezdi-Kovacs pointed out that his parents' generation firmly believed at first that the Americans would liberate them from communism. "I remember my parents saying that one day General Eisenhower will come on his white horse," he recalled. Although the failure of Americans to intervene when Soviet troops crushed the 1956 uprising disillusioned many Hungarians, America still remained the symbol of freedom throughout the region. After the Velvet Revolution, when the citizens of the Czech town of Pilsen were finally free to commemorate the liberation of their city by American troops at the end of World War II, they did so with abandon. Young Americans in Prague joked that any American was guaranteed a one-night stand in Pilsen. Even in once-isolated Albania, the joyful anticommunist victors of the first free elections, in March 1992, rushed around Tirana waving an American flag.

In the new era, Eastern Europeans welcomed almost everything American, often with little regard to its value. In the space of one week in February 1991, I attended three gala premieres in Warsaw: of the film *Dick Tracy,* which, although it had flopped in the United States, drew a decked-out audience of the new capitalist class and cultural elite, and was replete with a Madonna lookalike cigarette seller and a jazz band in 1930s attire; of the Sam Shepard play *Tooth of Crime,* a pointless and pretentious piece of work, at least in its Polish version, which also brought out everyone who was anyone in Warsaw; and of *Metro,* an American-style musical, something of a cross between *Chorus Line* and *Hair,* which made up for its lack of originality with its sheer exuberance and dazzling laser lighting effects produced by Laser Media, the American company that handles the likes of Pink Floyd and Michael Jackson.

The last of those shows, *Metro,* proved to be the smash of Warsaw, playing to packed houses for more than a year. Even after its producers got carried away and in April 1992 moved the show to Broadway, where it was panned by the critics and forced to close after ten days, *Metro* continued its run in Poland. Poles also enjoyed the fact that *Metro* was staged at the theater in the Palace of Culture, the massive wedding-cake-shaped symbol of the despised Stalinist era. (An old joke asks: "Where can you see the best view of Warsaw?" The answer: "From the top of the Palace of Culture, because that is the only place where you won't see the Palace of Culture.") The total adulation of all things American that particular week in February may also have been prompted by delight at the outcome of the Gulf War, which was seen as not so much an American triumph over Iraq but as a triumph of American technology over Soviet technology. "It's wonderful how they gave it to the Russians," Poles told me enthusiastically.

American mass culture was enthusiastically invited in or flattered by imitation. McDonald's opened with great fanfare in Budapest, Prague, and Warsaw, and spawned numerous local imitators. New stores boasted names written in English, since that was seen as prestigious and sophisticated. Barbie dolls and Teenage Mutant Ninja Turtles were the rage in new toy stores like Kidi Land in Warsaw. Some Poles were willing to pay as much money for a flashy American car like a Pontiac Trans Am as they would for a Mercedes. "Poles think that whatever is American is the best," explained Henry Olczak, a Polish American who launched a General Motors dealership in Warsaw.

Even many of those who were hurt by the sudden flood of pop culture from across the Atlantic were largely free from bitterness. I was taken aback when Andrzej Wajda, the famed Polish film director, began marveling at the technical wonders of a film like *Terminator 2* or the pacing of a movie like *Presumed Innocent.* Referring to the latter, he told me: "In this film, there's more artistry than in any European film." That did not mean Wajda and other well-known directors were not troubled by the flood of American films and their difficulty in getting their own films screened, but they rarely directed any anger at Hollywood. "I like American films, although I'll never make an American-style film," said Hungary's Kezdi-Kovacs. As for their dominance, he shrugged: "That's the price you pay for freedom. People have the right to choose the films they see."

Most Eastern Europeans felt that there was poetic justice in the new symbolism: the former Communist Party headquarters in Warsaw being transformed into the seat of the new stock exchange and a banking center housing, among others, the offices of the Polish-American Enterprise Fund, the American-funded project aimed at developing the private sector; the U.S. Embassy in Prague renting a portion of the complex that made up the city's old Lenin Museum, using it for an American cultural center and foreign commercial service; and Madison Avenue–style advertising appearing everywhere, transforming previously uniform trams into multicolored rolling advertisements for Camel cigarettes, Barbie dolls, Stimorol chewing gum, Casio watches, and an assortment of other products.

Inevitably, some people began having second thoughts about the scope and speed of those changes. In the March 30, 1991, issue of *Polityka,* a Polish weekly that continued to appeal to an audience that considered itself a part of the enlightened left, psychologist Pawel Boski declared that the proliferation of advertising represented a simple about-face. "There has been a change of decor," he wrote. "American-style advertisements have replaced the old party slogans." In Prague, Czech intellectuals fretted about the "McDonaldization" of their beautiful city and the Americanization of culture. "Too much American freshness (Wrigley's Spearmint), too many Big Macs, too many kitschy movies, stupid television shows, true-to-life Barbies and *Playboy* magazines are changing Czechoslovakia in the same way they changed America," Ivan Rossler, the director of entertainment at Czech Radio, wrote in the spring of 1992 in *Prognosis,* an English-language publication in Prague. "They are forming an avalanche that may even stifle the last remnants of intellect that escaped post-totalitarian brainwashing."

Such strident voices remained in the distinct minority, but there was no doubt that increasing familiarity with Americans and the products of their culture did begin to foster new attitudes in place of the blind admiration of the past. One measure was the reception that young Americans received when they flocked to Czechoslovakia after the Velvet Revolution, often on English-teaching programs, and then to find other jobs. It was enough to identify oneself as an American to find a warm welcome anywhere, even among those who were normally suspicious of outsiders—particularly anyone who looked different.

In December 1990, Sandy Chen, an Asian-American from Boston, arrived in the Czech town of Chrudim and dropped into a pub, producing a dramatic effect on the older men assembled there. "Everyone stopped drinking, their glasses hoisted in midair," Chen recalled. As he ordered his beer, the silence continued, until his dress—Levi's, L. L. Bean jacket, and Nikes—prompted the bartender to ask cautiously if he wasn't American. When Chen confirmed his suspicion, all the tension in the room evaporated. "American, American, okay," the bartender reassured him. One of the customers came up and asked him about the Boston Bruins. But if the reception remained warm in smaller towns and cities, Prague, which was the prime magnet for Americans, began to take Americans more in stride. Chen, who later moved to Prague and set up his own consulting firm, reported that his nationality alone no longer assured him of special treatment.

In the early days of the postcommunist era, young Americans showed up at ministries and other government offices and could almost instantly be offered some vague "advisory" role; the job would not pay much, but it looked awfully good on a recent college graduate's résumé. That started to change as Czech officials began to recognize that they had to be more selective—and that Americans were not automatically qualified to reveal the secrets of how to make things work better. In the spring of 1992, I met John Allison, a former editor of *American Bookseller* in New York, who worked first as an aide for Prague's mayor and later as a floating editor of English texts and speeches for Havel's Castle staff. "Nobody would now think that, just because I am an American, I possess some special knowledge," he said. "In the beginning, in City Hall, they did."

Some of the young Americans were more apt to warn of the dangers of taking their countrymen too seriously than were many Czechs. Allison produced a mock ad in *Prognosis* spoofing the kinds of conferences that had proliferated in the region, proclaiming the virtues of the American way. Entitled "DOING THE RIGHT THING: Promoting the Growth of Democratic Freedom in the New Free Europe—Paths to Progress, Roads to Renewal," the conference featured a speech by Larry "J.R." Hagman entitled "This Here Land Is Your Land: Spreading the Word of Freedom," a talk by Jerry Rubin on "How You Can Become a Democracy Distributor," and a banquet at McDonald's followed by Ronald McDonald's remarks on "Verification of Nuclear Arsenal Dismantlement in the Former Soviet Republics." Convinced that the advertisement was genuine, some readers called in with indignant protests about the arrogance of the conference's organizers.

But anti-Americanism was still extremely hard to find—except in Slovakia. Just as they exhibited more anti-Western feelings in general than their neighbors, the Slovaks were more likely to spin conspiracy theories about America. According to a study conducted by the Center for Social Analysis in Bratislava in January 1992, 44 percent of Slovaks expressed fear that American influence was too strong. This flew in the face of the fact that Slovakia had attracted minimal attention from American businesses or politicians, and exhibited far fewer signs of creeping Americanization than the Czech Republic. The only explanation for this seemingly bizarre perception was that Slovak nationalists blamed the Americans for the decline of their arms industry, claiming that pressure from Washington had cost them sales and jobs.

The willingness of a large part of the Slovak population to base broader conspiracy theories on such arguments demonstrated another trait that distinguished them from the Czechs, Poles, and Hungarians, who were moving fastest toward integration with the West. Those peoples also had their extreme nationalists, who were just as eager to spin conspiracy theories, including those of the anti-American variety, but they usually played to much smaller audiences. Slovak distrust of the West and America was far more commonplace, and it undoubtedly contributed to the sense that they were slipping backward into the second tier of nations, which have a far longer way to go to qualify as new Europeans.

Among those already in that category, a more balanced view of America was beginning to appear. Even in Poland, the fascination of young people with everything American began to be tempered by increasing realism. Professor Jerzy Wilkin, the director of the American Studies Center Program, which was established in 1991, pointed out: "Our students want to learn the most about America, but they want to do so without myths, to do so sympathetically but objectively." That is likely to be the pattern in Poland, Hungary, and the Czech Republic. The United States will continue to exert a powerful grip on the imagination of those new Europeans, and they will retain a stronger instinctive sympathy for their neighbor across the Atlantic than many Western Europeans, but slowly they will begin to see America, not just *Ameryka*.

At nightfall on a late-summer day in 1992, the Przemysl railroad station in southeastern Poland quickly filled up with Ukrainians, Russians, and other travelers from the former Soviet Union. The wooden benches in the waiting room were already full of people positioning themselves for a fitful night's sleep, while others hunkered down on air mattresses or spread out newspapers in the station's pedestrian tunnel. Maria, a middle-aged seamstress from the Ukrainian city of Lvov just across the border, was settling down there with her companion, Lyuba, an elevator operator, amid their nylon bags crammed with everything from an electric saw to cheap clothing that they hoped to sell to Poles during the next few days. Fearful of thieves, they planned to sleep in shifts.

But they were not complaining. "I like Poland," Maria told me. "You have everything here." Lyuba agreed. "Poland is a small America," she said. Estimating that they would earn about $100 in a few days if they managed to sell their goods and then bought up Western and Polish products they could resell at a profit back home, Maria pointed out that this represented more than five times what she and her husband, a painter, made each month on their regular jobs. With three children and a salary of 1,000 rubles, or $5 a month, Lyuba needed the cash even more. "My husband doesn't work—he drinks vodka," she declared, flicking her forefinger at her neck in the familiar gesture to describe a drunkard. "If I didn't go back and forth, we'd starve."

So back and forth they went, not just Ukrainians but a vast assortment of nationalities across borders that had previously been impenetrable for them. The border they crossed the most often was the one with Poland. Hungary was too expensive for them, Russians and Ukrainians explained, and Czechoslovakia was not particularly welcoming, since customs officers there were strict and literal about their regulations; the Czechs were considered the Germans of Eastern Europe, more inclined to play by the rules than anyone else. Polish customs officials did not represent that kind of problem: either they could be slipped a bottle or two of vodka, or they often made only perfunctory checks. And the Poles, who had always been keen traders, provided plenty of opportunities for their neighbors from the east to peddle their wares.

In the summer of 1992, when I set out to see several border areas, the war in what once was Yugoslavia and the violent attacks on foreigners in Germany created the impression that the downfall of communism had only opened the way to nationalist strife, a settling of all ethnic scores. Even the acrimonious if peaceful Czech-Slovak divorce proceedings seemed to confirm that trend. But the situation along Poland's eastern border, as well as along some other borders in the region, demonstrated that just the opposite was also happening. New, more positive relationships were developing between at least some nationalities as they were coming into broader contact with one another, diminishing rather than fanning historical animosities. In those cases, economic self-interest was proving more important than traditional fears and prejudices.

Nowhere was this more evident than in border towns like Przemysl.

With a population of about seventy thousand, the town was initially poorly prepared to host some twenty thousand visitors a day from the East, arriving in trains, buses, and cars. Some treated Przemysl only as their first stop in a tour of Polish towns and cities, but others went no farther. The authorities acted quickly to make them feel welcome. Instead of the one market it had had earlier, by the time of my arrival the city boasted seven, offering basic but adequate facilities for foreign and a growing number of local traders from the whole region for set fees. "This is good business for the city," Deputy Mayor Leszek Krzywon told me. "This helps the municipal budget and, thanks to the influx, our unemployment is not too high."

At the Polonia soccer stadium, which was quickly transformed into the largest bazaar, Ukrainians and Russians peddled their wares in the stands—tools ranging from screwdrivers to saws and drills, lamps, rugs, plastic suitcases, toothpaste, cigarettes, and the usual assortment of communist pins and medals. One man offered me a Stalin medal, assuring me with a gold-toothed smile: "My uncle was awarded this."

Poles rented the booths below the stands, selling Asian electronic goods, counterfeit Levi's jeans and Lacoste shirts, and colorful winter coats with an assortment of dubious Western labels. The sellers had one main concern: that rising prices and the elimination of shortages across the border would gradually eliminate the opportunities to make a quick profit that kept the visitors coming. "If the Ukrainians stopped coming, it'd be really bad," said Wojciech Kochman, a twenty-two-year-old Pole quoting prices on his jackets in Russian to potential customers. "I survive on this trade." In the town's regular shops, the refrain was similar: without the customers from the East, who bought large amounts for resale back home, they would have a tough time making ends meet.

To a large extent, the Ukrainians, Russians, and others were simply repeating the earlier experiences of the Poles, which may also have accounted for the largely friendly reception they received. The visitors from the East were no longer seen as Big Brother's envoys but as the poorer neighbors from next door who were seeking to better their lot in strikingly familiar fashion. In the 1980s, when Poland had neither a convertible currency nor many consumer goods, Poles could travel relatively freely. They became the master peddlers of the region, taking advantage of the huge price and currency differentials between East and West to buy low and sell high whatever was in demand—which was just about everything.

There were multiple, convoluted combinations: the Poles from border towns like Przemysl would take jeans across to the Soviet Union, sell them there, and purchase Soviet radios and other cheap electronic goods, sell those products in Hungary for forints, which they exchanged on the black market into dollars, then travel to Turkey to buy leather jackets, which they would sell in Yugoslavia, where they would buy alcohol, which they would sell on the way back in Hungary, and return with hard cash. I discovered another variation when I visited the Moldavian capital of Kishinev in 1990 and found my hotel full of Poles. A couple of local black-marketeers explained that the Poles sold them anything they wanted from Germany—and pulled out a Neckermann mail-order catalogue to prove it. The Poles would include Moldavia in a broad eastern-southern-western loop, picking up orders along the way and bringing the goods the Moldavians had pointed out in the German store's catalogue on their next trip.

Many Poles had also worked illegally in West Germany or the United States. They earned meager wages and skimped on everything, living in squalid conditions and eating next to nothing in order to save their precious earnings. But once they brought their dollars back home and converted them at black-market rates, their small sums were transformed into small fortunes by local standards.

I met Michal Hrynkiw, an ethnic Ukrainian who lived in Przemysl, on a hillside at the edge of town, where he was building a house for his grown son. In the late 1980s, he had spent two years as a construction worker in Chicago, working "on the black," which is how Poles describe illegal employment abroad. As we talked, he pointed out that he was directing the construction of the house, but that the real work was being performed by Ukrainians he had employed from across the border, who were as willing to work fourteen-hour days as he had been in Chicago. "It's the way America was for us in the old days, when the dollar was so strong," he said. "You work hard because no one will pay you if you don't. This is America for them." It was an analogy he relished, including its implication about what was happening to Poland now that, at least in the eyes of the Ukrainians, it was clearly on the western side of the East-West divide. "We'll build America here," he chuckled. But he was at least partially serious: by that, he meant that he saw real possibilities for growth in Poland.

The Ukrainian construction workers naturally focused on their earnings, pointing out that they could make in two days of construction work for Hrynkiw what they would earn in a good month back home; their three-week stay would produce a tidy sum. But when I asked a gangly young worker named Stas his impressions of Poland, he did not focus only on the difference in living standards. He cited "the cultural level" of Poland. "People live better here and treat each other better here," he added. It was a useful reminder of how quickly public mores had changed in Poland from the days when, as in the former Soviet Union, hostility was commonplace and a Pole had to reckon with the possibility that any encounter—in a store, an office, or a bus—could lead to personal humiliation. For the Ukrainians, who were only beginning to emerge from the shadow of the old system, those habits, nurtured by a political system that had specialized in demeaning the individual, were still all too present.

The numbers of former Soviet citizens visiting Poland were in the millions, seven million in 1991 alone, and that kind of traffic was by no means all tension-free. On the Ukrainian side of the border, near Przemysl, the waiting period for passenger cars seeking to enter Poland could be up to several days—if drivers did not pay standard bribes. In late 1991 and early 1992, Polish travelers were attacked on several occasions when they refused to pay up or did not pay whatever was deemed enough, prompting angry protests from the Polish authorities and even brief closures of the border crossing. By the time I visited the crossing point, such violent incidents had subsided, but Polish customs officers reported sharp increases in the amounts of contraband—especially alcohol and cigarettes—they were confiscating from the visitors. "It's dramatically different from before, when it was just personal belongings," Customs Officer Wieslaw Tylinski explained as he showed me several storage rooms crammed with confiscated bottles of vodka and cartons of cigarettes. "Now we find whole truckloads of goods."

Some of the visitors were also involved in more serious crimes, such as car-theft rings, arms sales, and extortion, with organized gangs expanding their mafialike activities to the new Polish terrain, occasionally triggering bloody shoot-outs. Prostitution, both organized and freelance, was widespread. In another southern Polish town, a Ukrainian ambulance had cruised the streets offering the services of two "nurses" on board, which were decidedly not of a medical nature.

In Przemysl, the authorities reported only minor crimes and no serious violence. Prostitution was not particularly evident, although one Ukrainian peasant learned about the perils of Poland the hard way. He dispatched his wife to Przemysl to sell some belongings, only to have her disappear. When a neighbor invited him over to distract him with a new soft-porn video smuggled in from Poland, the peasant received the shock of his life: his wife was playing the leading role.

Nor had old tensions, spawned by a long history of bloody Polish-Ukrainian conflicts, all disappeared, particularly among the older generation. Eugenia Kaczmasz, a cleaning lady in her sixties, vividly re-counted how members of her family and friends had been murdered by Ukrainians during World War II. "I don't want any contact with Ukrainians," she insisted. "It'd be best if they all stayed over there." Przemysl's small ethnic Ukrainian community remained bitter over the refusal of Polish Catholics to turn over a Carmelite church that had been a Ukrainian Eastern-rite cathedral until 1946. Pope John Paul had planned on returning the church to the Ukrainians on his visit to Przemysl in June 1991, but angry protests by local Polish Catholics forced him to assign them another church.

Nonetheless, most of Przemysl's inhabitants and the Ukrainian visitors from across the border maintained that they got along just fine, dismissing past conflicts as irrelevant. "I don't care about history," said Zdzislaw Gardzewik, the director of Scorpio, a Polish trading company seeking to expand its Ukrainian business; he recognized that the future lay with more sophisticated, large-scale transactions. "If we delved into history, there would be no trade at all."

I had thought there would be more complaints from local Poles about the influx from the East, and I searched extensively for negative comments to balance the positive assessments I was hearing. The town's unemployed, I assumed, would not be pleased with Ukrainian illegal workers in their midst. But when I stopped Mariusz Blaszczyszyn, a twenty-six-year-old who had been jobless for a year, he seemed genuinely not to harbor any resentment against the Ukrainians who eagerly snapped up what Poles considered to be low-paying jobs. "No Pole would work for that kind of money on construction," he said. "They are no competition for us." He had bounced in and out of a couple of jobs, and his ambition was to obtain a loan to start up a small general store, which would also serve as the local video-rental shop, in a nearby rural area where no such facility existed. "I'd like to build something which has a future," he said.

I had also figured that the local police would have plenty of complaints about the Ukrainians. But police spokesman Adam Stachurski, a sixteen-year veteran of the force, downplayed the law-enforcement problems generated by the constant visitors and expanding trade, praising the new contacts as vital to the town's development as a gateway to the East. Then, at the end of a lengthy discussion, he let slip that he was resigning from the police in two weeks' time to get a piece of that action. His brother was already making good money arranging the shipment of Western products to Ukrainian firms across the border, and he planned to follow his example. He smiled broadly as he escorted me to the door. "I intend to get to real work," he declared.

After long delays and clear indications that the Soviet Foreign Ministry still harbored resentment about the reporting I had done from Moscow during the end of the Brezhnev era, which had led to my expulsion, I finally received a multiple-entry visa in 1991, making it easier for me to travel in and out as needed. Going back and forth between the most advanced countries of Eastern Europe and the disintegrating Soviet Union was a bit like switching channels between very different programs set in different eras. In that early period of the 1990s, the Soviet Union, or later the Commonwealth of Independent States, was still struggling with the old system and seeking only to reach the starting point for real reforms, while Hungary, Poland, and Czechoslovakia, or at least what soon became the Czech Republic, had already embarked on the path of reforms, even if they were still a long way from completion. They were on the road marked "to Europe," while the destination of their eastern neighbors was still far from certain.

Almost every border crossing provided me with a reminder of the gap between these two worlds, and how the East-West boundary had effectively shifted eastward, as was evident in Przemysl. In the spring of 1991, I traveled from Warsaw to Moscow by train. During the habitual changing of the wheels for the wide-gauged track that begins on the Byelorussian side of the border at Brest, my train stood beside another train, which had also just arrived from Poland. As two Polish businessmen and I looked on, the wagon just opposite us came alive. One woman was busily pulling sweater after sweater from her stuffed nylon bag and triumphantly holding them all up, while another was shedding one sweater after another off her back, and still another was peeling off several pairs of jeans she had been wearing. They were all visibly in a gleeful mood, having made it past the Soviet customs officials with their acquisitions from Poland, and they were showing them off to each other. "Many of us did the same thing a few years ago," said one of the Polish businessmen, smiling at the virtuoso performance. "You have to live."

Some Poles, Hungarians, and Czechs may still have had serious doubts about the extent of their countries' Westernization, but not the Russians, Ukrainians, and others who made such voyages. In late 1991, on a flight from Warsaw to Moscow, I sat beside Boris Kharlov, a factory director from the Urals. He had just spent a week in Poland arranging to barter the engines his factory produced for Polish food shipments. We chatted about his trip and his impressions of Poland, and then I asked whether he had ever been to the West. "No, this is my first time," he replied, perfectly seriously.

A friend from my earlier days in Moscow, Victor Erofeyev, who had emerged from years on the Soviet literary blacklist and won acclaim for his writing at home and abroad, described his sensations as he returned from a long trip abroad in September 1991, right after the unsuccessful coup attempt by Soviet hard-liners. "After you cross the Polish-Soviet border, it's immediately a different world of eternal Russia. You can throw away your watch—time stands still," he said, referring to the endless lines in the bank where he had to pick up the rubles he had left behind, since no one was allowed to take rubles in or out of the country. "You've been to Paris, London, Monte Carlo, and now . . ."

His voice trailed off, then picked up again. "That's the difference between Poland and Russia. You cross from Germany into Poland, and of course you see that it's poorer, dirtier. But it's still Europe. People do not feel like slaves. They know their own worth; they feel their dignity and what they want to do in life. You cross the Soviet border and, even after the putsch and the miracle of what happened, people are still slaves, still lost and afraid of what the *nachalniki* [bosses] will do."

Erofeyev's generalizations for dramatic effect may have been a bit too sweeping, but his basic point was one that many Eastern Europeans who have experience in Russia agreed with. During the same postcoup period, I talked with Rudolf Slansky, the Czechoslovak ambassador to Moscow. He warned against postcoup euphoria and discussed the psychological traits that made Russians so different from his own people. "The Russians have in their blood the traditions of Russian society—in addition to what the seventy years [of communism] did to them," he said. "Those are the traditions of communal life, of little experience with life in a bourgeois society, a relatively shallow experience with market economics, the tradition of autocratic rule and submission to it. These are not only the traits of *Homo sovieticus* but also of *Homo russicus*. These people have simply forgotten a lot of what they knew, and there's much they didn't and couldn't learn."

Given those perceptions, many Eastern Europeans had distinctly mixed feelings as the Soviet Union began to unravel. On the one hand, the disintegration of the empire was a dream come true; on the other, they were far from certain they liked all the consequences. "It's necessary, it must happen," Czechoslovakia's Foreign Minister Dienstbier told me in the fall of 1990. But he cautioned: "You cannot imagine what could happen if there are wars inside the Soviet Union." About the same time, Antoni Kaminski, a Polish sociologist, offered an offhand remark as we strolled through Warsaw's old town that revealed his ability to keep events in perspective. Noting the brisk private sales of Soviet Army coats, hats, and even arms around the city, he observed: "The demoralization of the Soviet Army is one of the most threatening processes, but it would be even more threatening if they weren't demoralized."

Poland and particularly Czechoslovakia were hit hard by the collapse of trade with the East as the Soviet economy plunged into a virtual free-fall, and it took time for them to reorient themselves westward. They worried about the possibility of a flood of refugees they were not equipped to handle. Until the August 1991 coup attempt, the Poles, in particular, also fretted about the capabilities of the Kremlin hard-liners. Since Soviet troops did not withdraw from Poland as quickly as they did from Czechoslovakia and Hungary, Polish officials felt especially nervous about anything that could reverse the course of events.

This produced one of Walesa's least heroic moments: his reaction to the coup attempt in Moscow. As soon as he heard the news from the Kremlin, the Polish president called his predecessor and old nemesis, General Jaruzelski, who gave him the advice not to interfere in internal Soviet affairs. Then, while other former Solidarity activists denounced the use of force and immediately proclaimed their support for "democratic Russia," he made a public appeal for calm without offering a single word of condemnation of the coup. He only reached Yeltsin by phone after the coup collapsed. Facing reporters on the lawn of the presidential palace, he claimed that he had tried to call earlier without success, but added: "I wasn't in a hurry, because in these kinds of situations I like to win." Many Poles cringed at that admission, but Walesa was convinced that he had acted as a leader responsible for the fate of his nation, if no longer as a dissident proclaiming bold stands based on moral principles.

For all their ambivalence and fears, most Eastern European leaders recognized the extent of the collapse of the Soviet system earlier than their Western counterparts and expressed less alarmist views than those appearing frequently in the West. There was less instinctive clinging to familiar relationships with the unified Soviet Union than there was by the Bush administration. Havel spoke of the transformation of the Soviet empire when I interviewed him in July 1991, before the coup attempt accelerated events. "It doesn't make sense to delay or oppose this transformation," he insisted.

In January 1992, a time when Western officials and commentators were portraying the breakup of the Soviet Union in particularly gloomy terms, Hungarian Foreign Minister Jeszenszky was intent on offering a contrary view. "Nobody can doubt that there are very great problems arising from [the breakup of] the Soviet Union," he told me. "But I don't share the attitude which can be perceived in various Western media that this is a tragedy." He emphasized the accomplishment represented by the elimination of the threat of nuclear war, and he offered a more upbeat assessment of post-Soviet prospects. "I won't say that democracy and a market economy can be established in the former Soviet Union as quickly as in Hungary. But the way has been opened and the Leninist utopia has been officially discarded."

The Eastern Europeans were keenly aware of the potential for friction with the newly independent former Soviet republics. There were plenty of lingering resentments and suspicions rooted both in more distant history and in recent events. The Poles and Lithuanians, for instance, have long held radically different views of their common history. The Poles saw the union of their two countries between 1385 and 1572 as a period of triumph and cooperation, whereas the Lithuanians resented what they saw as Polish domination, particularly the Polonization of their culture and nobility. Between the two world wars in this century, the Poles hardly endeared themselves to the Lithuanians by seizing Vilnius, leaving them deprived of their current capital. Though many Polish Solidarity activists and intellectuals supported Lithuania's drive for independence as the Soviet Union began to collapse, mutual recriminations, rather than the impulse to make common cause against the old Soviet enemy, dominated the Polish-Lithuanian relationship in the early 1990s.

The major source of tension was the status of the ethnic Polish minority in Lithuania. Following the failed putsch in Moscow, Lithuania cracked down hard on its Poles, dissolving regional Polish councils that it claimed had backed the Kremlin hard-liners. Both Lithuanian officials and local Poles agreed that the KGB had sought to exploit traditional tensions between the two communities to weaken Lithuania's drive for independence. That proved relatively easy to do. Most of the Polish intellectuals who had lived in Lithuania either perished during the war or moved to Poland afterward, leaving a poorly educated population which felt threatened by the revival of Lithuanian nationalism and was susceptible to Kremlin propaganda. If the Lithuanians' decision to dissolve the Polish regional councils could be explained as a questionable but understandable reaction to what they viewed as disloyalty, their refusal to allow new elections in the Polish districts until November 1992 could hardly be justified. In effect, the Poles' democratic rights were suspended for over a year, and the Lithuanians used this period as an opportunity for a general redrawing of electoral districts, which, among other consequences, diluted the representation of the Poles. Against that backdrop, serious cooperation between Vilnius and Warsaw proved extremely difficult.

But the newly emerging political relationships and personal contacts between Poles and their other eastern neighbors—Ukrainians, Byelorussians, and Russians—produced a far more favorable evolution. I frequently encountered Poles who expressed surprise at how radically their views of those nationalities had been revised in a very short period. On one level, they had been forced to acknowledge that the Russians and other nationalities had proved capable of extraordinary behavior that had brought about the end of the communist system. After Yeltsin rallied his supporters at the Russian White House and foiled the coup attempt, Senator Andrzej Celinski, the sociologist who had served as a close adviser to Walesa during the 1980s, marveled: "This is something transcendental. This is the best proof that God exists." For all their reservations about the Lithuanians, many Poles also admired their courage in standing up to the Kremlin. On another level, the abolition of the Soviet system allowed people who had been focused on their resentments born of subjugation to allow other feelings to surface.

Russia may have been the imperial power for centuries, but the East has always exerted a powerful grip on the imagination of many Poles. "Polish intellectuals know Russian literature much better than they do French literature," Russian writer Erofeyev pointed out. "On the one hand, they don't want to have anything to do with Russia; and on the other, their souls are flying to the East." However violently, their destinies had been intertwined for centuries. After viewing an excellent production of *The Accused Dmitry Karamazov* at a Warsaw theater, my wife, Christina, congratulated one of the actors for how Russian he looked in the play. "None of us knows what Tartar may have grabbed my grandmother," he shot back with a mischievous grin.

Poland's eastern neighbors also felt the element of shared heritage. Sergei Grigoryants, the veteran former dissident and political prisoner who edits *Glasnost* magazine in Moscow, looked very much at ease when we met at a Warsaw café on a hot summer day in 1992. "With all its problems, Poland will be the Western model for the Eastern Slavic world," he said, adding that Poland was the "most European" part of that Slavic world. This, he continued, made it easier for Russians to feel that they are Europeans in Poland than in Western Europe. "In London, Paris, or Rome, you feel that the gap with the West is too wide.

You come to Poland and you feel more comfortable," he concluded. "There are Slavic traditions—the better part of Slavic traditions—which are more Western. I like coming here."

Although the Poles, Czechs, and Hungarians have turned westward, they have the opportunity to develop new, healthier relationships with their eastern neighbors—who, if things proceed on course, will seek to emulate some of their achievements. Hungarian Foreign Minister Jeszenszky repeatedly stressed in our conversations that this was another reason it was so important for his country, Poland, and the Czech Republic to succeed, so that they could provide their eastern neighbors with a positive example. Though looking toward their integration with the West, they had not forgotten about the East. It was too early yet to predict the extent to which cooperation would replace conflict in their relationships with their eastern neighbors, but, at the very least, there were signs of promising new beginnings.

The town of Cheb is located on the Czech side of the Czech-German border, but its picturesque historic town square, featuring imposing frame houses with high roofs and dormer windows, exemplifies a colorful mixture of Gothic and Baroque architecture which is unmistakably German. That is no accident. Starting in the eleventh century, Cheb—or Eger, as it was called by the Germans—was a cultural crossroads, a town inhabited almost completely by Germans, although it always belonged to Bohemia. That arrangement lasted until Hitler seized the Sudetenland, including Cheb, in 1938. At the time, thirty-two thousand of Cheb's thirty-five thousand inhabitants were German. After the war, when the Sudetenland was returned to Czechoslovakia, the Germans of Cheb were among about three million ethnic Germans who were forcibly expelled from the region. For the ensuing four decades, Cheb's new Czech inhabitants rarely learned anything about the town's German heritage aside from the fact that Goethe used to visit the town or that Schiller wrote his *Wallenstein* trilogy there, and there was only a trickle of traffic across the border with what was then West Germany.

When I visited Cheb in the summer of 1992 as part of my swing around border regions, the situation was dramatically different. Germans were once again streaming across the border, and Czechs were free to travel the other way. German cars clogged Cheb's main thoroughfare, whose name had been changed from Karl Marx Street to Europe Street after the Velvet Revolution. Most of the Germans came for a combination of shopping and sightseeing, taking advantage of cheap Czech prices for food, alcohol, cigarettes, and gas, or to visit ancestral homesteads and such famous Bohemian spas as Frantiskovy Lazne and Karlovy Vary—or Franzensbad and Karlsbad, in German. Some also came for the young Czech prostitutes who lined Europe Street and other roads near the border, flagging down the German cars and trucks at all hours of the day and night.

Local Czechs sometimes complained about the prostitution and the traffic congestion, and they chafed a bit at feeling so poor when they crossed the border themselves, since most German prices were prohibitive for those on normal Czech salaries. But the overwhelming majority of the people I talked to were delighted by the way their town had been transformed, and local restaurants, shops, and other businesses were benefiting from the cross-border traffic. "Before 1989, it was the end of the world here," said Frantisek Hubacek, who had quit his accounting job to run a pension that caters primarily to Germans. "Now it feels like a crossroads again, like the center of the world."

Some of Cheb's residents benefited even more from the open borders by commuting daily to jobs on the other side. An estimated three thousand Czechs from the Cheb district had found jobs across the border, producing a labor shortage in Cheb. On the day I visited the local employment office, 1,434 job openings were listed, while only 232 people were listed as unemployed. To remedy this situation, local businesses employed about four hundred of their own "guest workers" from points farther, sometimes much farther, east—Romania, Ukraine, even Vietnam.

I visited the apartment of Olga Gregoridesova, who had been working for a year at a porcelain factory in the German town of Waldsassen, six miles across the border. She commuted there with four other women from Cheb, all of whom considered themselves unbelievably lucky to have landed their new jobs. Whereas Gregoridesova's colleagues who did similar work in Cheb earned about $130 a month, she was earning over $1,000. Her husband, a solderer who worked for a construction company that had obtained German contracts to build temporary housing for Yugoslav refugees, earned about $230 a month. "My wife brings home the money," he said cheerfully.

The results were visible in their apartment, which displayed a brand-new Japanese TV and stereo set. As a result of Gregoridesova's earnings, they were also able to shop for fashionable clothing for their three daughters, in German stores. Her salary was modest by German standards, which explained why there was a shortage of workers and she could be hired legally by a German firm. But it had transformed their lives.

Gregoridesova had no complaints about either her employers or her German co-workers. "They accept us very well. There is no evidence of animosity," she said, and added that the German workers had come to visit Cheb and she had shown them around. She confessed that the attacks on foreigners in Rostock and other German cities that summer had made her nervous, but she noted that most of the violence had occurred in former East German territory. "The West Germans are more peaceful, more quiet," she concluded.

Other Czechs also alluded frequently to the differences between the former East Germans and West Germans. They were sometimes offended by visiting East Germans who "acted like kings" because they now carried German marks in their pockets; before unification, the East Germans had lived in conditions similiar to the Czechs', and their new arrogance did not sit well. The Czechs also were quick to point out how poorly the East Germans were adjusting to a more open society where everyone had to fend for himself.

Jana Zieczowska, a nurse from Cheb who worked in a hospital in the formerly West German town of Selb, about twenty miles away, recounted how the hospital had initially hired East Germans as well as Czechs. "The East Germans came and they expected to make a lot of money for not much work," she said. "The West Germans have a much better relationship with the Czechs than with the East Germans." Most of the East Germans soon quit when they saw how much work was demanded of all members of the staff; only those who had escaped to West Germany before unification, who had displayed a genuine desire to live in different conditions, had stayed on. Zieczowska and other Czechs expected to work hard to justify their employers' decision to hire them and to keep earning their new salaries—in her case, about $1,700 a month.

The continuing distinction between the two parts of Germany was evident elsewhere as well. Cheb bordered directly on the former West German region, but just a few miles north there was the Vojtanov border crossing to former East German territory. On a visit there, I could hardly spot a single car with Czech plates in the heavy flow of traffic in both directions; all the cars looked German. Checking with the border guards, I confirmed my impression: on a daily basis, they explained, about thirty thousand Germans and only about six hundred Czechs crossed that border. Just outside of Cheb, at the Svaty Kriz border-crossing point to West Germany, which had only been opened in the spring of 1992, the proportions were completely different: about six thousand Germans and four thousand Czechs crossed there daily. I asked Captain Peter Milca, the director of the Czech side of the border crossing, what accounted for that huge disparity. He looked at me as if he had a question of his own—about my mental capacity. "Who would go to East Germany if he could go to the West?" he replied.

Although the border region had already undergone a major transformation, Jaromir Bohac, the director of the Cheb archive whose life was the history of the town, had even broader ambitions. In 1990, he had launched a local organization called Euroregio Egrensis, which was supported by the International Institute for National Rights and Regionalism in Munich. Pointing out that Europe has about thirty cross-border regions, Bohac said his dream was "to see the region as one without borders," where the formal borders would not be questioned but would diminish in practical importance as cooperative efforts to address regional problems would increase. Euroregio Egrensis had organized conferences to discuss those problems, and eventually he hoped that a regional council would emerge, with representatives from both sides of the border. That summer had already featured a Festival Mitte Europa of concerts, plays, operas, and workshops sponsored by both the Czech Republic and Bavaria and Saxony, with the events taking place in various Czech and German locations. Here the old, hazy concept of Mitteleuropa no longer seemed quite so abstract.

Such initiatives, Bohac explained, could help Czechs and Germans to live and learn about each other, re-establishing the connections that had been severed since the Munich Pact of 1938. "The problem is that the Czechs living here must accept that this was a German town with a German culture," he said, acknowledging the psychological difficulty of that task. He also expressed the hope that a gradual narrowing of the huge difference between the standards of living of Czechs and Germans would eliminate the most common source of occasional friction. There was more than a hint of an unusual passion in this scholarly archivist as he spelled out his hopes—and, near the end of our discussion, he revealed its possible source.

I had asked about his age, since I was curious whether he had been born during or after the war and what that indicated about his family's origins. It turned out that he was born in July 1945, the son of a Czech who had been sent as a forced laborer to the region and a local German woman. His parents had had to keep their love affair a secret until the end of the war, when they were finally free to marry. He smiled. "I was born one week after the wedding."

Despite such encouraging progress, the new Europeans and the Germans still had a lot of emotional obstacles and deep-seated prejudices to overcome. Only the Hungarians were almost completely free of any phobias about the Germans, and vice versa. Hungary and Germany had been allies during the two world wars, although Hungary was known as a distinctly unenthusiastic and unreliable partner during the second conflagration. Perhaps most significantly, they did not have a common border, which was the surest guarantee of conflicts in earlier eras. In more recent times, many Germans felt a particular sense of gratitude toward Hungary because it had opened its border to Austria in 1989, allowing thousands of East Germans to use that route to flee to the West. The Hungarian government, which was still communist at the time, had ignored the angry protests of the Honecker regime and insisted on sticking to its policy of abolishing the Iron Curtain, thus setting the stage for the collapse of the Berlin Wall.

But Poland was a completely different case. For centuries, the Germans, like the Russians, had been the enemy, the oppressor, the force that had not only robbed Poles of their independence but tried to strip them of their national identity as well. Sometimes Poland was merely the natural battlefield for showdowns between the Germans and the Russians, its destruction a somewhat haphazard by-product of their warfare. At other times—the successive partitions of Poland at the end of the eighteenth and beginning of the nineteenth centuries, and the Molotov-Ribbentrop Pact of 1939, which provided for the division of the country between Hitler's Germany and Stalin's Soviet Union—the two great powers meticulously planned its destruction.

The communist era only reinforced the easily aroused prejudices of Poles against Germans, and Germans against Poles. This was deliberate policy, nothing accidental. For decades, successive Polish communist governments placed all blame for the country's poor living standards on the war, and "the German threat" was invoked to maintain a psychological climate of fear to justify Poland's "alliance" with the Kremlin, explained by the necessity of obtaining the protection of the Russians against the possibility of a new onslaught from the Germans. During my visits to Poland in the 1960s, first as a tourist and then as an exchange student, I was struck by the pervasive feeling that the war had only just ended. Given the wholesale destruction of life in Poland during the war, it was only natural that memories remained much more vivid there than in the West. The unnatural part was the all-out propaganda effort to ensure that Poles would constantly relive their worst nightmares about the Germans.

This was literally true. Brought up on a diet of Polish films about the war and other constant invocations of the worst Nazi atrocities, even

Poles who were born after 1945 found themselves waking with a start from nightmares in which they were prisoners in concentration camps or tortured by SS men. I heard about that from my Polish peers when I was an exchange student in Krakow in 1968, and I was reminded of this later when Christina, whom I had married, kept having such nightmares for several years after she had moved to the United States.

The first newsreel I saw when I arrived in Poland in 1968 showed grisly pictures of Nazi atrocities in Poland twenty-five years earlier, then immediately switched to shots of West German maneuvers near the Czech border. The invasion of Czechoslovakia to crush the Prague Spring, which had just taken place, had been portrayed by the Polish authorities as a firm rebuff to West German "revanchists" seeking to repeat the seizure of the Sudetenland in 1938. On August 23, 1968, two days after the invasion, the Polish army newspaper *Zolnierz Wolnosci* wrote:

> In recent months, droves of tourists from Western countries, and particularly from the Federal Republic of Germany, have crowded into Czechoslovakia. Many of them were reminiscent of the tourists who had invaded Czechoslovakia in droves in 1938 and, when Hitler's armies crossed into that country, turned out to have been officers of the Wehrmacht. Let it be added that recently these sorts of tourists appearing on the Polish-Czechoslovak border were increasingly frequently noted. . . .

In theory, the anti-German propaganda was designed to convince the Poles that the West Germans were the successors to the Nazis, while the East Germans were their "progressive, socialist allies," who had always rejected fascism. If the anti-German barrage succeeded in keeping alive fears of all Germans, it failed abysmally in this effort at differentiation. In fact, the East Germans were particularly despised, because they were seen as both unreconstructed German fascists and communists, making them an incarnation of everything Poles hated that flowed from the East and the West.

On my first trip to Poland, in 1964, I found myself at a soccer match in Warsaw where the opposing sides were an East German and a Soviet team. The biggest dilemma expressed by several of the fans was which of "the bastards" they wanted more to see lose. A macabre joke of about the same period expressed similar sentiments, although it reflected the even more intense hatred of the Russians who were the oppressors of that era. Poland is invaded simultaneously by East German and Soviet forces, hardly a farfetched scenario in those times, and a Polish soldier has to decide whom to shoot at first. He decides on the Germans. "Business before pleasure," he says.

On the East German side, the feelings were mutual. Unlike the West Germans, the East Germans were allowed to delude themselves that they had no moral responsibility for the Nazi era, the Holocaust, or the destruction of Poland. Their regime felt no compunctions about fanning anti-Polish hatred when this suited its purpose, keeping alive the worst undercurrents left over from the previous era to prevent ideological contamination from their disruptive and often unpredictable Polish neighbors. As Poles repeatedly clamored for freedom, the East German government portrayed them as troublemakers, strikers who were jeopardizing the living standards of all Eastern Europeans; they were described as lazy and, by implication, dirty. The term *Untermenschen* was not specifically used, but the sentiment was unmistakable. Many East Germans already resented the relative freedom of Poles, who could travel via East Germany to West Berlin, something the East Germans had no chance of doing. So they were easily swayed by propaganda campaigns in which the Poles figured as the villains.

East Germans were also more inclined to be true believers, more willing to accept the contorted logic of their official ideology as representing a higher moral truth rather than a grotesque charade. One day in the fall of 1981, when communist regimes throughout the region were intensifying their rhetoric to justify the looming crackdown on Solidarity, I was waiting for a plane in the Russian Black Sea town of Sochi along with a group of East German tourists. I struck up a conversation with a schoolteacher from the group, who proceeded to lecture me sternly on the dangers of "fascism" in Poland, and how it was everyone's duty to prevent the "counterrevolutionary forces" from succeeding there. Her eyes glowed as she declared: "I know fascism." So did I, and I got away from her as soon as I could.

Many West Germans had at least made an effort to overcome old prejudices and recognized that, even if some of their views had not changed, they were best left unspoken. The Polish–West German reconciliation during the détente period of the 1970s helped significantly to reduce official and personal tensions. Increased travel between the two countries initially contributed to the breaking down of many negative stereotypes: young Poles discovered that West Germans were not the successors to the Nazis portrayed by earlier Polish propaganda, and many West Germans admired the Poles' persistent quest for greater freedoms and broader contacts with the outside world.

In the 1980s, when growing numbers of Poles either sought asylum in West Germany or worked illegally there, anti-Polish sentiment revived in West Germany, although usually it still fell far short of the kind of open hatred that was routinely apparent in East Germany. Piotr Jankowiak, a German language instructor at the University of Poznan who traveled frequently to both parts of Germany, explained the difference: "In West Germany, you can encounter anti-Polish feelings on occasion, but you don't feel a general hostility. In East Germany, you feel that the street doesn't like us."

In the new postcommunist era, Polish-German relations got off to a shaky start when Chancellor Helmut Kohl refused to provide an unequivocal guarantee that a unified Germany would recognize the permanence of the Oder-Neisse Line as the border between the two countries. Afraid of alienating right-wing voters, he waffled, providing Poles a solid reason to be nervous about German unification. But an intense lobbying effort by Prime Minister Mazowiecki's government succeeded in finally convincing Kohl, in late 1991, to agree to a treaty that put the border issue to rest.

The results were dramatic. In the spring of 1990, I talked to Professor Karl Jonca, a German specialist at the University of Wroclaw, who was appalled by Kohl's behavior, his seeming tolerance of right-wing fantasies of reclaiming former German territory. "He has shown that you can't trust the Germans, which is what my grandfather always said," he declared. But a year later, after the treaty was signed and ratified, he had radically revised his opinion. "Kohl has shown through his Polish policy that he wants a genuinely united Europe," he told me. Jonca was particularly impressed that, once Kohl's government had dealt with the border issue, the chancellor appeared to get tougher on his right-wing coalition partners. He rejected their demands that the friendship treaty include special rights for the German minority in Poland, something that had an ominous sound to many Poles; instead, he accepted the Polish government's pledge to give equal treatment to all groups.

Jonca was no isolated example. Opinion polls showed that a growing number of Poles considered unification to have been a positive development. After the agreement on their borders and the decision by Germany to abandon visa requirements for Poles in April 1991, some Poles talked effusively of a new era in the relations with their former enemies. "Poland has a great opportunity to establish new relations with Germany," said historian Adam Bromke. "Poles and Germans will go together into a united Europe."

Unlike the more fortunate Czechs, the Poles have a border only with the old East Germany, which meant that the situation on the border it-self proved more volatile, especially after the visa barriers were removed. The German media had warned of an "onslaught" of Polish shoppers once the restrictions disappeared, and the spring of 1991 was marked by numerous incidents. East German neo-Nazis repeatedly attacked Polish visitors, shouting "*Sieg Heil,* Polish swine, Poles go home, Poles out." But soon it became apparent that as a rule more East Germans were crossing over to the Polish side to shop there than vice versa, and the hysterical predictions of a Polish "onslaught" proved inaccurate. Free to travel all over Europe since visa restrictions no longer applied in most cases, Poles traveled to a wide variety of destinations and no longer focused so heavily on Germany.

When I visited the Polish-German border in June 1991, I found Polish merchants eagerly welcoming the flow from the other side. "The more Germans here, the better," said Marek Dudziak, who was selling cigarettes, butter, and asparagus at an outdoor market in the border town of Slubice. Dudziak admitted he was cautious about visiting Frankfurt an der Oder, across the river, because of the frequent beatings of Poles. But he seemed determined to take an optimistic view, arguing that this was a temporary phenomenon. "I heard that, when the French-German border opened up, there were the same kinds of incidents," he said.

Czechoslovakia took longer to work out the terms for a friendship treaty with Germany: it was not until February 1992 that Havel and Kohl signed the document in Prague. The treaty negotiations had been delayed by wrangling over how to deal with the Munich Pact of 1938 and the expulsion of the Sudeten Germans after the war. In the end, the Czech side acknowledged that the expulsion was wrong, while the Germans dropped their claim for compensation for the three million expellees. The debate preceding the treaty was longer and more acrimonious than the debate in Poland before the signing of its treaty with Germany, since many Czechs were outraged that they should concede any wrongdoing to the nation that was responsible for the war and their country's dismemberment. The signing ceremony was marked by protests from an angry, mostly elderly crowd, who booed the two leaders and shouted "Shame" and "Treason" at Havel. But, like the Poles, most Czechs seemed inclined to put the main disputes behind them quickly.

The older generation of Poles and Czechs continued to be nervous about the Germans, but the young and middle-aged had far less of "a German complex." Anti-German suspicions were reflected in Polish laws that require foreigners to get special permission to buy property, and the Czechs expressed concern about the dominance of German investment in their country. To offset the Germans' "natural advantage" in Eastern Europe, explained Zdenek Drabek, a senior official in the Federal Ministry of Economics, "we need to do more investment promotion in the United States, Canada, and elsewhere." But this did not mean trying to shut the Germans out. Given their historical ties and proximity, many Czechs saw no alternative to a strong German presence. "It is our fate, the Germans," shrugged Czech Privatization Minister Tomas Jezek, when I asked about his feelings on the subject.

Polish fears about German economic dominance gave way to concern that the Germans were not investing enough, since they were preoccupied with the Eastern part of their own country. Government officials openly lobbied for more German involvement. "I believe that German investments in Poland should be much bigger," Foreign Minister Krzysztof Skubiszewski said in early 1992. Popular attitudes were also changing, still betraying some trepidations but striking generally positive notes. In the Mazurian Lakes region of what used to be East Prussia, I talked with Adam Kochanowski, an enterprising young farmer who had transformed his old German farmhouse into a boarding house, attracting both Polish and German guests. "For the next ten years, the Germans will be absorbing the East Germans. Then they'll seek to expand eastward economically," he predicted. "But I'm happy about that because by then we'll really be Europeans and this can take place on the basis of partnership." Then he added: "Although it's hard to be an equal partner with the Germans, because they are so rich."

Both Poles and Czechs recognized that their road to Europe ran through Germany, whatever their misgivings and lingering animosities. Observing the evolution of popular attitudes and the situation in border areas, I became convinced that the Poles and the Czechs were ready to develop a new partnership with the Germans as part of their broader partnership with other Western European nations. Whatever doubts I had were more focused on the Germans themselves than on their eastern neighbors.

Germany's persistent problems in taming the violence against foreigners, which escalated sharply in the summer and fall of 1992, raised serious questions about its ability to overcome the legacy of hatred and intolerance, particularly in the former East German regions. The strength of the neo-Nazi movement was one cause for concern; another was the insistence of Chancellor Kohl and other German politicians that "Germany is not an immigrant country." Such assertions ignored nearly six million foreigners who lived permanently in Germany and encouraged the notion that anyone with a non-German background was an outsider with no rights to equal treatment. For all their ethnic problems, France and Britain had increasingly acknowledged the multicultural nature of their societies; the Germans had not even begun to follow suit. In that sense, they were hardly expressing an attitude that acknowledged the realities of the new Europe.

This leads to the broader issue of Germany's place in the new Europe. According to some pessimists, the question is whether Germany is to be a part of Europe, or Europe is to be a part of Germany. That way of framing the question may be unduly alarmist, but there is no doubt that all of Germany's partners, not just the Eastern Europeans, will be asking themselves how far Germany will go to adapt its behavior to new European norms. Particularly in its dealings with its still-weak Eastern neighbors, it could be tempted to try to dictate the terms of its relations rather than working in the spirit of a new form of cooperation, although it was careful to avoid giving that impression in the early stages of the postcommunist era. The Poles and the Czechs, not to mention the Hungarians, are ready for a new cooperative relationship with Germany. The question is whether Germany is also ready.

History and politics divided them for most of this century, but Cieszyn on the Polish side of the Czech-Polish border and Cesky Tesin on the Czech side are two parts of the same town. When my trip around border areas brought me there in August 1992, the local inhabitants were rediscovering that reality. Just by flashing their passports, they could walk or drive across the two bridges over the Olza River to visit the other side. Twice a week, on market days, hordes of Czechs came to shop at an enormous outdoor bazaar on the Polish side, bringing back the current bargains—at the time, wicker baskets, folding doors, baby carriages, and Hula Hoops. Many Poles crossed daily to the Czech side to take advantage of the cheaper prices for beer and meat, or to book inexpensive tours to the West through Czech travel agencies. In the evenings, Poles drifted over to the Jazz Club on the Czech side, and Czechs came over for concerts on the Polish side.

"When people talk about a Europe without borders, this has a specific meaning here," boasted Cieszyn Mayor Jan Olbrycht when he greeted me at City Hall. The relaxed atmosphere represented an astounding turnaround. Right up until 1991, relations between Poles and Czechs were severely strained, particularly in border towns like Cieszyn–Cesky Tesin. They demonstrated that the new Europeans faced the task of forging new relationships not only with their eastern and western neighbors, but also among themselves.

In earlier centuries, under successive Polish, Bohemian, and Austrian rulers, the town and the entire province had functioned as a single entity. But in the aftermath of World War I, when Poland and Czechoslovakia emerged as independent states, Czechoslovakia tried to seize the disputed territory by force, resulting in the partition of the province and the town, leaving a large Polish minority on the Czech side. Taking advantage of Czechoslovakia's dismemberment under the Munich agreement, Poland annexed Cesky Tesin in 1938. After World War II, the old partition was restored and, despite the official line of "socialist brotherhood," traditional animosities thrived in a climate of separation and mutual suspicion. When Solidarity gained momentum in Poland in 1981, Czechoslovakia's hard-liners slapped on new travel restrictions, requiring Poles to obtain formal invitations before they could go across to the other side. For the rest of the 1980s, it was often easier for Poles living in Cieszyn to visit Western Europe than Cesky Tesin.

Some Czechs claimed that the official propaganda against Solidarity did not have much of an impact. "We silently applauded the Poles," Bohumil Muron, the mayor of Cesky Tesin, told me. "At home, we watched Polish TV and we would cheer. In public, we had on our masks." Muron attributed such behavior to the differences in the temperament of Czechs and Poles. "Czech pragmatism dictated that we tolerate the system and endure it," he said. "The Poles were more willing to fight for freedom, to act on their own."

Muron's analysis of national character was generally accepted by both Czechs and Poles. For Havel and other Czech dissidents during the communist era, their commitment to liberation from within, defying the censors and openly challenging the authorities, may have been based in part on rational calculation, but it was also a tremendous romantic leap of faith, atypical of the Czechs, who had not taken up arms against any oppressor since the Battle of White Mountain in 1620, when Hapsburg armies crushed the rebellion of Czech Protestants. For the Poles, such a romantic leap of faith was far more typical—in spirit, if not in tactics, akin to the nineteenth-century uprisings. That was why Polish dissidents were joined by a far broader spectrum of supporters in a struggle that was both rational and irrational, calm and desperate. And that was why Havel and other Czech activists found themselves fairly lonely during much of their dissident journey.

But Muron's interpretation misrepresented the impact of the anti-

Polish campaign waged by the Czechoslovak communists. Like their East German counterparts, they were intent on defending their country from ideological contamination by Solidarity, and they had no qualms about stirring up the most negative national feelings to achieve that goal. Poles had tended to dismiss the Czechs as cowards because of their submissiveness toward authority, whereas the Czechs often dismissed the Poles as an undisciplined, dishonest people prone to self-destructive escapades. During the 1980s, some Czechs did sympathize with the Poles, but many reacted the way the authorities hoped they would, accepting their portrayal of the Poles as troublemakers jeopardizing peace and progress in the region.

In those days, Czech stores were relatively well stocked, while the Poles endured chronic shortages. Since shoppers were seen as enemies rather than customers under the old system, Poles who did manage to cross the border were often greeted with outright hostility. Some Czech stores featured signs that read "POLES ARE NOT SERVED HERE."

Even after the Velvet Revolution, Czechoslovakia resisted appeals by the Polish side to lift the travel restrictions. Since Czechoslovakia lagged behind Poland in getting reforms started, eliminating price subsidies, and achieving currency convertibility, cross-border traffic was still seen as more of a threat than an opportunity. But when Czechoslovakia's economic reforms began in earnest in 1991, Prague finally yielded. The inhabitants of Cieszyn and Cesky Tesin were the most immediate beneficiaries.

Not everything went smoothly. Some inhabitants of Cesky Tesin complained about the sudden overcrowding in their stores and continued to eye the Poles suspiciously. Czech shopkeepers sometimes accused Poles of shoplifting and other forms of stealing; even less serious concerns could be transformed into sweeping generalizations about the bad habits of the Poles. I stopped in at the office of Adria, a new private travel agency in Cesky Tesin which was prospering because 60 percent of its clients were Poles. I expected Prymus Radim, its young manager, to be delighted by the impact of the open border on his business, but he was hardly ecstatic. "We have our problems," he said, shaking his head. "The Poles are not very honest—they try to cheat us."

"In what way?" I asked.

"They make reservations and then cancel them. If a Czech makes a reservation, he sticks to it."

It had not occurred to Radim that the Poles were acting like normal customers in most Western countries, who feel free to change their plans.

The Czechs were more like the Germans, who also make their holiday plans months in advance and rarely change them. For Radim, this was the only proper and "honest" form of behavior.

But there were signs of new attitudes among the Czechs, generated by the combined impact of the economic reforms and the opening of the border. New private shopkeepers professed a far different credo from that of their predecessors in the state stores, who had tried to keep the Poles at bay. "They say Czechs are prejudiced against Poles, but every customer is our master, whether he is a Czech or a Pole," said Jana Bojkova, the manager of a butcher shop that received a steady stream of Polish customers. And Czechs were discovering the benefits of easy access to the Polish side and its broader array of shopping opportunities. "This is good for both the Polish and the Czech economies," said Otto Rohac, an engineer from the nearby Czech city of Ostrava who was shopping at the Cieszyn bazaar. "They should open more border-crossing points."

Even though local Polish officials were the most vigorous proponents of opening up the border, they, too, had occasional complaints. They carped that they had to initiate most of the new contacts and proposals for cooperation, whereas their Czech counterparts tended to be simply reactive. Popular attitudes about the Czechs also reflected some of the old prejudices, portraying them as a plodding, subservient people who put on superior airs. Some Polish merchants echoed the same kinds of complaints about Czech customers as their Czech counterparts did about Polish customers. "They complain about Poles stealing, but look at this," said Franciszek Okruta, showing me how he had tied together his wicker baskets at the Cieszyn bazaar. "They steal, too."

Such complaints were relatively rare, however, and overshadowed by the delight of Polish merchants, including Okruta, that the Czech customers were providing them with new business. The wicker-basket salesman did not seem terribly concerned about his apparent brush with Czech shoplifters. "If it wasn't for the Czechs, I couldn't even pay the costs of this stand," he quickly added.

Even the old derisive Polish characterization of the Czechs as "a nation of waiters" ready to serve any master lost its sting in Cieszyn. When I visited the Targowa Restaurant, I learned that its owner, Piotr Banczyk, had hired several waiters who commuted from Cesky Tesin. "The Czechs are the best waiters in Europe," he asserted, with no hint of irony. "They are trained very well." Although the communist era had led to the dramatic deterioration of service in Czech restaurants, he explained, the old training methods, which dated from the Hapsburg days, had remained intact. "As an employer, I value the Czechs," he added, praising them for their generally conscientious work habits as well.

No one was under any illusion that all the old animosities had evaporated overnight. "This is ideal terrain for extremists and nationalists," Cieszyn Mayor Olbrycht warned, pointing out that the historical disputes could easily be revived. "This is why the contacts have to be made as broad as possible." To that end, the two parts of the town had already staged joint cultural festivals, and a new merchants' association had published the first map of the entire town and directory of businesses on both sides; until then, each side had published maps that ended at the Olza River, not even acknowledging the existence of the other half of the town. Though the results were still far from a love-in, the abnormality of division had been replaced by normal cooperation. For Cieszyn and Cesky Tesin, that was an impressive step forward.

In the late communist period, the cooperation between dissidents from Poland, Czechoslovakia, and Hungary provided a sense of broader purpose to all three movements. Although the number of activists directly involved in such contacts was relatively small, they would prove to be important political players in the postcommunist era. The stage seemed to be set for the forging of close ties between the new governments and the peoples of the region, with the dissidents-turned-politicans leading the way in encouraging those new relationships.

During the early 1990s, real progress was made in that direction, not just in easing tensions in border areas like Cieszyn–Cesky Tesin, but also in improving the relations between governments. At the first summit meeting of leaders of the three countries, in Bratislava in April 1990, the Poles pushed hard for greater cooperation, arguing that such efforts were necessary for regional stability and also for maximizing the chances for success of the participants' efforts to integrate themselves into Western European institutions. The subsequent summit, in February 1991 in the Hungarian town of Visegrad, led to the informal anointing of "the Visegrad triangle," as the threesome's new ties were called.

The single strongest motivation for this process was spelled out by Havel at the summit meeting in Prague in May 1992. "If we join our voices, our demands will be heard more strongly than if we act individually," he said. By presenting a relatively united front, the three countries signed association agreements with the European Community in December 1991, which they hoped would serve as the first step toward eventual full membership. They also pressed the West for admission to, or at least closer involvement with, NATO and other security organizations. Although the Western nations were initially cool to that idea, they did grant observer status to all three countries in the North Atlantic Assembly, which promotes ties between NATO nation parliamentarians and the defense alliance, and frequently invited officials from Poland, Czechoslovakia, and Hungary for meetings with NATO leaders and strategists.

For all the signs that regional cooperation was proving to be more than a purely rhetorical exercise, its proponents faced formidable obstacles. The first was the inevitable absorption of the new politicians in their own nations' complex problems. "Since the change of system in Eastern Europe, I often feel that I know much less about the diverging experiences of these countries," confessed Hungary's Miklos Haraszti, who had helped organize transnational protests in his dissident days. "Before, it was easier to know what was going on." Despite major differences in each country's situation during the communist era, the dissidents instinctively recognized the similarities in the struggles of their neighbors, and, more important, they had the time and energy to study their experiences.

In the faster-paced new era, when parliamentarians were faced with drafting new laws on every conceivable subject and consumed by the daily infighting of their new parties, this was often no longer the case. If the emergence of a new provincialism was somewhat understandable, I was still surprised by its scope; the preoccupation with local events frequently seemed to block out even the most rudimentary information about what was happening nearby. In early 1991, the deputy foreign editor of a major Hungarian newspaper asked me in all seriousness: "What about the shortages in Poland?" The elimination of food shortages had been the biggest instant success of the Mazowiecki government when it had implemented economic reforms a year earlier, a breakthrough that received extensive coverage in both the Polish and the foreign press. If the lesson of Western societies is that all politics is local, the new Europeans were sometimes learning that lesson all too well.

Personal rivalries also complicated the task of bringing Poland, Czechoslovakia, and Hungary closer together. Walesa's jealousy of the acclaim Havel received after he was first elected president of Czechoslovakia did not augur a good relationship between the two leaders; the former electrician was wary of the Czech intellectual, who suddenly appeared to be pushing him out of the international spotlight. But after an initial bumpy period, Havel won Walesa over. During Walesa's first official visit to Prague, in September 1991, Havel took him out for an evening at a local pub, which broke the ice between them. In subsequent meetings, Havel worked hard to ensure that Walesa never felt slighted.

As former dissidents, Havel and Foreign Minister Dienstbier attached considerable importance to nurturing such ties. Vaclav Klaus had a very different attitude, verging on open contempt for the triangular negotiations, when he served as Czechoslovakia's minister of finance. He bristled when Westerners lumped the Czechs together with their neighbors. Nothing irritated him more during his early months in office than to be dubbed "a Polish Balcerowicz," a reference to his Polish counterpart, who had launched reforms earlier than he did. Smugly superior in his attitudes toward other Czech politicians, he was convinced that any comparisons with a Pole could only be demeaning.

On the eve of the June 1992 elections which led to Klaus' assuming the job of Czech prime minister, I talked with Josef Zieleniec, one of his chief aides, who was about to become his foreign minister. Although he had been born in Poland and spent most of his childhood there before his family moved to Czechoslovakia, Zieleniec reflected Klaus' frosty attitudes toward his former countrymen. He claimed that he and Klaus were for continued "collaboration" with Poland and Hungary, but left no doubt that they intended to downgrade the importance of regional cooperation drastically. "We are not convinced that the integration of these countries is necessary for our future integration into Europe," he said. "It could be counterproductive. We don't want to create a second Europe here."

The implication was clear: the Czech Republic would concentrate on expanding its ties with the wealthy Western Europeans, who were far more important partners than Poland and Hungary. After the Czech-Slovak split in January 1993, Klaus continued to speak dismissively of the Visegrad triangle: in an interview with the French daily *Le Figaro,* he said the regional grouping was "a process artificially created by the West, and Czechs were not interested in it." Trying to undo the damage of this inaccurate characterization, Zieleniec again insisted that the Czech Republic continued to support regional cooperation, only that it did not want the creation of "alternative structures" to the European Community. But, like Klaus, he left little doubt that he sees his country as more Western than its neighbors, which made his nods toward regional cooperation blatantly perfunctory. "For all our one-thousand-year history, we have been part of Western Europe," he told me.

Klaus and Zieleniec were far from alone in thinking originally that they might be better off in dealing with the Western Europeans on their own. A strong element of internal competition was present from the beginning in the drive by all three countries for full membership in the European Community. Although he professed a firm commitment to regional cooperation, Hungarian Prime Minister Antall provided a distinctly ambivalent answer when I asked him, during an interview in October 1991, whether Hungary was seeking entry before the others. After pointing out what he considered to be Hungary's lead in switching to a market economy and achieving political stability, he declared: "We would not consider it right if we had to wait because of the other two. But this does not mean that we don't want integration with the Poles and the Czechoslovaks." Unlike the Czechs, the Hungarians were generally sympathetic to the Poles; they considered them kindred spirits, since both peoples had been prone to launching doomed uprisings against foreign oppressors. But they looked disapprovingly at the political turmoil in Poland in the early 1990s, and nervously at the revival of Slovak nationalism in Czechoslovakia.

As Czechoslovakia split into two, the Visegrad triangle faced new difficulties. "The triangle can simply become a square," Havel said optimistically, alluding to the need to deal with a separate Slovakia; others talked about the continuation of "the Visegrad process," to avoid any suggestion that former Soviet republics would not be able eventually to become part of this broader cooperation. The Czechs and the Hungarians were especially careful not to convey the impression that they were planning to lock the Slovaks out of future joint efforts. "It is not the aim of the Czech or the Hungarian government to isolate Slovakia," Hungary's Antall declared in August 1992 during a visit by Klaus—his first official trip abroad as Czech prime minister. "It is a common interest of both the Czechs and the Hungarians to help Slovakia find its place in Europe."

Such carefully phrased diplomatic rhetoric could not disguise the fact that the Hungarians were convinced that they faced a long, difficult future with an independent Slovakia, or that, privately, they shared the perception of the Czechs that Slovakia would not be able to keep pace with the other members of the old Visegrad triangle in developing closer political and economic links with Western Europe. The immediate frictions that surfaced over the status of Slovakia's Hungarian minority only confirmed them in those beliefs. When I interviewed Antall in September 1992, he stressed that the new Slovak constitution did not provide "adequate guarantees" for national minorities, and signaled that his government would be pressing for close monitoring of that situation. "We believe that the situation of national minorities is not an issue of domestic policy," he said. "This is an issue that has to be monitored and followed up on the international level."

Despite the occasional rhetorical blasts of extreme right-wingers like parliamentarian Istvan Csurka that suggested a different course, the Hungarian government did nothing to justify the charges of some Slovak nationalists that they still harbored ambitions to reclaim the territories they had lost as a result of the First World War. Amid all the turmoil in Eastern Europe in the early 1990s, the Hungarians, the Poles, and the Czechs managed to persevere with the remarkably broad transformation not only of their political and economic institutions but also of something deeper, how they were seen by others and how they viewed themselves. They were determined to prove that they were no longer the children of a region doomed to perpetual turmoil, warfare, and conquest, but the inhabitants of societies that could find peaceful ways of living together and of tapping the best, rather than the worst, instincts of their citizenry. They were intent on demonstrating that they deserved to be a part of the broader European family of nations which had achieved relative peace and prosperity in the aftermath of the Second World War.

When they talked about reaching "European" standards of behavior, they may have been endowing the concept of "Europe" with some of the same mystical qualities that they had long associated with the concept of *Ameryka*. After all, Western European nations have hardly freed themselves completely from their own history of hatred and intolerance, or organized perfectly run civil societies living harmoniously with each other; even as they officially proclaimed the need for greater European unity, they were torn by new, bitter debates about just how much unity they really wanted. But the Western Europeans were able to benefit from four decades in which they were free to pursue those goals, while the Eastern Europeans were trapped in a system that did everything to negate them.

Nonetheless, the Poles, Czechs, and Hungarians are endowed with a knowledge that offers them the conviction that they can orient themselves in the same direction. History has taught these new Europeans something about how the quirks of fate affect human potential. Writing about the personal transformations of his acquaintances during the Nazi occupation of his native Poland, Kazimierz Brandys ruminated in his novel *Rondo:*

> With each passing day I was more and more convinced that in each person we know we are given only one of many possible ver-

sions of his or her humanity. Similarly, while living in a community, we know only its revealed form. At the same time, there exist other, hidden variants, shapes and forms we know nothing about. Perhaps everything that is imagination, yearning for beauty or freedom, issues from those hidden layers that remain inside or above us.

If some of that imagination and yearning were released in the extraordinary transformation of Eastern Europe, it is natural that other parts were not, or were quickly suppressed again, this time not so much by edict as by the pressures of ordinary life. The new Europeans are only human, and normal people quickly revert to more familiar patterns of behavior after periods of historic upheavals when they played roles they themselves did not know they were capable of. But that does not diminish their previous accomplishments in overthrowing a grotesque system of oppression. Nor does it mean an end to their struggle to establish their new identities in the new circumstances they helped to create. That struggle will continue to be marked by bitter disappointments along with successes, but it may yet revive and resuscitate a continent that has often become too complacent in its thinking, forgetting that there are other forms of existence, both hidden and revealed.

NOTES

The bulk of the material in this book comes from my own reporting. The personal stories and quotations are based on countless interviews I conducted with the people described in these pages. As a general rule, I have sought to attribute quotations or information that came from other sources within the text, but in some cases either that was awkward or it required more elaboration. In the chapter notes below, I have provided such references where I felt it was necessary. In lieu of a formal bibliography, I have included the books I referred to or found particularly useful as background reading.

INTRODUCTION

Tadeusz Konwicki, *Bohin Manor* (New York: Farrar, Straus and Giroux, 1990).

Quotations from Henryk Sienkiewicz taken from Norman Davies' review of *With Fire and Sword,* translated by W. S. Kuniczak (New York: Copernicus Society of America/Hippocrene Books, 1991), *New York Times Book Review,* June 30, 1991.

Quotation from Witold Gombrowicz taken from Marek Pieczara, "Pornografia," in Polish monthly *Konfrontacja,* March 1991.

Josef Skvorecky, *The Engineer of Human Souls* (London: Picador, 1986).

Ivan Klima, *Love and Garbage* (New York: Alfred A. Knopf, 1991).

George Konrad, *The Loser* (New York: Harcourt Brace Jovanovich, 1982).

Luigi Barzini, *The Europeans* (New York: Simon and Schuster, 1983).

ONE: RESISTANCE, REBELLION, AND LIFE

Vaclav Havel's speech at the Hebrew University in Jerusalem on April 26, 1990, as quoted in *New York Review of Books,* September 27, 1990.

Zbigniew Bujak retold his story to me, but I also drew upon his earlier account as published in Maciej Lopinski, Marcin Moskit, and Mariusz Wilk, *Konspira* (University of California Press, 1990). Originally published by the underground Polish press in 1984, it provides revealing first-person accounts by Bujak and other activists about their underground activities.

Milan Kundera, *The Book of Laughter and Forgetting* (New York: Penguin Books, 1983).

Czeslaw Milosz, *The Collected Poems 1931–1987* (New York: Ecco Press, 1988).

Vaclav Havel, *Politics and Conscience* (Stockholm: Charta 77 Foundation, 1986). Not directly quoted here, but also important, was Havel's *The Anatomy of Reticence: Eastern European Dissidents and the Peace Movement in the West*, from the same publisher, in 1985.

Vaclav Havel et al., *The Power of the Powerless* (London: Hutchinson, 1985).

Adam Michnik, *Letters from Prison and Other Essays* (University of California Press, 1985).

Yuri Orlov's quote about dissidents comes from Paul Goldberg, *The Final Act* (New York: William Morrow, 1988).

Miklos Haraszti, *The Velvet Prison: Artists Under State Socialism* (New York: New Republic/Basic Books, 1987).

George Konrad, *Antipolitics* (New York: Harcourt Brace Jovanovich, 1984).

Karl Schlögel, *Die Mitte liegt ostwärts: Die Deutschen, der verlorene Osten und Mitteleuropa* (Berlin: Siedler, 1986).

Milan Kundera, "The Tragedy of Central Europe," *New York Review of Books*, April 26, 1984.

TWO: THE COMMUNIST AFTERLIFE

The quotation from Edward Ochab is taken from Teresa Toranska, *Them: Stalin's Polish Puppets* (New York: Harper & Row, 1987).

The quotes from Kiszczak come from *General Kiszczak Mowi . . . Prawie Wszystko* (Warsaw: BGW, 1991).

General Jaruzelski elaborated on his version of events in his memoir, *Stan Wojenny Dlaczego . . .* (Warsaw: BGW, 1992).

Peter Schneider, *The German Comedy: Scenes of Life After the Wall* (New York: Farrar Straus Giroux, 1991).

The discussion of Vondra and Havel on lustration and religion appeared in Adam Michnik's interview with them in *Gazeta Wyborcza*, November 30, 1992.

The findings of Jaroslav Basta were summarized in *Gazeta Wyborcza* on September 23, 1992.

Havel's interview for *Mlady Svet* was reprinted in *New York Review of Books*, August 15, 1991.

THREE: OUTSIDERS AS INSIDERS

Jaroslaw Kurski, *Wodz* (Warsaw: Pomost, 1991).

Bruce F. Pauley, *The Habsburg Legacy 1867–1939* (Malabar, Fla.: Robert E. Krieger, 1972).

Tadeusz Konwicki, *The Polish Complex* (New York: Penguin Books, 1984).

The public-opinion surveys cited in this chapter were prepared for the Center for Social Analysis in Bratislava. They include "Aktualne Problemy Cesko-Slovenska" from November 1990, "Aktualne Problemy Slovenskej Spolocnosti" from May 1991, and "Aktualne Problemy Cesko-Slovenska" from January 1992.

Vaclav Havel, *Summer Meditations* (New York: Alfred A. Knopf, 1992).

Miklos Haraszti, *A Worker in a Workers' State* (New York: Penguin Books, 1977).

FOUR: TO MARKET

Bartlomiej Kaminski, *The Collapse of State Socialism: The Case of Poland* (Princeton, N.J.: Princeton University Press, 1991). As the title indicates, this is an analysis

of the unraveling of the old economic system.
Jerzy Baczynski's "The Stench of Capitalism" appeared in the August 24, 1991, issue of *Polityka*.

FIVE: POISONED AIR, POISONED BODIES
Ministry of the Environment of the Czech Republic and the Czechoslovak Academy of Sciences, "Environment of the Czech Republic," 1990.
The figures on energy efficiency were taken from the November–December 1988 issue of *World Watch*, p. 28.
Czechoslovak Academy of Sciences and the Federal Committee for the Environment, "National Report of the Czech and Slovak Federal Republic: United National Conference on Environment and Development Brazil," Prague, June 1992.
Donald Forbes, "Soviet Army Leaves Environmental Catastrophe in Hungary," Reuters, August 1, 1991.
Christopher Davis and Murray Feshbach, *Rising Infant Mortality in the USSR in the 1970s* (Washington, D.C.: United States Bureau of the Census, 1980).
Nick Eberstadt, *The Poverty of Communism* (New Brunswick, N.J.: Transaction Books, 1988). This book elaborates on some of the findings of Davis and Feshbach and looks at Eastern Europe, along with other communist societies.
Life-expectancy figures, along with some environmental data, came from the Czechoslovak report to the Rio conference, and from the following Hungarian and Polish reports: Hungary's National Report to the United Nations Conference on Environment and Development, 1992; the Polish National Report for the UN Conference, "Environment and Development," UNCED-Brazil, 1992.
Ministry of Welfare, Republic of Hungary, *Health in Hungary: Where Do We Stand?* (Budapest, 1992).
Ministry of Environmental Protection, Natural Resources and Forestry, *The State of the Environment in Poland: Damage and Remedy* (Warsaw, 1992).

SIX: LIFE WITHOUT CENSORS
Adam Zagajewski, *Solidarity, Solitude* (New York: Ecco Press, 1990). This is a collection of his essays from the 1980s.

SEVEN: GOD AND THE DEVIL
Andrzej Micewski, *Cardinal Wyszynski* (New York: Harcourt Brace Jovanovich, 1984). A biography of the powerful late Polish primate.
Kosciol Katolicki w Polsce 1918–1990. A handbook put out by the Polish Catholic Church that provides a detailed rundown on vocations and other statistics.
The Zetkin quote appears in Robert C. Tucker, *The Lenin Anthology* (New York: W. W. Norton, 1975).
Aleksander Smolar, "Jews as a Polish Problem," *Daedelus*, Spring 1987.
Wladyslaw T. Bartoszewski, *The Convent at Auschwitz* (New York: George Braziller, 1991).
Alan Adelson and Robert Lapides, *Lodz Ghetto: Inside a Community Under Siege* (New York: Viking, 1989).
"Campo dei Fiori" is from Czeslow Milosz, *The Collected Poems 1931–1987*.
Andrzej Bryk, "The Hidden Complex of the Polish Mind: Polish-Jewish Relations During the Holocaust," in *My Brother's Keeper*, ed. Antony Polonsky (Oxford: Routledge, 1990).
Mark Yamamoto's article appeared in *The Prague Post*, December 3–9, 1991.

EIGHT: NEIGHBORS
Kazimierz Brandys, *Rondo* (New York: Farrar, Straus & Giroux, 1989).

INDEX

ABOUT THE AUTHOR

Andrew Nagorski is Warsaw Bureau Chief for *Newsweek* magazine. A winner of two Overseas Press Club awards, he has also reported from Hong Kong, Moscow, Rome, Bonn, and Washington. He described his expulsion from Moscow in *Reluctant Farewell: An American Reporter's Candid Look Inside the Soviet Union*. He and his wife, Christina, have four children.